Conserving Biodiversity in Areas beyond National Jurisdiction

Conserving Biodiversity in Areas beyond National Jurisdiction

Edited by

David Freestone

BRILL
NIJHOFF

LEIDEN | BOSTON

Library of Congress Cataloging-in-Publication Data

Names: Freestone, David, editor.
Title: Conserving biodiversity in areas beyond national jurisdiction / edited by David Freestone.
Other titles: International Journal of Marine and Coastal Law.
Description: Leiden ; Boston : Brill Nijhoff, 2019. | Includes index. | Includes article originally published in International Journal of Marine and Coastal Law.
Identifiers: LCCN 2019001003 (print) | LCCN 2019001420 (ebook) | ISBN 9789004391703 (ebook) | ISBN 9789004391697 (pbk. : alk. paper)
Subjects: LCSH: Marine biodiversity conservation—Law and legislation. | Law of the sea. | Environmental law, International.
Classification: LCC K3488 (ebook) | LCC K3488 .C66 2019 (print) | DDC 346.04/695616—dc23
LC record available at https://lccn.loc.gov/2019001003

Typeface for the Latin, Greek, and Cyrillic scripts: "Brill". See and download: brill.com/brill-typeface.

ISBN 978-90-04-39169-7 (paperback)
ISBN 978-90-04-39170-3 (e-book)

This book is printed on acid-free paper and produced in a sustainable manner.

Contents

Foreword

For more than a decade the United Nations General Assembly (UNGA) has been discussing the question of the conservation and sustainable use of biodiversity in areas beyond national jurisdiction. Despite the prescience, the scope and the apparent comprehensiveness of the huge 1982 UN Convention on the Law of the Sea, a number of aspects of the regime of the high seas were left unfinished, or at least unimplemented. Some of these were addressed by the 1995 UN Fish Stocks Agreement dealing with straddling or highly migratory fish stocks, but a number of key governance questions raised by the huge increases in human activities in, and impacts upon, the open ocean still remain unresolved. These issues, raised first at the Ad Hoc Working Group (2004–2015) and then at the Preparatory Commission (2016–2107), have been the subjects of important debates within the academic literature as well as on the floor of the United Nations.

In December 2017, by Resolution 72/249, the UNGA agreed to convene an intergovernmental conference "to consider the recommendations of the Preparatory Committee on the elements and to elaborate the text of an international legally binding instrument under the United Nations Convention on the Law of the Sea on the conservation and sustainable use of marine biological diversity of areas beyond national jurisdiction, with a view to developing the instrument as soon as possible." The Intergovernmental Conference will initially have four negotiating sessions stretching into 2020, but in light of the complexity of the issues to be addressed, it seems likely that the negotiations may well extend beyond that period.

As the Editor-in-Chief of the *International Journal of Marine and Coastal Law* I have been able to publish, and also to commission, a number of articles which cover some of the key issues in these debates. This volume is a collection of some of those articles published over the last decade.

I am grateful to the authors for allowing me to republish these in the current volume and to my publisher Marie Sheldon at Brill Nijhoff, for agreeing to collect them together so that they can be made available in an accessible format for the substantive negotiations of the newly proposed International Legally Binding Instrument on the conservation and sustainable use of biodiversity in areas beyond national jurisdiction.

David Freestone
Washington DC

Acknowledgements

I am grateful to a number of people for their help with the preparation of this volume.

Primarily I am grateful to the authors of the papers included here that were originally published in the International Journal of Marine and Coastal Law. They have kindly agreed to allow me to republish these in the current volume. These are republished in their original form and the locations of the original versions are listed below.

Most of my work on this volume was done during the glorious English summer of 2018, when I was fortunate enough to spend a number of weeks at Oxford University as a Visiting Fellow at the Oxford Martin School in the wonderful Old India Institute Building on Broad Street. I was made enormously welcome by the Director of the OMS, Charles Godfray and his team, particularly Laura Lauer and Julian Laird. The Visiting Fellows programme is directly supported by Lilian Martin, whom I was delighted to be able to meet.

My nomination for this Fellowship was the work of the Co-Directors of the OMS Sustainable Oceans Project: Catherine Redgwell, Alex Rogers and Richard Bailey. My thanks to them also, but particularly to Catherine who also hosted me so generously at All Souls College; both she and her colleague, Akis Papastavridis, went out their way to make my stay most enjoyable as well as productive.

The original plan was to complete the volume by the start of the substantive negotiations in September 2018, but I am confident that they will still be of considerable relevance in 2019.

Finally I am grateful to Teresa Mackey, my colleague at the Sargasso Sea Commission, who at the last minute was able to master the indexing software for me and who spent a considerable amount of time preparing the subject index for me.

The chapters of this volume first appeared as follows:

David Freestone, 'Principles Applicable to Modern Ocean Governance' was first published (2008) 23 IJMCL 385–391;

Alex G. Oude Elferink, 'Coastal States and MPAs in ABNJ: Ensuring Consistency with the LOSC' was first published (2018) 33 IJMCL 437–466;

Vasco Becker-Weinberg, 'Preliminary Thoughts on Marine Spatial Planning in Areas beyond National Jurisdiction' was first published (2017) 32 IJMCL 570–588;

Richard Barnes, 'The Proposed LOSC Implementation Agreement on Areas beyond National Jurisdiction and Its Impact on International Fisheries Law' was first published (2016) 31 IJMCL 583–619;

Dire Tladi, 'The Proposed Implementing Agreement: Options for Coherence and Consistency in the Establishment of Protected Areas beyond National Jurisdiction' was first published (2015) 30 IJMCL 654–673;

David Freestone and Kate K. Morrison, 'The Signing of the Hamilton Declaration on Collaboration for the Conservation of the Sargasso Sea: A new paradigm for high seas conservation?' was first published (2014) 29 IJMCL 345–362;

Andrew Friedman, 'Submarine Telecommunication Cables and a Biodiversity Agreement in ABNJ: Finding New Routes for Cooperation' was first published (2017) 32 IJMCL 1–35;

Gunnar Sander, 'International Legal Obligations for Environmental Impact Assessment and Strategic Environmental Assessment in the Arctic Ocean' was first published (2016) 31 IJMCL 88–119;

Gaute Voigt-Hanssen, '"Light" and "heavy" options for benefit-sharing in the context of the United Nations Convention on the Law of the Sea' was first published (2018) 33 IJMCL 683–705;

Thomas Vanagt, Arianna Broggiato, Laura E. Lallier, Marcel Jaspars, Geoff Burton, and Dominic Muyldermans, 'Mare Geneticum: Balancing Governance of Marine Genetic Resources in International Waters' was first published (2018) 33 IJMCL 3–33;

Harriet R. Harden-Davies, 'Research for Regions: Strengthening Marine Technology Transfer for Pacific Island Countries and Biodiversity Beyond National Jurisdiction' was first published (2017) 32 IJMCL 797–822.

Abbreviations

ABM	Area-Based Management
ABMT	Area-Based Management Tool
ABNJ	Areas beyond National Jurisdiction
ABS	Access and Benefit Sharing
APEI	Areas of Particular Environmental Interest
BBNJ	Biodiversity beyond National Jurisdiction
CBD	Convention on Biological Diversity
CCLR	Carbon and Climate Law Review
DOALOS	Division of Ocean Affairs and Law of the Sea
EBSA	Ecologically or Biologically Significant Area
EEZ	Exclusive Economic Zone
EIA	Environmental Impact Assessment
EU	European Union
FAO	Food and Agriculture Organization (of the UN)
ICCAT	International Convention for the Conservation of Atlantic Tunas
IJMCL	International Journal of Marine and Coastal Law
ILBI	International Legally Binding Instrument
ILM	International Legal Materials
IGC	Inter-Governmental Conference
IA	Implementing Agreement
IMO	International Maritime Organization
IOC	Intergovernmental Oceanographic Commission
ISA	International Seabed Authority
ITLOS	International Tribunal on the Law of the Sea
ITPGRFA	International Treaty on Plant Genetic Resources for Food and Agriculture
IUCN	International Union for Conservation of Nature and Natural Resources
IUU	Illegal, Unreported and Unregulated (Fishing)
LOSC	UN Law of the Sea Convention
MARPOL	International Convention for the Prevention of Pollution from Ships
MGR	Marine Genetic Resources
MPA	Marine Protected Area
MSP	Marine Spatial Planning
MSY	Maximum Sustainable Yield
NAFO	Northwest Atlantic Fisheries Organization
NEAFC	North-East Atlantic Fisheries Commission

OSPAR	Oslo and Paris Convention
PrepCom	Preparatory Commission
PSSA	Particularly Sensitive Sea Areas
RFMO	Regional Fisheries Management Organization
SEA	Strategic Environmental Assessment
SIDS	Small Island Developing State
SPA	Specially Protected Area
SPAMI	Specially Protected Area of Mediterranean Interest
SSC	Sargasso Sea Commission
TS	Territorial Sea
UNCLOS	United Nations Conference on the Law of the Sea
UNEP	United Nations Environment Programme
UNESCO	United Nations Educational, Scientific and Cultural Organization
UNFSA	United Nations Fish Stocks Agreement
UNGA	United Nations General Assembly
UN	United Nations
UNTS	United Nations Treaty Series
VME	Vulnerable Marine Ecosystems

PART 1

Introduction

INTRODUCTION

The UN Process to Develop an International Legally Binding Instrument under the 1982 Law of the Sea Convention: Issues and Challenges

David Freestone

On Christmas Eve of 2017, the UN General Assembly decided by Resolution 72/249 "to convene an Intergovernmental Conference, under the auspices of the United Nations, to consider the recommendations of the Preparatory Committee on the elements and to elaborate the text of an international legally binding instrument under the United Nations Convention on the Law of Sea on the conservation and sustainable use of marine biological diversity of areas beyond national jurisdiction, with a view to developing the instrument as soon as possible."[1]

This momentous decision to initiate the negotiation of an International Legally Binding Agreement (ILBI) under the 1982 UN Convention on the Law of the Sea (LOSC)[2] was a long time in the making. Ever since 2006 the UN General Assembly (UNGA) had been discussing the issue of the conservation and sustainable use of biodiversity in the high seas and the deep seabed, the so called marine areas beyond national jurisdiction (ABNJ). Over more than a decade the discussions have raised a large number of important and often controversial questions regarding the regime established by the LOSC for these areas as well as its implementation.

This volume collects together a number of diverse and detailed perspectives on the BBNJ process and examines some of the key challenges and the opportunities that it presents. The BBNJ IGC presents the first opportunity, since the negotiation of what became the UN Fish Stocks Agreement in 1995,[3] to look in detail at possible gaps in the LOSC high seas regime and in the way that it has been implemented. A lot of important issues are on the table.

1 UN A/RES/72/249 at http://undocs.org/en/a/res/72/249.

2 United Nations Convention on the Law of the Sea (Montego Bay, 10 December 1982, in force 16 November 1994) 1833 *UNTS* 396.

3 Agreement for the implementation of the Provisions of the United Nations Convention on the Law of the Sea of 10 December 1982 Relating to the Conservation and Management of Straddling Fish Stocks and Highly Migratory Fish Stocks (adopted 4 December 1995, entered into force 11 December 2001) 2167 *UNTS* 3.

 | DOI:10.1163/9789004391703_002

This introduction starts with some background as to why the UN parties are concerned about the issue of biodiversity in ABNJ. A lot of major technological developments have taken place since the finalization of the negotiations of the LOSC in 1982 and human impacts, both direct and indirect, on the open ocean and its resources have expanded and continue to expand. It then looks at the legal and institutional framework contained within the LOSC for the regulation of the high seas and then at the way this has been implemented in practice by the relevant competent bodies. This section also includes a brief discussion of issues raised by moves to establish marine protected areas in the high seas under existing law.

The following section then summarizes the evolution of the BBNJ process within the UN General Assembly and the final section seeks to outline the key messages from the articles reproduced here and attempts to draw out the important issues which will need to be addressed in the ongoing Inter-Governmental Conference. This is an ongoing and dynamic process, but hopefully this volume will provide some useful insights and approaches to the issues being faced within that process.

1 The Challenges to Marine Biodiversity in ABNJ

A major part of the challenge is that we still know very little about the high seas and the deep sea bed—the ecosystems that cover more than half of our planet. It has often been remarked that we know more about the surface of the moon than about the deepest parts of the ocean. However, we do know beyond doubt that humankind has already had major negative impacts upon the ocean everywhere. The past thirty years have seen unparalleled expansion of human activities and impacts on the ocean, and on the high seas in particular. A decade ago, in 2008, the Census of Marine Life project highlighted the fact that anthropogenic pollution has already affected ecosystem functioning in the deep ocean and that millions of organism have been destroyed before they have even been identified by science.[4] In 2018, a major study suggested that only 13% of the oceans remain truly wild—untouched by human impact.[5] We know that plastics and other wastes are accumulating in the great gyres of

4 R Danovaro, *et al.*, 'Exponential Decline of Deep-Sea Ecosystem Functioning Linked to Benthic Biodiversity Loss' (2008) 18 *Current Biology* 1.

5 K Jones, *et al.*, 'The Location and Protection Status of Earth's Diminishing Marine Wilderness' (2018) 28 *Current Biology* 2506–2512. (August 6, 2018) https://www.cell.com/current-biology/issue?pii=S0960-9822(17)X0017-1. doi.org/10.1016/j.cub.2018.07.081.

the Pacific and the Atlantic, contaminating and suffocating pelagic creatures; and ultimately finding their way back into the food chain upon which we humans depend.

At the same time, scientists have discovered valuable new resources in high seas areas: ocean hydrothermal vents with temperatures of 300 to 600°C containing gold and other valuable minerals like copper, silver, and zinc used in electronics such as mobile phones and laptop computers. The vent systems are also home to accompanying *hyperthermophile* and *extremophile* life-forms—crabs, bivalves, tube worms and shrimp-like creatures as well as microbes—that process hydrogen sulphide instead of oxygen and that function in very deep ecosystems where the ambient water temperature may be over 100°C. These are already proving to have important bio-technology and pharmaceutical value, although the profits to be made from their exploitation have probably been much exaggerated. Also deep cold-water corals—much slower-growing than their shallow tropical water counterparts but equally colourful and very diverse—are proving far more common than initially thought, and are highly vulnerable to ocean-floor fishing equipment. Cold seeps and huge frozen methane deposits have been discovered, with potential for exploitation, albeit with risks of major damage to the global atmosphere.[6]

Sustained demand for fish, particularly high value fish, has accelerated fishing pressures and pushed fishing efforts into more extreme environments, such as the Southern Ocean, as well as into deeper waters. Heavy exploitation of valuable deep-sea species has meant that some stocks are on the verge of extinction before scientists have discovered much about them. Bottom-trawling for stocks that spawn on seamount ecosystems can eliminate whole year groups as well as destroy the very sea-bed ecosystems that attract them.

High seas fish stocks are a particularly high-value source of protein for human consumption—but there is evidence of serious depletion in the larger pelagic species, such as tunas and billfishes, resulting in fishing for smaller species, lower down the trophic levels.[7] This gives rise to serious questions about the impact of such fishing on the whole marine ecosystem and its long-term sustainability. Economists, as well as biologists, have begun to voice concerns for sustainability, in light of the huge amounts of money spent each year to support fisheries.[8]

---

6 According to the UNFCCC, methane MH_4 has a global warming potential over 20 years that is 56 times that of CO_2 as a greenhouse gas. *Climate Change 1995, The Science of Climate Change: Summary for Policymakers and Technical Summary of the Working Group I Report*, page 22.

7 See D Pauly, *et al.*, 'Fishing Down Marine Food Webs', (1998) 279 *Science*, 860, 862–863.

8 See study by the World Bank and FAO, *The Sunken Billions: The Economic Justification for Fisheries Reform* (Washington, DC: The World Bank, 2009), that estimates that USD 1.05 is

The international science community has also, albeit somewhat late in the day, become more vocal about the role of the oceans in relation to climate change. While it is well known that the oceans are the most important global sink for CO_2, research from *inter alia* the Census of Marine Life mentioned above indicated that the processes that absorb carbon depend heavily on ocean species—including the tiniest life-forms.[9]

Warming of the oceans and rises in sea level prompted by the resulting increases in volume and fed by melting glaciers and ice-caps have already attracted public attention. In addition, the increased atmospheric carbon load—currently estimated at about 410 parts per million (ppm) in the atmosphere[10]—is already beginning to affect ocean acidity levels. Research suggests that, at 450 ppm, corals and shellfish, and perhaps even plankton, may have problems in creating and maintaining their carbonate structures.[11] These issues, which affect waters both inside and outside national jurisdiction, pose governance issues far beyond the remit of the 1982 LOS Convention, even though some entrepreneurs have already seen opportunities for generating lucrative "carbon offsets" by using as yet unproven ocean fertilization techniques in an attempt to generate algal blooms that might fix more carbon in the ocean.[12]

The relevant international framework provided by the UN Framework Convention on Climate Change (UNFCCC)[13] and its science advisory body—the Intergovernmental Panel on Climate Change—have barely started to focus on these issues. There is for example no substantive mention of the

---

spent for every USD 1 of fish produced. This figure was raised higher by the 2016 study which argues that it results in lost economic opportunities of more than $80 billion per annum. *The Sunken Billions Revisited: Progress and Challenges in Global Marine Fisheries. Environment and Development.* The World Bank, Washington, DC. https://openknowledge.worldbank.org/handle/10986/24056 License: CC BY 3.0 IGO.

9 R Danovaro, *et al.*, above n 4.

10 And the highest levels for 3 million years. 410.79 ppm in June 2018. *Per* Mauna Loa Observatory, Hawaii (Scripps UCSD), Preliminary data released November 21, 2018. https://www.co2.earth/.

11 O Hoegh-Guldberg *et al.*, 'Coral Reefs under Rapid Climate Change and Ocean Acidification' (2007) 318 *Science*, 1737–1742.

12 See D Freestone and R Rayfuse, 'Ocean Iron Fertilization and International Law', (2008) *Marine Ecology Progress Series*, 227–233 (in Theme section: 'Implications of Large-scale Iron Fertilization of the Oceans', available at <www.int-res.com/articles/theme/m364ThemeSection.pdf>); R Rayfuse, M Lawrence and K Gjerde, 'Ocean Fertilisation and Climate Change: the Need to Regulate Emerging High Seas Uses', (2008) 23 *IJMCL* 297–326.

13 UN Doc Distr. General A/AC.237/18 (Part II)/Add.1.15 May 1992. 1771 *UNTS* 107.

ocean in either the text of the 1992 UNFCC[14] or of the 1997 Kyoto Protocol.[15] The 2015 Paris Agreement only contains a single reference to the ocean in its preamble.[16] However, in 2016 the IPCC decided to prepare a special report on climate change and the oceans and the cryosphere which will be released in 2019.[17]

2 The Existing Legal and Institutional Framework for Governance of ABNJ

Under the LOSC, coastal states have jurisdiction over living and non-living resources in their exclusive economic zones (EEZS) out to 200 nautical miles from their baselines and over continental shelf resources out to the legal limit of their continental shelf.[18] Beyond that point, the LOSC gives the International Seabed Authority (ISA) jurisdiction over the exploration and exploitation of the resources of the "Area",[19] and the superjacent waters are high seas.

Part VII of the LOSC covers the rights and duties of States on the high seas. Article 87 of the Convention provides for "Freedom of the high seas" making it clear that the high seas are open to all States, whether coastal or landlocked. It then itemises six specific freedoms, namely: freedom of navigation; freedom of overflight; freedom to lay submarine cables and pipelines, subject to Part VI; freedom to construct artificial islands and other installations permitted under international law, subject to Part VI; freedom of fishing, subject to

14 There is a mention of sea-level rise in the preamble and a reference to oceans in a list of sinks and reservoirs in Art 4(1)(d) UNFCCC. See D Freestone, "Can the UN Climate Regime respond to the Challenges of Sea Level Rise?"(arguing that its financing regime might be the most relevant way it is likely to assist) (2013) 35(2) *University of Hawai'i Law Review* pp. 671–685.

15 FCCC/CP/1997/L.7/Add.1, Decision 1/CP.3 Adoption of the Kyoto Protocol to United Nations Framework Convention on Climate Change, Annex, reprinted in (1998) ILM 22.

16 Annex to FCCC/CP/2015/L.9/Rev (12 December 2015).

17 Decided at the IPCC 43rd Session in Nairobi, Kenya, 11–13 April 2016. During its 45th Session (Guadalajara, Mexico, 28–31 March 2017), the Panel approved the outline of the *Special Report on the Ocean and Cryosphere in a Changing Climate* (SROCC) to be finalized in September 2019. See https://www.ipcc.ch/report/srocc/.

18 On the outer limit of the continental shelf, see Part V, and C A Fleischer, 'Continental Shelf beyond 200 Nautical Miles', in D Vidas (ed.), *Law, Technology and Science for Oceans in Globalisation* (Leiden: Martinus Nijhoff, 2010) 423–589.

19 Art 133(a) LOSC. See further below.

the conditions laid done in section 2;[20] and freedom of scientific research, subject to Parts VI and XIII.[21]

Article 87(1) also makes the point, reiterated in detail in other provisions, that these freedoms are not unconditional. They may only be exercised "under the conditions laid down by this Convention and by other rules of international law." Article 87(2) reinforces the point still further when it states that these freedoms shall be exercised by all States with due regard for the interests of other States in their exercise of the freedom of the seas, and also with due regard for the rights under the Convention with respect to the Area. Indeed, the only specific additional restrictions that can be made to the exercise of these rights are by international agreements that are binding only on the States which are party to them.

A really significant obligation imposed by Part XII of the LOSC relates to the Protection and Preservation of the Marine Environment, which extends to the high seas and international seabed area. Article 192 obliges all States to "protect and preserve the marine environment" and Article 194(5) specifies that measures under Part XII are to include "those necessary to protect and preserve rare or fragile ecosystems as well as the habitat of depleted, threatened or endangered species and other forms of marine life." Article 197 further obliges States to:

> [C]o-operate on a global basis and, as appropriate, on a regional basis, directly or through competent international organizations, in formulating and elaborating international rules, standards and recommended practices and procedures consistent with this Convention, for the protection and preservation of the marine environment, taking into account characteristic regional features.

Part XI of the Convention establishes the international regime for the exploration and exploitation of seabed mineral resources in "the Area" overseen by the International Seabed Authority (ISA).[22] It designates the Area and its mineral resources as the Common Heritage of Mankind, and mandates the ISA to

---

20 Arts 116–120.

21 Part VI places limits on research activities on the continental shelf where it extends under the high seas. Part XIII sets out general provisions and co-operative requirements concerning the conduct of marine scientific research.

22 Under Art 133, "resources" means "all solid, liquid or gaseous mineral resources *in situ* in the Area at or beneath the seabed including polymetallic nodules". This is important given debates about the extent to which living resources comprise part of the regime for the Area, or are subject to the freedom of the high seas.

administer the resources for the benefit of mankind. In addition to provisions for the sharing of financial and other economic benefits from mining activities, it also envisages the development of detailed rules and regulations for the prevention of damage from mineral exploration and extraction activities and for the conservation of the flora and fauna of the seabed.[23] The ISA is currently in the process of developing the regulations which would be applicable to seabed mining.[24]

However, these rules do not apply to activities such as deep-sea bottom fishing, marine scientific research, cable-laying or potential new activities such as bio-prospecting, ocean fertilization and other forms of marine geo-engineering.[25] Hence, there is a major *lacuna* in the LOSC regime relating to management and conservation of deep-sea or seabed living resources and for exploration and exploitation activities unrelated to seabed mining.[26]

A range of other global and regional treaties do regulate specific activities which take place in ABNJ, such as fishing, ocean dumping and navigation. But of course these detailed sectoral treaties are again only binding on States parties. So, the problem of proper (ie integrated and generally applicable) governance in ABNJ is exacerbated by the somewhat incomplete patchwork of treaties that exists. A number of experts have conducted detailed reviews of existing organizations with jurisdiction over activities in ABNJ which show that there are serious gaps in coverage.[27] In relation to sectoral activities, these gaps are both functional as well as geographic. This is not necessarily a defect

23 Art 145.

24 Revised draft Regulations on Exploitation of Mineral Resources in the Area [ISBA/24/LTC/WP.1/REV.1]. See https://www.isa.org.jm/news/international-seabed-authority-legal-and-technical-commission-issues-working-draft-exploitation.

25 See above n 11; also K Scott, 'Regulating Ocean Fertilization under International Law: The Risks' (2013) 2 CCLR 108.

26 Although note the unequivocal obligations to 'protect and preserve the marine environment' and to 'protect and preserve rare or fragile species and ecosystems in all parts of the marine environment, as well as the habitat of depleted, threatened or endangered species and other forms of marine life'; see Arts 192 and 194(5) LOSC.

27 K Gjerde, H Dotinga, S Hart, E J Molenaar, R Rayfuse and R Warner, Regulatory and Governance Gaps in the International Regime for the Conservation and Sustainable Use of Marine Biodiversity in Areas beyond National Jurisdiction (IUCN 2008) <http://cms-data.iucn.org/downloads/iucn_marine_paper_1_2.pdf>. See also: D Freestone, 'Problems of High Seas Governance' and K Gjerde, 'High Seas Fisheries Governance: Prospects and Challenges in the 21st Century' in D Vidas and PJ Schei (eds.) The World Ocean in Globalisation: Challenges and Responses (Martinus Nijhoff 2011). For an excellent wider discussion of the ABNJ legal regime, see: R Warner, Protecting the Oceans beyond National Jurisdiction: Strengthening the International Law Framework (Martinus Nijhoff 2009).

in the basic Convention regime itself, but it is a serious defect in the way that it has been implemented.

In fact, the *lacunae* in implementation are vividly shown by the LOSC provisions relating to the monitoring and reporting of potentially polluting activities. These prescient provisions, which envisage a form of environmental assessment, are quite rigorous but are based entirely on good faith implementation by States parties; there is no international process for receiving or reviewing these reports or even for publicizing them. The LOSC provides that:

> ... States shall keep under surveillance the effects of any activities which they permit or in which they engage in order to determine whether these activities are likely to pollute the marine environment. (Article 204(2))
>
> States shall publish reports ... or provide such reports at appropriate intervals to the competent international organizations, which should make them available to all States. (Article 205)
>
> When States have reasonable grounds for believing that planned activities under their jurisdiction or control may cause substantial pollution of or significant and harmful changes to the marine environment, they shall, as far as practicable, assess the potential effects of such activities on the marine environment and shall communicate reports of the results of such assessments ... (Article 206)

Although there are international treaty requirements for prior environmental impact assessment for the permitting of human activities in some areas of the ocean, such as the Southern Ocean under the Madrid Protocol,[28] or for some activities such as ocean dumping, this is very much the exception rather than the rule.[29] The 2010 decision of the Parties to the London Convention and

---

28 The Protocol on Environmental Protection to the Antarctic Treaty (signed in Madrid on October 4 1991 and entered into force in 1998), (1991) 30 *ILM* 1455. Annex 1 is on Environmental Impact Assessment. For text see http://www.ats.aq/documents/recatt/Att008_e.pdf.

29 See R Warner and S Marsden, *Transboundary Environmental Governance: Inland, Coastal and Marine Perspectives* (Ashgate, 2012).

Protocol,[30] which establishes an assessment framework in relation to ocean fertilization, represents an important step forward on this front.[31]

Much work remains to done in relation to emerging new concerns in ABNJ. As we saw above, the Census of Marine Life and other projects have highlighted the major impacts that human activities have already had on marine biodiversity and the importance which biodiversity at all trophic levels plays in maintaining ocean ecosystem health and functions.[32] This research has also made it clear that despite the strong and unequivocal obligations to protect the marine environment in the LOSC discussed above, insufficient attention is directed at conservation of marine ecosystems outside areas of national jurisdiction.

For example, experience at the national level has demonstrated beyond doubt the beneficial effects that the establishment of marine protected areas has on the conservation of biomass, even though these are often established in the face of strident opposition from user groups, particularly fishermen.[33] General international law, and indeed the LOSC itself, does not provide a mechanism for the establishment of conservation or other areas on the high seas that would have objective status and would thus be binding on all States.

An important result of the sectoral approach in the treaty regimes applicable to ABNJ is that although the parties to all these treaties must have regard to the sweeping obligation of Article 192 to protect and preserve the marine environment, the modalities by which this is done vary widely from regime to

30 Resolution LC-LP.2(2010) on the Assessment Framework for Scientific Research Involving Ocean Fertilization, adopted on 14 October 2010. Available at http://www.imo.org/OurWork/Environment/LCLP/EmergingIssues/geoengineering/Documents/OFassessmentResolution.pdf. Convention on the Prevention of Marine Pollution by Dumping of Wastes and Other Matter 1972, 1046 *UNTS* 120; 1996 Protocol to the 1972 Convention on the Prevention of Marine Pollution by Dumping of Wastes and Other Matter, 2006 *ATS* 11.

31 See P Verlaan, 'Marine Scientific Research: its Potential Contribution to Achieving Responsible High Seas Governance' in D Freestone (ed.) *The 1982 Law of the Sea Convention at 30: Successes, Challenges and New Agendas* (Martinus Nijhoff 2013); P Verlaan, 'Marine Scientific Research: its Potential Contribution to Achieving Responsible High Seas Governance' (2012) 27 *IJMCL* 805.

32 R Danovaro, *et al.*, above n 4.

33 There is wide range of literature on this. See, e.g. SE Lester et al., 'Biological effects within no-take marine reserves: a global synthesis' (2009) 384 *Marine Ecology Progress Series* 33–46; PB Fenberg et al., 'The science of European marine reserves: Status, efficacy, and future needs' (2012) 36 (5) *Marine Policy* 1012–102; K Grorud-Colvert et al., 'Marine Protected Area Networks: Assessing Whether the Whole Is Greater than the Sum of Its Parts' (2014) 9(8) *PLoS ONE* 9: e102298; GJ Edgar et al., 'Global conservation outcomes depend on marine protected areas with five key features' (2014) 506 *Nature* 216–220.

regime. Each sectoral regime has its own distinctive protection mechanisms and assesses differently the factors that need to be taken into account. The result is a number of distinct sectoral regimes designed to protect specific areas of the ocean from individual sector-specific risks.

The International Maritime Organization (IMO), for example, has authority to regulate maritime transport and vessel source pollution. The IMO convention, MARPOL 73/78,[34] provides for the establishment of "Special Areas" of the ocean, in which more rigorous regimes apply for the discharge of various substances from vessels. The IMO can also designate Particularly Sensitive Sea Areas (PSSAs) to denote areas of particular vulnerability to shipping activities with accompanying protection measures.[35] To date however, none have been established in the high seas.[36] Regional Fisheries Management Organizations (RFMOs) also have authority to establish a range of protection measures, including closing areas for fisheries management reasons.[37] As a result of pressure from the UN General Assembly (UNGA), States and RFMOs have been called upon to protect marine biodiversity, including 'vulnerable marine ecosystems' from significant adverse impacts of deep-sea bottom trawling.[38] In August 2008, the Committee on Fisheries of the UN Food and Agriculture Organization (FAO) adopted International Guidelines for the Management of Deep-Sea Fisheries in the High Seas which provide criteria for identifying 'Vulnerable Marine Ecosystems (VMEs)' and outline procedures for preventing significant adverse impacts from the impacts of bottom trawling including closure of areas and prior environmental impact assessments.[39] However, UNGA

34 International Convention for the Prevention of Pollution by Ships, 1973/78, (1978) 17 *ILM* 546.

35 Called Associated Protection Measures (APM). See IMO Assembly Resolution A.982 (24) *Revised guidelines for the identification and designation of Particularly Sensitive Sea Areas (PSSAs)*. Further details at: http://www.imo.org/OurWork/Environment/PollutionPrevention/PSSAs/Pages/Default.aspx; also see: K Gjerde and D Freestone (eds.) 'Special Issue: Particularly Sensitive Sea Areas: an Important Environmental Concept at a Turning Point' (1994) 9 *IJMCL* 431.

36 Although MARPOL Special Areas have been established in ABNJ e.g., in Antarctica. See also J Roberts et al., 'Area-based Management on the High Seas: Possible Application of the IMO's Particularly Sensitive Sea Area Concept' (2010) 25 *IJMCL* 483–522. More recently see David Freestone and Viva Harris, 'Particularly Sensitive Sea Areas beyond National Jurisdiction: Time to Chart a New Course?' in *International Marine Economy: Law and Policy* (Myron Nordquist, John Norton Moore and Ronan Long, eds.), Brill Nijhoff, 2017, 322–361.

37 See particularly, Richard Barnes below, Chapter 4.

38 UNGA Res 59/25 (17 November 2004) para 66; UNGA Res 61/105 (8 December 2006) paras 80–90.

39 FAO, *International Guidelines for the Management of Deep-sea Fisheries in the High Seas* (Rome 2009).

reviews recognize that despite some progress, much work remains to be done to effectively implement these procedures and RFMOs have yet to adopt similar provisions with respect to vulnerable marine species in the superjacent water column.[40]

The International Seabed Authority (ISA) has also recognised Areas of Particular Environmental Interest (APEIs) in relation to its work in the Clarion-Clipperton Zone in the Pacific.[41] This concept attracted a great deal of positive attention but there has been no attempt as yet to systematize this on a global level through the ISA Draft Seabed Mining Regulations which are currently under development.[42]

Since 2008, the Parties to the Convention on Biological Diversity (CBD) have developed a science-based process to "describe" Ecologically or Biologically Significant [marine] Areas (EBSAs).[43] These EBSAs have no legal status *per se* but they were developed as a deliberate parallel process to the BBNJ process to inform and advise sectoral managers of the importance of certain important high seas and other marine areas which might be impacted by their operations, and hence be appropriate for conservation measures. At their COP10, the CBD Parties decided to initiate the science-driven process to describe EBSAs. To that end, by Decision X/29 the COP requested its Executive Secretary to

---

40 UNGA Res 64/72 (4 December 2009) para 118. Reports on implementation of these obligations have been prepared, inter alia, by IUCN and the Deep Sea Conservation Coalition, see M Gianni, *Review of the Implementation of the UNGA Agreement to Protect Deep-sea Ecosystems on the High Seas* (Deep Sea Coalition 2009). Available at <www.savethehighseas.org>. Sea also G Wright *et al.*, *Advancing marine biodiversity protection through regional fisheries management: a review of high seas bottom fisheries closures*. Working Paper 14/14 (IDDRI Paris 2014). Available at http://www.iddri.org/Publications/Collections/Idees-pour-le-debat/WP1414_GW%20et%20al_fisheries%20closures%20ABNJ.pdf.

41 When the ISA Council approved the environmental management plan for the Clarion-Clipperton Zone, it decided that "... for a period of five years from the date of the present decision or until further review by the Legal and Technical Commission or the Council, no application for approval of a plan of work for exploration or exploitation should be granted in areas of particular environmental interest referred to in the annex" (Decision of the Council relating to an environmental management plan for the Clarion-Clipperton Zone, ISBA/18/C/22 26 July 2012. Available at http://www.isa.org.jm/sites/default/files/files/documents/isba-18c-22_0.pdf.

42 Revised draft Regulations on Exploitation of Mineral Resources in the Area [ISBA/24/LTC/WP.1/REV.1] see https://www.isa.org.jm/document/isba24ltcwp1rev1.

43 In 2008 the CBD COP 9 adopted Decision IX/20 on "Marine and coastal biodiversity" that adopted the scientific criteria, recommended by the Azores Workshop, for identifying ecologically or biologically significant marine areas (or EBSAs) in need of protection in open-ocean waters and deep-sea habitats. https://www.cbd.int/doc/meetings/mar/EBSAws-2014-01/other/EBSAws-2014-01-azores-brochure-en.pdf.

work with parties and competent organizations at international, regional, and sub-regional levels, to convene a series of regional workshops to facilitate the description of EBSAs. The intent is clear from the title of its Annex II: 'Scientific Guidance for Selecting Areas to Establish a Representative Network of Marine Protected Areas, Including in Open Ocean Waters and Deep-Sea Habitats.'[44] To date more than 150 EBSA sites have been "described" by this ostensibly non-political, scientific process, however international organizations have not to date been willing to rely on this process to adopt protection measures for such areas.[45]

It is also clear that treaty regimes that are established for primarily environmental reasons can also establish protected areas. However the majority of these are regional and if they were to seek to establish high seas protected areas these would only be binding on the parties to the respective regional treaties. International law does not allow the restriction of general international law rights—such as freedom of the seas—without the consent of affected states. So there is still no general mechanism to designate an area of the high seas as a marine protected area, allowing management planning for the area and protection from a suite of threats or from cumulative threats, or even to preserve important marine ecosystems in a precautionary way for future generations in the way that we take for granted on land (or in coastal waters). The Parties to the CBD seem to have expressed some frustration with this in their decision relating to the 2010 CBD Aichi Target 11, in that it would be difficult to meet this target without including some high seas areas. Target 11 provides that:

> [b]y 2020, at least 17 per cent of terrestrial and inland water areas and 10 per cent of coastal and marine areas, especially areas of particular importance for biodiversity and ecosystem services, are conserved through effectively and equitably managed, ecologically representative and well-connected systems of protected areas and other effective area-based

44 To date, more than 17 workshops have been held and more than 150 sites identified by the workshops. For a full list see https://www.cbd.int/EBSA/about.

45 For early experience regarding the Sargasso Sea EBSA See D Freestone and K Morrison, 'The Signing of the Hamilton Declaration on Collaboration for the Conservation of the Sargasso Sea' Chapter 6 below. Also D Freestone, D Johnson, J Ardron, S Unger, and K Morrison 'Can existing institutions protect biodiversity in areas beyond national jurisdiction? Experiences from two on-going processes.' (2014) 42 *Marine Policy* 167–175. And note the recent award of a seabed mining exploration licence by the ISA to Poland regarding a site on the Mid-Atlantic Ridge which covers the unique "Lost City" EBSA.

conservation measures, and integrated into the wider landscape and sea scape.[46]

Some Protocols to the UNEP Regional Seas treaties do provide for the establishment of Specially Protected Areas (SPAs) and in the Mediterranean, Specially Protected Areas of Mediterranean Importance (SPAMIs).[47] There have also been regional efforts to identify MPAs in ABNJ. The first high sea MPA, established in 1993 by agreement among France, Monaco, and Italy, was the famous Pelagos Whale Sanctuary in the Mediterranean Sea around Corsica, which was subsequently absorbed into the SPAMI system.[48] In 2010, the parties to the OSPAR Convention in the North-East Atlantic established six MPAs in ABNJ and a seventh in 2012. In the Southern Ocean, the Parties to the Convention on Conservation of Antarctic Marine Living Resources have to date established two huge MPAs: in 2010, the South Orkney Islands,[49] and in 2017, the world's largest MPA in the Ross Sea.[50]

---

46 For text see http://www.cbd.int/sp/targets/rationale/target-11/. This is now reflected in Sustainable Development Goal 14.5: UN A/RES/70/1/L.1. Text at https://unstats.un.org/sdgs/report/2016/.

47 The first such Protocol was the 1982 Protocol on Specially Protected Areas to the 1976 Barcelona Convention for the Protection of the Mediterranean Sea against Pollution. This was revised in 1995 to reflect the 1992 Biodiversity Convention and the more cutting edge approach of the 1990 Kingston Protocol on Specially Protected Areas and Wildlife (SPAW) to the Convention for the Protection and Development of the Marine Environment in the Wider Caribbean Region ("Cartagena Convention"). For text see D Freestone, 'Specially Protected Areas and Wildlife in the Caribbean' (1990) 5 *International Journal of Estuarine and Coastal Law* 362–382, 369. East Africa and the South East Pacific are also covered by similar measures. See Protocol Concerning Protected Areas and Wild Fauna and Flora in the Eastern African Region 1985, available at http://www.unep.org/NairobiConvention/The_Convention/Protocols/Protocol_Protected_Areas.asp) and Protocol for the Conservation and Management of Protected Marine and Coastal Areas of the South-East Pacific (1989).

48 Although note that as most Mediterranean states do not claim EEZs, the high seas begin 12 nm from the coast.

49 Which covers just under 94,000 square kilometres of high seas within which fishing, scientific research related to fishing, and discharges and dumping from fishing vessels are regulated. See K Scott, 'Conservation on the High Seas: Developing the Concept of the High Seas Marine Protected Areas' (2012) 27 *IJMCL* 849, 852. See also Report of the 2007 Workshop on Bioregionalisation of the Southern Ocean (Brussels, Belgium, 13 to 17 August 2007), available at http://www.ccamlr.org/en/system/files/e-sc-xxvi-a9.pdf; Report of the Workshop on Marine Protected Areas (Brest, France, 29 August to September 2011) para 2.2, available at https://www.ccamlr.org/en/system/files/e-sc-xxx-a06.pdf.

50 1.55 million km^2 area of the Ross Sea with special protection from human activities https://www.ccamlr.org/en/news/2016/ccamlr-create-worlds-largest-marine-protected-area.

While these initiatives are extremely important, technically they are only binding on the parties to the treaties which establish them. This is one of the key issues that the BBNJ process was intended to address from the start—the development of a mechanism to establish MPAs that would have objective legal status and be opposable to (i.e. binding on) all States.

3 The BBNJ Process within the UNGA

As we saw above, in 2004, in order to address the full range of issues particularly related to the conservation of biodiversity in areas beyond national jurisdiction, the UNGA agreed to the recommendation of the UN Informal Consultative Process on the Oceans and the Law of the Sea (UNICPOLOS) to establish an Ad Hoc Open-ended Informal Working Group to study issues relating to the conservation and sustainable use of marine biological diversity beyond areas of national jurisdiction.[51] This section will look in a little more detail at the various stages in that process.

Several important proposals were discussed at these meetings including a European Union proposal for a new implementing agreement to develop a more specific framework to address conservation and sustainable use of marine biodiversity beyond national jurisdiction within the LOSC framework. Issues highlighted in the discussions included the suggestions that this new global instrument should reflect the basic principles of ocean governance that have evolved over the last few decades,[52] as well as a process for the establishment and monitoring of MPAs in ABNJ, which as we have seen are still very rare even though protected areas have proven to be extremely effective in maintaining biodiversity in coastal contexts. Delegations also noted the absence of comprehensive environmental impact assessments (EIAs) for new activities in ABNJ, as well as the lack of co-ordination between those international organizations that are charged with regulating specific sectoral activities in high seas areas.

---

51 This Working Group held its first meeting in 2006, with further meetings held in 2008, 2010, 2011, 2012, 2013 and 2014. A final meeting was held in January 2015. For details of the meetings see the UN website at: http://www.un.org/Depts/los/biodiversityworkinggroup/biodiversityworkinggroup.htm.

52 It has also been suggested that the international community should reaffirm some of the basic principles that have been agreed in a wide range of existing instruments, including the Convention, in relation to national activities in ABNJ. See further below, Freestone, Chapter 1.

Other States indicated that improved implementation, rather than a new treaty, should be the first priority, but have not always elaborated their views on what exactly might be done to enhance implementation of existing treaties with respect to biodiversity conservation in general in ABNJ. In addition, the lively debates on improved governance of ABNJ and their resources gave rise to a controversy over the future regime for exploitation of marine genetic resources beyond national jurisdiction.[53] The G77 and China argued that the common heritage of mankind concept that the LOSC applies to the 'Area' and deep seabed minerals,[54] should also apply to the living resources of the deep ocean floor, many of which may have important industrial and pharmaceutical potential. They argued that, rather than being subject to the open access regime of the high seas as advocated by some States, if the drafters of the LOSC had been aware of these resources—rather than simply being aware of the famous 'manganese nodules'—they would doubtless have specifically included these living resources within the deep sea bed regime.[55]

These polarised positions produced stalemate in the discussions at the BBNJ Working Group. However, at the May 2011 Meeting there was an important breakthrough. It was agreed that the issue of the protection of biodiversity through conservation and management tools such as EIAs and MPAs should be linked with issues relating to benefit sharing of marine genetic resources, as a form of 'package deal.'[56] This was discussed further at the 2012 BBNJ Working Group meeting,[57] and at the UN Conference on Sustainable Development

53 For an excellent assessment of the issues and potential of bio-prospecting, see: D Leary *et al.*, 'Marine Genetic Resources: A Review of the Scientific and Commercial Interest' (2009) 33 *Marine Policy* 183.

54 See Art 138 LOSC: 'The Area and its resources are the common heritage of mankind.' Art 133 LOSC further provides that resources means 'all solid liquid or gaseous mineral resources *in situ* in the Area at or beneath the seabed, including polymetallic nodules.'

55 For records of these discussions see: http://www.un.org/depts/los/biodiversityworkinggroup/biodiversityworkinggroup.htm For a general flavor of various concerns, see particularly the Co-Chairpersons' summary of discussion, appended to Letter dated 16 March 2010 from the Co-Chairpersons of the Ad Hoc Open-ended Informal Working Group to the President of the General Assembly, UN Doc A/65/68 (17 March 2010). Available at: http://daccess-dds-ny.un.org/doc/UNDOC/GEN/N10/277/20/PDF/N1027720.pdf?OpenElement.

56 Recommendations of the Ad Hoc Open-ended Informal Working Group to study issues relating to the conservation and sustainable use of marine biological diversity beyond areas of national jurisdiction and Co-Chairs' summary of discussions, UN Doc A/66/119 (30 June 2011). Available on the UN website at: http://daccess-dds-ny.un.org/doc/UNDOC/GEN/N11/397/64/PDF/N1139764.pdf?OpenElement.

57 Held in New York, 7–11 May 2012; see: Agenda UN Doc A/AC.276/5 (7 May 2012). http://daccess-dds-ny.un.org/doc/UNDOC/GEN/N12/332/60/PDF/N1233260.pdf?OpenElement.

(Rio + 20) in June 2012. The Outcome Document of the Rio Conference, entitled 'The Future We Want' contained the following commitment:

> We recognize the importance of the conservation and sustainable use of marine biodiversity beyond areas of national jurisdiction. We note the ongoing work under the General Assembly of an ad hoc open-ended informal working group to study issues relating to the conservation and sustainable use of marine biological diversity beyond areas of national jurisdiction. Building on the work of the ad hoc working group and before the end of the sixty-ninth session of the General Assembly we commit to address, on an urgent basis, the issue of the conservation and sustainable use of marine biological diversity of areas beyond national jurisdiction, including by taking a decision on the development of an international instrument under the United Nations Convention on the Law of the Sea.[58]

Acting on this undertaking, the UNGA in Resolution 68/70 requested the Secretary-General to convene three more meetings of the BBNJ Working Group.[59] These took place between 1–5 April and 16–19 June 2014 and 20–23 January 2015. At that last meeting the Working Group decided, after protracted debate, to recommend to the UNGA that it:

> Decide to develop an international legally binding instrument under the Convention on the conservation and sustainable use of marine biological diversity of areas beyond national jurisdiction …[60]

The recommendations of the Working Group also envisage the establishment of a Preparatory Commission, to report to the UNGA with recommendations on a text. Those recommendations are to address the topics identified in the package agreed by the BBNJ Working Group in 2011:

58 Para 162 of the Annex to UNGA Res 66/288 (27 July 2012), UN Doc A/RES/66/288 (11 September 2012).

59 Para 200 of UNGA Res 68/70 Oceans and law of the sea (9 December 2013) UN Doc A/RES/68/70 (27 February 2012).

60 Recommendations of the Ad Hoc Open-ended Informal Working Group to study issues relating to the conservation and sustainable use of marine biological diversity beyond areas of national jurisdiction to the sixty-ninth session of the General Assembly, para 5. Advance and unedited copy of the recommendation is available at http://www.un.org/depts/los/biodiversityworkinggroup/documents/ahwg-9_report.pdf.

> ... namely the conservation and sustainable use of marine biodiversity in areas beyond national jurisdiction, in particular, together and as a whole, marine genetic resources, including questions on the sharing of benefits, measures such as area-based management tools, including marine protected areas, environmental impact assessments and capacity building and the transfer of marine technology.[61]

In August 2015 the UNGA, by Resolution 69/292, (in other words, just within the time limit established by the Rio Plus 20 Decision) accepted the BBNJ Working Group's recommendation for the establishment of a Preparatory Commission, to begin work in 2016 and to report to the UNGA in 2017 with specific text recommendations for an ILBI.[62]

Four sessions of the Preparatory Commission were held: in March and August of 2016 and in March and July of 2017. Early in the morning of the day after its final session was due to end on 21 July 2017, after a protracted and contentious all day and evening session, the Preparatory Commission, despite having been unable to reach consensus on all of the proposed elements of an ILBI, did reach consensus to recommend that the UNGA:

> ... take a decision, as soon as possible, on the convening of an intergovernmental conference, under the auspices of the United Nations, to consider the recommendations of the Preparatory Committee on the elements and to elaborate the text of an international legally binding instrument under the Convention.[63]

Then, on 24 December 2017 by Resolution 72/249,[64] the UNGA agreed to convene an intergovernmental conference 'to consider the recommendations of the Preparatory Committee on the elements and to elaborate the text of an international legally binding instrument under the United Nations Convention

61 Ibid., para 6.

62 A/RES/69/292 (6 July 2015): Development of an international legally binding instrument under the United Nations Convention on the Law of the Sea on the conservation and sustainable use of marine biological diversity of areas beyond national jurisdiction.

63 Paradoxically it could not reach consensus on the proposed elements of the ILBI set out in the report. An advance unedited version of the Report of the Preparatory Commission is at: http://www.un.org/depts/los/biodiversity/prepcom_files/Procedural_report_of_BBNJ_PrepCom.pdf.

64 A/RES/72/429: Intergovernmental Conference on an international legally binding instrument under the United Nations Convention on the Law of the Sea on the conservation and sustainable use of marine biological diversity of areas beyond national jurisdiction (General Assembly resolution 72/249).

on the Law of the Sea on the conservation and sustainable use of marine biological diversity of areas beyond national jurisdiction, with a view to developing the instrument as soon as possible.' It also decided that the negotiations shall address the topics identified in the package agreed in 2011.[65]

The Intergovernmental Conference will initially have four substantive sessions. The first Organizing session took place in New York 16–18 April, where Ms. Rena Lee of Singapore was elected President of the Conference. The first negotiating session took place 4 to 17 September 2018, guided by an 'Aid to Discussions' issued by the President.[66] Two further sessions are planned for 2019 and a fourth in 2020.

The first substantive negotiation session was generally regarded as a success.[67] There were calls for the preparation of a "zero draft" of a treaty for the second session in March 2019. The President's final statement at the end of the Session however talked of preparing "as part of the preparations for the second session of the conference, a document with the aim of facilitating focused discussions and text-based negotiations, containing treaty language and reflecting options concerning the four elements of the package." Apparently it is planned that this will be ready by 14 February 2019. In concluding her closing statement to the Session the President said that she believed that "we are firmly on the path to achieving our mission. It will not always be smooth sailing, we will not always paddle in the same direction, but if we continue in our cooperative, flexible and committed mode, we will reach our destination one day."[68]

4 The Issues before the Intergovernmental Conference

In addition to the 2011 "package deal" issues up for discussion which form the agenda of the negotiations, there are a number of cross cutting issues. One of which is likely to be an elaboration of the principles upon which the ILBI is based and which should be used for its interpretation and further elaboration. As the "Elements" paper, produced by the PrepCom Chair indicates,[69] even this area is not free from controversy, particularly relating to the issue of

65 See above.

66 Presidents Aid to Discussions, of June 25, 2018 at http://undocs.org/en/A/CONF.232/2018/3.

67 See e.g. R Tiller *et al.*, 'The once and future treaty: Towards a new regime for biodiversity in areas beyond national jurisdiction.' (2019) 99 *Marine Policy* 239–242.

68 http://undocs.org/en/A/CONF.232/2018/7.

69 See *Chair's non-paper on elements of a draft text of an international legally-binding instrument under the United Nations Convention on the Law of the Sea on the conservation and*

whether the common heritage of mankind—which in the 1982 LOSC is clearly restricted to "the Area" and its resources—should be extended to cover other resources of ABNJ—particularly marine genetic resources found beyond national jurisdiction.

In the early days of the BBNJ discussions, the present author was asked to put together for IUCN a number of "principles of modern high seas governance" that might underpin a new legal instrument. After a number of iterations these were presented in October 2008 at the Barcelona World Conservation Congress at a session chaired by the then IUCN President, Minister Valli Moosa of South Africa.[70] The paper reproduced below on "Principles Applicable to Modern Ocean Governance introduces them, particularly the idea of "conditional freedoms of the seas."[71]

The ten principles are simply listed below,[72] with a few explanatory footnotes to highlight key sources and developments since the 2008 paper was published—particularly the work of the International Tribunal of the Law of the Sea (ITLOS) in its Advisory Opinions 17 and 21.[73] All have been generally accepted by the international community in a range of global and regional instruments, as well as in the decisions of many international courts and tribunals. All, however, require much more rigorous implementation in the development of a robust and appropriate system of international governance for the high seas. There has some support for the enumeration of all or some of these principles as a part of the ILBI.

---

sustainable use of marine biological diversity of areas beyond national jurisdiction, (Dated 28/02/17), particularly Part III and pages 16–18 that list nearly 50 principles or approaches. At http://www.un.org/depts/los/biodiversity/prepcom_files/Chair_non_paper.pdf.

70 http://www.iucn.org/about/work/programmes/marine/marine_our_work/marine_governance/?1694/IUCN-President-Valli-Moosa-to-launch-10-principles-to-save-the-high-seas.

71 David Freestone, 'Principles Applicable to Modern Ocean Governance.' Chapter 1 below. First published (2008) 23 *IJMCL* 385–391.

72 For a more detailed discussion see D Freestone, 'Modern Principles of High Seas Governance: The Legal Underpinnings', (2009) 39 *International Environmental Policy and Law* 49.

73 See *Responsibilities and Obligations of States Sponsoring Persons and Entities with Respect to Activities in the Area, Advisory Opinion*, ITLOS Reports 2011, 10 [Seabed Disputes Chamber Advisory Opinion]. For comment, see D Freestone, 'ITLOS Case 17 with respect to Activities in the Area,' (2011) 105 *American Journal of International Law*, 755–761 Also ITLOS Case 21 *Request for an Advisory Opinion submitted by the Sub-Regional Fisheries Commission (SRFC)*, Advisory Opinion, ITLOS Reports 2015. For comment see D Freestone, 'Case 21' (2016) 1 *Asia-Pacific Journal of Ocean Law and Policy*, 126–133.

Principles of High Seas Governance

1: Conditional Freedom of the Seas
2: Protection and Preservation of the Marine Environment[74]
3: International Cooperation[75]
4: Science-Based Approach to Management[76]
5: The Precautionary Approach[77]
6: The Ecosystem Approach
7: Sustainable and Equitable Use[78]
8: Public Availability of Information[79]
9: Transparent and Open Decision-Making Processes[80]
10: Responsibility of States as Stewards of the Global Marine Environment[81]

Many of these principles as contained within this passage from the 2012 "Rio plus 20" Outcome Document "The Future We Want":

> We therefore commit to protect, and restore, the health, productivity and resilience of oceans and marine ecosystems, and to maintain their biodiversity, enabling their conservation and sustainable use for present and future generations, and to effectively apply an ecosystem approach

74 Art 197 LOSC. See Principle 3 below.

75 Declaration of Principles of International Law, UNGA Resolution 2625 (XXV), of 24 October 1970. Adopted without a vote; it is generally accepted as being declaratory of customary international law.

76 E.g., Article 119 LOSC requires states to base their fisheries conservation and management measures on 'the best scientific evidence available' as well as environmental and economic factors and 'generally recommended inter-national minimum standards.' Also Art 5 UNFSA.

77 UN Doc A/CONF.151/26 (Vols. I–V), of 12 August 1992. See also the 1995 UNFSA, Art 6 and Annex II. Also ITLOS Case 17 on Responsibilities and Obligations of States Sponsoring Persons and Entities with Respect to Activities in the Area, AO, ITLOS Reports 2011, p. 10.

78 Principle 4 1992 Rio Declaration, permeates other principles, Agenda 21 and numerous other instruments. In 1997 it was considered by the International Court of Justice in the *Gabcikovo–Nagymaros Case* between Hungary and Slovakia.

79 See also 1998 ECE Aarhus Convention on Access to Information, Public Participation in Decision Making in Environmental Matters Signed 25 June 1998, entered into force 30 October 2001.

80 Article 12 UNFSA provides for 'transparency in the decision-making process and other activities or sub-regional and regional fisheries management organisations and arrangements.' Note also the Almaty Guidelines.

81 In ITLOS Advisory Opinions in Cases 17 and 21—see above n 00—ITLOS has set out high standards of due diligence for state responsibility.

> and the precautionary approach in the management, in accordance with international law, of activities impacting on the marine environment, to deliver on all three dimensions of sustainable development.[82]

As we saw from the PrepCom Chair's Elements non-paper,[83] there are a lot of other principles in contention including the Adjacency issue which Oude Elferink addresses below. Included also in that list is the important concept of "due regard" included in the submissions of a number of countries, including the US and China and the EU.

Alex Oude Elferink discusses the possible role of coastal States in designating and managing MPAs in ABNJ.[84] This became a controversial issue in the PrepCom discussions; in particular, the issue of "Adjacency" has been presented as an important concept in the managing of ecosystems in ABNJ, for reasons connected with oceanographic as well as ecological connectivity, including the migratory patterns of animals as well as human activities. A number of delegations, including the Pacific SIDS argued that the principle was needed to "address the interest of adjacent coastal states" and that "activities in ABNJ should not impact activities within national jurisdiction."

Oude Elferink reviews these concepts and the PrepCom discussions, arguing that adjacency may not be the most appropriate concept to capture ecological and oceanographic connectivity. Interestingly, he examines the provisions of the Convention on Migratory Species (CMS) that requires Range States of migratory species to cooperate to reach a favorable conservation status for migratory species. In the context of an ILBI, a concept similar to that of "Range State" could, he suggests, include all States under whose jurisdiction or control activities and processes are taking place that affect a proposed MPA. All those States could be included in the development of instruments/programs/measures aimed at protecting or restoring the biodiversity and ecosystem of the MPA.

He points out that the concept of adjacency only occurs in the text of the LOSC in relation to the regime for fisheries. And the similar concept of compatibility—a creation of Art 7 of the 1997 UN Fish Stocks Agreement UNFSA—is also strictly related to fisheries. However he is primarily concerned that the introduction of this new concept might undermine the delicate balance of interests between coastal states and high seas users reflected in

82 At para 58.

83 Above, n 69.

84 Alex G. Oude Elferink, 'Coastal States and MPAs in ABNJ: Ensuring Consistency with the LOSC. Chapter 3. First published (2018) 33 *IJMCL* 437–466.

the LOSC. He points out that a modern expansive interpretation of the existing LOSC requirements of "due regard" would address the concerns that coastal state have in relation to these issues. A different approach, he argues "would detract from the jurisdictional framework contained in the LOSC, and would imply a departure from the understanding that the ILBI has to be fully consistent with the LOSC."

Adjacency as espoused at the PrepCom, he thinks, signals a priority of coastal State interests. By contrast, he concludes, "the two-way street requirement of 'due regard,' which is both applicable to coastal States and to States carrying out activities in ABNJ, expresses the need for complementarity and integration of measures across jurisdictions."

5 The 2011 Package Deal

The 'package deal' agreed in 2011 and carried forward to the IGC contains four linked issues in relation to the conservation and sustainable use of biodiversity in ABNJ: marine genetic resources, including questions on the sharing of benefits, measures such as area-based management tools, including marine protected areas, environmental impact assessments and capacity building and the transfer of marine technology. This section will deal with them in a slightly different order—reflecting historically the origin of the whole process, which as we have seen was the original debate relating to MPAs and ocean governance.

5.1 *Measures such as Area-Based Management Tools, including Marine Protected Areas*

The term Area Based Management Tools (ABMTs) used by the Resolution covers a potentially wide range of issues including marine protected areas or sectoral area restrictions, and which can even be taken to include environmental assessments. Even though EA is given a separate status in the package, all these link to the notion of marine spatial planning

Vasco Becker-Weinberg in his chapter summarizes some of the key issues in the BBNJ debate.[85] He reminds us of the work that UNESCO has done on Marine Spatial Planning (MSP) in the context of management of areas under national jurisdiction. However, no existing international legal regime deals with MSP and the LOSC does not refer to it, but then, as Becker-Weinberg points out, the LOSC does not refer to marine genetic resources or biodiversity

85 V Becker-Weinberg, 'Preliminary Thoughts on Marine Spatial Planning in Areas beyond National Jurisdiction.' Chapter 4. First published (2017) 32 *IJMCL* 570–588.

either. So this is all new territory. Certainly, the LOSC Preamble does recognize that "the problems of the ocean space are closely interrelated and need to be considered as a whole".[86]

Becker-Weinberg cites the UNESCO definition of Marine Spatial Planning as "a public process of analyzing and allocating the spatial and temporal distribution of human activities in marine areas and to pursue ecological, economic, and social objectives that have been specified through a political process."[87] The Convention on Biological Diversity has also stressed the importance of area based management or MSP that addresses multiple management objectives as well as its relevance for improving decision based on the ecosystem approach and in relation to ecosystem-based management.[88]

So, the relevance of a tool such as this in the development of a more sophisticated and holistic approach to ocean governance, which many see as the objective of the ILBI negotiations, begins to appear obvious. Becker-Weinberg reminds us also that although the LOSC does not mention MSP, it does encompass a very carefully negotiated balance between the rights and responsibilities of coastal states in relation to their maritime zones and the resources found within them and the rights and obligations of *all* states in those areas. However, MSP extends beyond the traditional regulation of resource development and exploitation. He suggest that the "very concept of State jurisdiction solely based on sovereignty or functional jurisdiction, whereby States generally operate as either flag, coastal or port States, is one that must be reconsidered in light of new challenges facing the law of the sea, including BBNJ." In this respect, he suggests, MSP is relevant as an area based management tool that could achieve consistency between the rights of sovereignty and jurisdiction of coastal States and the overall interests of sustainable ocean governance. To some extent these issues have already been recognized at a regional level by

86 The LOSC Preamble goes on to acknowledge the need to establish a legal order for the seas and oceans which will facilitate international communication, and will promote the peaceful uses of the seas and oceans, the equitable and efficient utilizations of their resources, the conservation of their living resources, and the study, protection and preservation of the marine environment.

87 See http://msp.ioc-unesco.org/. Also see C Ehler and F Douvere, *Marine Spatial Planning: a Step-by-Step Approach towards Ecosystem-based Management* (IOC Manuals and Guides, n° 53, ICAM Dossier n° 6, Paris, UNESCO, 2009) 19–24.

88 Secretariat of the Convention on Biological Diversity and the Scientific and Technical Advisory Panel, Marine Spatial Planning in the Context of the Convention on Biological Diversity: A Study carried out in Response to CBD COP 10 Decision X/29 (Montreal, Technical Series No. 68) 11.

the European Union in its 2014 Directive establishing a framework for marine spatial planning.[89]

Within the BBNJ PrepCom there was substantial discussion of the use of MSP in the context of the ILBI. The "Non-Paper" issued by the chair of the PrepCom in 2017 quotes a definition put forward by one delegation which brings together some of the plethora of existing sectoral measures (or what might be called existing area based management tools) that might be considered. It is worth reproducing in full:

> Marine spatial planning is a cross-sectoral area-based management tool that provides a framework for the orderly and sustainable use of the oceans as envisioned by UNCLOS with a view to balance demands for development with the need to protect the marine environment. Sectoral area-based management tools (e.g. fisheries closures, Particularly Sensitive Sea Area (PSSAs), Areas of Particular Environmental Interest (APEIs)), other cross-sectoral ABMTs (e.g. MPAs), strategic environmental assessments (SEAs) and environmental impact assessments (EIAs) are an integral part of this overarching planning approach. Marine spatial planning approaches should be ecosystem-based, adaptive and include all relevant stakeholders in the area under consideration.[90]

This list of existing tools is not definitive, but it does demonstrate vividly that if the ILBI is seeking to develop a truly holistic system of governance, then Marine Spatial Planning—which is the systematic process of utilizing Area Based Management Tools (ABMTs) will be an important component of the tool chest, providing a process for bringing together and seeking to reconcile a host of different interests and expectations.

---

89 Directive n°2014/89/EU of the European Parliament and of the Council of 23 July 2014 establishing a framework for maritime spatial planning, Official Journal of the European Communities, L 257, 28.08.2014, 135–145. He also points out that the EU also has legislation on MGRs in relation to the Nagoya Protocol. See Regulation (EU) n° 511/2014 of the European Parliament and of the Council, of 16 April 2014, on compliance measures for users from the Nagoya Protocol on Access to Genetic Resources and the Fair and Equitable Sharing of Benefits Arising from their Utilization in the Union, *Official Journal of the European Union*, L 150/59, 25 May 2014.

90 *Chair's non-paper on elements of a draft text of an international legally-binding instrument under the United Nations Convention on the Law of the Sea on the conservation and sustainable use of marine biological diversity of areas beyond national jurisdiction*, 28/02/2017, available at http://www.un.org/Depts/los/biodiversity/prepcom_files/Chair_non_paper.pdf; at p. 9.

At the heart of the debate over ABMTs is the issue of Marine Protected Areas (MPAs) in area beyond nation jurisdiction. It will be recalled that the Aichi targets agreed by the Parties to the Convention on Biodiversity in 2010 require that:

> 10 per cent of coastal and marine areas, especially areas of particular importance for biodiversity and ecosystem services are conserved through effectively and equitably managed, ecologically representative and well connected systems of protected areas and other effective area-based conservation measures, and integrated into the wider ... seascapes.[91]

This target is reiterated by the 2015 UN Sustainable Development Goal 14.5 which requires conservation of "at least 10 per cent of coastal and marine areas, consistent with national and international law and based on the best available scientific information."[92] Given that the ocean covers 70% of the globe it will be extremely difficult to meet this target simply by conservation of areas within national jurisdiction, hence the pressure for a more systematic approach to conservation of high seas areas. As we saw above, there have been very few protected areas established in the high seas, despite the fact that a number of sectoral and regional organizations, including RFMOs have competence to regulate human activities in ABNJ.[93]

Richard Barnes looks specifically at RFMOs in his paper on the impacts of the ILBI on International Fisheries Law.[94] He suggests that the application of integrated governance principles and the use of area-based management tools and environmental impact assessment will necessarily influence fisheries

---

91 By Decision x/2, at the tenth meeting of the Conference of the Parties to the Convention on Biodiversity, held from 18 to 29 October 2010, in Nagoya, Aichi Prefecture, Japan, adopted a revised and updated Strategic Plan for Biodiversity, including the Aichi Biodiversity Targets, for the 2011–2020 period. Aichi Target 11: By 2020, at least 17 per cent of terrestrial and inland water, and *10 per cent of coastal and marine areas, especially areas of particular importance for biodiversity and ecosystem services*, [emphasis added] are conserved through effectively and equitably managed, ecologically representative and well connected systems of protected areas and other effective area-based conservation measures, and integrated into the wider landscapes and seascapes. https://www.cbd.int/sp/targets/.

92 SDG 14.5 By 2020, conserve at least 10 per cent of coastal and marine areas, consistent with national and international law and based on the best available scientific information. At https://sustainabledevelopment.un.org/content/documents/21252030%20Agenda%20for%20Sustainable%20Development%20web.pdf.

93 See above pp. 12–15.

94 Richard Barnes, 'The Proposed LOSC Implementation Agreement on Areas beyond National Jurisdiction and Its Impact on International Fisheries Law.' Chapter 5. First published (2016) 31 *IJMCL* 583–619.

regulation in ABNJ. Accordingly, he thinks, care should be taken to ensure that any innovative governance tools are adapted to existing institutional capacities and circumstances. His paper contains an excellent summary of the way certain themes have evolved during the process of the BBNJ Ad Hoc Working Group into the beginning of the PrepCom. He also points out that the negotiation mandate of the new Intergovernmental Conference reflects the continued faith in the success of package deal negotiations which of course underpinned the UNCLOS III process. He further reminds us that fisheries agreements do not only concern themselves with the conduct of fishing operations but also with the issue of entitlement to obtain access to the resources.

He suggests that there are two realistic options to address governance gaps. The first is to consider "collaborative institutional mechanisms to integrate fisheries with other environmental and resource-related activities." The second is to "advance a set of cross-cutting governance principles that can promote substantive integration by shaping the conduct of States, RFMOs and other institutions with mandates in ABNJ." And then suggests that either approach or some combination of the two could be accommodated within the proposed ABNJ ILBI. Both possibilities are explored well in his paper.

He may be excessively sanguine to imagine that RFMOs will radically change their behavior in response to hortatory professions of principles such as precaution—which are already articulated in the 1995 UNFSA (and also in their own constitutive instruments—see his chart, below). This has not been the Sargasso Sea experience which is discussed briefly below.[95] However he does provide a useful diagram of the range of suggestions for general structure of the ILBI reflected in the discussion so far:

Strong Integration

	Centralized	Decentralized
Strong Integration	**A1 Single ABNJ Management Authority** • ISA+ option • Single multi-sector institution with comprehensive planning/licensing authority, stablished under a binding instrument.	**B1 Composite Regional ABNJ Management Organizations** • Combined RFMO/regional environmental management regimes • Revised mandates and institutional arrangements governed under a strong binding agreement.
Weak Integration	**A2 ABNJ Advisory Body/Process** • Status quo • Non-binding guidelines advance through resolutions of the UNGA.	**B2 Coordinated Sectoral Management Organizations** • 'Enhanced status quo'. • Retain regional bodies, subject to structured coordination and revised obligations set out in a framework instrument.

Weak Integration

FIGURE 1.1

95 Freestone and Morrison, Chapter 7, below.

Barnes also provides a useful discussion of the relationship between Fisheries and ABMTs. He reminds us that at the PrepCom a number of delegations expressed the view that an integrated approach to the creation of marine protected areas could not be left to the RFMOs with some suggesting that an integrated approach will need to be mandatory—not purely hortatory.[96] The designation of Vulnerable Marine Ecosystems (VMEs) by RFMOs, documented by Barnes, was held up as a success story by some, although it is still subject to criticism outside the industry,[97] and its global coverage is by no means comprehensive.

Similarly, there are divided views on the issue of EIAs and fisheries. The LOSC does not contain any specific obligation requiring EIA for fishery activities. Article 206 LOSC, comments Barnes, "falls short of requiring a cross sectoral cumulative EIA of the kind that appears to be necessary in ABNJ, although it does not necessarily prevent it." He suggests however that a requirement for Strategic Environmental Assessment can be read into Art 206 LOSC, although as he puts it, that article "elides reference to strategic EIA."[98] By contrast the UNFSA Art 6(6) of the 1995 UN Fish Stocks Agreement (UNFSA) specifically requires assessment of new or exploratory fisheries, but only after fishing has begun.[99]

96 Eg Jamaica at his fn 89. Reflected in the position also taken by Dire Tladi below, Chapter 5.

97 See Barnes at p. 133 who highlights that "management measures are often limited to encounter protocols and 'move on' rules, which are set at too high a threshold to protect VMEs." See M Gianni, DEJ Currie, S Fuller, L Speer, J Ardron, B Weeber, M Gibson, K Sack, and A Kavanagh, *Unfinished business: a review of the implementation of the provisions of UNGA resolutions 61/105 and 64/72 related to the management of bottom fisheries in areas beyond national jurisdiction* (Deep Sea Conservation Coalition, September 2011). Available online at: http://www.savethehighseas.org/publicdocs/dscc_review11.pdf. See also the report of the UNGA Workshop to discuss implementation of paragraphs 80 and 83 to 87 of Resolution 61/105 and paragraphs 117 and 119 to 127 of Resolution 64/72 on sustainable fisheries, addressing the impacts of bottom fishing on vulnerable marine ecosystems and the long-term sustainability of deep-sea fish stocks: Letter dated 27 October 2011 from the Moderator of the Workshop to the President of the General Assembly. UNGA Doc A/66/566 (18 November 2011).

98 Art 206 LOSC provides: "When States have reasonable grounds for believing that planned activities under their jurisdiction or control may cause substantial pollution of or significant and harmful changes to the marine environment, they shall, as far as practicable, assess the potential effects of such activities on the marine environment and shall communicate reports of the results of such assessments in the manner provided in article 205."

99 Art 6(6)UNFSA: "For new or exploratory fisheries, States shall adopt as soon as possible cautious conservation and management measures, including, inter alia, catch limits and effort limits. Such measures shall remain in force until there are sufficient data to allow assessment of the impact of the fisheries on the long-term sustainability of the stocks, whereupon conservation and management measures based on that assessment shall be

So, he argues, there may be a customary international law duty to conduct an EIA, but he thinks this only becomes meaningful if the procedures for the EIA are then properly articulated within a legal instrument. The UNFSA and the constituent elements of some RFMOs do contain EIA obligations.[100] However, this does not go far enough and he thinks that "if the prospective IA is to make a difference, then it will need to move beyond generalities and articulate a meaningful EIA process."[101]

Barnes thinks that the development of EIAs through non-binding process such as the UN GA Resolutions on Bottom Fisheries 61/105 reflected in the FAO guidelines provides strong support for the evolution of these processes into binding rules. Although EIA is generally required of States, it needs to be linked to an effective decision-making process. Ideally, where there are reasonable grounds to believe that harm may occur, an EIA must be a prerequisite to fishing activities taking place: "No EIA" should mean "no fishing." However, it may be observed that in 2010 at the resumed Review Conference of the UNFSA, States adopted quite varied positions on this, with some rejecting the requirement of prior EIAs, and others calling for a judicious use of EIAs. Underlying this is a concern about the burdens that might be placed on the fishing industry. Such concerns are not unimportant, Barnes suggests, given that other, arguably wealthier sectors, such as commercial shipping (and submarine telecommunications cables—discussed below),[102] are not currently under similar pressures to conduct EIAs. Existing instruments place the responsibility in the hands of individual States. Ideally, Barnes argues there should be some degree of externality to any Strategic Environmental Review (SEA), otherwise the evaluation process will lack independence and legitimacy. Furthermore, it is arguable whether individual States are in the best position to conduct SEA for plans and programmes of activities that are actually set within regional or international bodies like RFMOs or the ISA. Here it would be logical for SEA to be carried out within that forum or through some other cross-cutting institutional mechanism.

Barnes concludes that the case for the inclusion of fisheries within the terms of the ILBI is very strong, given the importance States have attached to

implemented. The latter measures shall, if appropriate, allow for the gradual development of the fisheries."

100 See Barnes' table 1 at pp. 138–139, below. Oude Elferink notes that the lack of EIA for fisheries is due to fisheries having developed in parallel to environmental law, as opposed to being part of it. See AG Oude Elferink, 'Environmental Impact Assessment in Areas beyond National Jurisdiction' (2012) 27(2) *IJMCL* 449–480;

101 At p. 132.

102 Freidman, Chapter 8, below.

integrated/ecosystem-based approaches, and when considering the practical impact of ABMTs on fisheries or the need to account for the impact of fisheries when assessing cumulative impacts on the marine environment. Indeed, the case against the inclusion of fisheries largely rests on the existence of a dedicated regime for fisheries through the UNFSA and various RFMBs.

In his paper Dire Tladi looks at the whole question of the relationship between regional organizations—particularly Regional Fisheries Management Organizations and the central governance structure envisaged for the ILBI.[103] He thinks that the key issue is the extent to which the regional and proposed central systems will be "compatible."

Many States negotiating the ILBI have very different perspectives as to the respective roles of global and regional ocean governance. Some appear to envisage, or fear, that a new ILBI could create a centralized global ocean governance system analogous to the seabed exploration and mining regime administered by the International Seabed Authority (ISA). Such a new hypothetical Ocean Governance Authority would thus, for example, be able to adopt rules that were automatically binding on all States, including rules designating marine protected areas in ABNJ. It could render new and existing maritime activities subject to environmental impact assessments and strategic environmental assessments, requiring proof that such activities were not likely to cause significant adverse effects, alone or in combination, before being allowed to proceed. It could oversee the way that regional bodies such as Regional Fishery Management Organizations (RFMOs) and sectoral bodies such as the International Maritime Organization (IMO) and the UN Food and Agriculture Organization (FAO) live up to their obligations to protect and preserve the marine environment, and it could require improvements where those bodies come up short.

Other States have a different vision for ocean governance. These emphasize that, consistent with the relevant UN General Assembly Resolutions, the negotiating process should "not undermine" existing legal instruments and frameworks and relevant global, regional, and sectoral bodies.[104] They have thus proffered a minimalist view that would rely on the existing framework of regional and sectoral bodies to implement existing, and perhaps new, obligations to conserve marine biodiversity.

---

103 Dire Tladi, 'The Proposed Implementing Agreement: Options for Coherence and Consistency in the Establishment of Protected Areas beyond National Jurisdiction.' Chapter 6.
First published (2015) 30 *IJMCL* 654–673.

104 UNGA Res 69/292 (July 6, 2015).

As highlighted above, the experience of the Sargasso Sea project over the last eight years has been that that RFMOs and other sectoral organizations (such as the IMO and ISA) are often too narrowly focused on their particular sectoral concerns to perform a wider biodiversity or ecosystem-stewardship role, and that there is a clear need for a more holistic and integrated system of governance in order to conserve and sustain biodiversity and ecosystem functions in ABNJ.[105] In recounting the experience of the Signing of the Hamilton Declaration on Collaboration for the Conservation of the Sargasso Sea in March 2014, the authors explain the aspiration of the signatory governments and supporters that it would be a new paradigm for conservation of high seas area based on voluntary collaboration and working together through existing institutions.[106]

The Sargasso Sea project represents one of the few examples of state practice in relation to BBNJ, which justifies the reproduction of the full text of the Hamilton Declaration.[107] The Declaration authorizes the establishment of the Sargasso Sea Commission by the Government of Bermuda with a mandate of "Stewardship." The Declaration now has 10 Government Signatories[108] and the Commission has worked with a wide range of organizations with legal competences in the high seas. However, its experience is that sectoral organizations have been reluctant, or at least slow, to recognize the importance of conservation of unique high seas ecosystems, or the significance of EBSAs to their activities, or the impacts that their activities might be having on EBSAs. This reflects a general reluctance to espouse precautionary action, despite the fact that so many instruments mandate it.[109] If the international community is sincere in is wish to conserve and sustainably use biodiversity in areas beyond national jurisdiction, then the institutional framework for this needs to be improved.

---

105 *See* David Freestone, 'Governance of Areas beyond National Jurisdiction: An Unfinished Agenda?' in (J Barrett and R Barnes, eds.) *Law of the Sea: UNCLOS as a Living Treaty* (British Institute for International and Comparative Law, London 2016) 231–66.

106 David Freestone and Kate K. Morrison, 'The Signing of the Hamilton Declaration on Collaboration for the Conservation of the Sargasso Sea: A new paradigm for high seas conservation?' Chapter 7.
First published (2014) 29 *IJMCL* 345–362.

107 Below pp. 168–176, below.

108 Azores, Bahamas, Bermuda, British Virgin Islands, Canada, Cayman Islands, Dominican Republic, Monaco, UK and US.

109 D Freestone and K Gjerde, *Lessons from the Sargasso Sea: Challenges to the conservation and sustainable use of marine biodiversity beyond national jurisdiction.* Sargasso Sea Commission, 2016. At http://www.sargassoseacommission.org/storage/SargassoSea_in_page_format_1.pdf.

That framework could have a lighter touch than a full-time, comprehensive Ocean Governance Authority. It might, for example, be overseen by regular meetings of a Conference of Parties to the new ILBI, advised perhaps by a scientific advisory body or a legal, scientific, or technical commission ("scientific advisory commission"). That Conference of Parties might exercise a supervisory rather than a full governance role, reviewing environmental impact assessments and strategic environmental assessments for new ocean activities, as well as efforts by regional and sectoral bodies to integrate the new ILBI requirements into their existing roles.

Such a structure would recognize the important role of the regional and sectoral organizations, such as RFMOs, without (as Tladi terms it) "deferring" to them. Tladi thinks that the Conference of Parties should have a pre-eminent role in designating marine protected areas in ABNJ. In his scenario, a potential site that meets agreed, science-based criteria would be identified by a scientific advisory commission. The Conference of Parties could simply designate those areas as marine protected areas, but if such areas were within the jurisdictional area of a regional or sectoral body (such as an RFMO), then the Conference Secretariat or the scientific advisory commission itself would consult with those bodies to discuss appropriate conservation measures. The ideal outcome then would be for the RFMO to adopt appropriate conservation measures that could be endorsed by the Conference of Parties and thus be binding on all the parties to the ILBI. The support of the RFMO will always be useful and would greatly enhance the effectiveness of the ILBI process, but failure to act by the RFMO is not necessarily fatal. The Conference of Parties could nevertheless designate the area as an MPA. Such a decision would be universally binding on the parties to the ILBI—some of whom may also be parties to the RFMO. Such a situation would not, Tladi suggests, trigger a legal conflict, as no RFMO *obliges* its parties to fish in certain areas; it would be merely "incoherence between the obligation under the [ILBI] and the permissiveness of the RFMO." States Parties to the ILBI could be obliged to simultaneously pursue adoption of compatible conservation measures through the relevant organizations.

Certainly, in discussions of ocean governance, one key argument is that as a result of the fragmentation of organization on a sectoral and regional basis, there no centralized *system* of governance. In addition to fragmentation there are also governance gaps in that a number of activities are not systematically covered, or maybe not really regulated at all. Of these latter activities, the regulation of submarine telecommunication cables is often raised.

Unlike the regulatory framework established by the International Maritime Organization (IMO) or the International Seabed Authority or even the fisheries sector (although as we just saw, that framework is by no means comprehensive) there is no international body with authority to regulate the laying and maintenance of STCs. Freedom to lay submarine cables is entrenched as a freedom of the seas in Art 87, LOSC. The industry does have a sophisticated self-regulatory body—the International Cable Protection Committee (ICPC).

It is difficult to underestimate the importance of submarine telecommunication cables. As Andrew Friedman reports they are estimated to carry 98% of voice, data and internet traffic.[110] Moreover, ICPC has argued strongly that this network works perfectly well, that its impacts on the marine environment are minimal, and that is it too important to be subject to regulation which might restrict it effectiveness. It has submitted a formal submission to this effect to the BBNJ PrepCom arguing that it should be "expressly excluded" from the scope of the new instrument.[111]

However, all the BBNJ Working Group Recommendations, the Report of the PrepCom[112] and the 2017 UNGA Resolution 72/249 deciding to convene an intergovernmental conference to consider the recommendations of the PrepCom,[113] all specify that the new instrument is to be developed "under the United Nations Convention on the Law of the Sea". Hence, as Friedman points out, any elaboration of state rights or responsibilities inconsistent with those contemplated by the LOSC, including with respect to submarine cable activities on the high seas, would fall beyond the scope of the proposed negotiations. Under the LOSC, laying submarine cables, and attendant activities (e.g., surveying and repair by extension), are among the enumerated "freedoms" of the high seas. Hence, only a limited field of potential overlap remains between cables and the new instrument.

However, rather than exclude cables, Friedman suggests, a new instrument could instead formalize a flexible and cooperative approach with the cable industry to provide limited environmental management if and where necessary without restricting cable operations or network growth. This approach would be consistent with the LOSC and could also inform the ILBI negotiators approach to similar "low impact" activities in ABNJ.

110 Andrew Friedman, 'Submarine Telecommunication Cables and a Biodiversity Agreement in ABNJ: Finding New Routes for Cooperation.' Chapter 8. First published (2017) 32 *IJMCL* 1–35.

111 Submission by the ICPC to the PrepCom: Submarine Cables and ABNJ (1 August 2016) available at http://www.un.org/depts/los/biodiversity/prepcom_files/ICC_Submarine_Cables_&_BBNJ_August_2016.pdf.

112 UN A/AC.287/2017/PC.4/2.

113 UNGA Res 72/249 (24 December 2017).

One of the main concerns of the ICPC is that they might face the prior requirement of expensive EIAs for cable laying activities in ABNJ. While all cable-laying and replacement activities are preceded by extensive survey work these are not formal EIAs which would also require some other body to evaluate.[114] Friedman suggests three possible alternative approaches to the coverage of telecommunication cables in the ILBI: Specific Exclusion (as requested by the ICPC); second, silence regarding cables; or, third, a presumption of *prima facie* compliance with the ILBI. The last is his preferred choice. As he concludes, once the ILBI negotiations are underway, submarine cable operations will be only one of many activities in ABNJ facing implications. In addition to a raft of existing activities, the instrument will also need to address emerging activities, like high seas aquaculture and offshore power generation, with varying degrees of potential to affect biodiversity and the marine environment. He suggests that the way the negotiators respond to the issue of submarine cables will probably "chart a pathway for these other activities, particularly those that are likely to be similarly benign. In this way, the submarine cable industry can act as a critical first-mover in developing an efficient and effective regulatory regime."[115] The industry could also provide some useful parameters for the threshold requirements for EA for activities in ABNJ.

5.2 *Environmental Impact Assessments*

As we have seen, concerns about the need for the conservation of biodiversity in ABNJ are reflected in calls not only for the expansion of MPAs in ABNJ (themselves reflecting the CBD Aichi targets and the SDG 14.5 of 10 per cent of coastal and marine areas by 2020) but also calls for a more systematic process for the assessment of human impacts on the open oceans. These assessments are proposed not only for new activities, but there have also been calls for the

114 See following, cited by Friedman, D Burnett, D Freestone and T Davenport, *Submarine Cables in the Sargasso Sea: Legal and Environmental Issues in Areas Beyond National Jurisdiction*, Report from the Workshop held 23 October 2014 at George Washington University Law School, Washington, DC (16 January 2015) at p. 4. According to the workshop's participants, "[t]he submarine cable industry does not support the imposition of any requirement for an Environmental Impact Assessment (EIA) for cable laying operations in the Sargasso Sea or any other area which is beyond national jurisdiction. In its view, it is not legally required, there is no clear benefit and the costs of conducting an EIA are potentially onerous". Written up as A L de Juvigny, *et al.*, Submarine Telecommunication Cables in the Sargasso Sea" (2015) 30 *International Journal of Marine and Coastal Law* 371–378.

115 p. 210.

strategic assessment of existing activities—some of which have increased, and are continuing to increase rapidly.[116]

Gunnar Sander in his contribution looks in detail at the international legal obligations for EA in the Arctic.[117] He points out that the tools which have been developed at national and regional levels for such assessments are environmental impact assessments (EIA) and strategic environmental assessment (SEA), together known as environmental assessments (EA). His review is not simply a review of the individual applicable instruments applicable in the Arctic—he provides an interesting and thoughtful review of the *regime* for environmental assessments. Not only does he flag the constellation of instruments possibly applicable to this peculiar regional sea, but also the absence of specific instruments relating to activities in ABNJ. It is worth noting, as he does, that the Arctic Ocean is different from many other ocean areas in that it does have applicable regional conventions with assessment obligations, notably OSPAR but also the Espoo Convention.[118] The Arctic Council has also urged that any future exploitation of natural resources in the Arctic must be based on thorough impact assessments and has identified the need to consider a set of operational guidelines for assessing the impact of projects, plans.[119] By contrast the majority of regional seas conventions have provisions regarding EA that apply only to areas within national jurisdiction.

As we saw above the LOSC does have important requirements for environmental monitoring and reporting, but Sander describes them as "of low specificity." The LOSC requires that "when States have reasonable grounds for believing that planned activities under their jurisdiction or control may cause substantial pollution of or significant and harmful changes to the marine environment, they shall, as far as practicable, assess the potential effects of such

116 For example remote monitoring suggests that between 1992 and 2012 maritime traffic increased 300 percent, see Jean Tounadre, "Anthropogenic pressure on the open ocean: The growth of ship traffic revealed by altimeter data analysis" (2014) 21(22) *Geophysical Research Letters* 7924–7932. DOI: 10.1002/2014GL061786. See http://www.livescience.com/48788-ocean-shipping-big-increase-satellites.html.

117 Gunnar Sander, 'International Legal Obligations for Environmental Impact Assessment and Strategic Environmental Assessment in the Arctic Ocean.' Chapter 9, First published (2016) 31 *IJMCL* 88–119.

118 Convention on Environmental Impact Assessment in a Transboundary Context (Espoo, 25 February 1991, in force 10 September 1997) 1989 UNTS 310. Sander comments that Espoo and its protocols do not cover marine activities well and not all the Arctic Ocean coastal states are parties.

119 Sander at p. 213. Senior Arctic Officials' Report to Ministers, April 2009, section 3.2 (adopted by the Ministers). Available at http://www.arctic-council.org/index.php/en/document-archive/category/53-final-reports-and-statements.

activities on the marine environment and shall communicate reports of the results of such assessments ..."[120] However, the triggers for these requirements are unilaterally determined and reporting, if it takes place at all, is not done for any centralized body, nor is there any systematic process for reviewing these reports.[121]

Moreover, as Sander points out, these LOSC requirements are supplemented by general customary international law principles, although these are also with "low specificity," such as the no-harm principle, which involves obligations to exercise due diligence.[122] Also relevant are the precautionary principle and the duty of co-operation. However, the origins of detailed EA processes are at national level, first seen in the US in the 1960s. Indeed, Principle 17 of the 1992 Rio Declaration specifically envisages it "as a national instrument."[123]

So, as a case study, this assessment the Arctic—one of the most fragile but also more heavily regulated international areas—demonstrates there are still major gaps in the EA system. What Sander sees as the key weaknesses of the EA regime in the Arctic are also weaknesses of the global EA regime, namely:

- States' acceptance of existing instruments is far from complete.
- Major sectors are not covered, notably fisheries.
- International law does not clearly mandate EA at the domestic level for activities that could impact neighbours or commons.
- Weak coverage of ABNJ.
- Low marine relevance of existing instruments—such as the Espoo Convention.
- Strategic Assessments not covered well.

---

120 Art 206 LOSC. It also requires States to "keep under surveillance the effects of any activities which they permit or in which they engage in order to determine whether these activities are likely to pollute the marine environment."(Art 204) and to publish reports and "provide such reports at appropriate intervals to the competent international organizations, which should make them available to all States." (Art 205 LOSC).

121 R Warner, 'Oceans beyond Boundaries: Environmental Assessment Frameworks' (2012) 27 *The International Journal of Marine and Coastal Law* 481–499.

122 This is itself an evolving requirement. See e.g. *Pulp Mills on the River Uruguay* (Argentina v. Uruguay), International Court of Justice (ICJ), 20 April 2010, para 204. Available at http://www.icj-cij.org/docket/index.php?p1=3&p2=3&case=135&p3=4. And *Responsibilities and Obligations of States Sponsoring Persons and Entities With Respect to Activities in the Area*, Sea Bed Disputes Chamber Advisory Opinion, 1 February 2011, ITLOS Reports 2011, para 148. Available at https://www.itlos.org/cases/list-of-cases/case-no-17/.

123 "Environmental impact assessment, as a national instrument, shall be undertaken for proposed activities that are likely to have a significant adverse impact on the environment and are subject to a decision of a competent national authority". *1992 Rio Declaration on Environment and Development*, Available at http://www.unep.org/Documents.Multilingual/Default.asp?documentid=78&articleid=1163.

The lessons for the BBNJ ILBI negotiators are, he thinks, fairly clear. There is thematic and geographic fragmentation of EA requirements. So, EA requirements and minimum standards need to be included in the new instrument and they need to be much more specific. These could then act as a default mechanism for those activities not covered by specific regimes. Rather than attempt to develop detailed requirements for specific activities, he advocates generic rules for EIA and SEA for the ILBI that "are open to a broader set of tools and other values than the biophysical environment," and respond also to the call for integration on ocean governance issues.

There is also a major cross cutting issue here. While there is fifty years of experience of EA in certain parts of the world—this expertise is not uniform. There is a global need for high quality EA expertise, which would also be invaluable for the ongoing UN Regular Process for Global Reporting and Assessment of the State of the Marine Environment, which is now embarking on the Second World Ocean Assessment.[124] The ILBI presents an ideal opportunity to include this within it capacity building mandates.

Finally Sander reminds us that EA is a procedural requirement rather than a substantive regulation; it is not in itself a safeguard against developments with harmful effects.[125] Decisions then still have to be taken based on the EA findings. However best practice in the assessment community suggests it should be used upfront to help guide the planning process. When integrated in this way it can not only prevent harm but lead to better planning decisions. This takes us back to the need for an holistic approach, for there is currently no central planning process for activities in ABNJ. If the ILBI is to develop such a role then a form of marine spatial planning could be an important aspect of the Area Based Management Toolkit; EA would provide a vital tool for such a role.

5.3 *Marine Genetic Resources, including Questions on the Sharing of Benefits*

One of the key issues in the 2011 "package" is the issue of benefit sharing regarding marine genetic resources. This is probably the most complex and certainly likely to be one of the more controversial aspects of the negotiation.

---

124 See http://www.un.org/depts/los/global_reporting/global_reporting.htm.

125 Although it has been suggested that it could be linked to goals of sustainability and reduce discretion in decision making, see E Druel and KM Gjerde, 'Sustaining marine life beyond boundaries: Options for an implementing agreement for marine biodiversity beyond national jurisdiction under the United Nations Convention on the Law of the Sea' (2014) 49 *Marine Policy* 90–97.

In a most useful attempt to clarify some of the options available to the negotiators in relation to benefit sharing of MGRs, Gaute Voigt-Hanssen aims to provide a somewhat simplified overview of options of access and benefit-sharing drawing on existing models from international and national instruments.[126]

The problem, he explains, is that existing international models of benefit-sharing have all evolved in the context of national jurisdiction and cannot readily be put to use in areas outside national jurisdiction. However, in order to give readers and negotiators some idea of the complexity of the existing options available for both access to MGRs and benefit sharing from them, he roughly assigns them to two groups in terms of whether they involve monetary benefit sharing provisions. The substantive administrative burden associated with monetary benefit sharing, he suggests, makes them "heavy" in terms of the requirements for tracking, monitoring, reporting and enforcement.

He first highlights the fact others have pointed out above that the LOSC regime does not regard marine genetic resources as a recognised asset and has no specific rules regulating them. He then looks at the Nagoya Protocol to the CBD.[127] The Nagoya Protocol is based, he explains, on an assumption that biodiversity-rich provider countries will regulate access to genetic resources by making access for the user subject to prior informed consent. Requirements for benefit-sharing may be included in the access provisions and/or in a bilateral contract.

However, a more relevant model, Voigt-Hanssen suggests, is the International Treaty on Plant Genetic Resources for Food and Agriculture (ITPGRFA).[128] He reports that the ITPGRFA revolves around a system of facilitated access. To get access to a sample of one of the 64 food and feed crops *genera* listed on the annex of the Treaty, a Standard Material Transfer Agreement (SMTA) has to be signed. The SMTA has fixed terms and conditions on access and utilisation of these crops. The attractiveness of the system is its simplicity—the absence of a need to negotiate terms, which lowers administrative burdens

126 Gaute Voigt-Hanssen, '"Light" and "heavy" options for benefit-sharing in the context of the United Nations Convention on the Law of the Sea.' Chapter 10. First published (2018) 33 *IJMCL* 683–705.

127 2010 Nagoya Protocol on Access to Genetic Resources and the Fair and Equitable Sharing of Benefits Arising from their Utilization to the Convention on Biological Diversity, adopted 29 October 2010, entered into force on 12 October 2014. It has been ratified by 114 parties. For text see https://www.cbd.int/abs/text/default.shtml.

128 The International Treaty on Plant Genetic Resources for Food and Agriculture (Rome, 3 November 2001, in force 29 June 2004, 2400 UNTS 303).

and costs to both the Provider and the User. If products are later developed that are derived from the accessed material and the developer decides to restrict others from accessing the products through intellectual property restrictions, then the developer is obliged to pay a percentage of the sales of the product to the Benefit-Sharing Fund. This obligation to pay persists even if only a small amount of accessed material has been included in the product. The Fund is to be used to support conservation and further development of agriculture in developing countries.

So, a highly complex system based on a Nagoya model with individually negotiated contractual arrangements would be, he suggests, "double heavy," involving heavy administrative requirements to gain access and then complex benefit sharing requirements. Individually negotiated contracts for access would be "heavy" to negotiate and then "heavy" to enforce, with scope for wide national variations. It could also require an international supervisory authority to regulate the process. By contrast, another model would be a light, open science approach, requiring researchers and bio-prospectors to notify a designated authority of activities and then file detailed cruise reports of their work in ABNJ. The data would be in an open access data base (unless a fee was paid for a time bound embargo). Similarly a "light" benefit sharing approach could be essentially access to non-monetary benefits through a global or regional collection or database. He then explains how this might work. Finally another model would be "light access" with "heavy benefit sharing" in the case of commercialisation.

In the negotiations he suggests that developed countries generally appear to favour light-light approaches—expressing concern about inhibiting scientific research by a heavy regulatory system—and developing countries tend to favour the more heavy-heavy or light-heavy approach There are he points out many variations of these models, but there are lessons from previous instruments. First, clarify the material scope of the ILBI—i.e. no "creative ambiguity." Second, he suggests "there are few success stories in the regulatory history of monetary access and benefit sharing." He concludes that many developing countries are in need of capacity building to better conserve and sustainably use their own genetic resources before they commence utilizing genetic material from ABNJ. Taking part in cruises, laboratory work, product development, etc. related to genetic resources from ABNJ could prove beneficial for developing states in their utilization of national genetic resources. So, it is important that the design of the ILBI should give appropriate attention to these cross-cutting issues.

Following on the trail laid by Voigt-Hanssen, Broggiato, Vanagt and colleagues present a very thorough and perceptive analysis of the current situation, together with thoughtful and innovative approaches to addressing key problems.[129] As they stress, "a fair and effective regime regulating benefit-sharing of marine genetic resources (MGR) in areas beyond national jurisdiction (ABNJ) must consider inclusivity of developing states, as well as support scientific research and safeguard investments of the private sector." Early in their paper the authors look at the origin of the Freedom of the High Seas in the work of Hugo Grotius and argue that:

> Despite appearances … Grotius's heritage has not been slowly erased but rather operationalized … The current tendency to regulate these traditionally lawless areas is not occurring in a *mare clausum* type of policy, but rather following the recognition that there is a further need for sharing the resources provided by our planet. This comes with realizing the need for international cooperation and regulation to put the adequate frameworks in place within which such sharing can happen.

The paper sets out all three pillars of a possible access and benefit-sharing (ABS) regime: access; benefit-sharing; and compliance

Recent technical analysis shows uneven levels of access to MGR in ABNJ between a small group of developed countries and the rest of the world. The key factors include the cost of technology to sample in international waters and the deep-sea, and the cost of its maintenance; the scientific skills to undertake research on marine biodiversity; the cost and scientific skills to undertake molecular screening and biodiversity assessment; the scientific skills to analyse the data thereby produced.

In 1995, according to Glowka, only six countries (Finland, France, the United Kingdom, Japan, Russia and USA) had the technological, financial and human resources to directly access MGR *in situ* in ABNJ.[130] In 2012, this had risen to twenty-nine countries, both developed and developing, who had access to MGR from hydrothermal vents as members of *InterRidge*, (the International Cooperation in Ridge-Crest Studies),[131] a cooperation organisation, and of the

129 Arianna Broggiato, Thomas Vanagt, Laura E. Lallier, Marcel Jaspars, Geoff Burton, and Dominic Muyldermans: Mare Geneticum: Balancing Governance of Marine Genetic Resources in International Waters. Chapter 11. First published (2018) 33 *IJMCL* 3–33.

130 L Glowka, 'Evolving Perspectives on the International Seabed Area's Genetic Resources: Fifteen Years after the Deepest of Ironies' in D Vidas (ed.) *Law, Technology and Science for Oceans in Globalisation* (Martinus Nijhoff Publishers/Brill, Leiden/Boston, 2010) 397–419, at p. 415.

131 Available at www.interridge.org; accessed 18 January 2017.

Pacific Islands Applied Geoscience Commission.[132] However, notwithstanding the wider access to deep-sea sampling technologies, there are still very wide disparities. The authors remind us that the First UN World Ocean Assessment made the point that the current uneven research capabilities across the globe are the primary source of inequity amongst states, *more than disparities in accessing the resources in situ.*[133]

The UNGA Resolution text proposes that the ILBI negotiations should deal with "marine genetic resources including questions on the sharing of benefits." It does not mention access. However, Broggiato et al., consider that access should be part of the package to make it workable, but that should not mean restricted scientific access to resources *in situ*, nor excessive bureaucratic hurdles that would hamper scientific research.

They propose a facilitated procedure—that they have called their *Mare Geneticum* system—for those planning to access MGRs *in situ* from ABNJ. They have dubbed this the Obligatory Prior Electronic Notification (OPEN), which must be filed before any sampling cruise and updated after the cruise and which then must be available through an online registry. Identifiers will then be associated with each OPEN notification thus keeping track of cruise information, samples and the following steps in the research and development chain. This in itself will be an invaluable database on global marine biodiversity. Each OPEN notification would require acceptance of certain benefit sharing obligations including sharing data in public databases and the obligation to make payment in case of later commercialisation. An additional fee would be required for a temporary embargo on release of data (as commercial exploiters often require). A similar parallel arrangement would be required for researchers seeking to access MGRs from previously collected samples held *in vitro*.

Open access to all the data on marine biodiversity in ABNJ compiled by this system would then be freely available—the first non-monetary benefit. We are reminded that the commercial development of usable products from these samples is a long term and uncertain process.[134] Apparently only seven

132 Glowka, at p. 412.

133 DK Leary and SK Juniper, 'Addressing the Marine genetic resources issue: Is the debate heading in the wrong direction?' in C Schofield, S Lee and MS Kwon (eds.) *The Limits of Maritime Jurisdiction* (Martinus Nijhoff Publishers, Leiden, 2014) 769–785, at p. 773; and D Leary, M Vierros, G Hamon, S Arico, and C Monagle, 'Marine Genetic Resources: A Review of Scientific and Commercial Interest' (2009) 33 *Marine Policy* 183–194, at p. 187.

134 T Greiber 'Types of benefits and benefit sharing' in *IUCN information papers for the intersessional workshop on marine genetic resources in ABNJ* (IUCN Environmental Law Center, Bonn, 2013) 29–37, at 29.

pharmaceutical products derived from marine organisms are currently on the market. Of those seven, six are derived from species found in EEZs and the seventh—a fish species—occurs both within and beyond national jurisdiction. In addition, a further 28 products are in clinical trials and 250 undergoing preclinical investigation.[135]

The OPEN system could also require monetary payments at different stages in the product pipeline. As discussed above, if an embargo on release of data about samples collected *in situ* is requested, then an exclusivity/embargo fee would be required which could be on a sliding scale depending on issues such as the duration of the embargo, the level of research funding involved and (perhaps) the users financial capacity. These fees would be paid into a fund established by the ILBI.

The authors think a second payment step could also be envisaged, triggered by the commercialisation of a product which is derived from MGRs found in ABNJ. The percentage royalty to be paid would be contractually predetermined and fixed. It could be set by a process which ensures compatibility with equivalent payments under national Access and Benefit Sharing schemes.

The last part of the system would be an enforcement and compliance mechanism linked to a central tracking system derived from the OPEN registry. The authors are clear, however, that they regard the main benefits from this scheme as the non-monetary benefits. They summarise this argument as follows:

Above all, the authors feel, "the ILBI should emphasize and strengthen non-monetary benefit-sharing for the advancement of science and nature conservation through, *inter alia*:

- Open access to raw data and samples;
- Enhanced international research coordination and cooperation;
- Targeted training and sharing of expertise, methodology, guidelines and best practices;
- Standardized data management, taxonomy and species identification;
- Marine spatial planning in ABNJ, including protected areas;
- Ecosystem-based management;
- Development of marine conservation policies."

5.4 *Capacity Building and the Transfer of Marine Technology*

The last items in the list of issues to be addressed—but by no means the least important—are those of capacity building and the transfer of marine technology. Harriet Harden-Davies in her study of technology transfer in the South Pacific reminds us of the extensive coverage these issues receive in the LOSC

135 Broggiato, *et al.*, citing http://marinepharmacology.midwestern.edu/.

itself, but she also reminds of the slow progress that has been made on these issues in the 35 years or so since the conclusion of the LOSC.[136]

The thirteen articles of Part XIV of the LOSC oblige States to cooperate either directly or through international organizations. Article 268 in particular captures the key issues covered by this concept which are of relevance to the ILBI. It requires that States, directly or through competent international organizations, shall promote:

(a) the acquisition, evaluation and dissemination of marine technological knowledge and facilitate access to such information and data;
(b) the development of appropriate marine technology;
(c) the development of the necessary technological infrastructure to facilitate the transfer of marine technology;
(d) the development of human resources through training and education of nationals of developing States and countries and especially the nationals of the least developed among them;
(e) international cooperation at all levels, particularly at the regional, subregional and bilateral levels.

Harden-Davies' study looks generally at the mechanisms of scientific research and collaboration among the Small Island Developing States (SIDs) in the Pacific and specifically examines their capacity to engage in meaningful research on marine genetic resources. She reports that the South West Pacific region is a significant source of marine genetic resources and has been a target for marine bio-discovery activity. The discoveries she cites include compounds with anti-cancer properties derived from sponges collected in Guam and Palau and from fungal strains collected offshore from Fiji; and sterols with anti-fungal properties from a starfish collected off New Caledonia.[137] There are also marine genetic resource patents associated with the North Fiji Basin, Manus Basin, Tonga Trench and Kermadec Trench.[138]

Although Harden Davies' study concentrates on one particular region it does capture well the difficulties of establishing networks for scientific cooperation

---

136 Harriet R. Harden-Davies, Research for Regions: Strengthening Marine Technology Transfer for Pacific Island Countries and Biodiversity Beyond National Jurisdiction. Chapter 12.
First published (2017) 32 *IJMCL* 797–822.

137 D Skropeta, 'Deep-Sea Natural Products' (2008) 25(6) *Natural Product Reports* 1131–1166; D Skropeta and L Wei, 'Recent Advances in Deep-Sea Natural Products' (2014) 31(8) *Ibid.*, 999–1025.

138 P Oldham, S Hall, C Barnes, C Oldham, M Cutter, N Burns, L Kindess, *Valuing the Deep: Marine Genetic Resources in Areas Beyond National Jurisdiction* (One World Analytics, London, 2014). 1–241, at pp. 81, 82, 143, 158.

and of mobilizing resources for technology transfer with the least developed countries, particularly in relation to the sort of cutting edge technology which is involved in processing marine genetic resources and their derivatives.[139] The South Pacific region is particularly rich in regional organizations and has, through necessity, developed important coordinating mechanisms, through, for example, the unique role of the University of the South Pacific as well as others. These highlight however the intrinsic tension in the development of a mechanism under the ILBI which would specifically address technology transfer and capacity building related to MGRs in ABNJ, when there may be no existing national research infrastructure and capacity to deal with these issues at a national level.

As far as the ILBI is concerned, Harden-Davies notes there are proposals for the establishment of a Clearing House Mechanism, providing a central portal to access and exchange information on activities relating to biodiversity in ABNJ. This incidentally more than reinforces the same point made by Voigt-Hanssen above.[140] She notes that there will be issues of scope, as the technology and capacity building regarding ABNJ cannot be considered in isolation from national activities. Hence, the broader the scope the more meaningful it is likely to be at national levels but also the more resource intensive. Nevertheless a technology transfer/capacity building mechanism with a broad scope would be in accord with calls in a number of UNGA resolutions,[141] as well as with the terms of Sustainable Development Goal 14.A.[142]

Finally, she stresses the need for a funding mechanism. Absent from the Law of the Sea Convention but found in most international environmental law treaties since 1992, the technology and capacity building requirements of the new ILBI do highlight the need for a dedicated funding source.

The issue of funding, like "Principles" discussed above,[143] is one of the cross cutting matters which the negotiators will have to address, probably once the other key issues approach agreement. The famous PrepCom Chair's non paper also lists monitoring, review, compliance and enforcement, the settlement of

139 She highlights that some of the most successful initiatives have been at the North South institution to institution level.

140 Chapter 10.

141 E.g. UNGA Res A/71.L.26 at [247].

142 SDG 14.A: "Increase scientific knowledge, develop research capacity and transfer marine technology, taking into account the Intergovernmental Oceanographic Commission Criteria and Guidelines on the Transfer of Marine Technology, in order to improve ocean health and to enhance the contribution of marine biodiversity to the development of developing countries, in particular small island developing States and least developed countries." At https://sustainabledevelopment.un.org/sdg14.

143 At pp. 20–21, above.

disputes, position of non-parties, responsibility and liability and of course the requirement for coming into force.[144]

As we have seen there are still a large number of difficult issues still to be addressed. They are certainly not insuperable however and this collection has been designed to assist readers with a wider understand of many of the legal issues underlying this process, in the hope that it will also contribute to the process of finding ways forward.

---

144 Above n 69.

PART 2

The BBNJ Package Deal: Elements and Issues

CHAPTER 1

Principles Applicable to Modern Ocean Governance

David Freestone
Editor in Chief
International Journal of Marine and Coastal Law

Abstract

The establishment by the UN General Assembly of the Ad hoc Open-ended Informal Working Group to study issues relating to the conservation and sustainable use of biodiversity in area beyond national jurisdiction has highlighted the challenges that are faced in the governance of areas beyond national jurisdiction. This short editorial considers the ways in which the 1982 Law of the Sea Convention (LOSC) and subsequent instruments have developed principles which are particularly appropriate for high seas governance. It points out that the so called "freedoms of the high seas" are not unconditional freedoms but are subject to a number of important limitations and qualifications found both in the LOSC itself but also in other instruments such as the 1995 UN Fish Stocks Agreement and in customary law. It identifies 10 principles that should be applicable to the regulation of any human activities that affect the marine environment or biodiversity in ABNJ.

Keywords

Principles – Freedoms of the High Seas – UNGA, ABNJ, LOSC – UN Fish Stocks Agreement – precaution – ecosystem approach

In 2004 on the recommendation of the UN Informal Consultative Process on the Oceans and the Law of the Sea (UNICPOLOS) the UN General Assembly agreed to establish an Ad Hoc Open-ended Informal Working Group to study issues relating to the conservation and sustainable use of marine biological diversity beyond areas of national jurisdiction. This Working Group held its first meeting 13–17 February, 2006 and on the basis of its report the General

 | DOI:10.1163/9789004391703_003

Assembly agreed to convene a second meeting that was held from 28 April–2 May 2008.[1]

In October of 2007, in order to provide informed input into the deliberations of the UN Working Group, the IUCN and a group of partners hosted an important workshop of some fifty ocean law and policy experts, meeting in their personal capacity, to consider the challenges faced by High Seas Governance in the 21st century. The workshop was held at the law offices of the New York firm of Debevoise and Plimpton, 17–19th October 2007. The co-chairs report was made available early in 2008,[2] and a briefing was held at the UN in March as well as at an IUCN hosted side-event during the second meeting of the Working Group.[3]

At the October workshop I made a short presentation of the basic principles that should be applicable to modern ocean governance. What follows is my attempt to reduce this presentation to writing and to reflect the rich and thoughtful discussion that ensued.[4]

1 Ocean Governance: Where Have We Come From and Where Do We Need to Go?

An investigation into modern principles of ocean governance needs to start with some perspective. Over the last half century the law of the sea has evolved quite dramatically. In that period there were three UN Conferences on the Law of the Sea, including the nine years of UNCLOS III—one of the longest running treaty negotiations in UN history. Contrasting the relevant provisions of the 1958 Geneva Convention on Fishing and the Conservation of Living Resources of the High Seas with those of the 1982 Law of the Sea Convention reveals how modern thinking on fisheries and biodiversity conservation has changed in the quarter century between those two agreements. While the 1958 Convention provides that "All states have the right for their nationals to engage in fishing on the high seas subject ... (c) to ... provisions concerning conservation of the living resources of the high seas",[5] nevertheless, conservation programmes

1 Resolution 62/215 adopted on 22 December 2007.

2 The Co-chairs were: Kristina Gjerde, Rosemary Rayfuse, David Vanderzwaag and David Freestone. The Co-chairs Report is at: http://www.iucn.org/themes/marine/pdf/IUCN%20Workshop%20Co-Chairs%20Summary_FINAL%20VERSION.pdf.

3 http://www.un.org/Depts/los/biodiversityworkinggroup/biodiversityworkinggroup.htm.

4 In particular, this text has benefitted immeasurably from review and comment by Rosemary Rayfuse and by Kristina Gjerde, to both of whom I am extremely grateful.

5 Article 1(a), 1958 Geneva Convention on Fishing and the Conservation of Living Resources of the High Seas, 559 UNTS 285.

under Article 2 are to be designed to secure "a maximum supply of food and other marine products." In other words, the oceans were valued primarily as a source of food.

In comparison, the 1982 Convention represents a sea change: it introduced a major new principle—an unqualified obligation on all states to "protect and preserve the marine environment"[6]—as well as the active obligations to protect and preserve rare or fragile species and ecosystems in all parts of the marine environment, as well as the habitat of depleted, threatened or endangered species and other forms of marine life.[7] It also adopted a very different approach to the conservation of high seas living resources.[8] Article 116 expressly conditions the rights of states for their nationals to fish on the high seas by making them "*subject to*:

(a) their treaty obligations;
(b) the rights and duties, as well as the interests of coastal states, provided for *inter alia* in article 63, para 2 and articles 64–67; and
(c) the provisions of this section."

Not only are states obliged under Article 117 "to take or co-operate with other states in taking, such measures for their respective nationals as may be necessary for the conservation of the living resources of the high seas," but states are also, under Article 119, obliged to "[t]ake measures to 'maintain and restore populations of harvested species at levels which can produce MSY' based on the 'best scientific evidence available' to the states concerned, as qualified by relevant *environmental* and economic factors."

What these articles reflect is that freedom of fishing is not an absolute right—it is subject to conditions, including the duty to protect the marine environment. So, although the 1982 Convention talks of freedom of fishing, it is worth remembering that this is a *conditional* freedom. One can, and should, therefore talk about a conditional right of high seas fisheries and related activities, rather than an absolute right.

It is clear that the 1982 Convention reflects a much wider concern with the environmental dimension of marine regulation than its predecessors. Yet its provisions for high seas fisheries, including for stocks that move between EEZs and high seas, were soon recognized by many to be overly vague and general.[9] Its provisions still reflected the traditional view that the community interest

---

6 Article 192.

7 Article 194(5).

8 VII.§2: Conservation and management of the living resources of the high seas. Articles 116–120.

9 See Barbara Kwiatkowska, "The High Seas Fisheries Regime: at a point of no return?" (1993) 8 *IJMCL* 327–358; also David Freestone, "The Effective Conservation and Management of High Seas Living Resources: Towards a New Regime? (1994) 5 *The Canterbury Law Review* (NZ) 341–362.

is in minimizing interference in the exercise of high seas rights. This had proven to be ineffective in halting declines in these fish stocks. In the run up to the Rio Earth Summit—UN Conference on Environment and Development (UNCED)—in 1992 it became clear that the global agenda had moved on since the conclusion of the LOS Convention. Discussions at Rio focused on new approaches to ocean management and changes in the high seas regime for straddling fish stocks and highly migratory fish stocks.[10]

Agenda 21 of UNCED called for an international conference to address straddling fish stocks and highly migratory fish stocks, and the 1995 UN Fish Stocks Agreement (UNFSA) was the result.[11] This so-called "Implementation Agreement" introduced a large number of modern fisheries management principles into the international regime for straddling fish stocks and highly migratory fish stocks.[12] The UNFSA, *inter alia*, commits its parties[13] to the sustainable use of such stocks, endorses an ecosystem approach[14] and a precautionary approach to the conservation of these stocks;[15] addresses free riders by restricting the rights of non-members of Regional Fishery Management Organizations (RFMOs);[16] calls for transparency in decision-making processes and other activities of RFMOs;[17] and reinforces the power of non-flag states to take enforcement measures.[18] It also requires parties to protect biodiversity in the marine environment.[19] By establishing the parameters for the exercise of what could be called a "conditional" freedom to fish,[20] the UNFSA supports long term sustainability of highly migratory and straddling

---

10 See Agenda 21, Chapter 17, paras 17.44–69, particularly 17.50 calling for the Conference on straddling fish stocks and highly migratory fish stocks.

11 Agreement for the Implementation of the Provision of the United Nations Convention on the Law of the Sea of 10 December 1982 Relating to the Conservation and Management of Straddling Fish Stocks and Highly Migratory Fish Stocks, (1995) 34 ILM 1542.

12 See David Freestone and Zen Makuch "The New International Environmental Law of Fisheries: The 1995 Straddling Stocks Agreement", (1997) 7 *Yearbook of International Environmental Law*, pp. 3–49.

13 Currently the UNFSA has 71 parties. Interestingly this would not be enough to make a formal amendment to the LOSC regime, see David Freestone and Alex G. Oude Elferink, "Flexibility and Innovation in the Law of the Sea: Will the LOS Convention amendment procedures ever be used?" in *Stability and Change in the Law of the Sea: The Role of the LOS Convention* (Alex G. Oude Elferink, ed.) Martinus Nijhoff, 2005, pp. 163–216.

14 Article 5.

15 Article 6 with a clear methodology for its application to capture fisheries in Annex II.

16 *Ibid.*, Part III.

17 Article 12.

18 Article 23.

19 Article 5(g).

20 See Parts III–VI of the Agreement.

fish stocks. While the UNFSA only binds its parties and only applies to certain species,[21] its principles—particularly those of long term sustainability using the "best scientific evidence available", the ecosystem and the precautionary approach—are already recognized as important general principles for all fisheries management.[22] These principles therefore form an excellent foundation for a more widely applicable modern ocean governance regime.

Just as the UNFSA illustrates the way that international law has responded to the challenges of the modern age by recognizing new principles and concepts such as precaution, other international legal instruments now increasingly recognize the new paradigm of "sustainable use" or "sustainable development." First brought into the international arena by the 1987 Brundtland Commission on Environment and Development,[23] sustainable development has been hailed as a basic paradigm for the twenty-first Century.[24] Sustainable development, as defined by the Brundtland Commission (1987) is "development that meets the needs of the present without compromising the ability of future generations to meet their own needs." It thus reinforces the equitable notion of fairness to present and future generations as balanced by environmental limits and goals. A commitment to sustainable use can now be found in a raft of international instruments.[25]

---

21 There is still a need for modern governance structures to be effectively implemented in many RFMOs, including transparent science driven decision-making processes and a need for expanded enforcement of RFMO conservation and management measures.

22 UNGA resolution 61/105 paragraph 5 has called for these principles to be applied to all fish stocks: *Calls upon* all States, directly or through regional fisheries management organizations and arrangements, to apply widely, in accordance with international law and the Code, the precautionary approach and an ecosystem approach to the conservation, management and exploitation of fish stocks, including straddling fish stocks, highly migratory fish stocks and discrete high seas fish stocks…." Paragraph 19 specifically calls for UNFSA parties to apply the principles set forth in the Agreement to discrete high seas fish stocks.

23 GH Brundtland (ed.), *Our Common Future* (1987).

24 The principle of sustainable development was included as Principle 4 of the 1992 Rio Declaration on Environment and Development, and permeates other principles, Agenda 21 and numerous other instruments. In 1997 it was considered by the International Court of Justice in the Gabcikovo-Nagymaros Case between Hungary and Slovakia. Although the famous separate opinion of Judge Christopher Weeramantry, that sustainable development was a principle of customary international law, was not endorsed by the majority of the Court, it did however recognize the "need to reconcile economic development with protection of the environment … aptly expressed in the concept of sustainable development." [1997] ICJ Reports 78 at para 140.

25 In relation to fisheries the UN Fish Stocks Agreement, the FAO Code of Conduct on Responsible Fisheries, as well as the 2001 Reykjavik Declaration on Responsible Fisheries in the Marine Ecosystem, ftp://ftp.fao.org/fi/DOCUMENT/reykjavik/y2198too_dec.pdf.

General international law also recognizes important general principles which should also be born in mind with respect to the oceans. The 1970 UNGA Declaration of Principles of International Law, which is widely regarded as declarative of customary international law, declares that:

> All states have the *duty* to cooperate with one another ... in the various spheres of international relations, in order to maintain international peace and security and to promote international economic stability and progress ... (emphasis added).[26]

This fundamental general international law duty to cooperate is reflected in the law of the sea instruments discussed above, including Articles 117 and 197 of the Convention and Article 8 of UNFSA.

Another fundamental duty of States, originally recognised in the famous Principle 21 of the 1972 Stockholm Declaration, reproduced in Principle 2 of the Rio Declaration and also recognized in Article 3 of the Convention on Biological Diversity, is "to ensure that activities within their jurisdiction or control do not cause damage to the environment of other States or of areas beyond the limits of national jurisdiction." The concept of "responsible" high seas activities flows from this general duty. An example of its elaboration with respect to fisheries is the 1995 Code of Conduct for Responsible Fisheries and in the 2001 Reykjavik Declaration. While international lawyers readily recognize the concepts of liability and responsibility, there is more to this principle than simply legal responsibility. Given the depleted state of many capture fisheries and poor record of implementation of many existing legal instruments, there is a need to reaffirm and reinforce a positive duty of States to ensure that their nationals—whether natural or legal persons or vessels flying their flag—act in conformity with applicable conservation and management measures.[27] Given that breach of such an obligation is a breach of international law,[28] it may be helpful to enumerate the various ways in which that duty can be breached and to elaborate specific consequences for failure to comply with this duty, consistent with the principle of conditional high seas freedoms.

26 General Assembly Declaration on Principles of International Law concerning friendly relations and co-operation among States in accordance with the Charter of the United Nations. G.A. Res 2625 (XXV), October 24, 1970.

27 An agenda already recognized and mandated by both the UN General Assembly and the FAO Committee on Fisheries (COFI).

28 And breach of such a duty might have legal consequences—such as justifying counter-measures.

So, in recognizing that the international priorities and principles of international law have evolved in the quarter century since the 1982 Convention, it may again be time to consolidate and reaffirm them in one instrument. Reaffirmation of these principles could reinforce the collective responsibility of all States to ensure the conservation and sustainable use of marine biodiversity beyond areas of national jurisdiction. Reaffirmation could also help to:

- ensure that all activities in areas beyond national jurisdiction are held to the same minimum standards;
- ensure that principles, approaches and best practices are consistently applied across regions; and
- guide the elaboration of specialized regimes.

The following 10 principles may provide a useful starting point in identifying general principles of Modern Ocean Governance that should be recognized as applying to activities that may affect the marine environment or biodiversity beyond national jurisdiction:

- Conditional freedom of activity on the high seas;
- Protection and preservation of the marine environment;
- Conservation of high seas living marine resources and biodiversity;
- Sustainable and equitable use;
- Cooperation;
- Precautionary Approach (including prior EIA);
- Ecosystem approach;
- Use of best available science;
- Transparency;
- Responsibility of states to control the actions of their nationals and consequences for breach of international legal obligations.

It seems clear from the discussions at the April/May 2008 meeting of the UN Working Group that many of the findings of the 2007 IUCN Workshop have been taken very seriously by a number of Working Group members. One of the workshop's key proposals was that consideration be given to developing a Declaration of Principles of Modern Ocean Governance to be discussed by the General Assembly. IUCN itself may well be the appropriate body to take a lead on this, but in any event I hope very much that the principles discussed above will be useful in such a process.

CHAPTER 2

Coastal States and MPAs in ABNJ: Ensuring Consistency with the LOSC

Alex G. Oude Elferink
Netherlands Institute for the Law of the Sea, Utrecht Centre for Oceans, Water and Sustainability Law, Utrecht University, K.G. Jebsen Centre for the Law of the Sea, UiT, The Arctic University of Norway

Abstract

To address the question how a future instrument for areas beyond national jurisdiction (ABNJ) might give consideration to the rights and obligations of coastal States and other States in establishing marine protected areas (MPAs) in ABNJ, the current article discusses the options that have been tabled in this respect in the preparatory meetings for the intergovernmental conference that will be negotiating that instrument. In considering the current legal framework, the focus is on the United Nations Convention on the Law of the Sea (LOSC), as the new instrument is to be elaborated under the LOSC and is required to be fully consistent with it. The article analyses the relevant practice of four specific regions that have established MPAs in ABNJ. The article concludes that due regard is fundamental in addressing interactions between coastal States and other States and considers some options to provide it with specific content.

Keywords

areas beyond national jurisdiction (ABNJ) – high seas – due regard – coastal States – adjacency – marine protected areas (MPAs) – international legally binding instrument (ILBI) – biological diversity of areas beyond national jurisdiction (BBNJ) – continental shelf – exclusive economic zone

 DOI:10.1163/9789004391703_004

1 Introduction

The international community has committed itself to protecting at least 10 percent of marine and coastal areas by the establishment of protected areas.[*,1] Meeting this target implies that States will also have to designate marine protected areas (MPAs)[2] in areas beyond national jurisdiction (ABNJ).[3] This topic actually has been under consideration during the discussions on an international legally binding instrument (ILBI) under the United Nations Convention on the Law of the Sea on the conservation and sustainable use of marine biological diversity of areas beyond national jurisdiction that have been taking place at the United Nations. One of the controversial issues is how the rights of coastal States over their maritime zones should be taken into consideration in this connection. Due to, among others, the transboundary effects of activities in the marine environment and the fact that areas requiring protection may straddle ABNJ and coastal State zones, there is an obvious need to address this issue. As these considerations indicate, this may not only be a matter of giving

* Principal Investigator Nereus Program; Predicting Future Oceans; The Nippon Foundation. This article originates in the presentation MPAs adjacent to or adjoining areas under national jurisdiction: legal and practical challenges I gave at the BBNJ Workshop on the conservation and sustainable use of marine biological diversity beyond areas of national jurisdiction through a new legally binding instrument under UNCLOS convened by the Government of Portugal and the High Seas Alliance in Lisbon from 1 to 3 March 2017. I would like to thank the organizers for providing me this opportunity and the participants at the workshop for their feedback. I would like to thank Rui Chang for her research in preparation of this article and her contribution to preparing a first draft outline and Catherine Blanchard, Erik Molenaar, Rui Chang and two anonymous reviewers for commenting on a draft version of this article.

1 Aichi Targets, Target 11; available at https://www.cbd.int/sp/targets/default.shtml.

2 There is no generally accepted definition of the term MPA. For the purposes of this article it is not necessary to further address this matter.

3 If no MPAs were to be designated in ABNJ, coastal States would have to designate up to 20 per cent of their maritime zones as MPAs to meet Aichi Target 11. Moreover, to reach a comprehensive coverage of all types of ecosystems, MPAs have to include areas within and beyond national jurisdiction. Aichi Target 11 actually refers to "protected areas and other effective area-based conservation measures". The current discussions at the United Nations concerning an International legally binding instrument under the United Nations Convention on the Law of the Sea on the conservation and sustainable use of marine biological diversity of areas beyond national jurisdiction (ILBI) similarly refer to, e.g., "measures such as area-based management tools [ABMTs], including marine protected areas" (General Assembly Resolution A/RES/72/249—International legally binding instrument under the United Nations Convention on the Law of the Sea on the conservation and sustainable use of marine biological diversity of areas beyond national jurisdiction (available at http://www.un.org/en/ga/search/view_doc.asp?symbol=A/RES/72/249), para. 2). The current article only uses the term MPA and focusses on practice in relation to MPAs. This focus does not affect the outcome of the analysis contained in this article.

consideration to the rights of coastal States. The obligations of coastal States to protect and preserve the marine environment may require them to consider how the need to protect the marine environment in ABNJ, including MPAs in ABNJ, may affect the exercise of their rights as coastal States.

To address the question of how a future ILBI might give consideration to the rights and obligations of coastal States and other States in establishing MPAs in ABNJ, the current article starts with a discussion of the options that have been tabled in this respect in the preparatory meetings leading up to the intergovernmental conference that has been charged with negotiating the ILBI. Next, the article considers what the current legal framework has to say on this matter. This discussion focusses on the United Nations Convention on the Law of the Sea (LOSC).[4] The LOSC is generally recognized as the fundamental jurisdictional framework for oceans governance and the ILBI is to be elaborated under the LOSC.[5] A further section analyses the practice of four specific regions in order to determine how that practice has given consideration to the rights and obligations of coastal States and other States in establishing MPAs in ABNJ. A final section offers some concluding thoughts.

2 Discussions at the Preparatory Committee

Between 2016 and 2017 a Preparatory Committee (PrepCom), which had been established by the United Nations General Assembly, considered the negotiation of the ILBI at an intergovernmental conference.[6] During the discussions at the PrepCom, the possible role of coastal States in designating and managing MPAs proved to be one of the controversial issues. An overview of different options was provided by a non-paper prepared by the PrepCom Chair.[7] Under

4 United Nations Convention on the Law of the Sea (Montego Bay, 10 December 1982, in force 16 November 1994) 1833 *UNTS* 396.

5 For the relationship between the ILBI and the LOSC see also text below at (nn 28, 29).

6 General Assembly Resolution A/69/292 of 19 June 2015 (available at http://daccess-ods.un.org/access.nsf/Get?Open&DS=A/RES/69/292&Lang=E).

7 Chair's streamlined non-paper on elements of a draft text of an international legally binding instrument under the United Nations Convention on the Law of the Sea on the conservation and sustainable use of marine biological diversity of areas beyond national jurisdiction (Document of the fourth session of the PrepCom (10–21 July 2017) (available at http://www.un.org/Depts/los/biodiversity/prepcom.htm). As the non-paper observes, the document: 'provides a compilation of the ideas and proposals put forward by delegations without consideration for the level of support for these ideas and proposals. The inclusion of ideas and proposals in this document does not imply agreement to, or convergence of views on, such ideas and proposals among delegations' (*ibid.*, p. 1).

the heading of 'General principles and approaches', the non-paper listed the following items dealing with giving consideration to the rights and obligations of coastal States (and other States) in establishing MPAs in ABNJ:

- Due regard for the rights of others.
- Respect for the rights of coastal States over all areas under their national jurisdiction, including their continental shelves beyond 200 nautical miles where applicable.
- Respect for the sovereignty and territorial integrity of coastal States.
- Compatibility.
- Adjacency and requirement to consult adjacent States.[8]
- Recognition of the role of adjacent coastal States as well as other States.[9]

As the report of the fourth session of the PrepCom to the General Assembly indicates, this matter, like most matters concerning the ILBI, has been left for further consideration by the future intergovernmental conference. The report contains Recommendations to the General Assembly, which are divided into sections A and B. These include elements that may be considered in the further preparation of the ILBI.[10] As the report states, "Section A includes non-exclusive elements that generated convergence among most delegations" and "[b]oth sections are without prejudice to the positions of States during the negotiations".[11] The text in Section A dealing with the issue of coastal States in relation to MPAs in ABNJ illustrates the high level of abstraction of the "convergence among most delegations". Under the heading "Relationship to measures under relevant instruments, frameworks and bodies" it is provided that the text of an ILBI "would also address the relationship between measures under the instrument and those established by adjacent coastal States, including issues of compatibility, without prejudice to the rights of coastal States".[12] In the envisaged process of consultation and assessment of proposals on MPAs,

---

8 Next to the term 'adjacent' the term 'adjoining' has also been used in this context. The current article will use the term 'adjacent' throughout.

9 Chair's streamlined non-paper (n 7) at p. 11, para. 24. The non-paper's section on ABMTs and MPAs moreover includes references to the rights of coastal States, including the need to secure the agreement of coastal States adjacent to ABNJ in creating ABMTs (*ibid.*, p. 23, para. 107; see also *ibid.*, p. 24, paras 115–116 and p. 26, para. 131). For a further consideration of this list of items see below, current section.

10 Report of the Preparatory Committee established by General Assembly Resolution 69/292: Development of an international legally binding instrument under the United Nations Convention on the Law of the Sea on the conservation and sustainable use of marine biological diversity of areas beyond national jurisdiction (UN Doc. A/AC.287/2017/PC.4/2) (available at http://www.un.org/Depts/los/biodiversity/prepcom.htm), p. 7, para. 38.

11 *Ibid.*

12 *Ibid.*, p. 11, para. 4.2.

reference is made to a large number of interested parties, in which adjacent coastal States are merely included as a subcategory of all States.[13] As regards decision-making on issues concerning MPAs, the options are completely open, as the text states that it remains to be decided "how decisions [...] would be made, including who would make the decision and on what basis".[14] The text envisages that in this connection it would have to be considered how to involve coastal States adjacent to a proposed MPA.[15] Although Section A thus recognizes the need for further consideration of the role of adjacent coastal States, it does not imply any recognition of a special role for coastal States in this respect.

The list of options to deal with the rights of other States contained in the Chair's non-paper as cited above indicates the range of alternatives that have been suggested to address this matter. The concepts of "due regard" and "compatibility" do not imply a preferential role for either other States and other actors dealing with MPAs in ABNJ or for adjacent coastal States. The implications of these concepts to a large extent would have to be determined in light of the circumstances of the particular case.[16] The references to "respect for the rights", and the "sovereignty and territorial integrity of coastal States" imply a prioritization of the coastal State. The concept of "adjacency", with only a reference to consultation with the coastal State, would in comparison at first sight seem to suggest a limited role for coastal States.

Some further understanding of the various concepts that have been advanced in connection with possible interactions between MPAs in ABNJ and zones under coastal State jurisdiction may be gleaned from documents that States have submitted to the PrepCom and their statements during the PrepCom meetings. References to adjacency and the adjacent coastal State in general advance a prioritized coastal State position,[17] without providing

13 *Ibid.*, p. 12, para. 4.3.2, sub ii.

14 *Ibid.*, sub iii.

15 *Ibid.*

16 See also text below after (n 56); and at (n 72) et seq.

17 For a detailed discussion of the concept of "adjacency", which, however, does not necessarily reflect the views of States at the PrepCom, see DC Dunn, G Ortuño Crespo, M Vierros, D Freestone, E Rosenthal, S Roady, A Alberini, A-L Harrison, A Cisneros, JW Moore, MR Sloat, Y Ota, R Caddell, and PN Halpin, *Adjacency: How legal precedent, ecological connectivity, and traditional knowledge inform our understanding of proximity* (Policy Brief UN PrepCom 3; Nereus Scientific & Technical Briefs on ABNJ series) (available at https://www.researchgate.net/publication/318842160_Adjacency_How_legal_precedent_ecological_connectivity_and_Traditional_Knowledge_inform_our_understanding_of_proximity_POLICY_BRIEF_-_UN_PrepCom_3). Interestingly, the brief includes no discussion of the concept of "due regard". In relation to adjacency, the brief notes that: 'While the

much detail as to its precise content and implications. At the fourth session of the PrepCom, the Pacific small island developing States "requested including the adjacency principle to address the interests of adjacent coastal states".[18] The Cook Islands further commented on this point to the effect that "activities in ABNJ should not impact activities within national jurisdiction".[19] During the third session of the PrepCom, States also referred to the need for consent of the adjacent coastal State in taking decisions in relation to MPAs in ABNJ.[20]

---

legal definition of adjacency addresses geographic proximity, the ecological implications of adjacency involve oceanographic and ecological connectivity. An area adjacent to a national jurisdiction may be equally ecologically or biologically connected to areas on the other side of an ocean basin through oceanographic or migratory connectivity' (*ibid.*, p. 2). The policy brief further argues for: 'granting coastal States greater influence over management of those ABNJ resources to which they lie adjacent. Under this approach, those qualified adjacent states would be recognized as having the primary responsibility to coordinate with existing sectoral and regional organizations to become the leading architects of new regional conservation agreements' (*ibid.*, pp. 1–2). The brief subsequently also recognizes that this approach would imply 'extending the rights of coastal States' (*ibid.*, p. 9). It may be questioned whether oceanographic and ecological connectivity are best addressed through the concept of adjacency. Another approach could, for instance, consist of an adaptation of the concept of "Range State" contained in the Convention on the Conservation of Migratory Species of Wild Animals (CMS) (Bonn, 23 June 1979; in force 1 November 1983; 1651 *UNTS* 355), which would not require an adaptation of the jurisdictional framework contained in the LOSC. The CMS requires Range States of migratory species to cooperate to reach a favorable conservation status of migratory species. Article 1(1) (h) of the CMS defines the term "Range State": 'in relation to a particular migratory species means any State [...] that exercises jurisdiction over any part of the range of that migratory species, or a State, flag vessels of which are engaged outside national jurisdictional limits in taking that migratory species.' In the context of an ILBI, a concept similar to that of "Range State" could include all States under whose jurisdiction or control activities and processes are taking place that affect an MPA. All those States could be included in the development of instruments/programs/measures aimed at protecting or restoring the biodiversity and ecosystem of the MPA.

18 Summary of the Fourth Session of the Preparatory Committee on Marine Biodiversity Beyond Areas of National Jurisdiction: 10–21 July 2017 (*Earth Negotiations Bulletin* Vol. 25 No. 141), p. 8.

19 *Ibid.* See also Summary of the First Session of the Preparatory Committee on Marine Biodiversity Beyond Areas of National Jurisdiction: 28 March–8 April 2016 (*Earth Negotiations Bulletin* Vol. 25 No. 106), p. 4 (statement of the Federated States of Micronesia).

20 See, *e.g.*, Summary of the Third Session of the Preparatory Committee on Marine Biodiversity Beyond Areas of National Jurisdiction: 27 March–7 April 2017 (*Earth Negotiations Bulletin* Vol. 25 No. 129), pp. 5–7 (statements of Fiji and Mauritius). In some other instances, references to the adjacent coastal State are less explicit. For instance, a document submitted by Fiji refers to the need for cooperation (see, *e.g.*, Fiji's Submission for BBBN PrepCom (available at http://www.un.org/depts/los/biodiversity/prepcom_files/rolling_comp/Fiji.pdf), para. 45), whereas New Zealand argued for the "[re]cognition of the role of adjacent coastal states as well as other states" (Preparatory Committee

The concept of "compatibility" has been invoked by States that also support the concept of "adjacency".[21] In this connection, reference has been made to Article 7 of the Fish Stocks Agreement (FSA),[22] which elaborates the concept of "compatibility" in relation to straddling and highly migratory fish stocks.[23] As has been pointed out by the Pacific small island developing States, Article 7 specifically requires that measures for the high seas "do not undermine the effectiveness" of measures adopted by the coastal State.[24]

The concept of "due regard" has been juxtaposed to that of "adjacency". At the fourth session of the PrepCom, China, supported by the US, noted that "adjacency is not enshrined in [the LOSC and] [...] proposed "due regard" for coastal states' rights".[25] The concept of "adjacency" has also been explicitly opposed by Singapore, the Republic of Korea and Switzerland.[26] Support for the concept of "due regard" in relation to the rights of coastal States has also been expressed by the European Union and its Member States.[27] The documents submitted to the PrepCom and statements made during its meetings do not shed any further light on the content of the concepts of "respect for the rights of coastal States over their maritime zones" and that of "respect for the sovereignty and territorial integrity of coastal States".

---

on Conservation and Sustainable Use of Marine Biological Diversity of Areas Beyond National Jurisdiction; New Zealand Submission; December 2016) (available at http://www.un.org/depts/los/biodiversity/prepcom_files/rolling_comp/New_Zealand.pdf) p. 3).

21 See PSIDS Submission to the Second Meeting of the Preparatory Committee for the Development of an international legally binding instrument under the United Nations Convention on the Law of the Sea on the conservation and sustainable use of marine biological diversity of areas beyond national jurisdiction (BBNJ PrepCom); August 2016 (available at http://www.un.org/depts/los/biodiversity/prepcom_files/rolling_comp/PSIDS_second.pdf), p. 3; Summary of the Third Session (n 20) at p. 7 (statement of Chile).

22 Agreement for the Implementation of the Provisions of the United Nations Convention on the Law of the Sea of 10 December 1982 relating to the Conservation and Management of Straddling Fish Stocks and Highly Migratory Fish Stocks (New York, 4 August 1995, in force 11 December 2001) 2167 *UNTS* 3.

23 PSIDS Submission (n 21), p. 3. For a further discussion of the concept of "compatibility" see text *infra*, after (n 56).

24 PSIDS Submission (n 21). The Pacific small islands developing States in a similar vein invoked para. 199 of the International Tribunal for the Law of the Sea's (ITLOS) advisory opinion of 2 April 2015 in *Request for an advisory opinion submitted by the Sub-Regional Fisheries Commission (SRFC)* (*ITLOS Reports 2015*, p. 4) as the basis for cooperation (PSIDS Submission (n 21). Para. 199 of the opinion limits itself to referring to Article 63 of the LOSC, which has been further elaborated in Article 7 of the FSA.

25 Summary of the Fourth Session (n 18) at p. 8.

26 *Ibid.*

27 Written Submission of the EU and its Member States; Cross-cutting issues; 5 December 2016 (available at http://www.un.org/depts/los/biodiversity/prepcom_files/rolling_comp/European%20Union-cross-cutting_issues.pdf), p. 3.

3 Balancing the Rights and Obligations of Coastal States and Other States under Current International Law

3.1 *The Establishment of MPAs in ABNJ*

In view of the large measure of uncertainty surrounding the various terms that have been introduced at the PrepCom for defining the nexus between coastal States, other States and MPAs in ABNJ, it stands to reason to have a closer look at how this nexus has been conceptualized in the LOSC. This approach is in particular justified by the language included in the General Assembly Resolution convening the intergovernmental conference that is to negotiate the ILBI.[28] The Resolution provides that "the work and results of the conference should be fully consistent with the provisions of the United Nations Convention on the Law of the Sea".[29]

Before considering this matter, it is required to briefly consider the legal basis in the LOSC and the Convention on Biological Diversity (CBD) for designating and managing MPAs.[30] This is explained by the fact that the consideration of the role of coastal States in relation to MPAs in ABNJ has to be assessed in the light of that legal basis. Article 194(5) of the LOSC, which has a spatial focus, provides a basis for the designation of MPAs.[31] The Article does not explicitly

28 General Assembly Resolution A/RES/72/249 (n 3) at para. 1.

29 *Ibid.*, para. 8. The General Assembly Resolution that set up the PrepCom did not include this specific reference to the Convention, but provided that the PrepCom process "should not undermine existing relevant legal instruments and frameworks and relevant global, regional and sectoral bodies" (General Assembly Resolution A/69/292 (n 6) at para. 3). Identical wording is included in Resolution A/72/249 setting up the intergovernmental conference (Resolution A/72/249 (n 3) at para. 7). Although the implications of the terms "fully consistent" and "not undermine" are not completely clear, it should be assumed that being fully consistent with an instrument sets a higher threshold than not undermining an instrument (see also C Blanchard 'When "Not Undermining" Undermines The BBNJ Process Possible Effects of the "Not Undermining" Clause on the Upcoming Legally Binding Instrument' (paper presented at the Law of the Sea Interest Group of the 2017 Annual Conference of the European Society of International Law; on file with the author). For instance, the online Merriam-Webster Dictionary (https://www.merriam-webster.com/dictionary) defines the term consistent as "marked by harmony, regularity, or steady continuity; free from variation or contradiction [...]; marked by agreement" and defines the term undermine in terms of weakening something or someone.

30 Convention on Biological Diversity (Rio de Janeiro, 5 June 1992, in force 29 December 1993) (1992) 31 *International Legal Materials* 818.

31 Article 194(5) reads: 'The measures taken in accordance with this Part shall include those necessary to protect and preserve rare or fragile ecosystems as well as the habitat of depleted, threatened or endangered species and other forms of marine life.' For a further elaboration of this argument concerning Article 194(5), see EJ Molenaar and AG Oude Elferink, 'Marine protected areas in areas beyond national jurisdiction—The pioneering efforts under the OSPAR Convention' (2009) 5 *Utrecht Law Review* 5–20 at pp. 9–10.

identify specific States that are responsible for taking the measures it may require, but it does refer to the "measures taken in accordance with [Part XII]" of the Convention. Part XII contains provisions that are directed at all States and at specific categories of States, such as flag States, port States and coastal States. Three points may be noted in this connection. First, Part XII stresses the importance of cooperation.[32] Article 197 specifically refers to cooperation on a global or regional basis and, by including the requirement that such cooperation has to take "into account characteristic regional features", emphasizes the importance of cooperation at the regional level. Second, the focus of Part XII on measures for the prevention, reduction and control of pollution[33] indicates that States that are involved in activities in ABNJ also have a primary responsibility in taking such measures in relation to MPAs in ABNJ.[34] Third, Part XII also addresses the transboundary impacts of pollution. The relevant provisions in this connection impose obligations on the States under whose jurisdiction or control the activities concerned take place. That consideration also applies to coastal States in relation to MPAs in ABNJ.

The CBD, which is the other global instrument with most relevance to MPAs in ABNJ, provides that it is applicable to Parties "[i]n the case of processes and activities, regardless of where their effects occur, carried out under its jurisdiction or control".[35] That provision is also applicable in ABNJ. Article 5 of the CBD requires the Parties to cooperate in respect of ABNJ "for the conservation and sustainable use of biological diversity".[36] As has been argued by Drankier, Article 5 facilitates implementation of Article 8 of the CBD on *in situ* conservation, including through the establishment of MPAs, which is primarily targeted at individual States. She submits that this is of particular significance for dealing with MPAs in ABNJ.[37]

Taken together, the above provisions of the LOSC and the CBD indicate that the primary responsibility for dealing with MPAs in ABNJ rests on States under whose jurisdiction or control activities affecting biodiversity in ABNJ take

32 See, *e.g.*, LOSC, Articles 194(1), 202 and 207–212.

33 See, *e.g. ibid.*, Articles 194(1) and 196(1).

34 See also Molenaar and Oude Elferink (n 31) at p. 9.

35 CBD, Article 4. Article 4 further provides that this is "[s]ubject to the rights of other States". The CBD does not refer to the rights of adjacent coastal States in relation to ABNJ. Article 22 of the CBD, on the relationship to other agreements, implies that these rights are primarily defined in the LOSC.

36 Article 5 of the CBD does not contain an explicit reference to regional cooperation or regional characteristics similar to that contained in Article 197 of the LOSC. Article 5 refers to direct cooperation and cooperation through competent international organizations.

37 P Drankier, 'Marine Protected Areas in Areas beyond National Jurisdiction' (2012) 27 *International Journal of Marine and Coastal Law* 291–350 at p. 297.

place. Cooperation is a key element in this respect. These provisions do not suggest the existence of a specific competence for adjacent coastal States in dealing with MPAS in ABNJ.[38] This should not be taken to imply that the rights and duties of coastal States should not be taken into account in this regard. This requires a further consideration of the obligations of States in exercising jurisdiction or control over activities in ABNJ.

3.2 *The Rights of Coastal States and Other States in ABNJ*

The LOSC contains provisions that deal with the relationship between the competing rights and obligations of States in ABNJ and possible linkages with coastal States. Article 87 requires States to exercise their high seas freedoms "with due regard for the interests of other States in their exercise of the freedom of the high seas".[39]Article 87 does not refer to due regard for the rights of the coastal State in its maritime zones.[40] However, it is submitted that a "due regard" requirement also applies in this instance. Four arguments may be advanced to support this position. First, Article 58 of the LOSC, which deals with the rights and duties of other States in the exclusive economic zone (EEZ), provides that the high seas freedoms those States enjoy in the EEZ shall be exercised with "due regard to the rights and duties of the coastal State".[41] It would be curious if this "due regard" obligation in exercising a high seas freedom like navigation would cease to be applicable the moment a ship crosses the 200-nautical-mile limit and continues its voyage on the high seas. The same argument applies by analogy to any other activity taking place in the marine environment. Second, Part V of the Convention on the EEZ requires the coastal State to "have due regard to the rights and duties of other States".[42] Unlike the "due regard" provision of Article 58, this provision is not limited to the area of the EEZ, implying that it is also relevant where other States are

38 See also N Matz-Lück and J Fuchs, 'The impact of OSPAR on protected area management beyond national jurisdiction: Effective regional cooperation or a network of paper parks?' (2014) 49 *Marine Policy* 155–166 at pp. 156–157.

39 Next to their obligations under Part XII, States would also be bound by the requirement to pay due regard where other States in exercising their high seas freedoms have designated MPAS.

40 See also MC Ribeiro, 'South Atlantic Perspectives on the Future International Legally Binding Instrument under the LOSC on Conservation and Sustainable Use of BBNJ' (2017) 32 *International Journal of Marine and Coastal Law* 733–764 at p. 758 (n 107).

41 LOSC, Article 58(3). See also Dispute concerning delimitation of the maritime boundary between Bangladesh and Myanmar in the Bay of Bengal (Bangladesh/Myanmar); Judgment of 14 March 2012 (available at www.itlos.org/fileadmin/itlos/documents/cases/case_no_16/C16_Judgment_14_03_2012_rev.pdf), para. 475.

42 LOSC, Article 56(2).

exercising rights or acting in accordance with their duties in ABNJ.[43] There would not seem to be a justification for imposing this obligation on the coastal State and not on States carrying out activities in ABNJ that may affect the rights and duties of the coastal State in its EEZ. This argument is reinforced by the fact that the LOSC imposes a "due regard" obligation in other instances that require balancing the rights of States.[44] Third, the judgment of the ITLOS in *Bangladesh/Myanmar* provides support for the view that States carrying out activities in ABNJ have to have due regard for the rights and duties of coastal States in the EEZ.[45] Finally, Article 194(4) of the LOSC, read in conjunction with Article 194(5), indicates that States designating MPAs in any case have a "due regard" obligation to all other States, including coastal States.[46]

Part VI of the LOSC, in dealing with the rights and freedoms of other States in the waters superjacent to the coastal State's continental shelf, does not employ the term "due regard", but instead provides that the coastal State in exercising its rights "must not infringe or [...] unjustifiable interfere [...] with navigation and other rights and freedoms of other States".[47] However, the arbitral tribunal in *Chagos,* in a discussion of the words "unjustifiable interference" contained in Article 194(4) of the LOSC, observed that it considered them "to be functionally equivalent to the obligation to give 'due regard'".[48]

---

43 It may be noted that the chapeau of Article 56 refers to "Rights, jurisdiction and duties of the coastal State in the exclusive economic zone". However, that does not exclude a transboundary component to those rights, jurisdiction and duties (see also, *e.g.,* LOSC, Article 195).

44 For a further discussion see this section, below.

45 In paragraph 475 of the judgment, the Tribunal discusses the situation of concurrent jurisdiction—*i.e.,* one State having rights in the water column and the other in the seabed and subsoil. The Tribunal concludes that in such a situation of concurrent jurisdiction a State "must exercise its rights and perform its duties with due regard to the rights and duties of the other" (*Bangladesh/Myanmar* (n 41) at para. 475). The Tribunal in the quoted text refers to the situation of concurrent jurisdiction of two coastal States, but it is clear from the context that this finding is also applicable to a situation involving a coastal State and a State carrying out activities in ABNJ. Second, the Tribunal considers a situation of *vertical* concurrent jurisdiction (overlap of the high seas with the continental shelf or the water column of the EEZ with the continental shelf). However, there is no legally relevant difference with a situation of *horizontal* concurrent jurisdiction (*e.g.,* the EEZ and an adjacent area of the high seas).

46 For a further corroboration of this point see the text at (nn 47) et seq.

47 LOSC, Article 78(2). For a further discussion of the implications of the concept of "unjustifiable interference" see J Mossop, *The continental shelf beyond 200 nautical miles: Rights and responsibilities* (Oxford University Press, Oxford, 2016), chapter 7.

48 *Chagos Marine Protected Area Arbitration* (*Mauritius* v. *United Kingdom*), Award of 18 March 2015, para. 540; see also *Bangladesh/Myanmar* (n 41) at para. 475. This view is supported by the commentary of the International Law Commission (ILC) on Article 71 of its

That standard contained in Article 194(4) also applies to measures taken on the basis of Article 194(5), which provides, as was observed above, a legal basis and in its application may require the designation of MPAs in ABNJ. In the EEZ, the other States mentioned in Article 78(2) are required to give due regard to the rights and duties of the coastal State in relation to its continental shelf under Article 58(3) of the LOSC. The LOSC does not contain a similar "due regard" provision in relation to these other States for the high seas superjacent to the continental shelf. However, Mossop has observed that the existence of such an obligation is evident from the drafting history of the Convention on the Continental Shelf, which provided the basis for the substantive provisions of the continental shelf regime of the LOSC.[49] Article 79, dealing with cables and pipelines on the continental shelf, does employ the concept of "due regard", which is applicable to both the coastal State and other States.[50]

Due regard as a standard for balancing the interest of the international community and the coastal State is also included in Part XI of the LOSC. As a general rule, mineral resource activities "in the Area shall be carried out with reasonable regard for other activities in the marine environment".[51] The inclusive term marine environment includes marine areas within national jurisdiction. Article 142 provides that for mineral deposits that straddle the limits between the Area and an area under national jurisdiction mineral resource activities in the Area "shall be conducted with due regard to the rights and legitimate interests" of the coastal State. Article 142 does not impose a similar "due regard" obligation on the coastal State in such a situation. However, Article 137 on the legal status of the Area and its mineral resources would be applicable in this instance, implying a more stringent obligation than due regard. Article 137 provides, among others, that no State shall appropriate any part of the Area or its mineral resources.[52]

1956 Draft Articles on the Law of the Sea, which is the direct precursor to Article 78 of the LOSC and contains the words "unjustifiable interference" (*Yearbook of the International Law Commission* 1956, Vol. II, p. 299; the relevant text is reproduced below at (n 66).

49 Convention on the Continental Shelf (Geneva, 29 April 1958, in force 10 June 1964) 499 *UNTS* 312. J Mossop, 'The relationship between the continental shelf regime and a new international instrument for protecting marine biodiversity in areas beyond national jurisdiction' (2018) 75(1) *ICES Journal of Marine Science* 444–450 at p. 446.

50 LOSC, Article 79(5).

51 LOSC, Article 147(1).

52 Chircop, who refers to Article 142 as "one of the most one-sided provisions" of the Convention, seems to consider that Article 137 is not relevant in this context (A Chircop, 'Managing Adjacency: Some Legal Aspects of the Relationship Between the Extended Continental Shelf and the International Seabed Area' (2011) 42 *Ocean Development & International Law* 307–316, at p. 312). However, he submits that a customary law obligation

The LOSC provisions dealing with fish stocks that occur in the EEZ as well as in the adjacent high seas go beyond the requirement of "due regard" that generally controls interactions between coastal States and States carrying out activities in ABNJ. Article 116 of the LOSC, dealing with the right to fish in the high seas, provides that this right is, *inter alia,* subject to "the rights and duties as well as the interests of coastal States provided for, *inter alia*, in article 63, paragraph 2, and articles 64 to 67" of the LOSC.[53] Article 66 gives primary responsibility to the State of origin of anadromous stocks, and Article 67 gives primary responsibility to the relevant coastal State in relation to catadromous stocks. Fishing directed at catadromous stocks is only allowed within the limits of the EEZ.[54] Fishing directed at catadromous stocks beyond the limits of the EEZ is only allowed to avoid "economic dislocation for a State other than the State of origin".[55] Articles 63(2) and 64, dealing respectively with straddling and highly migratory fish stocks, envisage, in different terms, cooperation between the coastal State(s) and States fishing on the high seas.[56] Articles 63(2) and 64 have been further elaborated through Article 7 of the FSA, which deals with the compatibility of conservation and management measures established by the coastal State for the EEZ and those established for the relevant area beyond.[57] Superficially, the concept of "compatibility" might seem to display similarities with that of "due regard" as elaborated in the award in *Chagos*.[58] In both instances, the activities of one State that (may) affect the rights and duties of another State have to be further assessed to establish how adverse effects may be avoided or limited and certain considerations that should be taken into account are listed. However, the nature of the interaction between the States involved is different. Article 7 of the FSA requires, *inter alia,* that the

---

for coastal States to consult with the Authority concerning straddling mineral resources may exist (*ibid.*, p. 313).

53 LOSC, Article 116(b).

54 LOSC, Article 67(2).

55 LOSC, Article 67(2).

56 Article 63(2) requires the States concerned to "seek [...] to agree upon the measures necessary for the conservation of these stocks in the [area adjacent to the exclusive economic zone]" in which the straddling stock occurs. Article 64(1) requires the States concerned to "cooperate [...] with a view to ensuring conservation and promoting the objective of optimum utilization of [highly migratory stocks] throughout the region [in which fishing takes place], both within and beyond the exclusive economic zone".

57 For a further discussion of Article 7 of the FSA see, *e.g.,* AG Oude Elferink, 'The Determination of Compatible Conservation and Management Measures for Straddling and Highly Migratory Fish Stocks' (2001) 5 *Max Planck Yearbook of United Nations Law* 551–607.

58 See further text below, at (n 72) et seq.

measures for straddling fish stocks and highly migratory fish stocks applicable to the high seas "do not undermine the effectiveness" of measures taken by the coastal State(s) in accordance with Article 61 of the LOSC and States have to agree on compatible measures for both areas.[59] On the other hand, the requirement to pay "due regard" does not require this level of coordination—a State would in most instances be required to consult with other States, but does not need to agree with other States on what would be proper in regulating an activity[60]—and entails less deference to the rights and duties of the coastal State.

The concept of "adjacency" could be said to be reflected in Article 63 of the LOSC, which mandates cooperation between the coastal State and States fishing in the adjacent area.[61] Otherwise, the LOSC does not refer to adjacency in the context of addressing the relationship between coastal States and States carrying out activities in ABNJ.[62] The concept of "respect" that States had advanced during the PrepCom discussions does not feature in the text of the LOSC in the sense that other States in exercising their rights and fulfilling their obligations in ABNJ should respect the rights of the coastal State.[63]

The above overview indicates that under the LOSC the concept of "due regard" provides the general benchmark for addressing the relationship between coastal States and States carrying out activities in ABNJ. It is submitted

59 FSA, Article 7(2).

60 Article 7(2) of the FSA provides that "coastal States and States fishing on the high seas have a duty to cooperate for the purpose of achieving compatible measures in respect of [the stocks concerned]".

61 It should be realized that the content of the concept as reflected in the LOSC may differ from the specific content which States may want to accord the concept in the context of the ILBI (see also above text at (n 17)).

62 Articles 64, 66 and 67, without employing the terms adjacent or adjacency, also reflect a recognition of the fact that the occurrence of fish stocks within and beyond the EEZ requires addressing the rights and interests of the coastal States by means other than the generally applicable concept of "due regard". At first sight, the designation of MPAs in ABNJ might not seem to detract from the specific regimes set up under Articles 63, 64, 66 and 67 of the LOSC, as such a designation could contribute to the ensuring the conservation of the stocks concerned and also could enhance the conservation status of the stock in the EEZ.

63 Three references to the concept of "respect" are included in Article 51, which deals with existing agreements, traditional fishing rights and existing submarine cables in archipelagic waters. In this case the requirement of "respect" is imposed on the coastal State. Article 240(c) provides that "marine scientific research shall not unjustifiably interfere with other legitimate uses of the sea compatible with this Convention and shall be duly respected in the course of such uses". Article 242(1) requires States to promote cooperation on marine scientific research "in accordance with the principle of respect for sovereignty and jurisdiction".

that this also requires including this concept in the ILBI as the benchmark for dealing with the relationship between coastal States and other States. A different approach would detract from the jurisdictional framework contained in the LOSC, and would imply a departure from the understanding that the ILBI has to be fully consistent with the LOSC. The concept of "adjacency" only figures in the LOSC in the context of the regime for fisheries.[64] The concept of "compatibility", which is not included in the LOSC, elaborates on the rights and obligations of States to cooperate in relation of straddling fish stocks and highly migratory fish stocks. The use of these concepts in the context of fisheries management raises the question whether they should and can be applied equally in other contexts. However, even if this were to be the case, recourse to these concepts as a general standard could detract from the current role of "due regard" in addressing the interactions between coastal States and States carrying out activities in ABNJ under the LOSC. The latter argument applies equally to the concept of "respect", which does not figure in the LOSC at all.

4 The Content of the Concept of "Due Regard"

To obtain a clearer idea of the implications of the concept of "due regard", this section provides an overview of its content. Due regard and its 'functional equivalent' of "unjustifiable interference" have their origin in the work of the International Law Commission (ILC) and the 1958 United Nations Conference on the Law of the Sea (1958 Conference).[65] These sources provide little information about the content of these concepts. However, two points may be noted. The ILC in its comment on Article 71 of its draft project for a law of the sea convention stressed the need to weigh the interest involved, observing that:

> The case is clearly one of assessment of the relative importance of the interests involved. Interference, even if substantial, with navigation and fishing might, in some cases, be justified. On the other hand, interference even on an insignificant scale would be unjustified if unrelated to

64 See also Dunn *et al.* who, in advocating the concept of adjacency, only refer to Articles of the LOSC concerned with fisheries (Dunn *et al.* (n 18) at pp. 3 and 9).

65 The Convention on the High Seas actually uses the concept of "reasonable regard" (Geneva, 29 April 1958, in force 30 September 1962) 450 *UNTS* 11, Article 2. The equivalent provision of the LOSC uses the concept of "due regard" (LOSC, Article 87(2)).

> reasonably conceived requirements of exploration and exploitation of the continental shelf.[66]

The other point of note is that in reply to the criticism that concepts like "unjustifiable interference" were too vague, it was submitted that clarification could be achieved by judicial settlement. As was observed at the 1958 Conference by J.P.A. François, the former ILC rapporteur on the topic of the law of the sea:

> Any attempt to codify international law without using such expressions will prove vain. In contentious cases, the meaning will have to be decided by an impartial authority, to which disputes regarding the interpretation of these expressions in specific cases are to be submitted.[67]

Although the assessment that further elaboration of these concepts in a future international agreement would be impossible at present might be overly pessimistic, no such attempt was in any case undertaken during the negotiations of the LOSC. However, the dispute settlement mechanisms included in the LOSC have resulted in a significant clarification of the concept of "due regard". In *Bangladesh/Myanmar*, the ITLOS observed the parties owed each other a "due regard" obligation in exercising their rights and performing their obligations in an area in which one had sovereign rights over the water column and the other over the seabed and subsoil.[68] Next, the Tribunal observed that:

> There are many ways in which the Parties may ensure the discharge of their obligations in this respect, including the conclusion of specific agreements or the establishment of appropriate cooperative arrangements. It is for the Parties to determine the measures that they consider appropriate for this purpose.[69]

---

66 *Yearbook of the International Law Commission 1956*, Vol. II, p. 299; see also the statement of the Indian delegate to the same effect (United Nations Conference on the Law of the Sea; Official Records (A/CONF.13/42), Vol. VI, p. 12, para. 9).

67 United Nations Conference on the Law of the Sea; Official Records (A/CONF.13/42), Vol. IV, p. 34, para. 20; to the same effect see also *Yearbook of the International Law Commission 1956*, Vol. II, p. 299; Official Records (n 66), Vol. VI, p. 12, para. 9).

68 *Bangladesh/Myanmar* (n 41) at para. 475.

69 *Ibid.*, para. 476.

This finding was confirmed by the arbitral tribunal in *Bangladesh* v. *India*, in which a similar situation of overlap existed.[70] The tribunal further added that it was "confident that the Parties will act, both jointly and individually, to ensure that each is able to exercise its rights and perform its duties within this area".[71] These pronouncements provide little to no guidance to the parties on how to discharge their obligations, apart from stressing their contractual freedom. Perhaps most significantly, the arbitral tribunal in *Bangladesh* v. *India* stressed that these duties are owed jointly and individually. In the absence of agreement on cooperative measures, States are still required to assess how to ensure that due regard is given to the rights and duties of the other State(s). The specific course of action that is the outcome of that assessment would, in the case of disagreement, be open to judicial settlement.

Thus far, the most significant elaboration of the concept of "due regard" has been provided by the arbitral tribunal in *Chagos*. One of the issues before the tribunal was whether the United Kingdom, in establishing an MPA in the EEZ of the Chagos Archipelago, had given due regard to the fishing rights of Mauritius, as it was required to do under Article 56(2) of the LOSC. In assessing this question, the arbitral tribunal first pointed to the case-specific nature of "due regard", observing that the United Kingdom had "to have such regard for the rights of Mauritius as is called for by the circumstances and by the nature of those rights".[72] Unsurprisingly, the tribunal did not find:

> this formulation [to reflect] any universal rule of conduct. The Convention does not impose a uniform obligation to avoid any impairment of Mauritius' rights; nor does it uniformly permit the United Kingdom to proceed as it wishes, merely noting such rights.[73]

The tribunal subsequently formulated three criteria to arrive at a proper implementation of "due regard":
- Balancing of the rights involved;
- The consideration of alternative approaches; and
- Assessing the need for consultation with the other State concerned.[74]

70 *In the Matter of the Bay of Bengal Maritime Boundary* (*Bangladesh* v. *India*), Award of 7 July 2014 (available at http://www.pcacases.com/web/sendAttach/383), para. 508.

71 *Ibid.*

72 *Chagos* (n 48) at para. 519.

73 *Ibid.*

74 *Ibid.* In respect of the last point, the tribunal observed that in most cases "at least some consultation with the rights-holding State" would have been appropriate (*ibid.*).

As the reasoning of the tribunal indicates, due regard requires informed decision-making that provides evidence that the rights that are involved are properly identified and weighed. *Chagos* also indicates that the decision on how to implement due regard rests on the State that is exercising its rights or performs its obligations and does not require the concurrence of the other State concerned.

During the PrepCom, the Pacific small islands developing States in particular have pointed to the specific interests of developing States, including small island developing States, and in that connection have invoked the need for proportionate burden-sharing.[75] This raises the question how these concepts relate to the concept of "due regard". Paying due regard would require taking into account the rights and obligations of developing States and in that context seeking to avoid disproportionate burden-sharing. At the same time, the concept of "due regard", as is also evident from the discussion of *Chagos*, could lead to the result that these considerations are not (fully) taken into account. It may be questioned whether that provides an equitable solution to this matter.

5 Regional Practice in Respect of MPAS in ABNJ

Four regional frameworks for the protection and preservation of the marine environment have already dealt with the issue of MPAS in ABNJ.[76] These are the Nouméa, OSPAR, and Barcelona Conventions (South Pacific Ocean, North-East Atlantic Ocean and Mediterranean Sea respectively),[77] and the Hamilton Declaration (Sargasso Sea).[78] This section first briefly considers the relevant

75 See, *e.g.*, Fiji's Submission (n 20) at para. 27; PSIDS Submission (n 21) at p. 3. For a discussion of the concept of (dis)proportionate burden sharing see *e.g.* T Scovazzi, R Davis, Q Hanich and A Vrahnos, 'Defining a disproportionate burden in transboundary fisheries: lessons from international law' (2016) 70 *Marine Policy* 188–191.

76 The extensive experience of the Commission for the Conservation of Antarctic Marine Living Resources in respect of the designation of MPAS in ABNJ is not discussed in this section. Due to the absence of generally recognized coastal States that practice is of limited relevance to the matter that is under consideration in this article.

77 Convention for the Protection of the Natural Resources and Environment of the South Pacific Region (Nouméa, 24 November 1986, in force 18 August 1990, available at http://www.sprep.org/attachments/Legal/Files_updated_at_2014/NoumeaConvProtocols.pdf); Convention for the Protection of the Marine Environment of the North-East Atlantic (Paris, 22 September 1992, in force 25 March 1998) (1993) 32 *International Legal Materials* 1072; Convention for the Protection of the Marine Environment and the Coastal Region of the Mediterranean (Barcelona, 10 June 1995, in force 9 July 2004) 1102 *UNTS* 27.

78 Hamilton Declaration on Collaboration for the Conservation of the Sargasso Sea (adopted on 11 March 2014; available at http://www.sargassoseacommission.org/storage/

provisions of the above instruments and relevant practice in relation to these instruments and then provides an assessment in the light of the issue under consideration in this article.

5.1 *The Relevant Regional Practice*

The Nouméa Convention provides that its Convention Area is constituted by the EEZs of the States parties, and in addition also includes the "areas of high seas which are enclosed from all sides by the 200 nautical mile zones" of the Parties.[79] Article 14 envisages the possibility of designating protected areas in the Convention Area and further provides that "[t]he establishment of such areas shall not affect the rights of other Parties or third States under international law". Thus far the States Parties to the Nouméa Convention have not taken any action in relation to the establishment of MPAs in ABNJ.

The Barcelona Convention is applicable to the Mediterranean Sea.[80] Due to the dimensions of the Mediterranean Sea, it is entirely within 200 nautical miles from the surrounding coasts. However, because several coastal States of the Mediterranean Sea have not yet established a 200-nautical-mile zone, large parts of the water column beyond the territorial sea for the time being remain part of the high seas overlying the continental shelf. The possibility of establishing MPAs in the high seas of the Mediterranean Sea is envisaged under the Protocol Concerning Specially Protected Areas and Biological Diversity in the Mediterranean (SPAMI Protocol), which was adopted together with the revised Barcelona Convention in 1995, and also applies to the high seas areas of the Mediterranean Sea.[81] The Protocol provides that it is without "prejudice [to] the rights, the present and future claims or legal views of any State relating

documents/Hamilton_Declaration_with_signatures_January_2017.pdf). One could ask whether the Hamilton Declaration itself actually establishes an MPA. That case could be made (see, *e.g.*, Hamilton Declaration, paras 1–3, which recognize the Sargasso Sea's "high ecological and biological significance, its cultural importance and its outstanding universal value", affirm that the guiding principle of the Declaration is the Sargasso Sea's conservation and that to that end the signatories will collaborate in pursuing conservation measures). The Declaration in any case is relevant for the present analysis because of, among others, its identification of actors relevant for its further implementation.

79 Nouméa Convention, Article 2(a).

80 Barcelona Convention, Article 1(1). For a discussion of the Barcelona Convention see, *e.g.*, I Papanicolopulu, 'The Mediterranean Sea' in D.R Rothwell, AG Oude Elferink, T Stephens and KN Scott (eds.) *The Oxford Handbook of the Law of the Sea* (Oxford University Press, Oxford, 2015) 604–625.

81 Protocol Concerning Specially Protected Areas and Biological Diversity in the Mediterranean (SPAMI Protocol) (Barcelona, 10 June 1995, in force 12 December 1999); available at http://rac-spa.org/sites/default/files/protocole_aspdb/protocol_eng.pdf), article 2(1).

to the law of the sea, in particular, the nature and the extent of marine areas [...], as well as the nature and extent of the jurisdiction of the coastal State, the flag State and the port State".[82] The Protocol makes a distinction between MPAs and Specially Protected Areas of Mediterranean Importance (SPAMIs). Whereas the former may only be designated in areas under coastal State sovereignty or jurisdiction,[83] the latter may also be situated on the high seas.[84] In this case, a proposal to include an area in the list of SPAMIs may be submitted by "by two or more neighbouring Parties" to the Protocol.[85] The Protocol does not further define the term "neighbouring Parties", but its use in the Protocol suggests that it is intended to refer to States that are adjacent to the area of high seas concerned.[86]

The Pelagos Sanctuary is the only SPAMI that currently is located in part on the high seas.[87] The Sanctuary has been designated and is jointly managed by France, Italy and Monaco in accordance with the Agreement on the creation of a marine mammal sanctuary in the Mediterranean concluded by these States.[88] It is partly located in their waters and partly in the high seas area adjacent to these waters.[89] The Agreement provides that its parties "may invite any other interested State or international organization to accede to the [...] Agreement".[90]

The spatial scope of application of the OSPAR Convention is the North-East Atlantic (Maritime Area) and includes extensive areas of ABNJ.[91] In this connection, Article 1(a) provides that the Maritime Area includes "the sea beyond and adjacent to the territorial sea under the jurisdiction of the coastal state to *the extent recognised by international law*".[92] In 1998, the Contracting Parties to the OSPAR Convention concluded Annex V to the Convention concerned

---

82 *Ibid.*, Article 2(2).
83 *Ibid.*, Article 5.
84 *Ibid.*, Article 9(2)(b).
85 *Ibid.*
86 See *ibid.*, Articles 9(2)(b), 9(2)(c) and 9(3)(a).
87 Further information on the Pelagos Sanctuary is available on the website of the Sanctuary (http://www.sanctuaire-pelagos.org/en/).
88 Agreement on the creation of a marine mammal sanctuary in the Mediterranean (Monaco, 25 November 1999, in force 21 February 2001) 2176 *UNTS* 247.
89 *Ibid.*, Article 3.
90 *Ibid.*, Article 20.
91 OSPAR Convention, Article 1(a). On OSPAR's designation of MPAs in ABNJ see also, *e.g.*, Matz-Lück and Fuchs (n 38) at pp. 158–162; Molenaar and Oude Elferink (n 31).
92 Emphasis added.

with biodiversity.[93] Annex V requires the Contracting Parties to "develop means, *consistent with international law*, for instituting protective, conservation, restorative or precautionary measures related to specific areas or sites or related to particular species or habitats".[94]

Following the adoption of Annex V, the OSPAR Contracting Parties have worked towards the designation of a network of MPAs in their maritime zones and in ABNJ of the Maritime Area. Two OSPAR documents from 2003 set up a framework for the designation of MPAs in the Maritime Area. This concerned OSPAR Recommendation 2003/3 on a Network of Marine Protected Areas[95] and the 2003 Strategies of the OSPAR Commission for the Protection of the Marine Environment of the North-East Atlantic (OSPAR Strategies).[96] Recommendation 2003/3 distinguishes between MPAs within national jurisdiction areas and beyond the national jurisdiction of the OSPAR Contracting Parties.[97] The OSPAR Network of Marine Protected Areas (OSPAR Network) is to consist of MPAs within national jurisdiction, which are reported by the coastal State concerned, and MPAs in ABNJ, which have "been included as a component of the network by the OSPAR Commission".[98] Recommendation 2003/3 originally only set up a specific procedure in relation to MPAs within national jurisdiction, but was amended in 2010 to include a procedure for including MPAs in ABNJ in the OSPAR Network.[99] Recommendation 2003/3 as amended provides that each Contracting party is to report MPAs within its national jurisdiction. Any Contracting Party may take the initiative to make a proposal to the OSPAR Commission to include MPAs in ABNJ in the OSPAR Network.[100] The original OSPAR Strategies from 2003 already specified that the OSPAR Commission would be charged with designating MPAs in ABNJ.[101]

---

93 Annex V on the Protection and Conservation of the Ecosystems and Biological Diversity of the Maritime Area (23 July 1998; in force 30 August 2000); available at https://www.ospar.org/site/assets/files/1290/ospar_convention_e_updated_text_in_2007_no_revs.pdf).

94 *Ibid.*, Article 3(1)(b)(ii) (emphasis provided).

95 OSPAR Recommendation 2003/3 on a Network of Marine Protected Areas (Summary Record OSPAR 2003; OSPAR 03/17/1-E, Annex 9).

96 2003 Strategies of the OSPAR Commission for the Protection of the Marine Environment of the North-East Atlantic (Summary Record OSPAR 03/17/1-E, Annex 31).

97 OSPAR Recommendation 2003/3 (n 95) at para. 1.1.

98 *Ibid.*, paras 1.1 and 3.1.

99 OSPAR Recommendation 2010/2 (OSPAR 10/23/1, Annex 7).

100 See *ibid.*, paras 2.4–2.9, which contain the relevant amendments.

101 OSPAR Strategies (n 96) at section 4.4. Appendix 4 to the Guidelines for the Identification and Selection of Marine Protected Areas in the OSPAR Maritime Area contained in OSPAR Agreement 2003/17 as amended in 2007 (available at http://www.ospar.org/documents?d=32398) also make this distinction. Coastal states are requested to comply

The OSPAR Commission has thus far included seven MPAs in ABNJ within the OSPAR Network: the Charlie-Gibbs South, Milne Seamount Complex, Altair Seamount High Seas, Antialtair Seamount High Seas, Josephine Seamount High Seas, and MAR North of the Azores High Seas MPAs in 2010, and the Charlie-Gibbs North High Seas MPA in 2012.[102] Two of the MPAs designated by the OSPAR Commission in 2010 (Charlie-Gibbs South Marine Protected Area; Milne Seamount Complex Marine Protected Area) comprise the water column and seabed, which are both part of ABNJ. The other four areas designated in 2010 only concern the high seas water column superjacent to the continental shelf beyond 200 nautical miles of Portugal. All six decisions provide that they: "shall apply without prejudice to the rights and obligations of coastal States, other States and international organisations in accordance with [the LOSC] and customary international law".[103]

In addition, the preamble of all six decisions recognizes that they do not prejudice the rights of coastal States over their continental shelf.[104] In the case of the MPAs superjacent to the Portuguese continental shelf, the preamble adds that the procedure for designation is not intended to set a precedent for such MPAs and that future designations "will be decided on a case by case basis".[105] The general safeguarding clause of the 2012 decision on the Charlie-Gibbs North High Seas MPA, which covers waters superjacent to the continental shelf of Iceland, is identical to that of the six 2010 decisions.[106] The rights of the coastal State are in addition safeguarded in more specific

with a specific process for nominating MPAs under their jurisdiction. A note to Appendix 4 provides that this process does not "apply to any MPA that is the collective responsibility of all Contracting Parties. In such cases, the OSPAR Commission is responsible for data validation and final approval".

102 OSPAR Decision 2010/2 on the establishment of the Charlie-Gibbs South Marine Protected Area (OSPAR 10/23/1-E, Annex 36); OSPAR Decision 2010/1 on the Establishment of the Milne Seamount Complex Marine Protected Area (*ibid.*, Annex 34); OSPAR Decision 2010/3 on the Establishment of the Altair Seamount High Seas Marine Protected Area (*ibid.*, Annex 38); OSPAR Decision 2010/4 on the Establishment of the Antialtair Seamount High Seas Marine Protected Area (*ibid.*, Annex 40); OSPAR Decision 2010/5 on the Establishment of the Josephine Seamount High Seas Marine Protected Area (*ibid.*, Annex 42); OSPAR Decision 2010/6 on the Establishment of the MAR North of the Azores High Seas Marine Protected Area (*ibid.*, Annex 44); OSPAR Decision 2012/1 on the establishment of the Charlie-Gibbs North High Seas Marine Protected Area (OSPAR 12/22/1, Annex 6).

103 OSPAR Decisions 2010/1 and 2010/2 (n 102) at para. 2.2; and OSPAR Decisions 2010/3 to 2010/6 (n 102) at para. 2.3.

104 OSPAR Decisions 2010/1 to 2010/6 (n 102) at preamble.

105 OSPAR Decisions 2010/3 to 2010/6 (n 102) at preamble.

106 OSPAR Decision 2012/1 (n 102) at para. 2.3.

terms in the body of the decision.[107] The preambular considerations of the 2012 decision are more elaborate on the point of the rights of the coastal State and other states than the 2010 decisions, but essentially confirm that the rights of the coastal State over its continental shelf and other States in the superjacent waters are defined in the LOSC.[108] The difference in wording between the 2010 and 2012 decisions is likely to be explained by the differences in approach of the coastal States concerned. Portugal has designated the parts of its continental shelf concerned as MPAs, but Iceland has not.[109]

The Hamilton Declaration is an outcome of the work of the Sargasso Sea Alliance, which was led by the Government of Bermuda. It aims to conserve the Sargasso Sea high seas ecosystem.[110] Currently, the Declaration signatories are principally from North America and the Caribbean, but the Declaration also "[e]ncourages participation by any other interested government or regional economic integration organisation in efforts to conserve the Sargasso Sea ecosystem in accordance with this Declaration".[111] The area of collaboration for the Sargasso Sea is defined as the high seas and the Area as defined in Annex I to the Declaration. It excludes the EEZs of Bermuda and other adjacent coastal States,[112] and the continental shelf of adjacent States that are overlain by the high seas as defined in Annex I. The preamble of the Declaration indicates that it "is not legally binding and is without prejudice to the existing legal rights and obligations of the Signatories under international law or to the competences of regional and international organisations". The focus of the Declaration is on collaboration to achieve "conservation measures for the Sargasso Sea

107 *Ibid.*, para. 2.2.

108 *Ibid.*, preamble.

109 For a further consideration of this point see Matz-Lück and Fuchs (n 38) at pp. 161–162.

110 There are now nine signatory governments—Azores, Bahamas, British Virgin Islands, Canada, Cayman Islands, Monaco, UK and US. For a discussion of the Hamilton Declaration and background information to the Declaration and the Sargasso Sea Alliance see D Freestone and KK Morrison, 'The Signing of the Hamilton Declaration on Collaboration for the Conservation of the Sargasso Sea: A New Paradigm for High Seas Conservation?' (2014) 29 *International Journal of Marine and Coastal Law* 345–362; DF Freestone, 'Governance of Areas beyond National Jurisdiction: An Unfinished Agenda?' in J Barrett and R Barnes (eds), *Law of the Sea:* UNCLOS *as a Living Treaty* (British Institute of International and Comparative Law, London, 2016) 231–266.

111 Hamilton Declaration, paragraph 10.

112 According to Freestone and Morrison, the Bermudan EEZ was excluded from the area of collaboration at the last minute upon the request of the Government of Bermuda (Freestone and Morrison (n 110) at p. 352).

ecosystem through existing regional and international organizations with relevant competences".[113]

5.2 *Assessment of the Regional Practice*

The regional practice on the role of coastal States in designating MPAs in ABNJ is limited in scope, implying that one should in any case be careful in drawing general conclusions. The relevant practice makes clear that it is not intended to detract from the jurisdictional framework for the oceans contained in the LOSC and customary international law. Thus, these regional frameworks do not intend to alter the existing balance of rights and obligations between coastal States and States carrying out activities in ABNJ.[114] At the same time, these frameworks indicate that the current legal regime already allows for dealing with the obligations of States in relation to the establishment of MPAs in ABNJ. Further analysis of the experience in this regard could provide insights in how a future ILBI could enhance the effectiveness of these regional frameworks.

A regional approach to the designation of MPAs in ABNJ in principle implies that the coastal State(s) adjacent to the area involved will be part of the designation process. However, that does not mean that the adjacent coastal State has a different role from other participating States. In this connection, a distinction may be made between the role of different States as defined in the instruments concerned and the role of different States in practice. As regards the former point, only the SPAMI Protocol accords a special role to the coastal States that are adjacent to an area that is being considered for MPA designation. However, the case of the Mediterranean is not typical of the situation of ABNJ, which in principle are situated beyond the full suite of coastal State maritime zones that are permitted under the LOSC. Rather, once all Mediterranean coastal States have established an EEZ, any MPA that formerly might have been located in the high seas would be located in a maritime zone of one of the coastal States. The provisions of the SPAMI Protocol in all likelihood are intended to avoid the situation that the relevant coastal State(s) would be faced with the situation that there would be MPAs in their maritime zones on whose designation they had not had the final say.[115]

113 Hamilton Declaration, paras 3 and 8. For a discussion of initiatives in this respect see Freestone and Morrison, *ibid.*, at pp. 347–349.

114 Most of the States involved in this regional practice are coastal States. However, not all of them are always coastal States that are adjacent to the MPA being designated.

115 See in particular the way in which Article 9 of the SPAMI Protocol has been drafted. It could be asked whether the Mediterranean experience might serve as a precedent in relation to high seas enclaves of limited dimensions. Two arguments indicate that this may not be the case. First, these high seas enclaves are beyond the outer limits of the EEZ

It has been suggested that the practice under the OSPAR Convention provides evidence of according a special position to coastal states where the high seas overlap with their continental shelf beyond 200 nautical miles.[116] As is submitted by Ribeiro: "as demonstrated by the practice of OSPAR Contracting Parties, it is difficult to conceive of the designation of high seas MPAs without the [...] consent" of these coastal States.[117] However, on closer consideration, the sources on which she relies do not support that conclusion. First, she submits that this practice implies a recognition that the rights of the coastal State over its continental shelf cannot be violated in such cases of overlap.[118] The OSPAR decision to which she refers to substantiate this argument provides that it "does not in any way prejudice the sovereign rights and obligations of the coastal State over the continental shelf in accordance with [the LOSC]".[119] In other words, the decision confirms the jurisdictional framework contained in the LOSC. States cooperating at the regional level can designate an MPA in the high seas, leaving the rights of the coastal State over the continental shelf unaffected.

Moreover, as was set out above, in this case a mutual "due regard" requirement is applicable under the LOSC. This "due regard" requirement is part and parcel of the rights and obligations of the coastal State in relation to its continental shelf to which the decision refers. In support of the assertion that the designation of an MPA in the water column of the high seas overlying the continental shelf of a coastal State requires its consent, Ribeiro refers to three designations by OSPAR and a report prepared by the OSPAR Commission in 2014.[120] As was discussed above, *all* OSPAR decisions on the designation of MPAs in ABNJ state that they are without prejudice to the rights and obligations

---

and the continental shelf, whereas the high seas in the Mediterranean is in its totality within 200 nautical miles of the coast. Second, in the negotiation of the FSA, the matter of high seas enclaves was also considered, resulting in Articles 15 and 16 of the FSA. These articles do little to develop the legal framework the Agreement otherwise establishes (see also M Hayashi, 'The 1995 Agreement on Straddling Fish Stocks and Highly Migratory Fish Stocks: Significance for the Law of the Sea Convention' (1996) 26 *Ocean and Coastal Development* 51–69, at pp. 64–65; E Hey, 'Global Fisheries Regulations in the First Half of the 1990s' (1996) 11 *International Journal of Marine and Coastal Law* 459–490, at pp. 474–475). However, this does not exclude that the coastal States *de facto* would have more influence in the case of high seas enclaves than ABNJ in general even if the legal regime would be the same.

116 Ribeiro (n 40) at pp. 756–757.

117 *Ibid.*, p. 757.

118 *Ibid.*

119 As quoted in *ibid.* at (n 101).

120 *See* (n 102).

of coastal States and other States as defined in the LOSC and customary international law. The decisions have been adopted by the OSPAR Commission and the decision-making process does not accord a privileged position to specific coastal States.[121] The OSPAR Status Report's discussion of the designation of MPAs in ABNJ in the Maritime Area does not contain any indication that this requires the consent of a coastal State having a continental shelf beyond 200 nautical miles.[122]

6 Conclusions

The LOSC and the CBD indicate that the primary responsibility for dealing with MPAs in ABNJ rests on States under whose jurisdiction or control activities affecting biodiversity in ABNJ take place. Cooperation is the key element in this respect. These provisions do not suggest the existence of a specific competence for adjacent coastal State in dealing with MPAs in ABNJ.

Four concepts have been advanced at the PrepCom for addressing the role of coastal States and other States in the designation of MPAs in ABNJ: due regard, adjacency, compatibility, and respect for coastal State sovereignty or sovereign rights. In proposing specific concepts to the PrepCom, little to no elaboration of the implications of these concepts has thus far been provided. To further assess the implications of these concepts, the present article has considered how the LOSC and other relevant instruments have or have not relied on them in addressing the interaction between coastal States and States carrying out activities in ABNJ. The determination of existing legal relationships in negotiating an agreement that further elaborates the applicable legal framework provides a logical point of departure, as it indicates how further elaboration can be best accomplished, while building on existing frameworks. Moreover, the negotiations at the intergovernmental conference and its outcome are required to be fully consistent with the LOSC. This requirement would not be met if the ILBI would adopt an approach that does not take into account concepts contained

121 Article 13(1) of the OSPAR Convention provides that: "Decisions and recommendations [of the OSPAR Commission] shall be adopted by unanimous vote of the Contracting Parties. Should unanimity not be attainable, and unless otherwise provided in the Convention, the Commission may nonetheless adopt decisions or recommendations by a three-quarters majority vote of the Contracting Parties".

122 See OSPAR Commission, *2014 Status Report on the OSPAR Network of Marine Protected Areas* (compiled by Germany for OSPAR, 2015), pp. 18–21. However, the process leading up to the designation of MPAs in ABNJ by the OSPAR Commission in large part may have been driven by the wish to maintain consensus (see Matz-Lück and Fuchs (n 38) at p. 162).

in the LOSC or would change the legal relationship between coastal States and States carrying out activities in ABNJ as defined in the LOSC.

The present analysis of the LOSC points out that it does not contain the requirement of "respect for coastal State sovereignty or coastal State rights". The concept of "adjacency" is only employed in the context of fisheries and has been elaborated through the concept of "compatibility" in the context of the FSA, which has a different connotation from the concept of "due regard". Due regard is the concept that is generally applicable between coastal States and States carrying out activities in ABNJ under the LOSC. In light of the agreement that the ILBI is to be fully consistent with the LOSC, this conclusion indicates that due regard should also be the main concept for regulating the relationships between coastal States and States carrying out activities in ABNJ under the ILBI. As is apparent from the above discussion, due regard is a "two-way street". Coastal States are required to give due regard to the rights and obligations of States carrying out activities in ABNJ—also where this concerns measures to protect the marine environment—and *vice-versa.*[123] The analysis of the (limited) regional practice in relation to the establishment of MPAS in ABNJ indicates that the States concerned recognize that the LOSC and customary international law provide the jurisdictional framework for this exercise. In other words, it is accepted that due regard is part of the jurisdictional framework for dealing with the interactions between coastal States and States carrying out activities in ABNJ.

If the central place of "due regard" in the LOSC scheme for dealing with the interactions between coastal States and States carrying out activities in ABNJ will be included in an ILBI, it should be considered whether and how that concept could be further elaborated.[124] As was set out above, when the concept was introduced in a law of the sea context in the 1950s, it was argued that further clarification could be attained through third-party dispute settlement. Indeed, significant clarification has been achieved through the recent award in *Chagos*. However, arguments against continued reliance on that approach,

123 See also Ribeiro (n 40) at pp. 758–759.

124 As long ago as 2008 Treves submitted that the concept of "due regard" should be included in a future instrument dealing with ABNJ, indicating that it could be elaborated along the following lines: "It should state specific criteria for ensuring coexistence of different activities, and, if necessary, establish priorities, or mechanisms for dealing with conflicts. If a plurality of machineries is to be set up, each regime should make provision for the possibility of efficient contacts and cooperation between them" (T Treves, 'Principles and Objectives of the Legal Regime Governing Areas Beyond National Jurisdiction', in EJ Molenaar and AG Oude Elferink (eds), *The International Legal Regime of Areas beyond National Jurisdiction: Current and Future Developments* (Martinus Nijhoff Publishers, Leiden, 2010) 7–25 at p. 22; see also Mossop (n 49) at p. 449).

and which instead plead for dealing with the operationalization of due regard in the ILBI itself, are that the designation and management of MPAS in ABNJ may quite often require recourse to due regard. In those circumstances, the option of clarification by resort to compulsory dispute settlement may prove to be ineffective, due to its adversarial nature, which may complicate future cooperation, the costs involved, and the unwillingness to litigate. If it were found to be impossible to elaborate the concept of "due regard" in the ILBI, it could alternatively be envisaged to provide for elaboration through the institutional framework that may be set up by the ILBI. One point that might seem to require attention is the specific situation of developing States. To account for their limited capabilities, the ILBI could, for instance, explicitly provide that one aspect of due regard would be to achieve proportionate burden-sharing between developed and developing States.

It may finally be asked if there could be any justification for replacing the generally applicable concept of "due regard" by the concept of "adjacency" (or "compatibility") that only is relevant to the fisheries sector. The article by Dunn *et al.*, which makes a strong case for adjacency, submits in this respect that "extending the rights of coastal States" by reference to adjacency "would likely result in better stewardship of th[e] resources [concerned] given their interest in protecting the biodiversity and ecosystems within their EEZ".[125] It is questionable whether this is really the case. The record of coastal States in managing their maritime zones is far from perfect from an environmental perspective and coastal States may also be tempted to accord priority to resource development in their own maritime zones instead of protecting biodiversity (and the marine environment) in ABNJ. The experience in the OSPAR Commission is a case in point that a coastal State may be hesitant to accept an MPA proposal that has received broad support at the regional level. Prioritizing coastal State rights through the concept of "adjacency" can also be expected to lead to a push against international review mechanisms to assess the effectiveness of MPAS in ABNJ for which adjacency would be relevant. Such a push would be in line with the resistance of coastal States to international review of their compliance with international obligations in managing their maritime zones.[126] As was argued above, an alternative to relying on the concept of "adjacency" to reflect the ideas of oceanographic and ecological connectivity could be the adaptation of the concept of "Range State" included in the CMS to fit the

125 Dunn *et al.* (n 17) at p. 9.
126 See Treves (n 124) at pp. 8, 11–12.

circumstances of MPA management in ABNJ.[127] That concept could operate in a framework that also includes an operationalized "due regard" principle.

Effective protection of marine biodiversity and the marine environment is likely to often require transboundary cooperation. At a conceptual level "due regard" is more in line with this requirement than "adjacency".[128] Adjacency as espoused at the PrepCom signals a priority of coastal State interests. On the other hand, the two-way street requirement of "due regard", which is both applicable to coastal States and to States carrying out activities in ABNJ, expresses the need for complementarity and integration of measures across jurisdictions.

---

127 See (n 17).

128 At the same time, the difference between due regard and adjacency may be limited in practice. In most regional contexts, most of the participating States are likely to be States with maritime zones that are adjacent to the ABNJ of the area of application of the relevant regional organization. In addition, as the discussion of the practice in the OSPAR Commission also illustrates, the wish to keep all parties on board may be an important consideration in looking for a compromise solution.

CHAPTER 3

Preliminary Thoughts on Marine Spatial Planning in Areas beyond National Jurisdiction

Vasco Becker-Weinberg
Professor, Faculty of Law, Universidade Nova de Lisboa, Lisbon, Portugal

Abstract

The conservation and sustainable use of biological diversity in areas beyond national jurisdiction is one of the most controversial issues facing the law of the sea, and one that will probably be the scope of a new implementing agreement of the United Nations Convention on the Law of the Sea (LOSC). The agreement will address a set of challenges not on the agenda at the time LOSC was drafted, constituting an opportunity for addressing innovative notions, but also to question established ones as States attempt to ensure the compatibility between the former and the latter. One of the many challenges and a key aspect is the adoption of area-based management tools such as marine spatial planning. This article examines the existing legal gap regarding the conservation and sustainable use of biological diversity in areas beyond national jurisdiction and the use of marine spatial planning as an essential area-based management tool.

Keywords

marine spatial planning – areas beyond national jurisdiction (ABNJ) – implementing agreement – United Nations Convention on the Law of the Sea (LOSC)

1 The New Implementing Agreement

The scientific and commercial interest in marine genetic resources (MGR) is rapidly growing, as they are generally considered to have significant biotechnological and pharmaceutical potential.[1] These are unique organisms

1 The Convention on Biological Diversity defines 'biological diversity' as "the variability among living organisms from all sources including, inter alia, terrestrial, marine and other aquatic

 | DOI:10.1163/9789004391703_005

also found in areas beyond national jurisdiction (ABNJ), mostly in extreme conditions in ecosystems of the deep ocean, such as seamounts, hydrothermal vents, methane seeps and in diverse biological communities of the ocean floor.[2]

These are still early days in research and development of MGR and many challenge face bioprospecting, both regarding its legal status (as marine scientific research or as an extractive activity[3]) and its economic viability.[4]

The global interest in MGR also raises questions regarding benefit-sharing and ownership, particularly concerning intellectual property rights and the fact that most patents are under the jurisdiction of a very few States.[5] Indeed, the issue of access and benefit-sharing is central to the debate on conservation and sustainable use of marine biological diversity in areas beyond national jurisdiction (BBNJ) and can be framed in very simple terms as having, on the one hand, the advocates that consider MGR as part of the common heritage

ecosystems and the ecological complexes of which they are part; this includes diversity within species, between species and of ecosystems", and 'genetic material' as "any material of plant, animal, microbial or other origin containing functional units of heredity" and 'genetic resources' as "genetic material of actual or potential value". See Article 2 of the Convention on Biological Diversity (Rio de Janeiro, 5 June 1992, in force 29 December 1993) 1760 *UNTS* 79.

2 N Matz, 'Marine biological resources: some reflections on concepts for the protection and sustainable use of biological resources in the deep sea' (2002) 2–3 *Non-State Actors and International Law* 279–300, at pp. 280–283; J Mossop, *The Continental Shelf Beyond 200 Nautical Miles: Rights and Responsibilities* (Oxford University Press, Oxford, 2016) 21–33. Also see L Glowka, 'The deepest of ironies: genetic resources, marine scientific research and the Area' (1996) 12 *Ocean Yearbook* 154–178, at p. 154; T Scovazzi, 'Special report: Biodiversity in the Deep Seabed' (1997) 7 *Yearbook of International Environmental Law* 481–487, at p. 481; A Proelss, 'Marine genetic resources under UNCLOS and the CBD' (2008) 51 *German Yearbook of International Law* 417–446, at pp. 418–419; D Leary, 'International law and the genetic resources of the deep sea' in D Vidas (ed), *Law, Technology and Science for Oceans in Globalisation: IUU Fishing, Oil Pollution, Bioprospecting, Outer Continental Shelf* (Martinus Nijhoff, Leiden, 2010) 353–369.

3 Mossop (n 2) at pp. 110–113.

4 J Mossop identifies four stages: 1) collection of samples, 2) attempts to isolate, characterize and culture microbes, 3) screening of samples for useful qualities that may result in a commercial product, and 4) development of the product, including securing intellectual property rights, trials and sales and marketing. *Ibid.*, at pp. 31–33.

5 *Ibid.* Also see L Glowka, 'Marine genetic resources within and beyond the limits of national jurisdiction: challenges and opportunities posed by existing and emerging international legal frameworks and processes' in MC Ribeiro (ed), *30 Years After the Signature of the United Nations Convention on the Law of the Sea: The Protection of the Environment and the Future of the Law of the Sea* (Coimbra Editora, Coimbra, 2014) 251–290, at pp. 263–270.

of mankind,[6] mostly developing countries, thus implying no appropriation, peaceful use, common management, intergenerational responsibility, equitable access and benefit-sharing; and on the other hand, those that argue that MGR should be subject to the freedom of the high seas and the application of conventional intellectual property systems[7] as also a means of protecting and preserving these resources.[8]

Similar to some extent to what occurred during the Third United Nations Conference on the Law of the Sea (UNCLOS III), subjacent to the dichotomy of common heritage of mankind/freedom of the high seas are not only opposing ideological approaches but also real and extremely valuable economic interests regarding MGR. During UNCLOS III, which resulted in the United Nations Convention on the Law of the Sea (LOSC),[9] and largely influenced by the ideas supporting the establishment of a New International Economic Order,[10] an overwhelming number of States, particularly developing countries and those that had recently gained independence from colonial rule, were concerned that the awareness of the immense potential of the deep seabed could result in only the States that had, or could acquire, the know-how and the technological capability having access to and benefit from the development of the mineral resources found therein.[11]

This perception led to the acknowledgement by the United Nations of the common interest of mankind in the seabed and ocean floor and that its exploitation and use should be conducted in view of maintaining international peace and security and for the benefit of all mankind, taking into account the

6 JE Noyes, 'The Common Heritage of Mankind: Past, Present, and Future' (2011–2012) 10 *Denver Journal of International Law and Policy* 447–471, at p. 449.

7 These include the World Intellectual Property Organization and the World Trade Organization's TRIPS Agreement [*General Agreement on Tariffs and Trade Multilateral Negotiation (The Uruguay Round): Agreement on Trade-Related Aspects of Intellectual Property Rights, Including Trade in Counterfeit Goods*, 15 December 1993, 33, *ILM* 81; 15 April 1994, 1867 *UNTS* 3].

8 B-I Kim and S Lee, 'Existing legal framework relevant to marine genetic resources' in JM Van Dyke, SP Broder, S Lee and J-H Paik (eds), *Governing Ocean Resources: New Challenges and Emerging Regimes—A Tribute to Judge Choon-Ho Park* (Martinus Nijhoff Publishers, Leiden, 2013) 503–519, at pp. 503–506.

9 United Nations Convention on the Law of the Sea (Montego Bay, 10 December 1982, in force 16 November 1994) 1833 *UNTS* 3.

10 UNGA Resolution n° 3201 (S-VI), 1 May 1974. Also see UNGA Resolutions n° 3202 (S-VI), 1 May 1974, and n° 1515 (XV), 15 December 1960.

11 MW Zacher and JG McConnell, 'Down to the sea with stakes: the evolving law of the sea and the future of the deep seabed regime' (1990) 21–1 *Ocean Development and International Law* 71–103, at pp. 79–81.

special interests and needs of the developing countries.[12] The United Nations further envisaged international cooperation and coordination for the peaceful exploitation and use of the seabed and ocean floor.[13] As a result, the Committee on the peaceful uses of the sea-bed and the ocean floor beyond the limits of national jurisdiction was established for the purpose of, *inter alia*, studying the legal principles and norms that could promote international cooperation in the exploration and use of the seabed and ocean floor and to ensure that their resources would be exploited for the benefit of mankind.[14] However, the reduction of the common heritage of mankind to only include the exploration and exploitation of mineral resources of the Area, may be considered a significant limitation of the scope of the concept and of the said notion, which at the time also considered living resources.[15]

It is worth recalling that long before UNCLOS III, the International Law Commission (ILC) noted that the idea had been argued for the internationalization of the resources of the seabed, whereby their exploitation would be entrusted to international bodies, instead of coastal States.[16] Yet, at the time, the ILC did acknowledge that the circumstances presented "insurmountable practical difficulties" and "would not ensure the effective exploitation of natural resources necessary to meet the needs of mankind".[17] The ILC also recognized the possible conflict between the exploration and exploitation of the seabed and subsoil and the freedom of the seas, although concluding that this was not "a sufficient reason for obstructing a development which (…) can be to the benefit of mankind". In this respect, the ILC considered that

12 On the principle of the common heritage of mankind applicable to the Area and its resources see A-C Kiss, 'The common heritage of mankind: utopia or reality?' (1985) 40 *International Journal* 423–441; 'La notion de patrimoine commun de l'humanité' (1982) 175–2 *RCADI* 99–256, at pp. 109–119, 196–224; R Wolfrum, 'Hohe See und Tiefseeboden (Gebiet)' in W Graf Vitzthum (ed), *Handbuch des Seerechts* (Verlag C.H. Beck, Munich, 2006) 287–345, at pp. 338–340; R Wolfrum, *Die Internationalisierung staatsfreier Räume: die Entwicklung einer internationalen Verwaltung für Antarktis, Weltraum, Hohe See und Meeresboden* (Springer, Berlin, 1984) pp. 331–396; R Wolfrum, 'The principle of the common heritage of mankind' (1983) 43 *Zeitschrift für Ausländisches Öffentliches Recht und Völkerrecht* 312–337.

13 UNGA Resolution n° 2340 (XXII), 18 December 1967.

14 UNGA Resolution n° 2467 A (XXIII), 21 December 1968.

15 A Pardo, 'An opportunity lost' in BH Oxman, DD Caron, CLO Buderi (eds), *Law of the Sea: U.S. Policy Dilemma* (ICS Press, San Francisco, CA, 1983) 13–25, at p. 22. See UNGA Resolutions n° 2749 (XXV), 17 December 1970, n° 2574 (XXIV), 15 December 1969, Section D.

16 On the internationalization of marine natural resources see V. Becker-Weinberg, 'The internationalization of marine natural resources in UNCLOS', in R Lagoni, P Ehlers and M Paschke (eds) *Recent Developments in the Law of the Sea* (LIT Verlag, Berlin, 2010) 9–54.

17 (1956) 2 *Yearbook of the International Law Commission*, 253–302, at p. 296.

> [t]he necessary steps must be taken to ensure that this development affects the freedom of the seas no more than is absolutely unavoidable, since that freedom is of paramount importance to the international community.[18]

Currently no specific international legal framework deals with BBNJ. Certain international legal instruments are relevant, namely the LOSC and the CBD, but they can also clash.[19] They fail to provide legal rules that can settle many of the issues involving BBNJ, particularly as they do not deal with BBNJ.[20] On the one hand, although the LOSC provides for the compatibility and substantive integration of legal regimes at sea, and especially rules on access to and sharing of living resources, these are not applicable to the continental shelf within or beyond 200 nautical miles (nm).[21] On the other hand, the access and benefit-sharing regime of the CBD is not mandatory;[22] neither is it applicable to MGR of the deep seabed beyond the outer edge of the continental shelf.[23] Moreover, despite the fact that the CBD provides rules on conservation of biological diversity, sustainable uses of its components and fair and equitable sharing of the benefits from the use of genetic resources, it does not include specific mechanisms to that effect.[24] Likewise, it does not provide binding dispute settlement mechanisms.[25] In addition, there is a significant disparity between domestic legislation applicable to the control, access to and development of MGR, which, together with the absence of an international legally binding regime and the increasing resort to the protection of international intellectual property systems, creates an international environment ripe for conflict and competitive development of MGR or a first-come, first-served situation in ABNJ, particularly in the case of transboundary resources.[26]

---

18 *Ibid.*

19 Matz (n 2) at pp. 287–289; R Wolfrum and N Matz, 'The interplay of the United Nations Convention on the Law of the Sea and the Convention on Biological Diversity' (2000) 4 *Max-Planck-Yearbook of United Nations Law* 445–480, at pp. 477–480.

20 Preamble, para 4, and Articles 3 and 15(1) of the CBD.

21 Articles 61, 62, 77, 118 and 133 of the LOSC. On the relationship between the LOSC and the CBD, see Wolfrum and Matz (n 19) at pp. 445–480.

22 Article 15(2) of the CBD.

23 Proelss (n 2) at pp. 420–422, 424.

24 Article 1 of the CBD.

25 Article 27 of the CBD.

26 RJ McLaughlin, 'Managing foreign access to marine genetic materials: moving from capture to cooperation' in DD Caron and HN Scheiber (eds), *Bringing New Law to Ocean Waters* (Martinus Nijhoff Publishers, Leiden, 2004) 257–281, at p. 258.

It was precisely taking these concerns into account, and after almost a decade of work by the *Ad-Hoc* Open-ended Informal Working Group to study issues relating to the conservation and sustainable use of marine biological diversity beyond areas of national jurisdiction,[27] that the General Assembly of the United Nations started preparations in 2015 towards the elaboration of a new international legally binding agreement of the LOSC dealing with BBNJ.[28] A Preparatory Commission (PrepCom) was created to formulate substantive recommendations on elements of a possible draft text. Since its inception, three PrepCom meetings have been held at the headquarters of the United Nations, in New York, with a fourth meeting scheduled for July 2017,[29] after which the PrepCom will submit to the General Assembly of the United Nations a report on the said meetings and their outcome in order for a decision to be made on convening an intergovernmental conference to work on a new implementing agreement of the LOSC.

As in UNCLOS III, the negotiations of a new implementing agreement will be based on a 'package deal', this time focusing on the following items: MGR and access and benefit-sharing; area-based management tools, including marine protected areas (MPAs) and other effective area-based measures, such as marine spatial planning (MSP); environmental impact assessment (EIA) and strategic environmental assessment (SEA); capacity-building and transfer of technology, as well as to ensure the compatibility between BBNJ and other uses, such as high seas fisheries.[30] Other elements that might also be considered may include funding mechanisms and institutional arrangements necessary to ensure the effectiveness of the new implementing agreement, as well as the development of coordination mechanisms between existing organizations in order not to jeopardize their role and actions and to develop ways of enhancing their own intervention regarding BBNJ, including dealing with the threat of fisheries in the high seas.

These topics raise several questions that should be addressed in the new implementing agreement, such as determining which activities will be subject to EIA and SEA, what should be the conduct of States in this regard and which entity will carry out these assessments and make the final decision on which activities can take place and where. EIA and SEA are not expressly referred to in the LOSC, even though EIA has been considered a general obligation

27 UNGA Resolution n°59/24, 17 November 2004.

28 UNGA Resolution n°69/292, 19 June 2015. Also see UNGA Resolutions n° 68/70, 9 December 2013, and n° 66/288, 27 July 2012, paras. 158 and 162.

29 Details of the PrepCom meetings are available at http://www.un.org/Depts/los/biodiversity/prepcom.htm; accessed May 2017.

30 UNGA Resolution n° 69/292, 19 June 2015.

under customary international law whenever there is a risk that the proposed activity may have a significant adverse impact in a transboundary context, in particular, on a shared resource.[31] There is a need for common rules that should be included in the new implementing agreement.[32] Another important aspect to be considered in the new implementing agreement is the consistency between multilateral and regional institutions and legal instruments, particularly when considering the existing fragmentation and expanding soft law.

As mentioned, one intricate legal aspect that must be addressed in the new implementing agreement concerns the use of area-based management tools and in particular the creation and efficient management of MPAs. There is no single universally recognized notion of MPA and related concepts have different definitions.[33] Early examples of MPAs were established in maritime areas closer to the coasts, in the territorial sea. With the possibility for States to declare an exclusive economic zone (EEZ), MPAs have been created at greater distances, although still within national jurisdiction.

The possibility of establishing MPAs in the high seas has been the subject of discussion for several years and is central to the BBNJ debate.[34] The issue

---

31 *Responsibilities and obligations of States sponsoring persons and entities with respect to activities in the Area, Advisory Opinion (Request for Advisory Opinion submitted to the Seabed Disputes Chamber), 1 February 2011*, Case No. 17, paras. 145–149. Also see *Pulp Mills on the River Uruguay (Argentina v. Uruguay), I.C.J. Rep. 20 April 2010*, para. 204.

32 Mossop (n 2) at p. 245.

33 Article 2 of the CBD defines 'protected area' as a "geographically defined area, which is designated or regulated to achieve specific conservation objectives"; Decision VII/5 considers 'marine and coastal protected area' "an area within or adjacent to the marine environment, together with overlying water and associated flora, fauna, and historical and cultural features, which has been reserved by legislation or other effective means, including custom, with the effect that its marine and/or coastal biodiversity enjoys a higher level of protection that its surrounding". The International Union for Conservation of Nature defines a marine protected area as "a clearly defined geographical space, recognised, dedicated and managed, through legal or other effective means, to achieve the long term conservation of nature with associated ecosystem services and cultural values", available at https://www.iucn.org/theme/protected-areas/about, accessed May 2017. Also see International Convention for the Prevention of Pollution from Ships (London, 2 November 1973), modified by the Protocol of 1978 (in force 2 October 1978) 1340 *UNTS* 184 [MARPOL 73/78], cfr. Annexes I, II, IV, V and VI.

34 International Maritime Organization, *Report of the Legal Committee on the Work of its Eighty-Seventh Session*, 23 October 2003, paras. 194–203 (LEG 87/WP.3); UNGA, *Report of the* Ad Hoc *Open-ended Informal Working Group to Study Issues Relating to the Conservation and Sustainable Use of Marine Biological Diversity Beyond Areas of National Jurisdiction*, 20 March 2006, paras. 22–31 (A/61/65); OSPAR, *The North-East Atlantic Environment Strategy, Strategy of the OSPAR Commission for the Protection of the Marine Environment of the North-East Atlantic 2010–2020*, (OSPAR Agreement 2010–3); Meeting of the

is even more complex when considering the possibility of MPAs being located both within and beyond national jurisdiction, thus requiring coordinated management and clarification of the roles of coastal States and organizations. In the current legal framework and under the principle of the freedom of the high seas there is no possibility of imposing an MPA in the high seas on all States. Inspiration could perhaps be taken from regional efforts, such as that under the Convention for the Protection of the Marine Environment of the North-East Atlantic (OSPAR),[35] or also at global level with the International Maritime Organization.[36]

Also worth noting is how the concepts of capacity-building and transfer of technology will be implemented, and what parallel, if any, can be drawn from the existing regime provided in the LOSC. Likewise, the issue of dispute settlement is bound to be a subject of debate.

Overall and similar to the LOSC, there must be a real consensus or 'package deal' in the accommodation of interests in the new implementing agreement, and not the postponement of disputes regarding conflicting interests disguised as political compromise.[37] In the case of UNCLOS III, the compromise involved, in particular, on the one hand, navigational interests,

---

Conference of the Parties, Decisions X/29, VII/5, and IX/20, *Report of the Expert Workshop on Scientific and Technical Guidance on the use of Biogeographic Classification Systems and Identification of Marine Areas Beyond National Jurisdiction in Need of Protection*, 11 January 2010 (UNEP/CBD/SBSTTA/14/INF/4), and *Report of the Expert Workshop on Scientific and Technical Aspects Relevant to Environmental Impact Assessment in Marine Areas Beyond National Jurisdiction*, 8 March 2010, (UNEP/CBD/SBSTTA/14/INF/5); UNEP, *High Seas MPAs: Regional Approaches and Experiences* [*Side Event*], 12th Global Meeting of the Regional Seas Conventions and Action Plans, Bergen, Norway, 20–22 September 2012, ref. UNEP (DEPI)/RS.12/INF.6.RS.

35 Convention for the Protection of the Marine Environment of the North-East Atlantic (Paris, 22 September 1992, in force 25 March 1998), 32 *ILM* 1069; OSPAR Recommendation 2003/3 on a Network of Marine Protected Areas, as amended by OSPAR Recommendation 2010/2.

36 IMO Resolution A. 720(17), *Guidelines for the Designation of Special Areas and the Identification of Particularly Sensitive Sea Area*, 6 November 1991, consolidated and revised by IMO Resolution A. 982(24), *Revised Guidelines for the identification and designation of Particularly Sensitive Sea Area*, 1 December 2005; and IMO Resolution A. 927(22), *Guidelines for the Designation of Special Areas under MARPOL 73/78 and Guidelines for the Identification and Designation of Particularly Sensitive Sea Areas*, 29 November 2001. Also see IMO Resolution A. IMO Resolution A. 885(21), *Procedures for the Identification of Particularly Sensitive Sea Areas and the Adoption of Associated Protective Measures and Amendments to the Guidelines contained in Resolution A. 720 (17)*, 25 November 1999.

37 Pardo (n 15) at p. 15.

and on the other hand, resource-based interests.[38] It would seem that the compromise in the new implementing agreement will certainly include, amongst others, the limitation of the freedom of the high seas as a result of the growing awareness and interest of mankind for BBNJ, extending long beyond the current generation.

Indeed, as will be subsequently analysed, the new implementing agreement, when considering MSP, must take into consideration, on the one hand, the rights of States both within and beyond maritime areas subject to national jurisdiction, as well as, on the other hand, the need to achieve sustainable ocean governance.

2 Marine Spatial Planning

Early academic reflections underlined the importance of 'coastal zone management' and 'sea use planning' as "administrative efforts to organize, integrate, and co-ordinate the planning and management activities of various agencies with ocean-related responsibilities", and how these two concepts "envisage a highly sophisticated cross-sectoral approach to zoning: a system of interlocking zones, each designed to serve a specific unisectoral purpose but also designed within a larger framework of cross-sectoral planning and management".[39] However, the question was rightfully raised whether 'coastal zone management' and 'sea use planning' could be used at international level between two or more neighbouring States, or if these two concepts are limited to national level.[40]

No international legal regime deals with MSP and the LOSC does not refer to this concept. Nor does the LOSC refer to MGR or biodiversity. The Preamble does, nonetheless, recognize that "the problems of the ocean space are closely interrelated and need to be considered as a whole". The Preamble also acknowledges the need for establishing

> a legal order for the seas and oceans which will facilitate international communication, and will promote the peaceful uses of the seas and oceans, the equitable and efficient utilizations of their resources, the

38 EL Miles, *Global Ocean Politics: The Decision Process at the Third United Nations Conference on the Law of the Sea 1973–1982* (Martinus Nijhoff Publishers, The Hague, 1998) 4.

39 DM Johnston, *Theory and History of Ocean Boundary-Making* (McGill-Queen's University Press, Kingston, 1988) 57–58.

40 *Ibid.*

conservation of their living resources, and the study, protection and preservation of the marine environment.

The notion of interconnectivity of the maritime space is also present beyond the LOSC. Indeed, the United Nations Educational, Scientific and Cultural Organization (UNESCO) recognized that the governance of the marine space must be integral and not merely sectoral or restricted to the preservation of the marine environment in certain areas. UNESCO underlined the importance of rational organization of the use of the marine space and of the interactions between its uses. In order to achieve a balance regarding the development of such uses, it is necessary to protect marine ecosystems, and to achieve social and economic objectives in a transparent manner. In this regard, UNESCO considers MSP a public process of analysing and allocating the spatial and temporal distribution of human activities and to pursue ecological, economic, and social objectives. UNESCO expressly refers to the need for the adoption of governance models that include, on the one hand, planning measures that allow for sustainable development in time and space of different uses and activities, and on the other hand, implementation measures, control, monitoring, evaluation, research, stakeholder participation and identification of financial resources.[41]

Likewise, the CBD Secretariat emphasized the importance of implementing area-based management that address multiple management objectives, as well as the relevance of MSP to improve decision-making based on principles of the ecosystem approach and ecosystem-based management, built upon the Integrated Coastal Zone Management and the Integrated Coastal Area Management concepts, and the policies that support them, including the efforts to establish MPAs.[42]

Despite the absence of any reference to MSP therein, the LOSC provides rules that are relevant to this effect. This is foremost the case of the balance achieved in the LOSC between, on the one hand, the exercise of rights of sovereignty and jurisdiction by coastal States in their respective adjacent maritime areas and concerning the natural resources found therein, and, on the other

41 Available online at http://msp.ioc-unesco.org/about/marine-spatial-planning/; accessed January 2017. Also see C Ehler and F Douvere, *Marine Spatial Planning: a Step-by-Step Approach towards Ecosystem-based Management* (IOC Manuals and Guides, n° 53, ICAM Dossier n° 6, Paris, UNESCO, 2009) 19–24.

42 Secretariat of the Convention on Biological Diversity and the Scientific and Technical Advisory Panel, *Marine Spatial Planning in the Context of the Convention on Biological Diversity: A Study carried out in Response to CBD COP 10 Decision X/29* (Montreal, Technical Series No. 68) 11.

hand, the rights and freedoms and obligations of *all* States in these areas. The LOSC also underlines the importance of both global and regional cooperation, in particular regarding the protection and preservation of the marine environment.

Nevertheless, there is a significant difference between LOSC and the current development of MSP policies regarding the resource-based and sectoral perspectives that were predominant during UNCLOS III.[43] Activities at sea are no longer limited to considerations of resource development or merely deal with the consequences of offshore activities. This paradigm has changed dramatically since UNCLOS III. Today there are more competing uses and an increasing need for maritime space than three decades ago. The very concept of State jurisdiction solely based on sovereignty or functional jurisdiction,[44] whereby States generally operate as either flag, coastal or port States, is one that must be reconsidered in light of new challenges facing the law of the sea, including BBNJ.

Central to current maritime policies at national, regional and global level are the principles of integrated ocean use management and the ecosystem approach.[45] In this respect, MSP is relevant as an area-based management tool to achieve consistency between the previously examined rights of sovereignty and jurisdiction of coastal States and the overall interests of sustainable ocean governance.[46]

At regional level, the foremost example is perhaps that of the European Union (EU) and the adoption of the MSP Directive[47] to address the discrepancies

---

43 Y Tanaka, *A Dual Approach to Ocean Governance* (Ashgate, Farnham, 2008) 6–7; 'Zonal and integrated management approaches to ocean governance: reflections on a dual approach in international law of the sea' (2004) 19–4 *International Journal of Marine & Coastal Law* 483–514. Also see J-P Lévy, 'Ocean management and a new law of the sea' (1973) 1 *Ocean Management* 129–143; E Wenk, 'International institutions for rational management of ocean space' (1973) 1 *Ocean Management* 171–200; PC Jessup, 'L'exploitation des richesses de la mer' (1929) 29 *RCADI* 405–508, at p. 508.

44 M Gavouneli, *Functional Jurisdiction in the Law of the Sea* (Martinus Nijhoff Publishers, Leiden, 2007) 33.

45 L Juda, *International Law and Ocean Use Management: The Evolution of Ocean Governance* (Routledge, London, 1996) 285; T Potts, 'Marine spatial planning and various uses and interests relating to the marine environment' in D Hassan, T Kuokkanen and N Soininen (eds), *Transboundary Marine Spatial Planning and International Law* (Routledge, London, 2015) 42–59, at p. 57.

46 N Soininen and D Hassan, 'Marine spatial planning as an instrument of sustainable ocean governance,' in Hassan *et al.* (eds) *ibid.*, 3–20.

47 Directive n°2014/89/EU of the European Parliament and of the Council of 23 July 2014 establishing a framework for maritime spatial planning, *Official Journal of the European Communities*, L 257, 28.08.2014, 135–145.

between Member States regarding MSP, primarily because only a handful of Member States have legislation on MSP, even though legislation on MSP is not a pre-requisite of efficiency, but also to provide regional coordination on maritime planning and management and to tackle cross-border effects caused by the increasing development of offshore and competing economic activities. MSP is also valuable for the implementation of the EU's Integrated Maritime Policy (IMP)[48] and Marine Strategy Framework Directive, which establishes the regional approach and the background against which Member States shall take the necessary measures to achieve or maintain good environmental status in the marine environment by the year 2020 at the latest.[49] The IMP recognizes that all matters relating to "Europe's oceans and seas" are interlinked, that sea-related policies must be developed in a joined-up way, and that the adoption of common principles and guidelines must take into consideration marine ecosystems. The ambitious goals put forward by these policies have contributed significantly to enhance maritime cooperation and coordination on maritime affairs and related policies; at the same time they reinforce the capacity of the EU and of its Member States to address the challenges ahead facing ocean governance. In this regard it should also be highlighted that the EU adopted legislation on MGR.[50]

The principles applicable to the protection and preservation of the marine environment established in Part XII of the LOSC are similarly relevant to frame MSP in the law of the sea. These include the general obligation for all States to protect and preserve the marine environment,[51] including in the high seas,[52] of global and regional cooperation,[53] and of prevention of environmental harm.[54] States are also bound to protect and preserve rare or fragile

48 *Communication from the Commission to the European Parliament, the Council, the European Economic and Social Committee and the Committee of the Regions—An Integrated Maritime Policy for the European Union* COM(2007) 574 final.

49 Directive n°2008/56/EC of the European Parliament and of the Council of 17 June 2008 establishing a framework for community action in the field of marine environmental policy (Marine Strategy Framework Directive), *Official Journal of the European Communities*, L 164, 25.06.2008, 19–40.

50 Regulation (EU) n°511/2014 of the European Parliament and of the Council, of 16 April 2014, *on compliance measures for users from the Nagoya Protocol on Access to Genetic Resources and the Fair and Equitable Sharing of Benefits Arising from their Utilization in the Union, Official Journal of the European Union*, L 150/59, 25 May 2014.

51 Article 192 of the LOSC.

52 Articles 116–119 of the LOSC.

53 Article 197 of the LOSC.

54 Articles 194(2) and 206 of the LOSC. See *Request for Advisory Opinion submitted to the Seabed Disputes Chamber* (n 31) paras. 78, 145–149. Also see *The MOX Plant Case (Ireland v. United Kingdom), Request for provisional measures*, I.T.L.O.S. No.10, 2001, paras. 82, 84,

ecosystems and habitat of depleted, threatened or endangered species and other forms of marine life.[55] Other principles, such as the precautionary principle, polluter-pays principle, the notion of sustainable development and ecosystem approach were introduced after the LOSC, but are also fundamental for MSP.[56] This is the case of the precautionary principle and ecosystem approach that are referred to in the 1995 Fish Stocks Agreement.[57]

Undoubtedly and similar to BBNJ, despite the fact that the LOSC is the main framework for MSP, the different existing legal instruments resulting from the fragmentation of the law of the sea complement the existing legal order of the oceans. This is particularly relevant with respect to providing substantive principles for current MSP policies and to ensure their effectiveness.[58]

Recently, the Chair of the PrepCom published a 'non-paper' that intends to be a reference document to assist delegations in their consideration of the issues to be discussed.[59] The main purpose of preparing the 'non-paper' was to reflect different positions in a structured form and to provide an idea of the task ahead. It was not intended to compile in a single document the several submissions made by different delegations.[60]

89(1); see *Legality of the Threat or Use of Nuclear Weapons, Advisory Opinion, I.C.J. Reports 1996*, para. 29; *Pulp Mills on the River Uruguay (Argentina* v. *Uruguay), Judgment, I.C.J. Reports 2010*, paras. 55, 56, 113, 115, 19, 120, 158.

55 Article 194(5) of the LOSC.

56 S Marr, *The Precautionary Principle in the Law of the Sea* (Martinus Nijhoff, Leiden, 2003) 5–7.

57 Article 6 of the Agreement for the Implementation of the Provisions of the United Nations Convention on the Law of the Sea of 10 December 1982 relating to the Conservation and Management of Straddling Fish Stocks and Highly Migratory Fish Stocks (New York, 4 August 1995, in force 11 December 2001) 2167 *UNTS* 3.

58 D Hassan and N Soininen, 'United Nations Convention on the Law of the Sea as a framework for marine spatial planning' in Hassan *et al.* (eds) (n 45) 60–84, at p. 69.

59 *Chair's non-paper on elements of a draft text of an international legally-binding instrument under the United Nations Convention on the Law of the Sea on the conservation and sustainable use of marine biological diversity of areas beyond national jurisdiction, 28/02/2017*, available at http://www.un.org/Depts/los/biodiversity/prepcom_files/Chair_non_paper.pdf; accessed March 2017. Also see *Supplement to the Chair's non-paper on elements of a draft text of an international legally-binding instrument under the United Nations Convention on the Law of the Sea on the conservation and sustainable use of marine biological diversity of areas beyond national jurisdiction, 24/03/2017*, available at http://www.un.org/Depts/los/biodiversity/prepcom_files/Supplement.pdf; accessed May 2017.

60 *Submissions received from delegations in response to the Chair's invitation made at the second session of the Preparatory Committee, as reflected in paragraph 11 of his overview of the second session of the Preparatory Committee, due by 5 December 2016*, available at http://www.un.org/Depts/los/biodiversity/prepcom_files/rolling_comp/Prep_Com_webpage_submisions_by_delegations.pdf; accessed March 2017.

The 'non-paper' refers to MSP in several instances as an area-based management tool together with MPAs. It also includes a reference to a possible definition provided by one delegation.[61] Yet, the 'non-paper' reflects a significant absence of a substantial reflection thus far on the use of MSP in ABNJ.[62]

In the new implementing agreement on BBNJ, MSP should continue being discussed together with MPAs, as both are area-based management tools that are necessarily connected and strive to accomplish similar goals. Also, the connection between the two concepts is extremely relevant when preparing and ensuring the effectiveness of regulations and management rules applicable to MPAs and when implementing cooperation and coordination measures between States necessary to provide an integrated approach and safeguard the interconnectivity of the different maritime zones. Furthermore, MSP is a relevant tool when dealing with maritime areas both within and beyond national jurisdiction. In this case, the basis for acceptance of any new implementing agreement that may include activities in areas within national jurisdiction will require the adherence of coastal States. Overall, many of the complex issues that are raised and implied in the whole BBNJ debate are dependent on effective and legally binding planning tools.

Perhaps inspiration for rules on MSP in the new implementing agreement dealing with activities both within and beyond national jurisdiction could be taken from Article 142 of the LOSC. According to this provision, the development of deposits found in the Area that straddle the limits of national jurisdiction shall be conducted with due regard for the rights and legitimate interests of the relevant coastal States and that consultations shall be maintained in order to avoid trespassing on such rights and interests. The LOSC also provides that in the event that such activities in the Area result in the exploitation of resources found within national jurisdiction, the prior consent of the coastal State shall be required.[63] Mineral resources that are partially

61 "Marine spatial planning is a cross-sectoral area-based management tool that provides a framework for the orderly and sustainable use of the oceans as envisioned by UNCLOS with a view to balance demands for development with the need to protect the marine environment. Sectoral area-based management tools (e.g. fisheries closures, Particularly Sensitive Sea Area (PSSAs), Particularly Sensitive Sea Area (APEIs)), other cross-sectoral ABMTs (e.g. MPAs), strategic environmental assessments (SEAs) and environmental impact assessments (EIAs) are an integral part of this overarching planning approach. Marine spatial planning approaches should be ecosystem-based, adaptive and include all relevant stakeholders in the area under consideration". *Chair's non-paper* (n 59) at p. 9.

62 Also see the recently published paper *Chair's overview of the third session of the Preparatory Committee*, pp. 9 and 18, available at http://www.un.org/Depts/los/biodiversity/prepcom_files/Chair_Overview.pdf; accessed May 2017.

63 Article 142 of the LOSC.

located in the Area are also included in the concept of the common heritage of mankind[64] and therefore should too be appropriately developed for the benefit of mankind.[65] In this respect and as rightly noted, the reference to this concept should be considered as an "underlying philosophy", seeing that it "does not give indications concerning the formal or substantive contents of a legal regime in a general sense".[66] The terms and conditions applicable to the development of these resources must be, as a result, determined between the International Seabed Authority and the relevant coastal State(s). This too could be the case of MGR under the principle of common heritage of mankind.

The LOSC also states that the exploration and exploitation of the resources of the Area shall be carried out "to foster healthy development of the world economy and balanced growth of international trade, and to promote international cooperation for the over-all development of all countries, especially developing States".[67] The Area regime further provides that resources shall be orderly, safely and rationally managed in accordance with sound principles of conservation and the avoidance of unnecessary waste, and to ensure supply to consumers, the promotion of just and stable prices and of long-term equilibrium between supply and demand, and the conditions of access to markets for the imports of minerals produced from the resources of the Area and for imports of commodities produced from such minerals.[68] The LOSC establishes that there should be reasonable and reciprocal regard between the activities in the Area and other activities in the marine environment.[69] Although Article 142(1) does not expressly refer to the obligation of mutual restraint regarding "resource deposits in the Area which lie across limits of national jurisdiction," it would seem that this obligation would be implied in the duty of due regard in order to avoid causing damage to the relevant coastal State, seeing that the duty of due regard for the rights and interests of third States is connected with States' obligation to prevent and not to cause harm. In the event that either the coastal State or the Authority would cause damage, the relevant rules on

64 Article 136 of the LOSC.

65 Article 140 of the LOSC.

66 N Matz-Lück, 'The concept of the common heritage of mankind: its viability as a management tool for deep-sea genetic resources' in AG Oude Elferink and EJ Molenaar (eds), *The International Legal Regime of Areas beyond National Jurisdiction: Current and Future Developments* (Martinus Nijhoff Publishers, Leiden, 2010) 61–75, at p. 65. Matz-Lück concludes that "[i]t is a matter of methodology whether the common heritage concept is a legal principle from which one can deduct the necessary legal consequences or whether it is an idea that is reflected in different treaty provisions" (at p. 66).

67 Article 150 of the LOSC.

68 Article 150 lit. b), e), f) and j) and Article 13(1) of Annex III of the LOSC.

69 Article 147(1), (3) of the LOSC.

liability would be applicable.[70] In this respect, the Seabed Disputes Chamber considered that carrying out an EIA was a 'direct obligation' under the LOSC and a general obligation under customary international law and, consequently, "should be included in the system of consultations and prior notifications set out in article 142".[71] As a result, coastal States and the Authority must exchange information regarding mineral resources that may be found to straddle the demarcation line between the continental shelf and the Area, as well as adopt restraint regarding any action that may potentially cause harm to their legitimate interests. The recognition of a duty of information and an obligation of due regard does not imply, however, the obligation for coastal States and the Authority to cooperate in sharing these resources.

3 Observations

Despite the efforts of UNCLOS III and the resilience of the LOSC for more than thirty years during which human activity at sea has increased tremendously, the fragmentation of international law of the sea has resulted in important governance gaps. New usages and activities and many threats represented by climate change, sea level rise, ocean acidification and exhaustion of marine natural resources demand a prompt and efficient response that is not available under the current legal framework. Indeed, although not on the agenda of issues addressed during UNCLOS III, one of the existing governance gaps concerns BBNJ, which is undoubtedly today one of the most contentious issues in the law of the sea.

Notwithstanding the fact that several objectives and principles enshrined in many international legal instruments, as well as in customary international law, are applicable to BBNJ, in order to effectively address its conservation and sustainable use and effectively protect and preserve and avoid further degradation of the marine environment, a holistic and integrated approach, as mentioned in the Preamble of the LOSC, is necessary, to avoid piecemeal governance. It is vital when dealing with BBNJ that all States share common objectives and standards based on which a coherent decision-making process can take place. Moreover, it is also necessary to implement coordination and cooperation arrangements at regional and global levels between States and between organizations, as well as between the former and the latter. There is an

---

70 Article 187 lit. b) of the LOSC.

71 *Request for Advisory Opinion submitted to the Seabed Disputes Chamber* (n 31) paras. 145, 148.

intricate reality of international organizations that have a role in high seas governance at regional and multilateral level, but with significant areas of overlap and few coordination mechanisms in place between them. Furthermore, consensus is lacking on the relationship between BBNJ with regard to the seabed and the water column, as well as regarding which relevant legal principle it should be subject to: common heritage of mankind or freedom of the high seas.

As a result, and with many coastal States pursuing the extension and delineation of their outer continental shelf beyond 200 nm, it is necessary to avoid conflicts between usages and activities under the legal regimes of the continental shelf and of the high seas. In this regard, together with area-based management tools, such as MSP, regional and global cooperation is essential.

A paradigmatic case is that of bottom trawling that is undertaken under the freedom of the high seas but has a dramatic adverse effect on stocks and on the seabed environment. This continues to be the case despite the fact that the LOSC is the overarching legally binding framework for fisheries management in ABNJ, and that the 1995 Fish Stocks Agreement elaborates on requirements for the conservation and management of straddling and highly migratory fish stocks, as well as on the application of the precautionary and ecosystem approach and the protection of biodiversity in the marine environment. Regional Fisheries Management Organizations and arrangements have an important role regarding the conservation of BBNJ and in addressing the concerns raised by deep-sea fisheries and their impact on the sustainable use and protection of vulnerable marine ecosystems. Indeed, the reinforcement of flag State responsibility notwithstanding, promoting cooperation between these organizations on fisheries management in ABNJ is an indispensable component of a global approach to existing governance gaps.[72] For example, following the adoption of legislation on MSP,[73] Portugal banned bottom trawling in its national maritime space, including the extended continental shelf, but, alas, could only do

72 See Food and Agriculture Organization of the United Nations, *International Guidelines for the Management of Deep-sea Fisheries in the High Seas*, available at ftp://ftp.fao.org/docrep/fao/011/i0816t/i0816t.pdf; accessed May 2017. These guidelines provide policy directions on deep-sea fisheries, namely sustainable use and protection of vulnerable marine ecosystems and assessing potential impacts of bottom fishing in order to facilitate the adoption and implementation of conservation and management measures by Regional Fisheries Management Organizations and arrangements.

73 V Becker-Weinberg, 'Portugal's legal regime on marine spatial planning and management of the national maritime space', (November 2015) 61 *Marine Policy* 46–53. A more detailed analysis of Portugal's MSP legal regime see V Becker-Weinberg, *Ordenamento e Gestão do Espaço Marítimo Nacional: Enquadramento e Legislação* (Quid Juris, Lisbon, 2016) 11–55.

so regarding ships flying its flag.[74] Therefore, in order to ensure that this measure was also applicable to other vessels, Portugal had to seek the support of the member-States of the North-east Atlantic Fisheries Commission, although it was not entirely successful in doing so. Likewise, other relevant developments are being discussed in Portugal regard the adoption of a legal framework on classification and management of MPAs beyond the territorial sea, including in the extended continental shelf. Portugal has nominated twelve MPAs both within and beyond national jurisdiction[75] under the network established by OSPAR.[76] Amongst the most notable are Formigas Bank and Rainbow Hydrothermal Vent Field (Rainbow MPA), which were, respectively, the first OSPAR MPA and the first MPA in the extended continental shelf, even though when Portugal created the Rainbow MPA it had not yet submitted its proposal for the extension of the continental shelf.[77] In this case, regional cooperation is essential in order to impose an MPA on all States in ABNJ and ensure its effectiveness.

Another example that could potentially be considered when discussing possible opposing or conflicting interests and the need to frame the freedom of the high seas in order to safeguard BBNJ, could be that of the freedom to lay submarine cables and pipelines, which is included in the overall freedoms of the high seas.[78] Also in this case MSP could be a valuable tool to reconcile such distinctive interests, as long as the relevant global and regional cooperation mechanisms are in place.

Therefore, as an area-based management tool, MSP is essential to achieve a holistic and integrated approach, as long as the proper coordination and cooperation arrangements, at regional and global levels, are in place. Moreover, it

---

74 *Portaria* n° 114/2014, 28 May 2014, published in *Diário da República*, 1st Series, n° 102, 28 May 2014.

75 V Becker-Weinberg and M Martins, 'Marine protected areas: a strategy for Portugal' (2013) 5 *Maria Scientia* (Institute of Political Studies of the Portuguese Catholic University) 73–82, at p. 76.

76 *Final Statement of the Ministerial Meeting of the OSPAR Commission, Sintra, 22–23 July 1998*, Annex 45 Ref. § B-10.2; OSPAR Recommendation 2003/03.

77 On the Rainbow Hydrothermal Vent Field, see MC Ribeiro, 'The 'Rainbow': the first national marine protected area proposed under the high seas' (2010) 25 *International Journal of Marine and Coastal Law* 183–207. Portugal created the Rainbow MPA pursuant to its continental shelf rights as provided by Article 77 of the LOSC and in accordance with Article 192 of the LOSC, namely the adoption of the appropriate measures to protect the sensitive areas under its jurisdiction or sovereignty, which in the case of the Rainbow MPA only included the protection of the seabed and subsoil, without hindering the legal status of the overlying water column.

78 Article 87(1) lit. c) of the LOSC.

is also necessary that an ample and binding legal framework be implemented, allowing for a wide-ranging and transparent decision-making process. Only through such a comprehensive approach will it be possible to improve ocean governance and contribute to the avoidance of conflicts between uses and activities taking place under different legal regimes and having due regard for the interaction between areas within and beyond national jurisdiction.

CHAPTER 4

The Proposed LOSC Implementation Agreement on Areas beyond National Jurisdiction and Its Impact on International Fisheries Law

Richard Barnes
Professor of International Law, University of Hull, Hull, United Kingdom

Abstract

As the development of an implementation agreement on the conservation and sustainable use of marine biodiversity in areas beyond national jurisdiction gathers pace, it is important to consider how this might impact upon international fisheries law. Although the proposed agreement provides an opportunity to addresses governance gaps both generally and with respect to fisheries, we should not expect too much of it; not least because the inclusion *per se* of fisheries remains debated by States. Also, positive institutional developments are already occurring beyond this United Nations process. The proposed implementation agreement should not undermine existing laws, but it is unlikely to leave them untouched. The application of integrated governance principles, and the use of area-based management tools and environmental impact assessment will necessarily influence fisheries regulation in ABNJ. Accordingly, care should be taken to ensure that any innovative governance tools are adapted to existing institutional capacities and circumstances.

Keywords

areas beyond national jurisdiction (ABNJ) – international fisheries law – regional fisheries management organizations – United Nations Convention on the Law of the Sea (LOSC) implementation agreement – governance principles – area-based management tools – environmental impact assessment

 | DOI:10.1163/9789004391703_006

1 Introduction[1]

The United Nations Convention on the Law of the Sea (LOSC) establishes a broad framework for the regulation of our oceans.[2] However, it is not complete. One such gap concerns the regulation of marine resources in areas beyond national jurisdiction (ABNJ).[3] States have resorted, *inter alia*, to the negotiation of 'implementation agreements' to fill gaps in or resolve problems with the LOSC.[4] Two such agreements have been adopted and now it is likely that a third will emerge to deal with ABNJ.[5] On 13 February 2015, the *Ad-Hoc* Open-ended Informal Working Group to study issues related to the conservation and sustainable management of marine biological diversity beyond areas of national jurisdiction (BBNJ Working Group) concluded its work and recommended that the United Nations General Assembly (UNGA) initiate a process for the negotiation of an international legally binding instrument on the conservation and sustainable use of BBNJ.[6] On 19 June 2016, the UNGA accepted this recommendation and initiated this process through the adoption of UNGA Resolution 69/292.[7] This Resolution established a Preparatory Committee (PrepCom) to make substantive recommendations on the elements of a draft legal text. This was a significant step, the culmination of more than a decade of efforts focused on what is generally accepted to be a major gap in the scope

1 This article was delivered first at a workshop organized by the K.G. Jebsen Centre for the Law of the Sea at the University of Tromsø. My thanks to the Centre and colleagues at the workshop for their support, as well as Philomène Verlaan and David Freestone for their helpful feedback on the article.

2 United Nations Convention on the Law of the Sea (Montego Bay, 10 December 1982, in force 16 November 1994), 1833 *UNTS* 396.

3 ABNJ refers to the high seas and the Area—the deep seabed beyond the outer limits of the continental shelf.

4 On the development of the LOSC through a range of mechanisms, see generally, J Barrett and R Barnes (eds), *Law of the Sea: LOSC as a Living Treaty* (BIICL, London, 2016).

5 1994 Agreement relating to the implementation of Part XI of the LOSC of 10 December 1982 (New York, 28 July 1994, in force 28 July 1996), 1836 *UNTS* 42; The United Nations Agreement for the Implementation of the Provisions of the United Nations Convention on the Law of the Sea of 10 December 1982 relating to the conservation and management of straddling fish stocks and highly migratory fish stocks (New York, 4 August 1995, in force force 11 December 2001) 2167 *UNTS* 88 (Fish Stocks Agreement or FSA).

6 Letter dated 13 February 2015 from the Co-Chairs of the *Ad-Hoc* Open-ended Informal Working Group to the President of the UN General Assembly, UN Doc. 69/780, A/69/780, annex, section I.

7 UNGA Res. 69/292, UN Doc. A/Res/69.292, 6 July 2015.

of the LOSC.[8] It is for the UNGA decide whether to convene an intergovernmental conference to consider the recommendations of PrepCom, and elaborate the text of a legally binding instrument. This decision will be taken in 2018, and it is possible that a new agreement will be ready for adoption by 2020.

Although States generally recognize the need for a global instrument on the conservation and sustainable use of marine biodiversity in ABNJ, this general consensus masks important differences of opinion on the precise scope and content of such an instrument, and of its relationship with existing arrangements.[9] The process of developing a new agreement "should not undermine existing relevant legal instruments and frameworks and relevant global, regional and sectoral bodies".[10] As this article will show, this raised particularly difficult questions in respect of fisheries. Given that there is little agreement beyond the general topics to be covered in the proposed implementing agreement, one must be cautious about speculating too far on what future negotiations may bring. However, one can be reasonably certain that the agreement will articulate some general principles concerning the conservation and use of marine biological resources. It will also address the use of area-based management (ABM) tools, the use of environmental impact assessment (EIA) and mechanisms for capacity-building and technology transfer. For the most part fisheries issues are likely to remain governed by existing instruments. However, the scope of the proposed agreement means that fisheries will not be unaffected. First, many of the governance principles proposed for the prospective ABNJ implementation agreement (ABNJ IA) are likely to influence or shape the future mandates of regional fisheries management organizations (RFMOs), filling or addressing noted governance gaps. Second, two

---

8 On the governance gap see: K Gjerde, H Dotinga, S Hart, EJ Molenaar, R Rayfuse and R Warner, *Regulatory and Governance Gaps in the International Regime for the Conservation and Sustainable Use of Marine Biodiversity in Areas beyond National Jurisdiction* (IUCN, Gland, Switzerland, 2008); K Gjerde, 'High Seas Fisheries Governance: Prospects and Challenges in the 21st Century' in D Vidas and PJ Schei (eds), *The World Ocean in Globalisation: Challenges and Responses* (Martinus Nijhoff Publishers, Leiden, 2011), 99–113; D Freestone, 'The Final Frontier: The Law of the Sea Convention and Areas beyond National Jurisdiction' in HN Scheiber and M-S Kwon (eds), *Securing the Ocean for the Next Generation* (Law of the Sea Institute, Berkeley, CA, 2012), 1–15; D Freestone, 'Governance of Areas Beyond National Jurisdiction: An Unfinished Agenda' in Barrett and Barnes (n 4) 231–265.

9 This can be drawn from the discussions taking place within the BBNJ Working Group. See the Co-Chairs' summary of discussions in the Letter of 13 February 2016 (n 6), para 14.

10 UNGA Res. 69/292 (n 7), para 3.

key elements of the proposed ABNJ IA, i.e., ABM and EIA, necessarily entail some degree of overlap with or accommodation of fishing activities.

This article examines developments so far, focusing specifically on how they might affect fisheries regulation under international law.[11] After outlining the context of the ABNJ IA, the article reviews progress in the UN ABNJ process to date and examines the extent to which fisheries have featured in discussions. Although the debates were not conclusive of how fisheries will be accommodated in the proposed ABNJ IA, some general trends can be detected. This suggests that a broadly integrated approach, which builds on and is complementary to existing measures, will be preferred to radical approaches. The article then traces these discussions through the work of PrepCom. This is followed by an analysis of the potential contents of an ABNJ IA, focusing on those issues most likely to affect fisheries, i.e., governance principles, ABM and EIA. Within the ABNJ IA, the articulation and institutional support measures for governance principles will be absolutely critical. In the final section, the potential effects of this approach are assessed in existing fisheries regulation. Here I suggest that there will need to be some adaptation of RFMOs (in terms of substantive principles, expanded remits), efforts outside the IA to close institutional and substantive gaps (new RFMOs), and more formalized mechanisms for institutional cooperation and decision-making.

2 Context to the Proposed Implementing Agreement

2.1 *The LOSC and ABNJ*

The LOSC is a product of its time and so designed to deal with matters of which the negotiating States were then aware. This did not include the issue of marine genetic resources (MGR), biological diversity or indeed many issues related to the governance of the marine environment of ABNJ. Part XI of the LOSC was designed mainly to deal with mineral resources. That said, many of the LOSC's provisions were drafted in a way that would allow them to adapt to new situations.[12] Despite this flexibility, the discovery of the existence of

11 For a general review of developments, see R Long and M Chaves, 'Anatomy of a new international instrument for marine biodiversity beyond national jurisdiction. First impressions of the preparatory process' (2015) 6 *Environmental Liability* 213–229.

12 See for example, SV Scott, 'The LOS Convention as a Constitutional Regime for the Oceans' in AG Oude Elferink (ed), *Stability and Change in the Law of the Sea: The Role of the LOS Convention* (Martinus Nijhoff Leiden, 2005) 9–38; A Boyle, 'Further Development of the 1982 Convention on the Law of the Sea' in D Freestone, R Barnes and D Ong (eds), *Law of*

valuable marine resources with the potential to be exploited for their genetic potential, along with a growing awareness of the complex nature of deep sea ecosystems, has challenged the suitability of the LOSC as a self-contained regime for ABNJ. Much of this has focused on the tension between States holding to the applicability of the principles of freedom of the high seas and States advocating the application of the principle of the common heritage of mankind (CHM) to the resources constituting marine biological diversity.[13]

2.2 *UN-led Consideration of Marine Biodiversity—The BBNJ Working Group*

In 2004, the UNGA established the BBNJ Working Group.[14] The BBNJ Working Group would survey past and present activities of the UN and other intergovernmental organizations (IGOs), examine scientific, technical, economic, legal, environmental, socio-economic and other aspects of these issues. This would provide the basis for more detailed studies by States of these issues, and ultimately lead to recommendations on how to improve cooperation and coordination.[15] The BBNJ Working Group convened first in February 2006 and met periodically until it concluded its work in 2015.

The outcomes of discussions are contained in a series of reports and letters to the President of the UNGA.[16] These summaries indicate the general trends in discussion and positions of delegates, either as groups or collectively, without specifying views of individual States. It is interesting to note the careful use of language, even in these reports, designed to generate consensus. Thus a range of different terms is used to describe the views of delegations: 'some',

the Sea. Progress and Prospects (Oxford University Press, Oxford, 2006) 40–62; Barrett and Barnes (n 4).

13 This is widely discussed in the literature. See for example, D Tladi, 'Genetic Resources, Benefit Sharing, and the Law of the Sea: the Need for Clarity' (2007) 13(3) *Journal of International Maritime Law* 183–193; AG Oude Elferink, 'The Regime of the Area: Delineating the Scope of Application of the Common Heritage Principle and of Freedom of the High Seas' (2007) 22(1) *IJMCL* 143–176.

14 UNGA Res. 59/24, 17 December 2004, UN Doc. A/Res/59/24, 4 February 2005.

15 *Ibid.*, at paras 73–74.

16 Reports of the *Ad-Hoc* Open-ended Informal Working Group to study issues relating to the conservation and sustainable use of marine biological diversity beyond areas of national jurisdiction: 2006—UN Doc. A/61/65, 20 March 2006; 2008—UN Doc. A/63/79, 16 May 2008. Letter from the Co-Chairpersons of the *Ad-Hoc* Open-ended Informal Working Group to the President of the General Assembly: 2010—UN Doc. A/65/68, 17 March 2010; 2011—UN Doc. A/66/119, 30 June 2011; 2012—UN Doc. 67/95, 13 June 2012; 2013 UN Doc. A/68/399, 23 Sept 2013; 2014—UN Doc. A/68/82, 5 May 2014 and UN Doc. 69/117*, 23 July 2014; also footnote 9.

'several', 'many', 'other' and so on. Additionally, there are references to singular positions ('the view' or 'a view') and indeterminate collective positions ('delegations' or 'it'). The way in which the reports are composed tends to mask underlying ideological differences, but it definitely serves to build a sense of consensus.[17] Unfortunately, it also makes it difficult to provide a detailed analysis of State positions.

Little substantive progress was made at the first meeting in 2006, which focused on the organization of work and exchanges of views on the issues forming the remit of the BBNJ. There was a general consensus that the issues were important and concern for more effective implementation of existing legal commitments.[18] It was accepted that whilst the LOSC is the framework for oceans activities, other instruments are also relevant.[19] Fisheries were discussed, although no firm views were expressed, other than to note the potential for harm, and that other fora were relevant to dealing with them.[20] Much of the subsequent BBNJ discussions were characterized by growing consensus on core issues, but divergent views remained on the institutional implications of this.

By 2008, key issues of common concern began to emerge, including capacity-building, the implementation of effective EIA, and the development of ABM tools.[21] Consensus on these points continued to develop at the 2010 meeting, which highlighted the importance of expanding the knowledge basis for decision-making,[22] the general need for cooperation and coordination in implementation,[23] and capacity-building[24] There was also continued focus on ABM and EIA.[25] The 2011 meeting of the BBNJ Working Group presented a series of recommendations to the UNGA. This reflected a growing consensus between groups of States on the scope of a negotiating package.[26] Whilst it was generally accepted that the *status quo* was not an option, States were divided

17 This was manifest in the debate about whether or not MGR are part of the CHM regime. See for example UN Doc. 69/117*, para 12.
18 UN Doc. A/61/65, Annex I, paras 4 and 5.
19 *Ibid.*, at para 3.
20 *Ibid.*, at para 7.
21 UN Doc. A/63/79, para 54.
22 UN Doc. A/65/68, paras 31–37.
23 *Ibid.*, at paras 11–12 and 42–45.
24 *Ibid.*, at para 38.
25 *Ibid.*, at paras 14–18.
26 See S Hodgson, A Serdy, I Payne and J Gille, *Towards a Possible International Agreement on Marine Biodiversity in Areas Beyond National Jurisdiction.* IP/A/ENVI/2014-04 (European Parliament, 2014) p. 50.

on the precise way forward.[27] The BBNJ did not recommend an IA, but called for the initiation of a process that would address certain issues (general conservation and sustainable use of MGR in ABNJ, benefit-sharing, ABM, EIA, capacity-building and technology transfer), including through the development of an agreement under LOSC.[28] UNGA Resolution 66/231 consolidated the mandate of the BBNJ Working Group in line with the above recommendations.[29]

In 2012, the BBNJ Working Group met shortly before the Rio+20 Summit. By this stage it appears that a number of delegations were comfortable with the notion of an implementing agreement. However, insufficient consensus remained on this point. No decision on an implementing agreement was taken at Rio+20, although States made a strong commitment at a ministerial level to address this issue as a matter of urgency, and to reach a decision on the adoption of an agreement before the end of the UNGA's 69th session in August 2015.[30] This provided much-needed political momentum. One may note that the rate of progress in BBNJ discussions improved from 2013, with the use of intersessional meetings, and an invitation to the Co-Chairs of the BBNJ Working Group to submit their views on the scope, parameters and feasibility of an IA under the LOSC.[31] This latter point was built on in UNGA Resolution 68/70, which called upon States to submit their views on the scope, parameters, and feasibility of an IA.[32] However, a lack of consensus remained on the precise scope of a negotiating package.[33] Securing this was to become the main focus of the 2014 meetings. The BBNJ Group met twice (1–4 April and 16–19 June) in 2014. During the first meeting it was noted that the work of the BBNJ was reaching a critical stage, where decisions needed to be made.[34] Thus discussions covered questions of form (soft law or binding agreement?), as well as potential substantive and procedural aspects of an instrument.[35] Also, whether such matters should be addressed through an instrument falling under the

27 UN Doc. A/66/119, paras 42–43.
28 *Ibid.*, at Annex, para 1.
29 UNGA Res. 66/231, paras 167–168.
30 See Report of the United Nations Conference on Sustainable Development (Rio de Janeiro, Brazil 20–22 June 2012) UN Doc. A/CONF.216/16, para 162.
31 UN Doc. A/68/399, Annex, para 1(d) and (e).
32 UNGA Res. 68/70, para 201.
33 UN Doc. A/68/399, para 50.
34 UN Doc. A/68/82, para 14.
35 *Ibid.*, at paras 31–48. UN Doc 69/117*, paras 23–81.

LOSC.[36] A preference for a binding instrument emerged,[37] and at the 2015 session, the recommendation to develop a legally binding instrument was taken.

On 19 June 2016, the UNGA adopted UNGA Resolution 69/292,[38] which put in motion the process for formally developing an IA. It established a PrepCom open to all Member States of the UN, its specialized agencies and parties to the LOSC, and it was charged with making recommendations to the UNGA on the elements of a draft text of a binding agreement.[39] As a final comment, it is worth noting that although States have driven this process, both IGOs and non-governmental organizations (NGOs) provided considerable input.[40]

2.3 *PrepCom's First Meeting*

The progress made by the BBNJ Working Group meant that the material scope of PrepCom's mandate is quite clear. It is to address the following issues:

> the conservation and sustainable use of marine biological diversity of areas beyond national jurisdiction, in particular, together and as a whole, marine genetic resources, including questions on the sharing of benefits, measures such as area-based management tools, including marine protected areas, environmental impact assessments and capacity-building and the transfer of marine technology.[41]

PrepCom hosted its first meeting between 6–8 April 2016, with a second meeting scheduled between 26 August and 9 September 2016.[42] The meeting was well attended, but was by no means universal, despite the aim of the UNGA to be as inclusive as possible through the participation of all States, IGOs and

36 UN Doc. A/69/177*, para 11.

37 *Ibid.*, at paras 13–16.

38 UNGA Res. 69/292, (n 7).

39 *Ibid.*, at para 1(a).

40 R Warner, 'Conserving marine biodiversity in areas beyond national jurisdiction: co-evolution and interaction with the law of the sea' in DR Rothwell, AG Oude Elferink, KN Scott and T Stephens (eds), *The Oxford Handbook of the Law of the Sea* (Oxford University Press, Oxford, 2015) 52–76.

41 UNGA Res. 69/292, (n 7), para 2.

42 There is no formal record of PrepCom discussions, other than the Chair's overview of PrepCom's first session. Available online at: http://www.un.org/depts/los/biodiversity/prepcom_files/PrepCom_1_Chair's_Overview.pdf. However, a daily report on the discussions was published in *Earth Negotiations Bulletin* online at: http://www.iisd.ca/oceans/bbnj/prepcom1/.

NGOs, not just States Parties to the LOSC.[43] It was attended by 91 States Parties, 10 Non-States Parties, seven IGOs, five UN specialised agencies, five UN-funded programmes and agencies, 17 NGOs and two private commercial groups.[44] Notably only one RFMO, the South East Atlantic Fisheries Organisation (SEAFO), attended, despite the importance of the ABNJ IA to fisheries. PrepCom will report to the UNGA by the end of 2017, although this does not mean a draft text will be presented at this point. Rather, an intergovernmental conference will be convened at a date to be agreed before the end of the UNGA 72nd session (September 2017) to consider and elaborate the text of a binding agreement.

PrepCom procedures are the same as those applicable to the UNGA, with participatory rights afforded to the European Union (EU) as per the LOSC's Meetings of States Parties.[45] In order to secure the widest possible agreement, PrepCom shall work, as far as possible, on the basis of consensus.[46] Consensus has been facilitated through the use of informal working groups arranged on the basis of the four key aspects of the proposed agreement: Mr. Carlos Sobral Duarte (Brazil)—MGR, including benefit-sharing; Mr. John Adank (New Zealand)—ABM tools; Mr. René Lefeber (the Netherlands)—EIAs; and Ms. Rena Lee (Singapore)—capacity-building and the transfer of marine technology. It seems, however, that securing a text is the priority, as allowance is made for the draft text presented to the UNGA to contain provisions where consensus is lacking.[47]

The emphasis on integration at PrepCom is significant. It marks the continued faith in the success of package deal negotiations that underpinned the LOSC. More specifically, it would appear to fundamentally link questions of international fisheries regulation to the development of the IA. As discussed below, this is perhaps the most challenging issue faced by PrepCom. Indeed, the main divergence of opinion during the first meeting was the relationship between the new instrument and fisheries regulation. It is to this question we turn now.

43 UN General Assembly Res. 69/292 (2015), para 1(a).

44 Long and Chaves (n 11), at 220.

45 See (n 43), at para 1(j).

46 *Ibid.*, at para 1(g)–(h).

47 See (n 43), at para 1(i).

3 Fisheries and Governance Issues at the BBNJ Working Group and PrepCom

3.1 *Fisheries and Governance Gaps*

High seas fisheries and RFMOs have been subject to a high degree of criticism, much of it noting the need for reform.[48] Although fisheries regulation was not the principal object of the BBNJ Working Group's mandate, it was no surprise to see many delegations raise this issue at the first BBNJ meeting in 2006.[49] In later meetings, several fisheries-specific gaps were raised by delegates, including a lack of effective flag State control over fishing vessels operating in ABNJ, the need to improve port State control, limited regulatory tools (for example, scope for market-based controls on fisheries), weak performance reviews of RFMOs, gaps in the geographical and species coverage of RFMOs, and failure to implement controls on bottom-trawl fishing.[50] Whilst such issues are important, the identification of regulatory gaps in fisheries management could have been more complete, and this might have served to reinforce calls to include fisheries within a new regime. For example, the FSA does not explicitly cover discrete high seas stocks, and some gaps exist in the coverage of such stocks by RFMOs.[51] The FSA provides a framework for RFMOs and other arrangements, but it does not require conformity with its provisions.[52] Many but not all species are regulated by RFMOs.[53] Geographic gaps in RFMO

48 See the material cited in footnote 8. Also KM Gjerde, D Currie, K Wowk and K Sack, 'Ocean in Peril: Reforming the Management of Global Ocean Living Resources in Areas beyond National Jurisdiction' (2013) 74(2) *Marine Pollution Bulletin* 540–551; A Cox, R Renwrantz and I Kelling, *Strengthening Regional Fisheries Management Organizations* (OECD, Paris, 2009); MW Lodge, D Anderson, T Løbach, G Munro, K Sainsbury and A Willock, *Recommended Best Practices for Regional Fisheries Management Organizations* (Chatham House, London, 2007); AD Rogers and M Gianni, *The Implementation of UNGA Resolutions 61/105 and 64/72 in the Management of Deep-Sea Fisheries on the High Seas* (International Programme on the State of the Ocean, London, 2010); S Cullis-Suzuki and D Pauly, 'Failing the High Seas: A Global Evaluation of Regional Fisheries Management Organizations' (2010) 34(5) *Marine Policy* 1036–1042.

49 UN Doc. A/61/65, paras 9 and 23.

50 See, for example, UN Doc. A/63/79, paras 40 and 42; UN Doc. A/67/95, para 30; UN Doc. A/68/82, para 47.

51 Y Takei, *Filling Regulatory Gaps in High Seas Fisheries. Discreet High Seas Fish Stocks, Deep-sea Fisheries and Vulnerable Marine Ecosystems* (Martinus Nijhoff, Leiden, 2013) p. 4.

52 See Gjerde *et al.* (n 8), at 9.

53 Lodge *et al.* (n 48), at xviii.

coverage include the Arctic, Central and Southwest Atlantic.[54] Small vessels may be exempted from the FAO Compliance Agreement.[55] More generally, institutional oversight of RFMOs is lacking; no single institution is responsible for coordinating RFMO activities, or is independently mandated to review the performance of RFMOs, port States and flag States.

Delegations expressed divergent views on fisheries issues, but one point of agreement was that poorly regulated fishing was the main threat to marine biodiversity in ABNJ. At its first meeting in 2006, the BBNJ Working Group identified illegal, unregulated and unreported (IUU) fishing and destructive fishing practices as the greatest threat to ABNJ.[56] Some delegations observed the existence of perverse incentives and profit from IUU fishing as one of the key drivers of harm.[57] However, whilst this point was not disputed, concern with the socio-economic drivers of IUU fishing does not seem to have featured in later BBNJ Working Group discussions. In 2008, the Working Group focused on identifying anthropogenic impacts on BBNJ, and particular attention was placed on "unsustainable fishing activities, including overfishing, overcapacity, by-catch, destructive fishing practices, illegal, unreported and unregulated fishing; non-participation and non-compliance with global and regional fisheries instruments".[58] Thereafter, these threats seem to have been accepted as a given, with subsequent discussions focusing on how to address knowledge gaps about the precise impacts of human activities on ABNJ.[59] These discussions in turn contributed to consensus on the need for any ABNJ regime to be underpinned by sound knowledge. In this respect many delegates took the view that collection and sharing of data was critical to promoting conservation and sustainable use of marine biological diversity.[60] At the 2012 meeting, it was noted that since the inception of the BBNJ process, pressures on marine resources had increased and that human activities, including overfishing, had continued to put the oceans at risk.[61] In 2014, it was noted that "unsustainable fishing, in particular overfishing, illegal, unreported and unregulated fishing

54 For a general appraisal of RFMOs, see R Rayfuse, 'Regional Fisheries Management Organizations' in Rothwell *et al.* (n 40) 439–462.

55 Article II(2) of the Agreement to Promote Compliance with International Conservation and management Measures by Fishing Vessels on the High Seas 1993 (Rome, 24 November 1993, in force 24 April 2003), 2221 *UNTS* (No. 39486).

56 *Ibid.*, at para 33, and Annex I, paras 7–8.

57 *Ibid.*, at para 37.

58 UN Doc. A/63/79, para 13.

59 See for example: UN Doc. A/61/65, paras 19, 45 and 45; UN Doc. A/68/399, para 33.

60 UN Doc. A/65/68, para 34; UN Doc. A/68/399, para 33.

61 UN Doc. A/67/95, para 14.

and certain destructive fishing practices, was the greatest threat to marine biodiversity in those areas".[62] This presented States with something of a dilemma because if the subject-matter of an ABNJ agreement excluded fisheries, then how could it establish a workable regime for the conservation and sustainable use of ABNJ?

In general, delegations were of the view that implementation could be enhanced by securing universal participation in the LOSC and other agreements.[63] This point is worth stressing, because the adoption of an ABNJ IA will not resolve the gaps in RFMO coverage. This is something that depends upon the political will of States, as well as suitable socio-economic conditions. This latter point may require some degree of support for developing States. Already obligations of support, by way of capacity-building measures, exist under the FSA.[64] However, this would not necessarily result in all gaps being closed, particularly those that cut across different sectors. To this end several delegations also raised the issue of how existing institutions could develop and adopt initiatives, guidelines and regulations within existing mandates.[65]

Unfortunately, the question of how to address governance gaps in fisheries provoked quite polarized views during the BBNJ discussions. Some delegations took the view that a lack of political will to implement existing instruments would not be resolved by a new international instrument.[66] Some delegations adopted the position that the FSA and other fisheries instruments and RFMOs were the appropriate means for dealing with fisheries matters.[67] Others doubted that RFMOs had the capability or competence to deal with all fisheries issues in ABNJ because they lacked a holistic approach/capacity, had either a single-species mandate, or lacked mechanisms for dealing with non-fisheries issues such as vulnerable ecosystems.[68] Given the noted existence of regulatory gaps, as opposed to implementation issues, other delegations appeared to support the inclusion of fisheries within subsequent measures for ABNJ.[69] Some delegations observed that there was a need for new RFMOs to close geographic gaps and for existing RFMOs to have their mandate strengthened.[70]

62 UN Doc. A/68/82, para 10. Also UN Doc. 69/117*, para 8.
63 UN Doc. A/65/68, para 43.
64 See FSA, (n 5), Art. 25.
65 UN Doc. A/67/95, para 40.
66 UN Doc. A/68/82, paras 47 and 73.
67 UN Doc. A/61/65, para 24; UN Doc. A/65/68, para 44.
68 UN Doc. A/61/65, para 25.
69 UN Doc. A/69/82, para 47.
70 UN Doc. A/66/119, para 55.

Amidst these uncertainties and divergence of opinions, one thing did seem clear: a lack of will to expand the competence of RFMOs beyond fisheries matters.[71] More generally, the Co-Chairs' Report and Summary specifically raised the importance of identifying gaps, with the aim of securing an effective legal framework.[72] This was not limited to 'legal' gaps, but included issues of participation and implementation.[73] This left matters open on how best to progress, including on key issues related to fisheries.

During PrepCom, the tension between delegations favouring either the inclusion or exclusion of fisheries re-emerged. Indeed, this was probably the dominant feature of discussions. On the one hand, Iceland, Japan, and the Russian Federation were quite robust in their view that fisheries were not to be included within an international legally binding instrument on ABNJ.[74] On the other hand, a larger number of delegations or groups (the African Group, Costa Rica, Indonesia, Jamaica, New Zealand, Norway, Peru, and the USA) issued statements favouring the inclusion of fisheries.[75] This appears to indicate a change in position by some States from that adopted at the BBNJ Working Group who were originally equivocal about the inclusion of fisheries. Whether or not this trend continues will become clearer at subsequent meetings. The IUCN favoured inclusion, and this seems implicit in the views of Greenpeace, the High Seas Alliance, the Natural Resources Defense Council and Pew, who advocated a comprehensive binding instrument.[76] It is likely that RFMOs will have more prominence at the August/September 2016 meeting, and with greater clarity on the position of RFMOs, it is expected that more States will clarify their position on the inclusion of fisheries in the ABNJ IA.

Given that States appear to have accepted that the proposed ABNJ IA should address governance gaps, there appear to be two realistic options for going forward. The first is to consider collaborative institutional mechanisms to integrate fisheries with other environmental and resource-related activities. The second is to advance a set of cross-cutting governance principles that can promote substantive integration by shaping the conduct of States, RFMOs and other institutions with mandates in ABNJ. It is possible that either approach or

71 UN Doc. A/63/79, para 24.
72 UN Doc A/67/95, Annex, paras 29–47.
73 *Ibid.*, at para 31.
74 *Earth Negotiations Bulletin* (2016) vol. 25/97, pp. 1–2; *Earth Negotiations Bulletin* (2016) vol. 25/98, p. 2.
75 *Ibid.*
76 *Ibid.*

some combination of the two could be accommodated within the proposed ABNJ IA. These positions are considered in turn.

3.2 *Integrated Approaches to the Conservation and Sustainable Use of Marine Biological Diversity*

The need for greater integration between different sectoral activities is generally recognized, but remains a significant challenge in a decentralized legal system.[77] From the outset, delegations to the BBNJ Working Group attached importance to enhanced cooperation in respect of ABNJ via existing mechanisms, including through RFMOs, and between RFMOs and regional arrangements for the protection of the marine environment.[78] This was reiterated in the recommendations of the BBNJ to the UNGA in 2010, which called upon States and competent international organizations to cooperate as appropriate through regional seas conventions and RFMOs.[79] The importance of integration was highlighted by some delegations in 2011[80] and 2012.[81] It is notable that some delegations called for a coordinated cross-sectoral approach which would take into account the *cumulative* impact of human activities in ABNJ.[82] It is precisely this potential for cumulative impacts from different sectoral activities that provides a strong justification for integrated management, and is discussed further below.

Once the idea of a legally binding instrument started to gain traction at the BBNJ meetings, discussions tended to focus on the relationship between a new agreement and existing fisheries agreements. This manifested itself in discussions about 'complementarity'—the idea that existing mandates are not infringed, nor existing efforts duplicated.[83] However, beyond this, the records reveal little about how this idea could be accomplished. It is suggested that this could be achieved through the inclusion of a carefully drafted 'conflicts clause'

---

77 See R Rayfuse and R Warner, 'Securing a Sustainable Future for the Oceans beyond National Jurisdiction: The Legal Basis for an Integrated Cross Sectoral Regime for High Seas Governance for the 21st Century' (2008) 23(3) *IJMCL* 399–421, at 413; K Scott, 'Integrated Oceans Management. A New Frontier in Marine Environmental Protection' in Rothwell *et al.* (n 40), 463–490; J Harrison, 'The Law of the Sea Convention Institutions', in Rothwell *et al.* (n 40), 373–394.

78 UN Doc. A/63/79, para 24.

79 UN Doc. A/65/68, para 12.

80 UN Doc. A/66/119, para 14.

81 UN Doc. A/67/95, para 13.

82 UN Doc. A/66/119, para 14.

83 UN Doc. A/67/95, para 29; UN Doc. A/68/82, para 41. Also, UNGA Res. 69/292, (n 10).

in an IA.[84] Alternatively it could be secured through a treaty provision that requires compatibility of approaches, similar to Article 4 of the FSA.[85] Ideally both provisions should be utilized because this would help drive collaboration and sharing of practices across different institutions and sectors. One delegation did suggest that an IA should be limited to areas that were not covered by existing institutions.[86] However, it was not clear whether this referred to geographic areas or substantive issues or both. Regardless of which approach was intended, such an *ad hoc* approach to gap-filling should be avoided because it would result in unnecessary complexity and fragmentation.

As noted above, an integrated approach was part of PrepCom's mandate.[87] All participants supported this, either explicitly through the language of cooperation, or through calls to respect existing institutions and mandates. During the discussions, the general principle of integration quickly manifested itself in specific contexts, such as calls for cumulative EIA and inclusive approaches to ABM. For example, the African Group noted that an integrated approach to the creation of marine protected areas (MPAs) cannot be advanced through RFMOs, presumably due to their limited mandates.[88] Jamaica called for a binding instrument to adopt an integrated approach inclusive of fisheries.[89] Given the prevailing consensus for cross-cutting integrated approaches, something that cannot be ignored if the ABNJ incorporates provisions on ABM and EIA, the question is how best to secure this.

Arguably, several options for integration exist.[90] The archetypes are mapped out in Fig. 1.

84 See Art. 311 of the LOSC. This is governed under Article 30 of the Vienna Convention on the Law of Treaties 1969 (Vienna, 23 May 1969, in force 27 January 1980), 1155 *UNTS* 331. See further O Corten and P Klein (eds), *The Vienna Conventions on the Law of Treaties. A Commentary* (Oxford University Press, Oxford, 2011), vol. 1, p. 764.

85 See UN Doc. 69/117*, para 31.

86 UN Doc. 69/117*, para 19.

87 UNGA Res. 69/292, (n7).

88 *Earth Negotiations Bulletin* (2016) vol. 25/102, p. 1.

89 *Earth Negotiations Bulletin* (2016) vol. 25/98, p. 2.

90 See also: IUCN, *An International Instrument on Conservation and Sustainable Use of Biodiversity in Marine Areas Beyond National Jurisdiction. Matrix of Suggestions* (IUCN, Gland, 2016), section 6. Available online at http://cmsdata.iucn.org/downloads/iucn_bbnj_matrix_december_2015.pdf.

Strong Integration

Centralized		Decentralized
A1 Single ABNJ Management Authority • ISA+ option • Single multi-sector institution with comprehensive planning/licensing authority, stablished under a binding instrument.	**B1 Composite Regional ABNJ Management Organizations** • Combined RFMO/regional environmental management regimes • Revised mandates and institutional arrangements governed under a strong binding agreement.	
A2 ABNJ Advisory Body/Process • Status quo • Non-binding guidelines advance through resolutions of the UNGA.	**B2 Coordinated Sectoral Management Organizations** • 'Enhanced status quo'. • Retain regional bodies, subject to structured coordination and revised obligations set out in a framework instrument.	

Weak Integration

FIGURE 1 Scenarios and characteristics of institutional arrangements for ABNJ

A1—This would involve the creation of a new supra-national institution responsible for the management of all activities in ABNJ, including deep seabed mining, deep and high seas fisheries, marine scientific research, tourism, and environmental protection. It may be likened to an International Seabed Authority (ISA) + option, with defined institutional structures, governance principles, and decision-making authority and associated compliance mechanisms. Through such processes the body (as opposed to individual States, or regional arrangements) would be responsible for adopting a management plan for ABNJ, identifying specific regulatory options and securing their implementation.

A2—This perhaps reflects the *status quo*. Different sectoral bodies retain their discrete functions and consider ABNJ only peripherally. Centralized consideration of ABNJ is left to informal UN processes centred on the UNGA, which continues to issue or commission guidelines on specific activities. These guidelines may be followed by States or other institutions at their discretion.

B1—Fully integrated regional marine management organizations are established to regulate deep seabed mining, deep and high seas fisheries, marine scientific research, tourism, environmental protection. These could be based on the existing regional arrangements for different ocean areas (e.g., NE Atlantic, NW Atlantic and so on), with their geographic mandate extended and coordinated to cover all ABNJ. They would be authorized to use a system of marine spatial planning and associated tools to regulate all activities within the region.

B2—Existing bodies retain their sectoral mandates, but extend their sectoral remits to ABNJ to ensure gaps are filled. They are mandated/encouraged to coordinate their sectoral activities through *ad-hoc* interactions based upon a set of governance principles and specific management tools.

The discussions at PrepCom are at too early a stage to reveal States' clear preferences for one or the other approach. However, delegations were alert to the consequences of both approaches, and it is possible to gauge the direction of change from reports of the BBNJ Working Group and PrepCom. As noted above, a strong/holistic approach has significant implications for the structure and functioning of existing sectoral arrangements for fisheries. This also holds true for pollution control regimes, such as MARPOL and regional seas arrangements. This approach would require profound institutional reform—something that States appear to be set against. A decentralised approach is more realistic, and it would ensure that existing approaches are preserved. However, it leaves many questions unanswered about how fisheries should be integrated within any future regime. Integration could be secured through procedures to ensure that relevant interests, concerns, standards and approaches are taken into account within different agencies. Already this is occurring outside of the UN processes. A good example is the Memorandum of understanding (MOU) between the NE Atlantic Fisheries Commission (NEAFC) and the OSPAR Commission adopted in September 2008, which recognizes respective competences and areas of shared concern, and establishes processes for sharing of information, joint discussions and common approaches to the application of precautionary approaches and ABM.[91] There is little reason why such an approach to information-sharing and advisory input could not form part of other joint initiatives between different sectoral institutions.[92] This approach has the advantage of organic, adaptive development and could generate stronger traction than a heavy-handed, top-down approach. To an extent, the proposed implementation regime is a default regime—one designed to tackle matters left unresolved by other instruments. As such the pathway is already set against more radical reform of ABNJ governance. Taking a purely fisheries perspective, it should be recalled that existing fisheries arrangements are not only concerned with the conduct of fisheries activities, but also about entitlement to obtain access to resources. It is critical that States within RFMOs and regional arrangements have relatively stable access to and control over fisheries, and they are unlikely to risk compromising such entitlements. Whilst States may be willing to accept wider governance responsibilities for fisheries

91 A similar agreement was agreed between OSPAR and other institutions: the International Seabed Authority (2011) and the North Atlantic Salmon Conservation Organization (2013). A collaborative arrangement was also adopted between OSPAR and the Sargasso Sea Alliance in 2012. These are Available online at http://www.ospar.org/about/international-cooperation/memoranda-of-understanding.

92 UN Doc. A/65/68, para 34.

in ABNJ, it is difficult to imagine that they would explode existing access arrangements to do this.

3.3 *Governance Principles for ABNJ and Fisheries*

The second approach to addressing governance gaps is to advance a holistic set of governance principles for ABNJ. Already some fruitful discussion of such principles has occurred,[93] and during the BBNJ discussions, a high degree of consensus on such principles appeared to prevail.[94] The report of the 2014 BBNJ meeting compiled a list of these principles, including: balance between competing uses of the oceans and between conservation and sustainable use; protection and preservation of the marine environment, equitable utilization; cooperation; precautionary approach; decision-making based on best available science; ecosystem approach; integrated approach; adaptive management; public participation in decision-making processes; involvement of regional and sectoral stakeholders; open and transparent processes; public availability of information; CHM; freedom of the high seas; common but differentiated responsibilities; special requirements of developing countries, including land-locked States; duty not to transfer damage or hazards or transform one type of pollution into another; polluter-pays principle; cumulative impacts; flexibility and ability to address cumulative pressures; solidarity; and flag State jurisdiction as a basis for enforcement on the high seas. This list comprises a mix of established legal principles (e.g., precautionary principle) and other ideas, approaches, rules and attributes (e.g., solidarity, cumulative impacts and adaptive management). It is also clear that there is potential overlap/repetition of principles, so some degree of rationalization will be necessary as the discussions advance.

It is quite likely that some of these principles/approaches will form a substantive part of the proposed instrument, perhaps in a manner similar to Article 5 of the FSA. This is important because this will likely require existing RFMOs with an ABNJ mandate to respect such principles when adopting conservation and management measures. It may even require amendment of constituent instruments where existing mandates are too restrictive or ambiguous. To help indicate the extent to which such principles will affect existing RFMOs, Table 1 (in the Appendix) shows the extent to which a number of key principles

93 See the Chair's summary (n 42). More generally, see the articles by D Freestone, AG Oude Elferink and RA Barnes in the special issue of (2012) 27(2) *IJMCL*.

94 See the Informal Co-Chairs' overview of issues raised during the first round of discussions on the scope, parameters and feasibility of an international instrument under the LOSC. Appendix, UN Doc. A/69/82, 4 May 2014.

are found within the constituent instruments of Regional Fisheries Bodies (RFBS) and the FSA.[95]

As the table indicates, the main gaps are in respect of cross-sectoral integration, transparent decision-making, and obligations to protect and preserve the marine environment and biodiversity. Such gaps tend to arise in respect of RFMOs established before the FSA 1995. The table only encompasses the constituent agreements of the various bodies, and some RFMOs have advanced these principles/approaches through management decisions. For example, ICCAT adopted a precautionary approach to the implementation of conservation and management measures in 2015,[96] and NAFO adopted a precautionary approach framework in 2004.[97] However, this falls someway short of a systematic approach to the governance of ABNJ.

A more detailed analysis of these provisions reveals qualitative variations in the way core principles are used in RFBS. Some instruments refer to integrated approaches, but this is generally quite weak and limited to exhortations to cooperate with other interested organizations.[98] Even within the FSA, such cross-sectoral cooperation seems to be limited to provisions on developing States.[99] In contrast, as noted above, OSPAR has developed links with NEAFC. Also, a MOU has been adopted between WCPFC and the Secretariat of the

95 RFBS includes both advisory bodies and those competent to adopt binding conservation and management measures. The table includes: Asia-Pacific Fisheries Commission (APFIC), Commission for the Conservation of Antarctic Marine Living Resources (CCAMLR), Commission for the Conservation of Southern Bluefin Tuna (CCSBT), Fishery Committee for the Eastern Central Atlantic (CECAF), General Fisheries Commission for the Mediterranean (GFCM), Inter-American Tropical Tuna Commission (IATTC), International Commission for the Conservation of Atlantic Tunas (ICCAT), Indian Ocean Tuna Commission (IOTC), Northwest Atlantic Fisheries Organization (NAFO), North-East Atlantic Fisheries Commission (NEAFC), North Pacific Anadromous Fish Commission (NPAFC), North Pacific Fisheries Commission (NPFC), South East Atlantic Fisheries Organisation (SEAFO), South Indian Ocean Fisheries Agreement (SIOFA), South Pacific Regional Fisheries Management Organisation (SPRFMO), West and Central Pacific Fisheries Commission (WCPFC) and Western and Central Atlantic Fishery Commission (WECAF).

96 ICCAT Resolution 15/12 Concerning the Use of a Precautionary Approach in Implementing ICCAT Conservation and Management Measures: Available online at https://www.iccat.int/Documents/Recs/compendiopdf-e/2015-12-e.pdf.

97 NAFO/FC Doc. 04/18. Available online at http://archive.nafo.int/open/fc/2004/fcdoc04-18.pdf.

98 See for example, WECAFC, SPRFMO and SIOFA. CCAMLR is perhaps strongest in this respect, given that it is linked to the broader Antarctic treaty system.

99 FSA (n 5), Art. 24.

Pacific Regional Environmental Forum.[100] It goes beyond the scope of this article to analyse this in detail, but it may be noted that the relationships are complex, and often undermined by lack of experience and institutional capacity on both sides.[101]

Elsewhere, APFIC refers to prevention of pollution, but only insofar as it affects resources, and this falls some way short of a general commitment to protection of the environment.[102] In contrast, NAFO is quite detailed in referring to the actual environmental impacts of fishing.[103] In some it is difficult to determine whether an approach or principle is included. For example, in the WCPFC an ecosystem-based approach might be implicit from the Preamble and Articles 5(d), 12(2)(c), and 13(3), but it is not mentioned directly.[104] All RFBs refer to the use of science and data, but some do not refer to the use of best available science.[105] Although most instruments refer to some form of stock assessment process, this falls some way short of best practices used in EIAs, and often does not consider the impact of fishing on the wider environment.[106] Transparency of decision-making and availability of information also vary qualitatively.[107] Indeed, IUCN has noted that 10 out of 13 RFMOs made no open access to primary data available.[108] This is despite Article 12 of the FSA

100 WCPFC Cooperates with the SPREP via a MOU: https://www.wcpfc.int/system/files/WCPFC-SPREP%20Memorandum%20of%20understanding.pdf.

101 See generally, UNEP, *Regional Oceans Governance Making Regional Seas Programmes, Regional Fishery Bodies and Large Marine Ecosystem Mechanisms Work Better Together* (UNEP, Nairobi, 2016).

102 Agreement for the Establishment of the Asia-Pacific Fishery Commission 19486 (Baguio, formulated 26 February 1948, Approved Washington 15–29 November 1948, in force 9 November 1948), 1615 *UNTS* 59), as amended 1996, Art. IV(b)(3). Most recent version Available online at http://www.fao.org/apfic/background/apfic-agreement/en/.

103 See Convention on Future Multilateral Cooperation in the Northwest Atlantic Fisheries 1978 (Ottawa, adopted, 24 October 1978, in force 1 January 1979), as amended in 2007, Art. III(i). Most recent text Available online at http://www.nafo.int/about/frames/convention.html.

104 Convention for the Conservation and Management of Highly Migratory Fish Stocks in the Western and Central Pacific Ocean 2000 (Honolulu, 5 September 2000, in force 19 June 2004). Available online at http://www.wcpfc.int/doc/convention-conservation-and-management-highly-migratory-fish-stocks-western-and-central-pacific.

105 See IATTC, NPFC, SPRFMO, WCPFC, and WECFC.

106 See the evaluation of ecological risk assessment conducted by the IUCN: E Gilman, K Passfield and K Nakamura, *Performance Assessment of Bycatch and Discards Governance by Regional Fisheries Management Organizations* (IUCN, Gland, 2012), section 4.3.

107 See T McDorman, 'Implementing Existing Tools: Turning Words into Action—Decision-Making Processes of Regional Fisheries Management Organizations' (2005) 20(3) *IJMCL* 423–457, at 428.

108 See (n 106), section 4.2.

requiring transparency in decision-making and 'other activities'. Only a few RFMOs explicitly adopt strong guarantees of transparent decision-making.[109] Similarly, whilst most RFBs support the dissemination of information and decisions, few indicate that this will be done publicly. Often key information on enforcement and compliance is unreported, undermining compliance culture within RFMOs.[110] Others include *caveats* about confidentiality.[111] Arguably this falls short of best practice, for example, as included within the Aarhus Convention.[112] Despite being a euro-centric regime, little percolation of requirements of openness and transparency into other RFMOs in which European States and the EU participate appears to have occurred.[113] References to sustainable use of resources are common. However, few references to equitable sharing of resources exist.[114] SIOFA is perhaps an exception, in that it refers to the special position of small island and other developing States. Whilst debates have taken place about the application of the CHM principle to MGR, it cannot be conceived that this would have any direct influence on fisheries. There is no such reference to this in any fisheries instrument and no State is advancing this view. That said, it is possible that an IA with provisions on benefit-sharing and capacity-building might influence some RFMOs to adopt more 'equitable' arrangements for access to fisheries. In summary, the way in which the principles are articulated varies considerably across different constituent instruments.

In general, the extent to which principles are found in agreements depends on a range of factors. Thus post-1995 agreements (including those amended since 1995) have tended to possess a stronger and more complete statement of principles as per the FSA. It is unsurprising that RFMOs, as opposed to advisory bodies, have stronger provisions on the use of science, data exchange, and

---

109 I.e., CECAF, ICCAT and IOTC.

110 See (n 106), section 4.5.

111 See for example, Convention on the Conservation and Management of Fishery Resources in the South East Atlantic Ocean 2001 (Windhoek, 20 April 2001, in force 13 April 2003), 2221 *UNTS* 189, Art. 6(3)(l). Available online at http://www.seafo.org/About/Convention-Text.

112 Convention on Access to Information, Public Participation in Decision-making and Access to Justice in Environmental Matter 1998 (Aarhus, 25 June 1998, in force 30 October 2001), 2161 *UNTS* 447.

113 The EU is a member of six tuna/highly migratory species RFMOs (AIDCP, CCSBT, IATTC, ICCAT, IOTC, and WCPFC) and 11 mixed RFBs (CCAMLR, Convention on the Conservation and Management of Pollock Resources in the Central Bering Sea (CCBSP), CECAF, GFCM, NAFO, North Atlantic Salmon Conservation Organization (NASCO), NEAFC, SEAFO, SIOFA, SPRFMO and WECAFC).

114 See the fifth recital of the preamble to the Convention on the Conservation and Management of High Seas Fishery Resources in the South Pacific Ocean 2009 (Auckland, 14 November 2009, in force 24 August 2012). Available online at http://www.sprfmo.int/assets/Basic-Documents/Convention-web.pdf.

co-operation. Several of these principles/approaches exist under general international law, and therefore apply to activities within ABNJ regardless of their inclusion within an RFMO constituent agreement. However, their inclusion would have symbolic value and arguably increase pressure on States and other RFMOs to implement measures consistent with these principles. Finally, this short review focuses on the constituent instruments. In recent years several RFMOs have started to adopt formal cross-sectoral mechanisms, not just with other fisheries bodies, but also with institutions responsible for environmental issues.[115] This may establish pathways leading to more sophisticated management mechanisms, such as ABM and comprehensive EIAs.

4 Fisheries and ABM

ABM is a collective term referring to a range of spatially determinate measures designed to prevent harm to the environment, conserve resources and/or coordinate activities. From the outset, there has been consensus that ABM tools, including a network of MPAs and associated fisheries measures, are important tools for conserving and managing marine biodiversity in ABNJ.[116] Initially, there appeared to be general support by States for addressing fisheries within ABM regimes.[117] Already several RFMOs (and other institutions: ISA, International Maritime Organization (IMO)) adopt some form of ABM, so the question is really about whether this requires better coordination of these or entirely new mechanisms.[118] However, the 2006 BBNJ meeting was silent on both the legal basis of and institutional support for ABM. Delegations have since adopted quite different positions on this. When this issue was raised in 2008, some delegations noted that a more comprehensive and integrated approach than currently existed was required.[119] Some delegations have noted that measures to protect spawning stocks or to establish catch or fishing limits for specific areas are a form of ABM.[120] Other delegations argued that progress needed to be made within existing arrangements, including RFMOs.[121] In 2010, some delegations noted that existing RFMOs and arrangements have a mandate to implement ABM tools, such as MPAs, both in relation to particular

115 See (n 91), and accompanying text.
116 UN Doc. A/61/65, para 59 and Annex I, para 10.
117 *Ibid.*, Annex I, para 10.
118 See Takei, (n 51), chapter 3.
119 UN Doc. A/63/79, para 28.
120 UN Doc. A/65/69, para 66.
121 UN Doc. A/63/79, para 30.

stocks and the effects of fishing activities on vulnerable marine ecosystems in the high seas.[122] Reference was made to the MOU between NEAFC and OSPAR as an example of how existing institutions could cooperate in developing ABM tools.[123]

In 2012, questions remained about the scope of MPA: what activities would be allowed therein, such as fisheries, and what role existing institutions, such as RFMOs, should have as regards MPAs.[124] By 2014, it appeared that the issue was becoming polarized: was a new global instrument required to secure effective ABM, or could this be achieved through existing regional and sectoral regimes? Noting the absence of any global regime for MPAs, one suggestion was to develop a regional framework for the designation and implementation of MPAs, following the RFMO/FSA model.[125] However, it was not clear whether this would be done through *ad hoc* arrangements or a coordinating instrument. As regional cooperation may be easier to secure than global agreement, and would allow for regional circumstances to be taken into account, one can see the attraction of this approach. However, one must also consider that regional fisheries are predominantly concerned with areas within national jurisdiction and they as yet do not provide complete geographic coverage.

Discussions at the second meeting of the BBNJ in 2014 are revealing as to the complexities of designating and managing ABM regimes in ABNJ. First, it was generally agreed that although existing mechanisms exist for ABM, these are neither plenary in scope, or fully developed and readily applicable to ABNJ.[126] Second, in ABNJ, the principal form of jurisdiction is by the flag State, and this means that the effectiveness of ABM is contingent on widespread global support.[127] This is precisely the same challenge facing existing RFMOs and one that any new regime will need to address.

It is not clear that significant progress was made at PrepCom on the relationship between fisheries and ABM. At a bare minimum, all States seemed to agree that some degree of coordination is required between an instrument containing ABM provisions and existing fisheries regimes. Several delegations suggested that the development of ABM should draw upon or involve

122 UN Doc. 69/117*, para 25.

123 UN Doc. A/65/68, para 59. More specifically, the MOU refers to cooperation between NEAFC and OSPAR regarding marine spatial planning and ABM (n 91), at point 1(d).

124 UN Doc. A/67/95, para 31.

125 UN Doc. A/69/82, paras 59–60.

126 UN Doc. 69/117*, paras 59–62.

127 *Ibid.*, at para 64.

RFMOs.[128] The African Group rightly emphasized that RFMOs cannot adopt an integrated approach to MPAs—this requires, at a minimum, coordination of efforts.[129] New Zealand and the US supported the inclusion of fisheries in a legally binding instrument.[130] However, there seemed to be little appetite for a significant revision of RFMO mandates. Hence, Norway noted the cost-effectiveness of relying on existing mechanisms, such as RFMOs to establish MPAs.[131] And New Zealand proposed setting criteria for ABM tools that could be used by RFMOs.[132] This approach could be effective, having been relatively successful with regard to the FSA, which influenced the standards and mandates of pre-existing RFMOs, as well as newly established RFMOs.[133] Furthermore, Norway noted the cost-effectiveness of relying on existing mechanisms, such as RFMOs to establish MPAs.[134] Following calls from Iceland, Japan and the Russian Federation to hear from RFMOs, it seems likely that RFMOs will be more actively engaged in subsequent meetings of PrepCom.[135]

If the proposed ABNJ IA is to include provisions on ABM, then this should be done consistently with existing legal instruments providing for ABM.[136] The LOSC, the FSA and the FAO Code of Conduct for Responsible Fisheries contain a limited range of provisions relevant to ABM,[137] but these are only obligations of a general nature, falling someway short of stronger ABM exemplified by, for example, the EU Habitats Directives or Maritime Spatial Planning

128 Australia, the EU, Papua New Guinea and the United States, *Earth Negotiations Bulletin* (2016) vol. 25/102, pp. 1–2.

129 *Ibid.*, at p. 1.

130 *Ibid.*

131 *Earth Negotiations Bulletin* (2016) vol. 25/99, p. 2.

132 *Earth Negotiations Bulletin* (2016) vol. 25/102, p. 1.

133 See D Diz Pereira Pinto, *Fisheries Management in Areas beyond National Jurisdiction. The Impact of Ecosystem Based Law Making* (Martinus Nijhoff, Leiden, 2013), chapter 5.

134 *Earth Negotiations Bulletin* (2016) vol. 25/99, p. 2.

135 *Ibid.*, at p. 2.

136 Other relevant mechanisms include: Whaling sanctuaries under Art V(1) of the International Convention for the Regulation of Whaling 1946 (Washington, 2 December 1946, in force 10 November 1948), 161 *UNTS* 72; Special Areas under Annexes I, II and V of International Convention for the Prevention of Pollution from Ships 1973 (London, 2 November 1973), as amended by Protocol of 1978 relating to the International Convention for the Prevention of Pollution from Ships of 1973 (London, adopted 17 February 1978, in force 2 October 1983) (MARPOL 73/78), 1340 *UNTS* 62; Particularly Sensitive Sea Areas (PSSA), as outlined in IMO Resolution A. 720(17) and revised in IMO Resolution A.927(22); Specially Protected Areas of Mediterranean Interest under the Protocol to the Barcelona Convention. See further T Scovazzi, 'Marine Protected Areas on the High Seas: Some Legal and Policy Considerations' (2004) 19(1) *IJMCL* 1–17.

137 See LOSC, Arts. 192, 194(5), FSA Arts. 5 and 6; FAO Code, Art. 10.1.1. Available online at http://www.fao.org/docrep/005/v9878e/v9878e00.htm.

regimes.[138] The most important agreement is the Convention on Biological Diversity, Article 8 of which encourages Contracting Parties to establish a system of protected areas as part of their commitments to '*in situ*' conservation of biodiversity.[139] As appropriate, guidelines should be adopted for the selection, establishment and management of such areas, along with regulatory or management measures. These general commitments were further developed through the Programme of Work on Marine and Coastal Biodiversity.[140] Such policy measures are principally focused on areas within national jurisdiction, although the Programme highlighted the importance of cooperation, information-gathering and the adoption of measures consistent with international law to protect biodiversity in ABNJ.[141] These measures are generally predicated upon the adoption of nationality/flag State measures. Measures of general application can only be secured through multilateral agreements.[142]

Some RFMOs utilize area-based management tools. In 2006, the GFCM declared three areas as Fisheries Restricted Areas to protect corals, cold hydrocarbon seeps and seamounts. In 2013, it adopted Resolution GFCM/37/2013/1, which seeks to establish and coordinate Fisheries Restricted Areas with Specially Protected Areas of Mediterranean Importance (SPAMIs), with a particular focus on high seas areas.[143] NEAFC has introduced closed areas in ABNJ, including Hatton and Rockall Banks, to bottom trawling and static gear in order to protect vulnerable marine ecosystems.[144] NAFO has established

138 See further R Long, 'The Marine Strategy Framework Directive: A New European Approach to the Regulation of the Marine Environment, Marine Natural Resources and Marine Ecological Services' (2011) 29(1) *Journal of Energy and Natural Resources Law* 1–44.

139 Convention on Biological Diversity 1992 (Rio de Janeiro, 5 June 1992, in force 29 December 1993), 1760 *UNTS* 79. under Art. 4(2), States can take measures as regards processes and activities beyond national jurisdiction. However, this would fall short of true ABM, as such measures are limited to control over nationals. As such they could only supplement true ABM through other measures.

140 COP 7 (2003) Decision VII/5. Available online at https://www.cbd.int/decision/cop/?id=7742.

141 *Ibid.*, at paras 54–62, and Objectives 2.1, 2.2, 2.4 and 3.2.

142 See further EJ Molenaar and AG Oude Elferink, 'Marine protected areas in areas beyond national jurisdiction. The pioneering efforts under the OSPAR Convention' (2009) 5(1) *Utrecht Law Review* 5–20.

143 Resolution GFCM/37/2013/1 on ABM of fisheries, including through the establishment of Fisheries Restricted Areas (FRAs) in the GFCM Convention area and coordination with the UNEP-MAP initiatives on the establishment of SPAMIs. Available online at http://www.fao.org/3/a-ax392e.pdf.

144 Recommendation IX:2008. These measures have since been continued: See Recommendation VIII:2010; Recommendation 14:2011; Recommendation 8:2012; Recommendation 19:2014. Available online at http://www.neafc.org/managing_fisheries/measures.

two closed areas to shrimp fisheries on the Flemish Cap.[145] In 2007, four seamount areas were closed to bottom fishing between 2007 and 2010,[146] and two further areas were closed in 2008.[147] A coral protection zone was established in 2008, which is also closed to bottom-gear fishing.[148] Following the adoption of conservation and management measures in 2015, there are now 13 areas closed to bottom fishing, six protected seamount areas, and one Coral Area Closure Zone.[149] Since 2006, SEAFO has closed a number of vulnerable marine areas to fishing. At present, 11 areas are closed to all fishing and one area to all fishing except pots and longlines.[150] In the Indian Ocean, the Southern Indian Ocean Deepsea Fishers' Association, which is comprised of the four main bottom-trawling companies in the region, has designated 13 Benthic Protected Areas (BPAs). BPAs are areas where bottom trawling and dredging is forbidden. However, these measures are limited to members; they cannot be imposed upon third-party operators. There is also little independent assessment, oversight or control of the designations.

The FAO's International Guidelines for the Management of Deep-Sea Fisheries in the High Seas promote the use of area-based management in vulnerable marine ecosystems (VMEs).[151] The Guidelines encourage both States and RFMOs to identify and designate VMEs.[152] VMEs should be closed to fishing "until appropriate conservation and management measures have been established to prevent significant adverse impacts on VMEs and ensure long-term conservation and sustainable use of deep-sea fish stocks ..." The Guidelines do not establish formal legal authority to manage fisheries. Indeed,

145 NAFO Conservation and Enforcement Measures 2006, NAFO FC/ Doc 06/1, Art. 12. This and subsequent NAFO measures are Available online at http://www.nafo.int/fisheries/frames/fishery.html.

146 This includes the Orphan Knoll, Corner Seamounts, Newfoundland Seamounts and New England Seamounts NAFO Conservation and Enforcement Measures 2007, NAFO FC/ Doc. 07/1, Art. 12.

147 Fogo Seamount Areas 1 and 2. See NAFO Conservation and Enforcement Measures 2009, NAFO FC/ Doc. 09/1, Art. 15.

148 NAFO Conservation and Enforcement Measures 2008, NAFO FC/ Doc. 08/1, Art. 15.

149 NAFO Conservation and Enforcement Measures 2015, NAFO FC/ Doc. 15/1, Art. 17. It is notable that two of these sites cover areas in the Sargasso Sea, combining the notion of VME and ecologically significant marine areas under the CBD. See further D Diz, 'The Seamounts of the Sargasso Sea: Adequately Protected?' (2016) 31(2) *IJMCL* 359–70.

150 Conservation Measure 30/15 on Bottom Fishing Activities and Vulnerable Marine Ecosystems in the SEAFO Convention Area. Available online at http://www.seafo.org/Management/Conservation-Measures.

151 FAO, *International Guidelines for the Management of Deep-Sea Fisheries in the High Seas* (FAO, Rome, 2009).

152 *Ibid.*, paras 21(ii) and 42–53.

they note the limits of existing institutional arrangements and call upon States to strengthen this.[153] The ABNJ IA could provide an opportunity to strengthen the legal basis for such measures. That said, marine ABM principles tend to be discretionary and facilitative for good reason: management should be adaptive and context-specific. The importance of flexibility suggests that it is unlikely that the prospective ABNJ IA will depart from this approach—perhaps preferring the exhortation of guiding principles and approaches.

The absence of detailed provisions on marine ABM means that the ABNJ IA is unlikely to generate acute legal conflicts with existing legal arrangements unless it adopts measures that run counter to fundamental principles of exclusive flag State jurisdiction in ABNJ. Herein lies the crux of the matter, as it is precisely this response to a lack of strong coordinated/centralized institutional management that is driving the ABNJ process. Detailed discussion of such issues was notably absent from the BBNJ meetings and PrepCom. Careful steps will need to be taken to secure the agreement on coordinated management within a system where the political preference is for decentralized State-centric decision-making.

5 Fisheries and EIA

EIA is a procedural tool used in many legal systems to ensure that the potential adverse environmental effects of an activity are understood before a decision is made to authorize it. The duty to conduct an EIA is part of customary international law.[154] However, it is questionable whether or not this applies to existing and/or new fisheries. The extent to which fisheries should be included within an EIA resulting from other non-fishing activities is also unclear. The LOSC does not contain a specific provision requiring an EIA for fisheries; instead, it establishes under Article 206 a rather basic requirement to consider the impacts of an activity when a State has reasonable grounds to believe that it may cause substantial pollution or significant harm to the environment.[155] Article 206 falls short of requiring a cross-sectoral, cumulative EIA of the kind

153 *Ibid.*, paras 26–28.

154 See *Case concerning Pulp Mills on the River Uruguay* (2010) ICJ Reports 14, para 204; *Responsibilities and obligations of States with respect to activities in the Area*, Advisory Opinion, 1 February 2011, ITLOS Reports 2011, p. 10, para 145.

155 See further, AG Oude Elferink, 'Environmental Impact Assessment in Areas beyond National Jurisdiction' (2012) 27(2) *IJMCL* 449–480; D Ma, Q Fang and S Guan, 'Current legal regime for environmental impact assessment in areas beyond national jurisdiction and its future approaches' (2016) 56 *Marine Policy* 23–30.

that appears to be necessary in ABNJ, although it does not necessarily prevent this. It also elides reference to strategic EIAs. Article 6(6) of the FSA requires assessment of new or exploratory fisheries, but this occurs only after the fishing has begun.

Given that fishing is considered to be a significant cause of biodiversity loss, it is no surprise that the connection between EIAs and fisheries was raised on several occasions during the BBNJ and PrepCom discussions.[156] In 2006, the BBNJ noted the potential for a new agreement to address the fragmentation and sectoral approaches and provide for the possibility of cumulative EIAs.[157] At the 2008 meeting, some delegates suggested that the approach taken in UNGA Resolution 61/105 to the assessment of impacts on fishing could be used as one model for EIA.[158] However, this suggests a non-binding commitment, and one that lacks the detail and structure required to undertake an effective EIA. As noted in some later debates, such obligations already exist under international law.[159] However, the quality of such obligations varies considerably across different sectors, and within fisheries instruments they tend to be quite general or non-binding.[160] In 2011, the development and implementation of procedures to assess the impact of activities, including fisheries, was proposed.[161] Thereafter, the discussion was focused on specific questions including: whether a new agreement would address the lack of political will for

156 See comments at PrepCom by Australia and Papua New Guinea noted in *Earth Negotiations Bulletin* (2016) vol. 25/102, p. 2; and Norway, *Earth Negotiations Bulletin* (2016) vol. 25/103, p 1.

157 UN Doc. A/61/65, para 55.

158 UN Doc. A/63/79, para 18, referring, it appears, to UNGA Res. 61/105, para 83. A similar reference was made in 2011 to UNGA Res. 64/72 concerning the impact of bottom fisheries on VMEs. This Resolution contains far more detailed provisions on EIA, but is still only guidance. UN Doc. A/66/119, para 54.

159 UN Doc. A/65/68, paras 52 and 56. Specific reference was made to LOSC Articles 205–6, the CBD and the FSA. More generally, see the Convention on Environmental Impact Assessments in a Transboundary Context 1991 (Espoo, 25 February 1991, in force 10 September 1997), 1989 *UNTS* 389, and the Protocol on Strategic Environmental Assessment to the Convention on Environmental Impact Assessment in a Transboundary Context 2003 (Kyiv, 21 February 2003, in force 11 July 2010), 2685 *UNTS* 140. Non-binding instruments include: UNEP Goals and Principles of Environmental Impact Assessment, UNEP Res. GC 14/25, 14th Sess (1987); Voluntary Guidelines on Biodiversity-Inclusive Impact Assessment, UNEP/CBD/COP/DEC/VIII/28, 15 June 2006; and the Voluntary Guidelines for the Consideration of Biodiversity in Environmental Impact Assessments and Strategic Environmental Assessments in Marine and Coastal Areas, UNEP/CBD/SBSTTA/16/7/Add.1, 11 April 2012.

160 See for example Art. 5(c) of the Fish Stocks Agreement, and the FAO, *International Guidelines for the Management of Deep-Sea Fisheries in the High Seas*, (n 151).

161 UN Doc. A/66/119, para 31.

expanding the scope of EIA, who would conduct and monitor EIAs in ABNJ, whether uniform standards could be agreed, and how the cumulative impacts of multiple stressors from different sectors would be addressed in any EIA process.[162]

Some progress on environmental assessment was made at PrepCom. At a minimum, it was recognized that the LOSC provides only a general framework, and there is a need to develop common or minimum standards as regards the content of EIAs.[163] The Chair's summary of discussions simply maps out in some detail a wide range of features of EIAs, but without indicating how EIA will actual develop.[164]

Despite the existence of a customary duty to conduct an EIA, this only becomes meaningful if the procedures for the EIA are then properly articulated within a legal instrument. As indicated in Table 1, the FSA and some RFMOs address EIA, albeit in quite general terms. This does not go far enough. Elferink notes that the lack of EIA for fisheries is due to fisheries having developed in parallel to environmental law, as opposed to being part of it.[165] If the prospective IA is to make a difference, then it will need to move beyond generalities and articulate a meaningful EIA process. Support for this has been emerging through non-binding instruments, and it is possible that the processes outlined therein may evolve into formally binding rules.

In 2006, the UNGA called States and RFMOs to conduct EIA prior to new fisheries in ABNJ. Paragraph 83(a) of UNGA Resolution 61/105 calls upon RFMOs "To assess, on the basis of the best available scientific information, whether individual bottom fishing activities would have significant adverse impacts on vulnerable marine ecosystems, and to ensure that if it is assessed that these activities would have significant adverse impacts, they are managed to prevent such impacts, or not authorized to proceed". Such an EIA provides a starting point for the adoption of other management measures, including ABM tools for VMEs. This was reiterated in UNGA Resolution 64/72 of 2009, which called for implementation of UNGA Resolution 61/105 by flag states and RFMOs in accordance with the FAO Guidelines on Deep Sea Fisheries. Furthermore, they should "ensure that vessels do not engage in bottom fishing until such assessments have been carried out".[166] Although a positive development,

162 UN Doc. 69/117*, paras 66–70.

163 *Earth Negotiations Bulletin* (2016) vol. 25/100, p. 2.

164 (n 42), at 13–16.

165 Elferink, (n 155), at 469.

166 UN Doc. A/Res/64/72, para 119(a).

these measures have been criticized for being too weak.[167] Limited EIAs have been produced or they are limited to specific features, such as corals or seamounts. States and RFMOs have been reluctant to close areas despite these EIAs. Instead, management measures are often limited to encounter protocols and 'move on' rules, which are set at too high a threshold to protect VMEs.[168] It is critical that insufficient controls have been placed on bottom trawling. If guidelines are currently unable to secure effective protection of valuable or important resources, then a stronger legally binding regime is necessary. Although EIA is generally required of States, it needs to be linked to an effective decision-making process. Ideally, where there are reasonable grounds to believe that harm may occur, an EIA must be a prerequisite to fishing activities taking place. No EIA should mean no fishing. However, it may be observed that at the resumed Review Conference of the FSA 2010, States adopted quite varied positions on this, with some rejecting the requirement of prior EIAs,[169] and others calling for a judicious use of EIAs.[170] Underlying this is a concern about the burdens that might be placed on the fishing industry. Such concerns are not unimportant, given that other, arguably wealthier sectors, such as commercial shipping, are not under similar pressures to conduct EIAs.

It may also be observed that many fisheries are established practices and it is commonplace for EIA only to apply to new activities. Some RFMOs have adopted the requirement for prior EIA for new fisheries. CCAMLR has led on this, requiring Contracting Parties to notify the Scientific Committee and submit a preliminary EIA.[171] Contracting Parties shall not authorize vessels flying their

167 See M Gianni, DEJ Currie, S Fuller, L Speer, J Ardron, B Weeber, M Gibson, K Sack, and A Kavanagh, *Unfinished business: a review of the implementation of the provisions of UNGA resolutions 61/105 and 64/72 related to the management of bottom fisheries in areas beyond national jurisdiction* (Deep Sea Conservation Coalition, September 2011). Available online at http://www.savethehighseas.org/publicdocs/dscc_review11.pdf. See also the report of the UN GA Workshop to discuss implementation of paragraphs 80 and 83 to 87 of Resolution 61/105 and paragraphs 117 and 119 to 127 of Resolution 64/72 on sustainable fisheries, addressing the impacts of bottom fishing on vulnerable marine ecosystems and the long-term sustainability of deep-sea fish stocks: Letter dated 27 October 2011 from the Moderator of the Workshop to the President of the General Assembly. UNGA Doc. A/66/566 (18 November 2011).

168 'Encounter protocols' require vessels that bring up a particular quantity of species, e.g., live coral or sponges, in their gear to 'move on' to a different fishing area. See Gianni *et al.*, *ibid.*

169 Iceland is reported to have objected to such a proposal by Greenpeace: See *Earth Negotiations Bulletin* (2016) vol. 7/65, p. 7.

170 *Ibid.*

171 Conservation Measure 21–01 (2010) Notification that Members are considering initiating a new fishery; Conservation Measure 22–05 (2008) Restrictions on the use of bottom

flag to participate in bottom-fishing without approval of the Commission.[172] Since 2014, NEAFC has required prior EIA of exploratory bottom-fishing in VMEs.[173] This approach has been replicated by SEAFO.[174] Exploratory bottom-fisheries in the NAFO regulatory area are subject to a preliminary EIA prior to authorization.[175] To reiterate, such EIAs are limited to new and exploratory fisheries. An exception to this is the SPRFMO. Since 2014, it has required that all bottom fishing activities undergo an EIA prior to approval.[176] Such measures do not require a new mandate under an ABNJ IA. However, it is arguable that they will be limited in their ability to deliver strategic or integrated EIA of fishing and other activities in ABNJ. In this respect, an IA could do much to advance and structure the conduct of strategic environmental assessments (SEAs).[177]

SEAs are "formalized, systematic and comprehensive processes of identifying and evaluating the environmental consequences of proposed policies, plans or programmes to ensure that they are fully included and appropriately addressed at the earliest possible stage of decision-making on a par with economic and social considerations".[178] A SEA is usually conducted by a public authority, as opposed to an EIA, which is triggered and driven by a private developer/actor. The SEA is intended to provide a broader framework for assessing a range of activities and may be better suited to integrating a wider range of factors into the EIA. As such it can be used to guide individual project/activity-level EIAs and decisions. In this sense the SEA and EIA are complementary and help ensure a more balanced consideration of public/private concerns. However, this approach presents some difficulties when transposed

---

trawling gear in high-seas areas of the Convention Area. Available online at https://www.ccamlr.org/en/conservation-and-management/browse-conservation-measures.

172 Para 6 of CM 22–05, *ibid.*

173 Recommendation 19 2014: Protection of VMEs in NEAFC Regulatory Areas as Amended by Recommendation 09:2015, Available online at http://www.neafc.org/managing_fisheries/measures/current.

174 See Conservation Measure 30/15 on Bottom Fishing Activities and Vulnerable Marine Ecosystems in the SEAFO Convention Area. (n 150).

175 NAFO Articles 18 to 20 of Conservation and Enforcement Measures of 2015, and Annex I.E. Available online at http://www.nafo.int/fisheries/frames/fishery.html.

176 Conservation and Management Measure for the Management of Bottom Fishing in the SPRFMO Convention Area (CMM 2.03). Available online at https://www.sprfmo.int/cmms/.

177 R Warner, 'Oceans beyond Boundaries: Environment Assessment Frameworks' (2012) 27(2) *IJMCL* 481–499.

178 B Sadler and R Verheem, *Strategic Environmental Assessment. Status, Challenges and Future Directions*, Report No 53 (Ministry of Housing, Spatial Planning and the Environment, The Hague, The Netherlands, 1996), 27.

to the international level where States are both sponsors and decision-making authorities. Existing instruments place the responsibility in the hands of individual States.[179] Ideally, there should be some degree of externality to the SEA, otherwise the evaluation process will lack independence and legitimacy. Furthermore, it is arguable that individual States are not in the best position to conduct SEA for plans and programmes of activities that are actually set within regional or international bodies like RFMOs or the ISA. Here it would be logical for SEA to be carried within that forum or through some other cross-cutting institutional mechanism. This would have the benefit of being inclusive of cumulative and inter-related activities, and could fit within current RFMO strategic planning activities. Whilst this could be burdensome, and it would not remove the need for individual EIAs, this approach, if done carefully, could reduce the burden on individual States or agencies responsible for conducting project-specific EIAs. This approach would be contingent on ensuring that individual EIAs take account of the SEA.

6 Pathways to Reform of Fisheries in ABNJ

Given the novelty of the topic, little has been written on the scope and content of the proposed IA.[180] Fortunately, as the above analysis indicates, a more extensive array of literature exists on the governance of ABNJ, which explores regulatory/governance gaps, maps out governance principles, and investigates specific regulatory options, such as ABM and EIA. Such literature provides fertile ground for speculation as to the potential shape and form of an IA on ABNJ.

Discussions at the BBNJ and PrepCom show that the challenge is not so much in identifying the relevant legal principles; these are well known and generally accepted. The greater challenge is to overcome current institutional limitations, where the decentralized nature of the international legal order presents particular challenges for the adoption of integrated approaches and the use of spatial or cross-cutting tools like ABM and EIA. There is considerable scope to develop and learn from existing regimes. ABM and EIA are well developed within domestic law and this can provide models for a legally binding instrument on ABNJ. Domestic regimes are notably moving towards greater integration both within ABM and EIA regimes, and across different

179 Articles 3, 4 and 10 of the SEA Protocol to the Espoo Convention, (n 159).

180 See Long and Chaves (n 11); Warner (n 40); also see S Hart, *Elements of a Possible Implementation Agreement to the LOSC for the Conservation and Sustainable Use of Marine Biodiversity in Areas beyond National Jurisdiction* (IUCN, Gland, 2008).

regulatory approaches. For example, marine spatial planning at the domestic and regional level increasingly takes account of all activities occurring within marine spaces, and, at an EU level, across different jurisdictions. This is already influencing practices at a regional level through OSPAR and NEAFC, where MOUs are in place to facilitate information sharing and coordination of activities. As a minimum, an ABNJ IA should encourage and structure such practices.

Fisheries did not feature explicitly in the original list of topics to be addressed in an IA. However, this is not the end of the matter. If it is to succeed, a comprehensive, legally binding instrument on marine biological diversity must deal with fisheries either directly or indirectly, through the mandating of strong cooperative mechanisms within existing institutional regimes. The case for the inclusion of fisheries is strong, given the importance States have attached to integrated/ecosystem-based approaches, and when considering the practical impact of ABM on fisheries or the need to account for the impact of fisheries when assessing cumulative impacts on the marine environment. The case against the inclusion of fisheries largely rests on the existence of a dedicated regime for fisheries through the FSA and various RFMBs. There appears to be no appetite for wholesale reform of RFMOs. The path of compromise is likely to see States address fisheries in ABNJ indirectly, through the development of principles of general application and the creation of more carefully structured cooperative mechanisms. This may follow a similar approach to that adopted in the FSA. Ultimately this may result in some moderate reform of RFMOs. This may help address some governance gaps. However, it will not result in significant change in the structure and authority of fisheries arrangements. This is likely to be reinforced through carefully drafted savings and compatibility clauses within an ABNJ IA.

It is important not to regard the proposed ABNJ IA as a panacea and to overburden it with expectations. In particular, efforts to addresses RFMO gaps in species and geographic coverage ought to be pursued through other fora, albeit influenced by discussions taking place during the UN's ABNJ process. Regardless of the direction that discussions on fisheries take at PrepCom, it is clear that developments will continue apace outside of the UN process. Already during the debates in the BBNJ, particular emphasis was placed on UNGA Resolution 61/105, which addressed the impacts of bottom fishing on VMEs (including ABNJ), and the work of the FAO in developing international guidelines on the management of deep-sea fisheries.[181] Furthermore, since the BBNJ Working Group first met, the following instruments have been

181 See UNGA Resolution 61/105, paras 82–90.

adopted: FAO International Guidelines on the Management of Deep-sea Fisheries in the High Seas in 2008[182] and the Convention on the Conservation and Management of High Seas Resources in the South Pacific Ocean 2009.[183] The FAO Agreement on Port State Measures to Prevent, Deter and Eliminate Illegal, Unreported and Unregulated Fishing was adopted in 2009 and entered into force on 5 June 2016.[184] Looking forward, there will be ongoing consideration of issues related to ABNJ during the Review Conferences of the FSA and at the Subsidiary Body on Scientific, Technical and Technological Advice of the CBD. At a regional level, conservation and management measures taken by RFMOs will continue to adapt to the complex socio-ecological realities of ABNJ. These fora and initiatives provide fertile means for cross-fertilization of ideas and approaches. Over the next couple of years they will inevitably influence the way in which fisheries issues are handled during PrepCom and the subsequent ABNJ IA negotiations.

182 See (n 151).
183 See (n 114).
184 Available online at http://www.fao.org/3/a-i1644t.pdf.

TABLE 1 Matrix of ABNJ governance principles in regional fisheries bodies

	Cooperation	Integrated approach—cross sectoral cooperation	Protection and preservation of the marine environment	Science-based management	Precautionary approach
FSA 1995	Art. 5	Art. 24	Art. 6	Art 5(b)	Art. 6
APFIC	Art. VII		Art. IV(b)(3)		
CCAMLR	Preamble	Arts. III and V	Arts. II and VI	Art. IX(1)(f)	Art. II(3)(c)
CCSBT	Preamble			Arts. 5 and 8	
CECAF	Art. 3		revised statute		
GFCM	Preamble		Art 5(d)	Art. 5(b)	Art. 5(c)
IATTC	Preamble	Art. XVI(2)	Arts. VII(1)(k) and XV(3)	Art. VII(1)(c)	Art. IV
ICCAT	Preamble			Art. IV	
IOTC	Art. IV(3)			Art. V(2)	
NAFO	Art. II			Arts. II and VI	
NEAFC	Preamble		Art. 2	Art. 4|(2)(a)	Art. 4(2) (b)
NPAFC	Art. IV(4)			Art. VII	
NPFC	Art. 7(2)(d)	Preamble	Art. 3(k)	Art. 3(b)	Art. 3(c)
SEAFO	Preamble		Art. 7	Art. 3(a)	Art. 7
SIOFA	Art. 2	Art. 16	Art. 4(e)	Art. 4(a)	Art. 4(c)
SPRFMO	Art. 3(1)(a)(vi)	Art. 31	Art. 3(1)(a)(ii)	Art. 3(1) (a) (v)	Art. 3(2)
WCPFC	Art. 5	Art. 22		Art. 5(b)	Art. 6
WECAFC		Arts. 2(c) and 11		Art. 6(g)	Art. 2(a)

Ecosystem-based approach	Sustainable and/or equitable use	Public availability of information	Transparent and open decision-making	Protection of biodiversity	Impact assessment
rt. 5(e)	Arts. 5(a) and 24	Art. 14(3)	Art. 12	Art. 5(g)	Art. 5(d)
	Art. IV(b)(i)	Art. IV (G)			
rt. II(3)(c)	Art. II(3)(c)	Art. IX (1) (d)			Art. XX(4)
	Art. 8(4)				
		Art 3(d)			
rt. 8(b)	Art. 2(2)	Art. 8(b)			
rt. VII(1)(f)	Art. II	Arts. XII (2) (j) and XVI(1) (a)	Art. XVI		
	Art. IV (2)(b)	Art. IV (2) (d)			
	Art. V(1)	Art. V (2)(a)			Art. XII(4)(b)
rt. VI		Art. IV (1) (b)			
rt. 4(2) (c)	Art. 2	Art. 11(2)		Art. 4(2)(d)	Art. 4(2)(c)
		Art. X(2)			
rt. 3(d)	Art. 3(a)	Art. 16 and 18	Art. 18	Art. 3(e)	Art. 3(h)
rt. 3(d)	Art. 2	Art. 6(3)	Art. 8(9)	Art. 3(f)	Art. 3(c)
rt. 4(a)	Art. 2	Art. 14	Art. 14	Art. 4(f)	Art. 7(1)(a)(i)
rt. 3(2)	Art. 2	Arts. 10(3), 18	Art. 18	Preamble	Art. 10
	Art. 5(a)	Arts. 10(1) and 13(3)	Art. 21	Art. 5(f)	Art. 5(d)
rt. 2(a)		Art. 6(f)			

CHAPTER 5

The Proposed Implementing Agreement: Options for Coherence and Consistency in the Establishment of Protected Areas beyond National Jurisdiction

Dire Tladi
Professor of International Law, University of Pretoria, Hatfield, Pretoria, South Africa

Abstract

The purpose of this article is to provide initial thoughts on potential conflicts between the mandates of Regional Fisheries Management Organizations (RFMOs) and any mechanisms for establishing Marine Protected Areas in the high seas and how these conflicts might be avoided. The article addresses first, whether the fears that may exist concerning the conflicts are, as a matter of international law, real and to the extent that they are real, how an Implementing Agreement (IA) might be shaped to avoid them. As the article is intended to provide only initial thoughts, the range of RFMOs and possible conflicts are only illustrative and are not intended to be comprehensive. With the potential conflicts in mind, the article then provides, in the third section, possible approaches that the drafters of the IA could adopt to avoid and/or mitigate these conflicts. Finally, the article offers some concluding remarks.

Keywords

Law of the Sea Convention – high seas – conservation – sustainable use – biodiversity – Implementing Agreement – regional fisheries management organizations (RFMOs) – marine protected areas

 DOI:10.1163/9789004391703_007

1 Introduction*

On 19 June 2015, the General Assembly of the United Nations (hereinafter the 'General Assembly') adopted a Resolution providing for an intergovernmental conference to negotiate a possible Implementing Agreement, referred to as an 'international legally binding instrument' (hereinafter the 'IA'), under the UN Convention on the Law of the Sea (hereinafter the 'Convention')[1] on the Conservation and Sustainable Use of Marine Biological Diversity in Areas beyond National Jurisdiction.[2] The Resolution also provides for a preparatory committee "to make substantive recommendations" on the elements of such a proposed IA.[3]

The adoption of the Resolution by the General Assembly marked the end of a protracted and complicated process within the General Assembly, but also the beginning of a new, potentially more complicated process. It marked the end of the discussions within the UN *Ad Hoc* Informal Working Group to Study Issues Relating to the Conservation and Sustainable Use of Marine Biological Diversity in Areas Beyond National Jurisdiction (hereinafter the 'BBNJ working group').[4] In the course of the deliberations, spanning a decade, the BBNJ working group focused its discussions on two interrelated issues, namely the legal regime applicable to marine genetic resources on the deep seabed and the question of conservation of marine biological diversity.[5] Various aspects of

* Member of the United Nations Commission on International Law. I wish to express my appreciation to Vita Onwuasoanya, Kristina Gjerde, Alexis Jackson, Andrew Friedman, Paulus Tak and Duncan Currie for their helpful comments on earlier drafts of this article. The flaws in the arguments and the errors remain entirely mine. This paper draws on the collaborative work of the author in various projects designed to reflect on what a possible Implementing Agreement under the Law of the Sea Convention might look like.

1 United Nations Convention on the Law of the Sea (Montego Bay, 10 December 1982, in force 16 November 1994) 1833 *UNTS* 3.

2 Paras. 1(k) and 2 of UN General Assembly Resolution on the Development of an International Legally Binding Instrument under the United Nations Convention on the Law of the Sea on the Conservation and Sustainable Use of Marine Biological Diversity of Areas Beyond National Jurisdiction, (A/Res/69/292), 19 June 2015.

3 *Ibid.*, at para. 1(b).

4 The BBNJ working group was established pursuant to para. 73 of UN General Assembly Resolution on Oceans and the Law of the Sea, (A/Res/59/24), 4 February 2004.

5 The issues were interrelated in both a formal and a substantive sense. They were interrelated in the formal sense in that the participants agreed that these two issues will be "addressed together and as a whole". See para. (b) of the Recommendations of the *Ad Hoc* Open-ended Informal Working Group to Study Issues Relating to the Conservation and Sustainable Use of Marine Biological Diversity Beyond Areas of National Jurisdiction, Annex to the UN General Assembly on Oceans and the Law of the Sea (A/Res/66/231), 24 December 2011. See also para. 162 of *The Future We Want* (A/Res/66/288), 27 July 2012. But the two issues were

the discussions have been considered by the author in other publications and will consequently not be repeated here.[6]

The question of fishing activities, in particular the potential relationship between Regional Fisheries Management Organizations (hereinafter 'RFMOs') and the IA, arises in relation to the second of the interrelated issues, namely conservation measures in areas beyond national jurisdiction. Conservation issues, in the context of the deliberations of the BBNJ working group and the future negotiations of an IA, are described as "measures such as area-based management tools, including marine protected areas, [and] environmental impact assessments".[7] To the extent that the IA would create an institutional mechanism for the establishment of marine protected areas (hereinafter 'MPAs') that could have an impact on fishing activities within those areas, questions may validly arise concerning the relationship between such an institutional mechanism and the mandate of RFMOs in any given area beyond national jurisdiction. For example, would the decision to establish an MPA in areas under the management of an RFMO, including by providing for 'no-take zones', interfere with the mandate of the said RFMO? Would the validity of an MPA in areas beyond national jurisdiction be dependent on the 'blessings' of the competent RFMOs? Would the establishment of MPAs without the consultation or cooperation of relevant RFMOs necessarily lead to a conflict of norms not readily resolvable by recourse to the rules of international law?

The purpose of this article is to provide initial thoughts on potential conflicts between the mandates of RFMOs and any mechanisms for establishing MPAs in the high seas and how these conflicts might be avoided. The article addresses first, whether the fears that may exist concerning the conflicts are, as a matter of international law, real and to the extent that they are real, how an IA agreement might be shaped to avoid them. The next section describes the conflicts that might arise. This is done principally by considering the scope

---

also substantively interrelated in that both pose a challenge to the ever-eroding notion that the freedom of the high seas is the fundamental principle of ocean governance.

6 For the most recent publications by the author on the subject see D Tladi, 'State Practice and the Making and (Re) Making of International Law: The Case of the Legal Rules Relating to Marine Biodiversity in Areas beyond National Jurisdiction' (2014) 1 *State Practice and International Law Journal* 97–116; D Tladi, 'The Common Heritage of Mankind and the Proposed New Treaty on Biodiversity in Areas Beyond National Jurisdiction: The Choice between Pragmatism and Sustainability' (2014) *Yearbook of International Environmental Law* (forthcoming).

7 See para. (b) of the Recommendations of the *Ad Hoc* Open-ended Informal Working Group to Study Issues Relating to the Conservation and Sustainable Use of Marine Biological Diversity Beyond Areas of National Jurisdiction (2011) (n 5) and para. 2 of General Assembly Resolution 69/292 (n 2).

of the proposed IA in relation to fisheries, as well as the mandates of various RFMOs. As the article is intended to provide only initial thoughts, the range of RFMOs and possible conflicts are only illustrative and are not intended to be comprehensive. With the potential conflicts in mind, the article then provides, in its third section, possible approaches that the drafters of the IA could adopt to avoid and/or mitigate these conflicts. Finally, the article offers some concluding remarks.

2 Potential Conflicts between the Mandates of RFMOs and the Proposed IA

2.1 *Fisheries and the Scope of the IA*

In many ways it can be, and has been, argued that the objectives of the proposed IA, insofar as it relates to the protection and conservation of marine biological diversity in areas beyond national jurisdiction, is unnecessary and will amount to duplication. The Convention already provides a duty on States to "protect and preserve the marine environment".[8] To this end, the Convention requires States, individually or collectively, to take measures for the conservation of the marine environment.[9] States are thus already obliged to adopt measures, individually or collectively, for the conservation of the marine environment and such measures could include, for example, MPAs. It is thus not necessary, so the argument goes, to adopt an IA for this purpose. This point has been made by those States that have not been supportive of an IA.[10] The United States, in particular, has made the following observations:

8 See, e.g., Art 192 of the UN Convention on the Law of the Sea. It has been noted that, as quantitative matter, 46 of the 320 Articles of the Convention "are devoted to the protection of the marine environment". See C Redgwell 'From Permission to Prohibition: The 1982 Convention on the Law of the Sea and the Protection of the Marine Environment,' in D Freestone, R Barnes and D Ong (eds), *The Law of the Sea: Progress and Prospects* (Oxford: Oxford University Press, 2006) 180–191, at 180.

9 See, e.g., Art. 194 (measures to prevent, reduce and control pollution of the marine environment), Art. 197 (cooperation on a global or regional basis), Art. 210 (pollution from land-based sources), Art. 211 (pollution from vessels) and Art. 212 (pollution from or through the atmosphere). Specifically with respect to areas beyond national jurisdiction, see Art. 117 (duty of states to adopt with respect to their nationals measures for the conservation of the living resources of the high seas), Art. 118 (cooperation of States in the conservation and management of living resources), Art. 145 (protection of the marine environment in the Area) and Art. 240 (general principles for the conduct of marine scientific research).

10 See para. 81 of the Co-Chairs' Summary of the Discussions at the *Ad Hoc* Open-ended Informal Working Group to Study Issues Relating to the Conservation and Sustainable

> The United States supports the establishment of MPAs in areas beyond national jurisdiction. This can already be done through cooperation among nations, including through existing regimes and otherwise, if States are willing to apply obligations relating to MPAs to their nationals and flagged vessels.[11]

It is certainly true that the Convention makes provisions for conservation measures; however, there appears to be consensus in academic literature that there has been increasing degradation of the marine environment even *post* the Convention.[12] As Gjerde has pointed out, notwithstanding the many provisions on conservation in the Convention, "fish stocks are declining", "there are rising biodiversity concerns" and "illegal, unreported and unregulated fishing activities are expanding."[13] Freestone is more direct.[14] Having reflected on the major environmental challenges facing the *post*-Convention marine environment, he states that "the 1982 Convention regime has not lived up to expectations in terms of delivering the instruments of international cooperation and governance that UNCLOS III drafters may have intended."[15] In another contribution, Gjerde and Rulska-Domino make the following observations:

> areas beyond national jurisdiction (ABNJ) contain perhaps the largest reservoir of biodiversity (the largest of species, communities and

Use of Marine Biological Diversity beyond Areas of National Jurisdiction (A/69/177), 25 July 2014 where "it was [further] observed that willing States were already capable of establishing marine protected areas on the high seas and the question was raised as to how a new agreement would overcome unwillingness on the part of some States to establish such areas beyond national jurisdiction."

11 See Submission by the United States, Scope, Parameters and Feasibility of an International Instrument under the United Nations Convention on the Law of the Sea: Informal Working Document Compiling Views of Member States, Prepared in Accordance with General Assembly Resolution 68/70, para. 201, 4 December 2014, at 34 (on file with author). See also United States, Scope, Parameters and Feasibility of an International Instrument under the United Nations Convention on the Law of the Sea: Informal Working Document Compiling Views of Member States, Prepared in Accordance with General Assembly Resolution 68/70, para. 201, 11 March 2014, at 58 (on file with author).

12 See, e.g., R Jozan, J Rochette and S Sundar, 'Oceans: The New Frontier' in P Jacquet, RK Pachauri and L Tubiana (eds), *Oceans: The New Frontier* (Paris: The Energy and Resources Institute, 2011) 17–24, at 20.

13 KM Gjerde, 'High Seas Management under the Convention on the Law of the Sea' in Freestone *et al.* (n 8), 281–307 at 281.

14 D Freestone, 'International Governance, Responsibility and Management of Areas Beyond National Jurisdiction' (2012) 27 *International Journal of Marine and Coastal Law* 191–204.

15 *Ibid.*, at 194.

> ecosystems) left on earth, but are under extreme pressure. Evidence of this impact may be found in the near collapse of commercially valuable fish stocks.... [and other impacts]. Despite the exponential increase of threats, the rules of and regulations for the conservation and sustainable use of marine biodiversity ... have not kept pace.[16]

Thus, although there certainly are provisions on the protection of the marine biodiversity in areas beyond national jurisdiction, the current state of the marine environment, including the ongoing loss of marine biodiversity and depletion of a number of fish stocks at a high rate, suggests that these provisions are not sufficient. One of the main reasons for the current ocean governance's inability to sufficiently address the degradation of the marine environment is the excessive emphasis on the Grotian notion of the freedom of the seas which, in essence, re-enacts Hardin's tragedy of the commons.[17] In this connection, the United States has noted that the proposed IA could not remedy this problem because States that decide to adopt MPAs "cannot ... obligate unwilling States to accept the designation of an MPA beyond national jurisdiction and abide by its management measures."[18]

In a sense, the proposed IA, similarly to the Fish Stocks Agreement,[19] would seek to give effect to the environmental obligations in the Convention by constraining, to some extent, the freedom of the high seas.[20] The IA would also seek to provide detail to the environmental protection obligations in the Convention which are largely regarded as too general and too vague, and lacking an institutional framework for implementation.[21] In the context of an MPA, an IA would spell out the requirements for when an MPA should be

---

16 KM Gjerde and A Rulska-Domino, 'Marine Protected Areas beyond National Jurisdiction: Some Practical Perspectives for Moving Ahead' (2012) 27 *International Journal of Marine and Coastal Law* 351–373.

17 See D Tladi, 'Oceans Governance: A Fragmented Regulatory Framework?' in Jacquet *et al.* (n 12), 99–110 at 103.

18 United States Submission, March 2014 (n 11), at 58.

19 Agreement for the Implementation of the Provisions of the Convention on the Law of the Sea of 10 December 1982 relating to the Conservation and Management of Straddling Fish Stocks and Highly Migratory Fish Stocks (New York, 4 August 1995, in force 11 December 2001) 2167 *UNTS* 88.

20 See, e.g., Art. 17 of the 1995 Agreement for the Implementation of the Provisions of the United Nations Convention on the Law of the Sea of 10 December 1982 Relating to the Conservation and Management of Straddling Fish Stocks and Highly Migratory Fish Stocks. See also Freestone (n 14), at 200–201, discussing what he terms "conditional freedom of the seas".

21 See, e.g., R Barnes, 'The Convention on the Law of the Sea: An Effective Framework for Domestic Fisheries Conservation?' in Freestone *et al.* (n 8), 233–260, at 233.

put in place, the decision-making processes for putting it in place and for the identification of specific measures to be adopted, and the legal effects of such an MPA. Whereas, as a matter of international law, these legal effects could apply only to States Parties of the IA, the existence of the IA would obviate the necessity for specific and individual State consent to each individual MPA established in areas beyond national jurisdiction. At any rate, the mere existence of a framework could result in an increased rate in the creation of high seas MPAs.

The question of whether fishing activities should be excluded from the proposed new IA first arose during what were referred to as "scope, parameters and feasibility" discussions. In December 2013, while the BBNJ working group was considering the possibility of an IA, the General Assembly requested the BBNJ working group to make recommendations to the Assembly on the "scope, parameters and feasibility of an international instrument under the Convention."[22] During the BBNJ working group's consideration of the scope, parameters and feasibility of an IA, several States suggested excluding fisheries from the scope of the debate in their entirety, as a regime was already in place governing fishing-related activities. Iceland, for example, warned that "care should be taken not to reopen issues that are already subject to a sufficient legal regime".[23] In particular, Iceland identified 'fisheries' as a regime which is subject to "the legal regime of the [Convention] that was complemented by the [Fish Stocks Agreement]," both of which "provide the framework for work of RFMOs".[24] In a similar vein, concerns have been raised within the Informal Consultations of States Parties to the Fish Stocks Agreement about the potential of the proposed IA to undermine the Fish Stocks Agreement.[25]

Whereas it is true that fisheries are governed by a regime underpinned by the Fish Stocks Agreement, the effectiveness of this regime greatly varies due

22 Para. 198 of the UN General Assembly Resolution on Oceans and the Law of the Sea (A/Res/68/70), 9 December 2013.

23 Submission by Iceland in the Informal Working Document of March 2014 (n 11) at 31.

24 *Ibid.* See also Submission by Japan in the Informal Working Document of March 2014 (n 11) at 35.

25 See para. 52 of the Eleventh Round of Informal Consultations of States Parties to the Agreement for the Implementation of the Provisions of the United Nations Convention on the Law of the Sea of 10 December 1982 relating to the Conservation and Management of Straddling Fish Stocks and Highly Migratory Fish Stocks, (ICSP11/UNFSA/INF.3), 14 May 2015, which states: "A delegation questioned how the implementing agreement being discussed within the context of the *Ad Hoc* Open-ended Informal Working Group to study issues relating to the conservation and sustainable use of marine biological diversity beyond areas of national jurisdiction would relate to the Agreement and whether such an implementing agreement could undermine the Agreement and affect fisheries."

to lack of coordination and integration.[26] More importantly, the scope of the Fish Stocks Agreement is limited to highly migratory and straddling fish stocks and does not extend to the management of broader biodiversity issues. Yet fishing constitutes one of the more serious threats to marine biodiversity in areas beyond national jurisdiction as a result of both overfishing and the use of destructive fishing practices.[27] The scope of the Fish Stocks Agreement is limited by its terms to the "conservation and sustainable use of straddling fish stocks and highly migratory fish stocks".[28] The Agreement is thus fisheries-specific, i.e., its scope does not extend to biodiversity in general. Although the Fish Stocks Agreement is limited to fish stocks, and in particular to straddling and highly migratory fish stocks, the Agreement requires, for example, the protection of "biodiversity in the marine environment" as a means to achieve this objective.[29] It does not spell out *how* biodiversity is to be protected, but the inclusion of the general obligation to protect biodiversity in the context of conserving fish stocks is an important illustration of the link between the fishing activities and the protection of the marine environment. Excluding fishing activities from the scope of an IA designed to address broader conservation of marine biological diversity in areas beyond national jurisdiction would thus make little sense. That said, the concerns raised about possible conflicts cannot be ignored. As Canada noted in its submissions on the scope, parameters and feasibility of an IA, the challenge in elaborating an IA covering fisheries is to "clearly identify how it would interact with existing international regimes".[30] The United States, which has not been supportive of the elaboration of an IA, takes the view that if an IA were to be elaborated, such an IA would need to cover fisheries, but has also stressed that to be effective, the IA would need to be based on "coordination with existing RFMOs".[31] In order to assess the possible approaches to the design of the IA, it is important to have an understanding of the various mandates of RFMOs.

26 Gjerde and Rulska-Domino (n 16), at 356 *et seq.*

27 *Ibid.*, at 362.

28 See Arts. 2 and 3 of the Fish Stocks Agreement.

29 See Art. 5 of the Fish Stocks Agreement.

30 Submissions by Canada in the Informal Working Document of December 2014 (n 11), at 12.

31 Submission of the United States in the Informal Working Document of December 2014 (n 11).

3 Survey of Mandates of RFMOs

A survey of the mandates of RFMOs reveals wide variations, in terms of both geographical scope and functional coverage.[32] In terms of geographical scope, RFMOs are limited to a particular area of the ocean. The geographical scope of the International Commission for the Conservation of Atlantic Tunas (hereinafter 'ICCAT'), for example, is limited to the Atlantic Ocean.[33] In many instances, the geographical scope of RFMOs is defined in terms of the parts of the ocean defined by latitude and longitude.[34] The geographical scope of the mandate of the Commission for the Conservation of Antarctic Marine Living Resources (hereinafter 'CCAMLR'), for example, is "the area south of 60° South latitude and ... the area between that latitude and the Antarctic Convergence".[35] Although there are many RFMOs covering different parts of the ocean, with varying degrees of overlap, some gaps in geographical coverage remain.[36]

---

32 Gjerde and Rulska-Domino (n 16), at 363.

33 See Art. I of the International Convention for the Conservation of Atlantic Tunas, (Rio de Janeiro, 14 May 1996, in force 21 March 1969) 673 *UNTS* 63 (hereinafter 'ICCAT').

34 For example, North East Atlantic Fisheries Commission is limited to "those parts of the Atlantic and Arctic Oceans and their dependent seas which lie north of 36° north latitude and between 42° west longitude and 51° east longitude" and "that part of the Atlantic Ocean north of 59° north latitude and between 44° west longitude and 42° west longitude". See Article 1(a) of the Convention on Future Multilateral Cooperation in North-East Atlantic Fisheries (London, 18 November 1980, in force 17 March 1982) 1285 *UNTS* 129. See also Art. I of the Convention on Future MultilateralCooperation in the Northwest Atlantic Fisheries establishing the Northwest Atlantic Fisheries Convention (NAFO), Ottawa, 24 October 1978, in force 1 January 1979) 1135 *UNTS* 369, and Art. 4 of the Convention on the Conservation and Management of Fishery Resources in the South East Atlantic Ocean, which established the Southeast Atlantic Fisheries Organization (SEAFO), (Windhoek, 20 April 2001 in force 13 April 2003), 2221 *UNTS* 189. See also Art 3 of the Convention on the Conservation and Management of Highly Migratory Fish Stocks in the Western and Central Pacific Ocean, (Honolulu, 5 September 2000, in force 19 June 2004) 2275 *UNTS* 43.

35 See Art. I of the Convention for the Conservation of Antarctic Marine Living Resources, (Canberra, 20 May 1980, in force 7 April 1982), 1329 *UNTS* 48.

36 Gjerde and Rulska-Domino (n 16) at 363. See, however, S Cullis-Suzuki and D Pauly, 'Failing the High Seas: A Global Evaluation of Regional Fisheries Management Organization' (2010) 34 *Marine Policy* 1036–1042, at 1036, where it is stated that only a few areas of the ocean remain that are not the subject of an RFMO. See also D. Freestone, 'Fisheries, Commissions and Organizations' in Rudiger Wolfrum (ed), *Max Planck Encyclopaedia of Public International Law* (2010, online edition), at 18, who states as follows: "Although the global network of tuna management commissions is quite comprehensive, there are a number of major gaps in the areas covered by the general fisheries commissions managing the conservation of high seas stocks of non-tuna species."

In addition to geographical limitation, the mandates of RFMOs are very often generally limited to the management of a specific type of resource, in particular fisheries, and do not address marine biodiversity in general. In many instances, the RFMO is concerned with a particular type of fishery.[37] Examples in this respect include ICCAT, the Indian Ocean Tuna Commission (hereinafter the 'IOTC') and the Inter-American Tropical Tuna Commission (hereinafter the 'IATTC'), whose functional scope concerns tuna and other species similar to tunas. ICCAT's mandate, for example, extends to "tuna and tuna-like fishes ... and other species of fishes exploited in tuna fishing".[38] Article VI of the ICCAT provides for the establishment of panels on the basis of species in order to, *inter alia*, keep the species under review[39] and make recommendations for joint action.[40] To date, however, only four panels have been established, covering tropical tunas (yellowfin, bigeye and skipjack), northern temperate tunas (albacore and Atlantic bluefin), southern temperate tunas (albacore and southern bluefin) and other species (swordfish, billfish and small tunas, as well as sharks, seabirds, and other species commonly caught as bycatch in the tuna fisheries).[41] Through these panels, Contracting Parties cooperate to optimize the exploitation of these species. Although ICCAT does seek to ensure, with various levels of success, that these species are not overexploited, it has no mandate to advance wider conservation objectives. For example, ICCAT will not designate an MPA in its Convention Area with the intent advance a wider environmental objective not directly linked to its mandate.

CCAMLR, though not technically an RFMO, provides a useful exception to the fisheries-specific management approach used by RFMOs. The objective of the CAMLR Convention is broadly "the conservation of Antarctic marine living resources".[42] Living resources are defined broadly to include, in addition to resources named specifically, "all other species of living organisms".[43] More importantly, the CAMLR Convention adopts an ecosystem-based management approach, which the RFMOs generally do not. For example, the CAMLR Convention defines the Antarctic ecosystem as "the complex of relationships of Antarctic marine living resources with each other and with their physical

37 *Ibid.*, at 362.
38 See Art. IV(1) of the ICCAT (n 33).
39 Art. VI(a) of the ICCAT (n 33).
40 Art. VI(b) of the ICCAT (n 33).
41 See for the establishment of the Panels, Item 17 (Establishment of Panels and Date and Place of their Meetings), Report of the First Meeting of the International Commission for the Conservation of Atlantic Tunas, Rome, December 1969, FAO Fisheries Reports, No. 84.
42 Article II(1) of the CAMLR Convention (n 35).
43 Article I(2) of the CAMLR Convention (n 35).

environment."[44] In general, however, the mandate of RFMOs is often limited in scope to fisheries, and in many instances, to specific types of fisheries; furthermore, the experience of the CCAMLR is not typical.

In the midst of the growing calls for an ecosystem approach to the management of the resources of the ocean,[45] some RFMOs have referred to the need to take into account broader biodiversity concerns. The parties to the North East Atlantic Fisheries Commission (hereinafter 'NEAFC'), for example, in an interpretative declaration, have declared that in carrying out its mandate, the Commission "shall ... take due account of the impact of fisheries on other species and marine ecosystems."[46] However, a survey of measures adopted recently by NEAFC shows that it has generally maintained a sectoral fisheries-related mandate, with few exceptions.[47] Among these is its recommendation with regard to vulnerable marine ecosystems.[48] This recommendation is aimed at protecting the broader environment by putting in place fisheries-specific measures, in particular restrictions on bottom-fishing, and was inspired by the provisions of UN General Assembly Resolution 61/105 on bottom-fishing.[49]

44 Article 1(3) of the CAMLR Convention (n 35).

45 See, e.g., para. 171 of the UN General Assembly Resolution on Oceans and the Law of the Sea (A/Res/69/245). More specific to fisheries, see para. 7 of the UN General Assembly Resolution on Sustainable Fisheries, including through the 1995 Agreement for the Implementation of the Provisions of the United Nations Convention on the Law of the Sea of 10 December 1982 relating to the Conservation and Management of Straddling Fish Stocks and Highly Migratory Fish Stocks, and related instruments (A/Res/69/109), 9 December 2014, which states as follows: "Calls upon all States, directly or through regional fisheries management organizations and arrangements, to apply widely, in accordance with international law and the Code, the precautionary approach and ecosystem approaches to the conservation, management and exploitation of fish stocks."

46 See NEAFC Declaration on the Interpretation of the Convention on the Future Multilateral Cooperation in North East Atlantic Fisheries, (AM 2005/21), available at http://www.neafc.org/system/files/London-Declaration.pdf (last accessed 8 September 2015).

47 See for a list of measures adopted by NEAFC: http://www.neafc.org/managing_fisheries/measures/current (last accessed on 8 September 2015).

48 See Recommendation on the protection of vulnerable marine ecosystems in the NEAFC Regulatory Area, Recommendation 19:2014, as amended by Recommendation 9:2015, available at http://www.neafc.org/managing_fisheries/measures/current (last accessed 8 September 2015). Whereas, for example, the Recommendation to Adopt Conservation and Management Measures for Deep-Sea Sharks in the NEAFC Regulatory Area from 2013, Recommendation 7:3013, http://www.neafc.org/managing_fisheries/measures/current (last accessed 25 September 2015), is technically not fisheries-specific; it remains a single-species and not general marine biodiversity-related recommendation.

49 See para. 83 of the UN General Assembly Resolution on Sustainable Fisheries, including through the 1995 Agreement for the Implementation of the Provisions of the United Nations Convention on the Law of the Sea of 10 December 1982 relating to the Conservation

The Western and Central Pacific Fisheries Commission (hereinafter the 'WCPFC'), "applies to all stocks of highly migratory fish within the Convention Area except sauries".[50] Although the members of the WCPFC are called upon to "protect biodiversity in the marine environment",[51] their Convention does not operationalize this broad aspiration. Instead, its primary objective is "to ensure, through effective management, the long-term conservation and sustainable use of highly migratory fish stocks".[52] Indeed, even the scope of application is not biodiversity and the marine environment, but "stocks of highly migratory fish within the Convention Area".[53] The mandate of the South Pacific Regional Fisheries Management Organization (hereinafter the 'SPRFMO') is similarly fisheries-specific, but provides some elements of broader marine environmental conservation.[54] Although the Convention on the Conservation and Management of High Seas Fishery Resources in the South Pacific Ocean refers in its objective to an "ecosystem approach" and safeguarding the "marine ecosystem in which [fishery] resources occur", these are in relation to its primary objective of "fisheries management" and "the long-term conservation and sustainable use of fishery resources."[55]

This very brief survey should illustrate that although there are many RFMOs, their functional mandates are limited and, to some extent, even their geographical scope is limited. In particular, not all geographical areas are covered and not all components of biodiversity are covered. More importantly, reliance on RFMOs, which are fisheries-specific, and in many cases limited to specific types of fisheries, entrenches the sectoral approach and may be inconsistent with an ecosystem-based approach. To these limitations of scope one might also add an issue not covered in this survey, namely the varying degrees of effectiveness

and Management of Straddling Fish Stocks and Highly Migratory Fish Stocks, and related instruments, (A/Res/61/105), 8 December 2006.

50 The Convention on the Conservation and Management of Highly Migratory Fish Stocks in the Western and Central Pacific Ocean (n 34), Art. 3.

51 See *ibid.*, at Art. 5(f).

52 *Ibid.* at Art. 2.

53 *Ibid.* at Art 3(3).

54 The SPRFMO is established under the Convention for the Conservation and Management of High Seas Fishery Resources in the South Pacific Ocean, November 2009, available at https://www.sprfmo.int/assets/Basic-Documents/Convention-and-Final-Act/Convention-web.pdf (last accessed 9 September 2015).

55 *Ibid.* at Art 2. Article 2 provides in whole as follows: "The objective of this Convention is, through the application of the precautionary approach and an ecosystem approach to fisheries management, *to ensure the long-term conservation and sustainable use of fishery resources and,* in so doing, to safeguard the marine ecosystems in which these resources occur." (Emphasis added.)

of RFMOs,[56] which may provide an additional reason for a more coherent and uniform approach of a global IA. Still, the RFMOs are a reality, and to be successful, the design of the IA has to take into account the existence of RFMOs and should promote coherence by avoiding conflict. An IA, properly designed, would serve to provide an integrated and more uniform approach to the establishment of MPAs, which cannot be achieved through sectoral RFMOs.

4 Possible Approaches for Achieving Coherence

4.1 *Range of Options: Choice between Deference and Non-recognition?*

There are a number of ways that the design of a new IA for the conservation and sustainable use of marine biodiversity in areas beyond national jurisdiction can take into account the existence of RFMOs. One option, the deferential or maximalist approach, would be for the responsibility for the establishment of MPAs in areas beyond national jurisdiction to be placed with the RFMOs themselves. The other side of the spectrum, the minimalist or non-recognition approach, would simply place the responsibility of establishing MPAs in areas beyond national jurisdiction in another, possibly new, entity without a formal role for the RFMOs in that process. Between these two extremes a continuum of options is available to the negotiators of the IA.

The deferential approach, although attractive because of reliance on existing mechanisms, is not without its problems. First, if the management measures adopted under the RFMO were applicable only to members of the respective RFMOs, then the deferential approach would mean the continuation of the *status quo*. In this respect, as noted by the United States in the reference above, States are already free to adopt MPAs and an IA that simply recognizes, without more, the ability of States to expand the competence of their RFMOs and then adopt measures with respect to their members, would be without any real effect.[57] Yet a deferential approach which extends the applicability of measures adopted by RFMOs to other States is problematic. Such an approach first assumes that such an expanded mandate is politically feasible or

56 See, e.g., Cullis-Suzuki and Pauly (n 36), for a study on the effectiveness of RFMOs. Having considered both theoretical and practical effectiveness, the authors, at 1042, reach the following conclusion: "In this regard, RFMOs have failed. It is evident from the results here that the priority of RFMOs—or at least of their member countries—has been first and foremost to guide the exploitation of fish stocks. While conservation is part of nearly all of their mandates, they have yet to demonstrate a genuine commitment to it on the water." See also Freestone (n 34) at para. 33.

57 United States Submission, March 2014 (n 11), at 58.

desirable. It would also raise the legal problem of the unwilling State identified by the United States, i.e., "[w]hat willing States cannot do is obligate unwilling States to accept the designation of an MPA beyond national jurisdiction and to abide by its management measures."[58] It appears that this same concern caused Argentina to state that the terms of reference of an intergovernmental conference "must explicitly rule out that such functions ... could be in the care of entities with limited participation such as RFMOs."[59] The approach would be legally problematic, because, as a matter of international law, States cannot be bound by rules to which they have not agreed. This legal problem could be overcome by adopting the Fish Stocks Agreement approach, i.e., ratification of the IA amounts to consent to abide by the management of RFMOs, including those to which a State may not be a member.

However, the solution of consent-through-ratification-of-the-IA would itself raise a number of difficulties. First of all, many States are likely to find such an approach unacceptable and indeed this may be one of the reasons for the slow rate of ratification of the Fish Stocks Agreement. Second, the legitimacy of a decision to establish a 'globally' binding MPA—or at least an MPA binding on all Parties to the IA—would likely depend on consistent, science-based criteria. Yet it cannot be assured that RFMOs would all apply consistent, science-based criteria. Moreover, this deferential approach would still suffer from the drawbacks of scope and inconsistency described above. Finally, and perhaps more importantly, this approach would still be largely dependent on a sectoral approach, which is one of the problems that the IA is supposed to remedy.[60]

The non-recognition approach would require either the creation of a new entity, or the expansion of the mandate of an existing entity, with the mandate to establish MPAs with measures binding on all State Parties to the IA, without the involvement of RFMOs (and other organizations with sectoral mandates in areas beyond national jurisdiction). This approach is attractive because, depending on the decision-making criteria, it avoids inconsistency and promotes an ecosystem approach. Nonetheless, it risks the possibility of conflict between the measures adopted by the mechanism of the IA and those adopted by the RFMOs. At any rate, General Assembly Resolution 69/292 already sets out that a basic principle to govern the negotiations of a new IA will be that

58 United States Submission, December 2014 (n 11), at 34.

59 Argentina Submission (courtesy translation) in the Informal Working Document of December 2014 (n 11), at 4.

60 See in this regard, the submission by Australia, in the Informal Working Document of December 2014 (n 11), at 5, which notes that although there are existing mechanisms, "the coordination of activities across sectors and the management of cumulative impacts over both time and geographical area is often poorly addressed, or lacking altogether."

the IA "should not undermine existing relevant legal instruments and frameworks and relevant global, regional and sectoral bodies."[61]

4.2 *Recognizing without Deferring to RFMOs: an Illustration*

It should be clear from the above analysis that the optimal approach will be that which recognizes the mandate (and even importance) of RFMOs without deferring to them. One option would be the creation of a 'new entity' (or structure) with some role for RFMOs at both the decision-making and implementation phases of MPA establishment. It is apposite to state here, although this falls outside the scope of this article, that a new entity does not mean a new international organization. Whereas a new international entity might well be a new international organization, there is clearly no appetite for the establishment of a new international organization.

A new entity could be comprised simply of a secretariat, which some States have argued could be the UN's Division for Ocean Affairs and the Law of the Sea (known as 'DOAOLOS'), a legal, scientific and/or technical commission (hereinafter the 'LSTC') and a decision-making body in the form of, for example, a Conference of the Parties (hereinafter the 'COP'). Much of how the structure would, in practice, function would depend on, for example, the rules pertaining to (procedural) decision-making, and the (substantive) criteria for the establishment of MPAs. These issues, important though they are, fall outside the scope of this article. It is important also to emphasize that, this being only an illustrative approach, there may be variations to this basic structure.

Bearing in mind the illustrative purpose of this paper, the COP might take decisions on the establishment of an MPA on the basis of a recommendation by the LSTC. The key question, as regards the relationship between an IA and RFMOs, is where, in this decision-making chain, RFMOs would fit. The agreement could make provision for the interaction, first and foremost, between the secretariat of the COP, in this case DOALOS, and the secretariat of the RFMOs. Second, in addition to States Parties to the IA, RFMOs (and other competent organizations) should be permitted to submit proposals for MPAs (and attendant measures) to the decision-making bodies.[62] Allowing an RFMO to make proposals for an MPA, in addition to building solid relationships of cooperation, will also enhance the possibility for compliance with any

61 Para. 3 of the UN General Assembly Resolution 69/292 (n 2).

62 Whether proposals are submitted to the Conference of the Parties, which then transmits to the LSTC, or the proposals are submitted directly to the LSTC, is a matter of detail that would be determined in the IA.

decision to establish an MPA as proposed, at least from the members of that particular RFMO.

Third, during its consideration of any proposal for an MPA, the LSTC should engage with all relevant sectoral organizations that may be affected by any proposed measures. This means, at a minimum, that the IA must provide for the LSTC to consider the implications of any proposed measures on activities subject to the competent RFMOs (or other competent organizations) in its assessment of the various proposals. However, more than that, to promote cooperation and coordination, the LSTC could be empowered by the IA to request that relevant RFMOs respond to any objections to a potential conflict with their own management measures and take any such objections into account in making its own recommendation to the COP. There are practical issues connected with this consultation process, in particular the modalities for consultation, which fall outside the scope of this article and which likely can only be addressed in memoranda of understanding with various RFMOs.

Fourth, any recommendation by the LSTC to the COP on the establishment of a MPA should spell out clearly the possible impacts on activities regulated by other organizations, including RFMOs, and the views of such organizations (including the extent to which the RFMO has rejected the measures as in conflict with its own). In making its own decision, in accordance with its own decision-making procedures, the COP should also be required to, together with other factors and the criteria established in the IA, take into account the recommendations from competent organizations. If, having taken into account the relevant factors and criteria, the COP decides to establish an MPA, with measures that might potentially have an impact on the activities regulated by another organization or which would require the cooperation of that organization, the decision of the COP would, *inter alia*, spell out the nature of the potential impact. In addition, the decision would request the secretariat to bring the decision to the attention of the relevant organization and request its cooperation in giving effect to the decision. For example, if the decision by the COP to establish an MPA would require the imposition of a no-take measure on certain tuna species in the Atlantic Ocean falling under the mandate of ICCAT, the decision would request that ICCAT adopt measures prohibiting the exploitation of such species.

Where the relevant RFMO itself adopts the measures required by the IA, then problems of conflict do not arise. It is only where, for whatever reason, the relevant RFMOs do not accept the measures affecting their areas of competence that questions of conflicts may arise. The recommendation to require comments by RFMOs to be taken into account is precisely to avoid, or at any rate reduce, the incidence of non-support by RFMOs of measures adopted under the IA. Support by the relevant RFMOs would significantly improve implementation and effectiveness of any measures adopted under the IA.

However, the question arises whether in every case the concurrence of RFMOs and other competent organizations is *necessary* for action. The answer is: whereas concurrence will *always* be useful, it is hardly always *necessary*. After all, the decision to establish an MPA by the mechanism under the IA, and the measures adopted thereunder, will be binding on the States Parties to the IA whether or not a comparable decision has been made by another competent organization, such as an RFMO. States Parties to the IA would not be freed from any obligations from implementing the measures just because they also happen to belong to an RFMO which has not adopted the said measure. This point is particularly important, given that it is inconceivable for an RFMO to take a decision *obliging* states to engage in (destructive) fishing activities, such that a conflict arises between *obligations* under the RFMO and the measure adopted under the IA. At best, there may be incoherence between the obligation under the IA and permissiveness of the RFMO.

A state under an obligation to prevent conduct under the IA is not released from the obligation by virtue of the freedom (or right) under an RFMO to permit such conduct nor can it claim a conflict of obligations. This is because the *right* to permit conduct is not the same as an *obligation* to permit conduct. To take, yet again, ICCAT as an example, the establishment by the COP of an MPA in part of the Atlantic Ocean, within the Convention Area of ICCAT, which includes within that MPA a prohibition on the exploitation of, for example, yellowfin tuna, places an obligation on a State Party to ICCAT to refrain from permitting the vessels under its jurisdiction to catch yellowfin tuna within said MPA. That such a State Party is permitted to do so under ICCAT measures does not affect its legal obligation under the IA to refrain from fishing (or permitting the fishing for) yellowfin tuna in this Area. Moreover, there would be no *conflict* between the measures, because ICCAT does not require but permits the taking of yellowfin. In this sense, consistent with General Assembly Resolution 69/292, this proposed approach would not 'undermine' the mandate of RFMOs, because it would not create conflicting obligations.

As a matter of international law, the only issue that should arise would be the applicability of the measures to non-States Parties to the IA. Non-States Parties to the IA, whether they are members of the relevant RFMO or not, could not be bound by the said measures where the RFMO has not adopted an equivalent measure. Non-State Parties to the IA who are party to an RFMO would be bound, under the rules of the RFMO, by a measure adopted under the IA which has also been adopted by the RFMO. As a matter of international law this latter situation is addressed by the need to obtain the concurrence of the RFMO. Not obtaining the concurrence of the RFMO essentially frees States Parties of RFMOs, who are not also State Parties to the IA, from any obligation under the adopted measures.

The current article is concerned principally with RFMOs. However, an international organization such as the International Seabed Authority (hereinafter the 'ISA') might pose slightly different challenges. The ISA does not merely adopt measures that constrain State behaviour. It itself acts by issuing licenses and permits for prospecting, exploration, and (eventually) exploitation.[63] However, even here, the principles described above would be applicable. A State Party to the IA would be prevented from engaging in or authorizing an activity prohibited by a measure establishing an MPA under the IA, even if such a measure were approved in accordance with the rules of the ISA. However, the ISA itself and other members of the ISA that are not party to the IA, would not be similarly constrained unless the ISA issued a decision adopting similar measures.

The legal position described above could result in very unsatisfactory results of implementation if the IA does not attract a significant number of ratifications and the RFMOs do not generally support the measures adopted under the IA. In such an eventuality it would mean that a minority of States are obligated to respect the measures, while a large number of States are free to ignore such measures—a recipe for ineffectiveness. This has two policy implications. First, it is imperative that once adopted, the IA attracts a significant number of ratifications from States. Second, all efforts to secure cooperation, coordination and eventually concurrence of other competent international organizations, including RFMOs, will be very important. In this regard, securing the recognition of the General Assembly in its annual resolutions on the law of the sea (including the fisheries Resolution), would also contribute to the increase of the effectiveness of the measures. Finally, it is important to state that, to be effective, the IA would need to place an obligation on States Parties to support, *in other fora*, the recognition of the measures adopted under the IA. This includes deliberations in RFMOs when the RFMO considers whether or not to support the measures, and also in the consultations on the annual General Assembly Resolutions on the law of the sea.

---

63 See Art. 162(2)(j) of the UN Convention on the Law of the Sea. See also, generally, Annex III to the UN Convention on the Law of the Sea, Basic Conditions of Prospecting, Exploration and Exploitation.

5 Conclusion

One of the main concerns raised about a possible IA is the extent to which it would be compatible with existing mechanisms. Whereas the fears are real, from the perspective of international law they should not be overstated. To this extent, UN General Assembly Resolution 69/292 requires that the mandates of existing mechanisms not be undermined. Thus, in drafting the new IA, it is important that coordination between existing mechanisms and organizations, on the one hand and, on the other hand, the new IA and the mechanisms established under it with a mandate to establish MPAs, be promoted.

It is argued in this article that the optimal approach to be taken in the design of an IA would be one that recognizes the important role of other organizations, in particular RFMOs, without deferring to them. This would require that the IA be based on a number of key principles. First, RFMOs and other organizations, within the functional and geographic area of competence, should be permitted to make proposals for the establishment of MPAs. Second, RFMOs should, while the proposals are being considered at expert body level, be consulted. Third, any decision to establish an MPA must take into account the views of the relevant RFMOs and request such an RFMO to adopt equivalent measures.

The approach described is, first of all, only illustrative; several other models and variations of the model may exist. Second, it should be recognized that the approach is, because of the structure of international law, necessarily imperfect. It leaves unconstrained states that are party neither to the IA nor to the relevant RFMOs. It also leaves unconstrained states that are party to an RFMO that has not adopted equivalent measures. However, it does provide the potential for cooperation between RFMOs and mechanisms under the IA, and a real prospect for strong measures for conservation and sustainable use of marine biodiversity in areas beyond national jurisdiction.

CHAPTER 6

The Signing of the Hamilton Declaration on Collaboration for the Conservation of the Sargasso Sea: a New Paradigm for High Seas Conservation?

David Freestone
Executive Secretary
Sargasso Sea Commission

Kate Killerlain Morrison
Former Deputy Executive Secretary
Sargasso Sea Commission

Abstract

The 2014 Hamilton Declaration on Collaboration for the Conservation of the Sargasso Sea is the first non-binding instrument designed to provide a framework for intergovernmental collaboration to promote measures to minimize the adverse effects of human activities on a unique high seas ecosystem. This short article provides some context for the work and achievements of the Sargasso Sea Alliance which promoted this Declaration and examines the text of Declaration—highlighting the fact that it endorses the establishment of a Sargasso Sea Commission and a permanent Secretariat. The text of the Declaration is annexed.

Keywords

Sargasso Sea – Hamilton Declaration – high seas – ANBJ – Bermuda – stewardship – precaution – ecosystem approach – LOSC

On 11 March 2014, in an historic event in Hamilton, Bermuda, the representatives from the governments of eleven countries and territories met to reaffirm their support for an initiative, led by the Government of Bermuda, to collaborate for the conservation of the Sargasso Sea ecosystem for the benefit of present and future generations.

 | DOI:10.1163/9789004391703_008

The centerpiece of the meeting was the signing of the "Hamilton Declaration on Collaboration for the Conservation of the Sargasso Sea."[1] The governments of the Azores, Bermuda, Monaco, the United Kingdom and the United States signed the Declaration. Representatives of the governments of the Bahamas, the British Virgin Islands, the Netherlands, South Africa, Sweden and the Turks and Caicos Islands spoke in support, together with observers from the Secretariats of five international organizations, the Oslo and Paris Commission (OSPAR) from the neighboring North-east Atlantic region, the International Seabed Authority, the Inter-American Convention for the Conservation of Atlantic Sea Turtles, the Convention on Migratory Species and the International Union for Conservation of Nature (IUCN).

The Hamilton Declaration is the result of a two-year negotiation between interested governments that are either located in the broader Sargasso Sea area, have an interest in species within it or more generally in high seas conservation. It is historic in that it is the first non-binding instrument designed to provide a framework for intergovernmental collaboration to promote measures, through existing international organizations, to minimize the adverse effects of human activities in an ecosystem that is primarily in areas beyond national jurisdiction (ABNJ). It also envisages the establishment of a Sargasso Sea Commission, to "exercise a stewardship role for the Sargasso Sea and keep its health, productivity and resilience under continual review."[2]

In an earlier contribution in this journal,[3] the current authors explained that the Sargasso Sea Alliance (SSA) was founded in 2010 and led by the Government of Bermuda.[4] The SSA aimed to build an international partnership to secure recognition of the ecological significance of the Sargasso Sea and the threats that it faces, as well as to use existing regional, sectoral and international organizations to secure a range of protective measures for all or parts of the Sargasso Sea to address those threats.[5] These objectives have now been assumed *de facto* by the Signatories to the Hamilton Declaration.

Unlike the Mediterranean, the Northeast Atlantic or the Southern Ocean, where previous efforts to protect high seas areas have been located, the Sargasso Sea lacks both a regional oceans organization to promote conservation and

1 Reproduced below as Appendix 1 to this contribution on pp. 168–176, below; also at: http://www.sargassoseacommission.org/about-the-commission/hamilton-declaration.

2 Paragraph 6 and Annex II of the Declaration, *op. cit.* (n. 1).

3 D. Freestone and K.K. Morrison, "The Sargasso Sea Alliance: Seeking to Protect the Sargasso Sea" (2012) 27 *International Journal of Marine and Coastal Law* 647–655.

4 The SSA Secretariat is based in the Washington DC office of the International Union for Conservation of Nature (IUCN).

5 See http://www.sargassoseacommission.org/about-the-sargasso-sea.

a regional fisheries management organization (RFMO). So the key relevant international organizations that have regulatory authority for the Sargasso Sea area beyond national jurisdiction are the International Maritime Organization (IMO)[6] for maritime traffic and vessel discharges and the International Seabed Authority[7] for seabed exploration and mining. In the fisheries sector the regulatory area of North-West Atlantic Fisheries Organization (NAFO) does extend as far south as 35°N into the northern-most part of the Bermuda Exclusive Economic Zone (EEZ)[8] and the International Commission for the Conservation of Atlantic Tunas (ICCAT) has regulatory authority over the whole area, but only over fisheries of "tuna and tuna-like species."[9]

1 Achievements of the Sargasso Sea Alliance to Date

The Hamilton Meeting was the culmination of some three years' work by the SSA, in bringing the importance of the Sargasso Sea to the attention of the international community and in working to develop specific protection measures for consideration by relevant bodies. In early 2012, after extensive research and having commissioned a number of studies,[10] the SSA published *The Protection and Management of the Sargasso Sea: The Golden Floating Rainforest of the Atlantic Ocean. Summary Science and Supporting Evidence Case.*[11]

This report was the basis for a submission in March 2012 by the Government of Bermuda on behalf of the SSA at a Convention on Biological Diversity (CBD)

6 In 1948, an international conference in Geneva adopted a convention formally establishing the IMO (the original name was the Inter-Governmental Maritime Consultative Organization, or IMCO, but the name was changed in 1982 to IMO). It currently has 170 Member States and three Associate Members; see http://www.imo.org/About/HistoryOfIMO/Pages/Default.aspx.

7 Established under Part XI of the 1982 UN Convention on the Law of the Sea, (1982) 21 ILM 1261.

8 1979 Convention on Future Multilateral Cooperation in the Northwest Atlantic Fisheries (NAFO), which applies to most fishery resources of the Northwest Atlantic except salmon, tunas/marlins, and sedentary species (e.g., shellfish). For text see http://www.nafo.int/about/overview/governance/convention/convention.pdf.

9 The International Commission for the Conservation of Atlantic Tunas (ICCAT) is discussed below; it is species-based and there is an FAO Advisory Body, WECAFC, with no management competence.

10 Twelve of these are available to download as pdfs in the Sargasso Sea Alliance Science Report Series at: http://www.sargassoseacommission.org/publications-and-news/sargasso-sea-alliance-science-report-series.

11 D. Laffoley and H. Roe (eds). Available at: http://www.sargassoseacommission.org/storage/documents/Sargasso.Report.9.12.pdf.

Secretariat workshop to consider the description of Ecologically or Biologically Significant Areas (EBSAs) in the mid-Atlantic region.[12] The case for the Sargasso Sea as an EBSA was discussed and adopted by the scientists at the workshop,[13] then forwarded as part of the Workshop Report to the CBD's Subsidiary Body on Scientific, Technical and Technological Advice (SBSTTA) meeting in April 2012 and ultimately the Conference of Parties (COP) in October 2012, where it was officially described as an EBSA.[14]

"Description" as an EBSA has no legal significance, but it is intended that the CBD process will be taken into account by other international processes charged with managing and conserving ocean resources.[15] The SSA was the first to use the EBSA description in proposals to such "international processes." The first occasion was September 2012, at the NAFO Fisheries Commission, and the second was at the November 2012 Meeting of the ICCAT Commission in Agadir.

At NAFO, a proposal for special conservation measures for the areas of the Sargasso Sea EBSA north of 35°N, and thus inside the NAFO Regulatory Area, was put forward by the European Union (EU)—at the suggestion of the UK—with strong US support. The NAFO Fisheries Commission requested the advice of the NAFO Scientific Council. This advice was considered at its June and September 2013 meetings, where the proposals were then sent for consideration by the new joint FC/SC Working Group on Ecosystem Approach Framework to Fisheries Management which is scheduled to meet in July 2014.[16]

At the 12–19 November 2012 meeting of the ICCAT Commission in Agadir, Morocco, in response to a proposal by Bermuda, the ICCAT Commission referred the question of the significance of the Sargasso Sea for tuna and tuna-like species to the Standing Committee on Research and Statistics (SCRS),[17] which

---

12 CBD Wider Caribbean and Western Mid-Atlantic Regional Workshop to Facilitate the Description of Ecologically or Biologically Significant Marine Areas (EBSAs), 28 February–2 March 2012 in Recife, Brazil.

13 The EBSA proposal garnered acclaim at the workshop, with several experts complimenting it for its thoroughness and scientific rigour.

14 CBD UNEP/CBD/COP/DEC/XI/17 (5 December 2012), at page 23, item 13.

15 Freestone and Morrison (n 3), at p. 654.

16 Northwest Atlantic Fisheries Organization (NAFO), NAFO/FC DOC. 12/24, Fisheries Commission's Request for Scientific Advice on Management in 2014 and Beyond of Certain Stocks in Subareas 2, 3 and 4 and Other Matters (Sept. 2012). See also: NAFO Scientific Council June 2013 Meeting. Section xiv—Sargasso Sea management measures (Item 15, at page 48). See also: NAFO FC Working Paper 13/20, FC Request #15.

17 See Resolution by ICCAT on the Sargasso Sea, Res. 12-12 (2012) in ICCAT, Report For Biennial Period 2012–13, Pt. I (2012)—Vol. 1 at p. 215, available at: http://www.iccat.es/

in turn referred it to its Subcommittee on Ecosystems. Bermuda and the SSA worked with that Subcommittee, and at the ICCAT Commission Meeting in Cape Town, South Africa, in November 2013, the chair of the SCRS reported that the ecosystem group "recognized that basic biological and ecological data provided for the Sargasso Sea offers a useful foundation for adopting the region as a basis for a case study ..."[18]

The SSA has also reached out to all the other international organizations relevant to its work in order to develop a network of collaborating organizations. These include the secretariats of regional organizations, such as OSPAR,[19] with which it signed a Collaboration Arrangement in 2011,[20] the Cartagena Convention,[21] the Abidjan Convention,[22] the Inter-American Convention for the Protection and Conservation of Atlantic Sea Turtles,[23] the International Seabed Authority,[24] the Convention on Migratory Species,[25] UNESCO[26] and the Western Central Atlantic Fishery Commission (WECAFC).[27]

Documents/BienRep/REP_EN_12-13_I_1.pdf.1. The SCRS will examine the available data and information concerning the Sargasso Sea and its ecological importance to tuna and tuna-like species and ecologically associated species. 2. The SCRS will provide an update on the progress of this work in 2014 and report back to the Commission with its findings in 2015.

18 ICCAT Report for the Biennial Period 2012–2013, Volume 2. Standing Committee on Research and Statistics. Appendix 9. Summary of the Report of the Inter-Sessional Meeting of the Sub-Committee on Ecosystems, at p. 336. Available at: http://www.iccat.es/Documents/BienRep/REP_EN_12-13_II_2.pdf.

19 The 1992 Convention for the Protection of the Marine Environment of the North-East Atlantic (the "OSPAR Convention") was formed from the merger of the Commissions of the 1972 Oslo Convention and the 1974 Paris Convention, and entered into force in March 1998; text at (1993) 32 ILM 1072 and at: http://www.ospar.org/html_documents/ospar/html/ospar_convention_e_updated_text_2007.pdf.

20 Collaboration Arrangement in August 2012 to "maximize opportunities for the sharing of research, expertise and practical experience in seeking to protect and manage the marine environment of the North Atlantic, particularly in Areas beyond National Jurisdiction."

21 1983 Convention for the Protection and Development of the Marine Environment of the Wider Caribbean Region. (1983) 22 ILM 221.

22 1981 Convention for Cooperation in the Protection and Development of the Marine and Coastal Environment of the West and Central Africa. (1981) 20 ILM 746.

23 1996 text at: http://www.iacseaturtle.org/eng-docs/Texto-CIT-ENG.pdf.

24 Established under Part XI of the 1982 UN Convention on the Law of the Sea. (1982) 21 ILM 1261.

25 1979 Convention on the Conservation of Migratory Species of Wild Animals. (1980) ILM 15.

26 With responsibility for the World Heritage Convention.

27 An advisory body established under Article IV of the FAO Constitution, text at: http://www.rlc.fao.org/en/about-fao/statutory-bodies/wecafc/.

Within the UN General Assembly in November 2012, on the basis of a proposal by the United Kingdom, the USA and South Africa, the Annual Composite Resolution on Oceans and Law of the Sea: "Noted the efforts of the Sargasso Sea Alliance—led by the Government of Bermuda—to raise awareness of the ecological significance of the Sargasso Sea."[28]

2 The Hamilton Declaration

The negotiation of the text of the Declaration was a two-year process. In December 2012, the SSA convened a two-day meeting at the Pocantico Center of the Rockefeller Brothers Fund in Tarrytown, New York. Official representatives from the governments of Bermuda, Belgium, Dominican Republic, Portugal, South Africa, Sweden, Trinidad & Tobago, the United States and the United Kingdom attended, as did a representative from the European Commission. In addition, representatives from international and regional organizations also participated as observers, including the UN Division of Ocean Affairs and Law of the Sea (DOALOS), the Regional Coordinators from the UN Environment Programmes for the Caribbean (the Cartagena Convention) and West Africa (the Abidjan Convention), the Secretariat of the Convention on Biological Diversity and the Caribbean Community (CARICOM). The Pocantico Meeting developed a negotiated text for review and consideration by the governments interested in signing it. The text was presented to the EU Council of Ministers Committee on Law of the Sea issues (COMAR) in Brussels in March 2013 and reviewed by COMAR on a number of occasions thereafter.[29]

A second meeting was held in Pocantico in November 2013 to finalize the text for signature. Together with a representative from the European Commission, official representatives from the following governments attended: Portugal, the Azores, the Bahamas, Belgium, Dominican Republic, the Netherlands and Monaco, the USA and the UK. The International Seabed Authority and the Canadian Senate participated as observers.

28 Para 199. For the 2012 Resolution, see: http://library.constantcontact.com/download/get/file/1109154724045-37/2012+oceans+and+los+resolution+as+passed.pdf.

The following year, this time on a proposal from the UK, the USA and the Bahamas, a similar text was agreed in the 2013 Resolution (see para 215). United Nations General Assembly. Sixty-eighth session. Agenda item 76 (a). Oceans and the law of the sea. A/68/L.18, page 37.

29 See http://www.sargassoseacommission.org/publications-and-news/newsletters?start=10.

2.1 *The Text of the Declaration*

The Declaration Preamble recognises, *inter alia*, the Government of Bermuda for its important leadership role in bringing to international attention the global significance of the Sargasso Sea and for initiating and continuing the process leading to the convening of the Hamilton Meeting. It reinforces the point that the framework for this collaboration is the 1982 UN Convention on the Law of the Sea, recognises the important scientific work of the SSA, and recognises explicitly that the Declaration "is not legally binding and is without prejudice to the existing legal rights and obligations of the Signatories under international law or to the competences of regional and international organisations."

After reiterating that the guiding principle of this Declaration is to conserve the Sargasso Sea ecosystem for the benefit of present and future generations, Paragraph 3 states that the basic objective of the Declaration is for the signatory states to agree to collaborate, to the extent possible, in pursuing conservation measures for the Sargasso Sea ecosystem through existing regional and international organizations with relevant competences. Paragraph 8 further develops this concept, entrusting the Sargasso Sea Commission (discussed below) with the role of developing proposals for such measures for consideration by the Signatories to the Declaration;[30] the Signatories may then decide whether to submit these or support them at relevant regional or international organisations.

2.2 *Institutions*

The Declaration establishes a "Meeting of Signatories" and endorses the establishment of a Sargasso Sea Commission with a Secretariat and supporting financial mechanism.[31] The Government of Bermuda will establish the Sargasso Sea Commission, composed of "distinguished scientists and other persons of international repute committed to the conservation of high seas ecosystems", serving in their personal capacity, to "exercise a stewardship role for the Sargasso Sea and keep its health, productivity and resilience under continual review."[32]

30 These might be proposals for measures before IMO, or the relevant RFMOs, etc.

31 The structure is very loosely modelled on the structure of The Memorandum of Understanding on the Conservation of Migratory Sharks, an instrument developed under the auspices of the Convention on Migratory Species. Text is at: http://sharksmou.org/sites/default/files/Migratory_Shark_MoU_English.pdf. As of February 2014, the MOU has 36 Signatories: 35 national governments and the European Union; see http://sharksmou.org/list-of-signatories.

32 Established in the first instance under the law of Bermuda, the Government of Bermuda, in consultation with the Signatories and Collaborating Partners, will select qualified

A small permanent Secretariat will assist both bodies and a financial mechanism to receive voluntary contributions from both public and private sources is to be established, including a dedicated fund in Bermuda.[33] There are no mandatory financial obligations but Signatories are invited on a voluntary basis, to support the work of the Commission.[34]

2.3 *Definition of the Sargasso Sea*

For the purposes of this Declaration, the Sargasso Sea is defined as the "area of collaboration", being the portion of high seas and the Area[35] under that portion of the high seas (excluding the exclusive economic zone (EEZ) and territorial sea around Bermuda, and the extended continental shelves of neighbouring states) shown on the illustrative map attached to the Declaration. The outer parameters of this map were generally described by the scientific experts attending the CBD Wider Caribbean and Western Mid-Atlantic Regional Workshop to Facilitate the Description of Ecologically or Biologically Significant Marine Areas (EBSAs), 28 February–2 March 2012 in Recife, Brazil, discussed above.[36] The EBSA definition included the Bermudian EEZ and waters up to the edge of the seamount on which the islands of Bermuda are situated (known as "the platform"), but for internal political reasons, arising from misinformation within Bermuda about the role of the Commission, the Bermudian authorities requested, at the last minute, that the Bermuda EEZ be excluded from the area of collaboration.

2.4 *Later Signatures and Collaborating Partners*

The Declaration remains open for signature by other interested governments.[37] Five out of the eleven governments attending the Hamilton Meeting signed and the others indicated an interest in signing in the future. Similarly, it is open to regional and international organizations, as well as other bodies and entities, interested in contributing to the efforts to conserve the Sargasso Sea ecosystem in accordance with this Declaration, to participate as "Collaborating Partners."[38]

---

individuals to serve on the Commission. Details of the Commission's initial mandate are set out in Declaration Annex II.

33 Paragraph 9.

34 Paragraph 7.

35 The Area is the seabed and ocean floor and subsoil beyond the limits of national jurisdiction. See 1982 UN Convention on the Law of the Sea, Article 1(1)(1).

36 See above.

37 Paragraph 10.

38 Paragraph 11.

3 Conclusions and Looking Forward

In the light of the decision made at the Rio Summit in June 2012, discussions continue within the UN General Assembly—through its *Ad Hoc* Open-ended Informal Working Group to study issues relating to the conservation and sustainable use of marine biological diversity beyond areas of national jurisdiction (known as BBNJ)[39]—regarding the possibility of negotiating a new instrument—including possibly a new implementing agreement to the LOSC.[40] The Hamilton Declaration is not an attempt to undermine that process, but to highlight the importance of iconic high seas ecosystems like the Sargasso Sea and the need for international collaboration to start sooner rather than later.

The work of the SSA and the signature of the Hamilton Declaration may indeed represent a possible new paradigm for high seas conservation. Regional treaty regimes, while still important, take a long time to negotiate, move slowly and cannot bind third parties.[41] The Alliance was funded by a group of forward-thinking private donors; it worked with the Government of Bermuda—and ultimately the United Kingdom—in a novel form of public-private partnership. The Hamilton Declaration is not a legal instrument, but the Signatories have agreed to work together through the international legal mechanisms that already exist. The Sargasso Sea Commission will not have international legal personality, nor will it have management authority *per se*. But its "stewardship" role does have the potential for it to be an important voice, to provide the scientific and policy underpinnings for monitoring and management by others, and to be the conscience of the Signatories. The appointment of the first Sargasso Sea Commission, by the Government of Bermuda, after nomination by and consultations with the Signatory Governments of the Declaration, is planned for August 2014.

39 For details of the meetings to date, see http://www.un.org/Depts/los/biodiversityworking group/biodiversityworkinggroup.htm. Discussed in Freestone and Morrison (n 3), at pp. 649–650.

40 *The Future We Want*, G.A. Res. 66/288, at 3, U.N. Doc. A/RES/66/288 ¶ 162 (11 September 2012), available at: http://www.un.org/ga/search/view_doc.asp?symbol=A/RES/66/288&Lang=E.

41 For a comparison of the OSPAR experience and the SSA, see D. Freestone, D. Johnson, J. Ardron, K. K. Morrison and S. Unger, "Can existing institutions protect biodiversity in areas beyond national jurisdiction? Experiences from two on-going processes," (2014) 42 *Marine Policy* (in press); http://dx.doi.org/10.1016/j.marpol.2013.12.007.

Appendix 1

Hamilton Declaration on Collaboration for the Conservation of the Sargasso Sea
Hamilton, Bermuda
11 March, 2014

WE, THE SIGNATORIES LISTED BELOW:

Recognising that the islands of Bermuda are the only land territory within the Sargasso Sea and that the Government of Bermuda has taken a leadership role in marine conservation;

Commending the Government of Bermuda for its important leadership role in bringing to international attention the global significance of the Sargasso Sea and for initiating and continuing a process leading to the convening of this meeting in Hamilton;

Recognising the challenges in protecting areas beyond national jurisdiction including effective monitoring and development of protection measures for important marine ecosystems in such areas;

Reaffirming that the 1982 United Nations Convention on the Law of the Sea sets out the legal framework within which all activities in the oceans and seas must be carried out, including the obligation to protect and preserve the marine environment;

Recognizing also that there are other international instruments that articulate how States may use their jurisdiction over vessels and persons to control certain activities in areas beyond national jurisdiction including within the Sargasso Sea;

Noting that the Sargasso Sea is the world's only holopelagic seaweed ecosystem, home to a wide diversity of species including several identified for protection by a range of regional and international instruments;

Recalling the findings of "*The Protection and Management of the Sargasso Sea: the golden floating rainforest of the Atlantic Ocean. Summary Science and Supporting Evidence Case*", including the identification of threats to the Sargasso

Sea, prepared by the Sargasso Sea Alliance on behalf of the Government of Bermuda;

Recognising that the ocean is a vital global resource; and

Acknowledging that this Declaration is not legally binding and is without prejudice to the existing legal rights and obligations of the Signatories under international law or to the competences of regional and international organisations.

We hereby:

Common Vision

1 Recognize that the Sargasso Sea is an important open ocean ecosystem, the majority of which lies beyond national jurisdiction, which deserves recognition by the international community for its high ecological and biological significance, its cultural importance and its outstanding universal value.

2 Affirm that the guiding principle of this Declaration is to conserve the Sargasso Sea ecosystem for the benefit of present and future generations.

3 Decide to collaborate, to the extent possible, in pursuing conservation measures for the Sargasso Sea ecosystem through existing regional and international organisations with relevant competences.

Geographical Area of Collaboration

4 Recognize the geographical area of collaboration of the Sargasso Sea is defined in Annex I.

Institutional Arrangements for Collaboration

5 Establish a Meeting of Signatories of the Hamilton Declaration composed of representatives from each Signatory that will meet either physically or virtually at regular intervals. Each Signatory will designate a focal point for communication among Signatories and with the Secretariat. The Meeting of Signatories will:

- Pursue collaboration and cooperation in furtherance of the common vision of this Declaration;

- Provide advice and guidance for the Commission (referred to in paragraph 6 below) in its role of promoting the conservation of the Sargasso Sea;

- Review and comment on the Commission's proposed work programme and action plans;

- Make proposals for Commission initiatives and activities;

- Review and comment on proposals developed by the Commission that Signatories, individually or jointly, may elect to submit for consideration by regional or international organisations with relevant competences;

- Review Commission financial reports;

- Develop rules relating *inter alia* to the process of nomination of individuals to serve on the Commission and to their length of service; and

- Develop other rules and procedures as appropriate.

6 Welcome the proposal of the Government of Bermuda to establish a Sargasso Sea Commission, to be based in Bermuda, as well as a Secretariat to assist the Commission and the Signatories. The Commission would, at the outset, be established under Bermudian law. It would be composed of distinguished scientists and other persons of international repute committed to the conservation of high seas ecosystems that would serve in their personal capacity. The Government of Bermuda, in consultation with the Signatories and Collaborating Partners (referred to in paragraph 11 below), will select qualified individuals to serve on the Commission. Details of the Commission's initial mandate are set out in Annex II.

7 Decide to consider the means and modalities by which Signatories could, according to their mandate and their means, support the work of the

Commission by the provision of assistance, subject to the availability of existing resources, either by financial contributions or by contributions in kind, including the assignment or secondment of staff, provision of equipment or services or coordination of existing activities.

8 Decide that the Commission will also develop, for consideration by the Signatories, proposals that the Signatories, individually or jointly, may submit to, or support at, regional or international organisations with relevant competences. In developing such proposals, the Commission will use the best available science, and apply an ecosystem approach and the precautionary approach, as appropriate. Such proposals may include:

8.1 Measures to control, minimize, and where possible, eliminate the adverse effects of international shipping activities which may be adopted through the International Maritime Organization (IMO);

8.2 Measures to minimize, to the maximum extent possible, the adverse effects of fishing activities, including for the protection of vulnerable marine ecosystems, which may be adopted through the Food and Agriculture Organization of the United Nations (FAO) and/or regional fisheries management organisations or arrangements; and

8.3 Any other measures to maintain the health, productivity and resilience of the Sargasso Sea and to protect its components, including the habitats of threatened and endangered species, from the adverse effects of anthropogenic activities.

9 Welcome the establishment of a financial mechanism including a dedicated trust fund to support activities in furtherance of this Declaration, including the work of the Commission and the Secretariat. The financial mechanism would be available to receive voluntary contributions from both public and private sources.

10 Encourage participation by any other interested government or regional economic integration organisation in efforts to conserve the Sargasso Sea ecosystem in accordance with this Declaration including by becoming a Signatory to this Declaration.

11 Encourage relevant regional and international organisations, as well as other bodies and entities, who wish to contribute to efforts to conserve

the Sargasso Sea ecosystem in accordance with this Declaration, to participate as Collaborating Partners by notifying the Secretariat of their interest in doing so.

Adopted in Hamilton, Bermuda on 11 March 2014

For the Government of Bermuda

For the Government of the Azores

For the Government of Monaco

For the Government of the United Kingdom of Great Britain and Northern Ireland

For the Government of the United States of America

Annex I

Geographical Area of Collaboration

For the purposes of this Declaration the Sargasso Sea is the portion of high seas and the Area[42] under that portion of the high seas, (excluding the exclusive economic zone (EEZ) and territorial sea around Bermuda, and the extended continental shelves of neighbouring states) shown on the illustrative map below.[43]

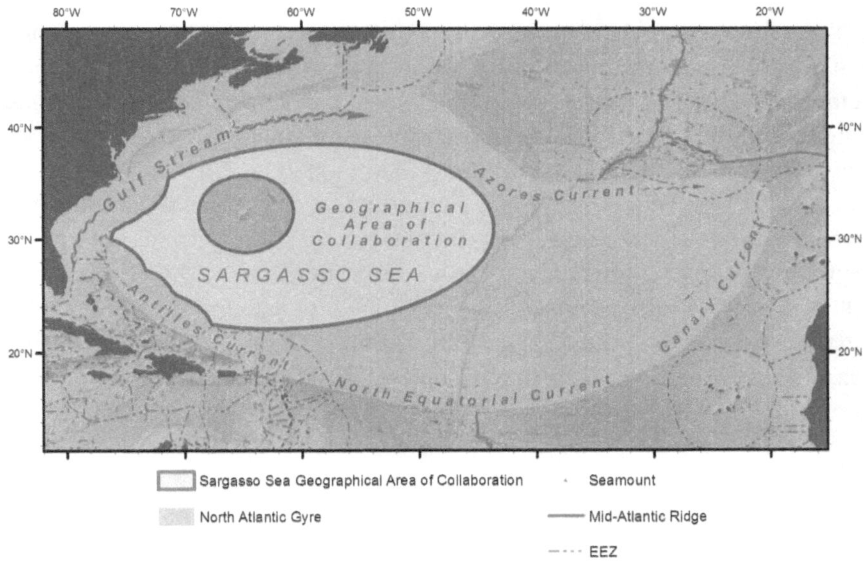

42 The Area is the seabed and ocean floor and subsoil beyond the limits of national jurisdiction. See 1982 UN Convention on the Law of the Sea, Article 1(1)(1).

43 The Geographical Area of Collaboration was generally described by the scientific experts attending the CBD Wider Caribbean and Western Mid-Atlantic Regional Workshop to Facilitate the Description of Ecologically or Biologically Significant Marine Areas (EBSAs), 28 February-2 March 2012 in Recife, Brazil, as meeting the CBD scientific criteria for an EBSA adopted by the Conference of the Parties to the CBD, at its ninth meeting, in annex 1 to Decision IX/20.

Scientific Note

The Sargasso Sea is an area of open-ocean situated within the North Atlantic subtropical gyre, and bounded on all sides by the clockwise flow of major ocean currents. The Gulf Stream and North Atlantic Drift form the western and northern boundaries, the Canary Current forms a more diffuse eastern boundary, and the North Equatorial Current and Antilles Current form the southern boundary. As these currents vary, the precise boundaries of the Sargasso Sea also vary. To refine this general location and to ensure that the area of interest incorporates a core area containing essential oceanographic and environmental characteristics the Sargasso Sea Alliance commissioned a new map based on criteria such as ocean current and eddy occurrence, remote sensing of *Sargassum* weed, and seabed topography. The resultant map agrees broadly with the overlap of previous delineations and is shown above. The Sargasso Sea study area occupies ~ 4,163,499 km2 in an area extending between 22°–38°N, 76°–43°W and centred on 30°N and 60°W. Because the Canary current is more diffuse and variable than the other currents the eastern boundary is more ill-defined, so the eastern boundary of the Sargasso Sea Alliance Study Area is pragmatically considered to lie to the west of the mid-Atlantic Ridge in the western basin of the Atlantic Ocean. Again for pragmatic reasons all of these boundaries were placed outside the EEZs of all adjacent countries or territories.[44]

44 See Laffoley, D.d'A and Roe, H.S.J., *et al.*, 2011. *The Protection and Management of the Sargasso Sea: the golden floating rainforest of the Atlantic Ocean: Summary Science and Supporting Evidence Case*, Sargasso Sea Alliance, pp. 7-8.

Annex II

Mandate of The Sargasso Sea Commission

Pursuant to paragraph 6 above, the Sargasso Sea Commission, which has no management authority, will:

a. Exercise a stewardship role for the Sargasso Sea and keep its health, productivity and resilience under continual review;

b. Develop a work programme and action plans for the conservation of the Sargasso Sea ecosystem;

c. Develop its rules and procedures as appropriate;

d. Develop a regular budget and generate necessary financial reports;

e. Serve as a focal point for the gathering and exchange of such information and data, develop a repository of information and scientific data relating to the condition of the Sargasso Sea ecosystem and make it publically accessible;

f. Foster and promote outreach, public awareness and scientific research and observation, and liaise with appropriate national, regional and international organisations to this effect;

g. Publish and/or publicise reports of the results of scientific research and, as appropriate, submit such reports to governments, national, regional and international organisations with relevant competences for their consideration;

h. Monitor the effects, including cumulative effects, of any anthropogenic activities in order to determine whether such activities are likely to have adverse impacts on the Sargasso Sea ecosystem and to assess the appropriateness and effectiveness of any measures being adopted for the conservation of the Sargasso Sea;

i. Liaise with the Signatories, as well as with other governments in the region and appropriate national, regional and international organisations with relevant competences, including those with competence in adjacent marine areas, to obtain a better understanding of issues of common concern and interest through, where appropriate, developing exchange of data, sharing of databases and collecting data in standardised formats;

j. Cooperate with governments, national, regional and international organisations with relevant competences in the development of environmental impact assessments, strategic environmental assessments and equivalent instruments;

k. Encourage cooperation among governments, national regional and international organisations with relevant competences in developing and promoting contingency plans for responding to any significant pollution incidents; and

l. Undertake such other tasks as may be deemed appropriate by the Meeting of the Signatories.

CHAPTER 7

Submarine Telecommunication Cables and a Biodiversity Agreement in ABNJ: Finding New Routes for Cooperation

Andrew Friedman
International Conservation Policy Officer, The Pew Charitable Trusts, Washington, DC, US

Abstract

In 2016, countries began meeting at the United Nations (UN) to prepare for negotiations to develop an international legally binding instrument on the conservation and sustainable use of marine biological diversity in areas beyond national jurisdiction (ABNJ). How the instrument will relate to submarine cables, if at all, remains to be decided. The preparatory committee will address a "package" of issues, among them the application of area-based management tools, including marine protected areas (MPAs) and environmental impact assessments (EIAs) to activities in ABNJ. EIAs and MPAs already affect submarine cable operations in national jurisdictions. In ABNJ, a new instrument should formalize a cooperative framework with the cable industry to provide limited environmental management where necessary without over-burdening cable operations. This approach would be consistent with the UN Convention on the Law of the Sea and could also inform governance with respect to other activities likely to be benign in ABNJ.

Keywords

submarine cables – areas beyond national jurisdiction (ABNJ) – high seas – marine protected areas – environmental impact assessments

1 Introduction

In the early morning hours of 24 January 2015, United Nations delegates came to a decision with momentous implications for ocean governance and the implementation of the United Nations Convention on the Law of the Sea

 | DOI:10.1163/9789004391703_009

(LOSC).[*,1] Following a lengthy and difficult negotiation, these delegates issued from their *Ad Hoc* Working Group[2] a consensus recommendation to the UN General Assembly (UNGA) to "develop an international legally-binding instrument under [the LOSC] on the conservation and sustainable use of marine biological diversity of areas beyond national jurisdiction [ABNJ]".[3] If successfully concluded, the new instrument would be the first implementing agreement under the LOSC in two decades and the first to focus principally on the conservation and sustainable use of biodiversity in ABNJ. Toward that end, the recommendation also called for convening a preparatory committee to develop "elements of a draft text"[4] and to decide by 2018 whether to initiate an intergovernmental conference.[5] This recommendation was adopted by the UNGA[6] and the first two meetings of this preparatory committee (PrepCom) were held from 28 March to 8 April and from 26 August to 9 September of 2016. The PrepCom will meet twice again in 2017, whereupon states must decide whether to go forward into a formal negotiating conference.

---

* J.D., New York University School of Law, 2008. I am particularly grateful to Doug Burnett, Kristina Gjerde, and Thorsten Thiele for their guidance, encouragement, and feedback, without which this article would not have been possible, to Nigel Irvine and Michael Costin for their technical expertise, to David Freestone and Philomene Verlaan for their thoughtful edits and comments, and to my wife and father for their patient editing as well—they have learned more about submarine cables than they ever wanted to know. I am also indebted to the International Cable Protection Committee for making available the scholarship which motivated me to write this article and attend the Rhodes Academy of Oceans Law and Policy in 2015. The views expressed herein are entirely my own and do not reflect those of any institutions or organizations with which I am affiliated. Any errors or omissions are likewise my own.

1 United Nations Convention on the Law of the Sea (Montego Bay, 10 December 1982; in force 16 November 1994) 1833 *UNTS* 396.

2 Known more formally as the *Ad Hoc* Open-ended Informal Working Group to study issues relating to the conservation and sustainable use of marine biological diversity beyond areas of national jurisdiction. See, e.g., UNGA Resolution 69/109, Oceans and the Law of the Sea (29 December 2014) (hereinafter "2014 LOS Resolution"), Preamble.

3 UN Doc. A/69/780, Letter dated 13 February 2015 from the Co-Chairs of the *Ad Hoc* Open-ended Informal Working Group to the President of the General Assembly (hereinafter the "Recommendations").

4 *Ibid.*, at para. 1(e)(i).

5 *Ibid.*, at para. 1(e)(ii) ("[B]efore the end of the 72nd session of the General Assembly [in September 2018] ... decide on the convening and on the starting date of an intergovernmental conference under the auspices of the United Nations, to consider the recommendations of the preparatory committee on the elements and to elaborate the text of an international legally binding instrument under [the LOSC]").

6 UNGA Resolution 69/292, Development of an international legally binding instrument under the United Nations Convention on the Law of the Sea on the conservation and sustainable use of marine biological diversity of areas beyond national jurisdiction (6 July 2015)

A question remains as to how the instrument will relate to submarine cables, if at all. The importance of submarine telecommunication cables to global commerce and information flow has been given full treatment elsewhere,[7] but here it bears repeating that such cables are estimated to carry 98 per cent of the world's voice, data, and internet traffic.[8] The UNGA has recognized that "they are vitally important to the global economy and the national security of all States".[9] Representatives of the submarine cable industry[10] and commentators[11] have argued forcefully that this network is too important to subject to regulations that might restrict its effective operation or dampen its growth. The International Cable Protection Committee (the "ICPC"), a non-governmental organization representing cable owners and operators worldwide, submitted a "white paper" just prior to the second session of the

(hereinafter "July 2015 Resolution"). This Resolution also provides several modalities that govern the preparatory committee, including the organization of its bureau and its obligation to "exhaust every effort to reach agreement on substantive matters by consensus". *Ibid.*, at para. 1(h).

7 See L Carter, D Burnett, S Drew, G Marle, L Hangodorn, D Bartlett-McNeil and N Irvine, *Submarine Cables and the Oceans: Connecting the World* (UNEP, 2010) (hereinafter "UNEP/ ICPC Report") 8; see also UN Doc. A/70/74, Report of the Secretary-General on Oceans and the Law of the Sea (30 March 2015) paras. 53–55 ("Functioning as the backbone of the international telecommunications system, submarine cables are a fundamental component of the critical global infrastructure").

8 *Ibid.*

9 2014 LOS Resolution (n 2), Preamble.

10 D Burnett, D Freestone and T Davenport, *Submarine Cables in the Sargasso Sea: Legal and Environmental Issues in Areas Beyond National Jurisdiction*, Report from the Workshop held 23 October 2014 at George Washington Law School, Washington, D.C. (16 January 2015) (hereinafter "Workshop Report") at p. 4. (According to the workshop's participants, "[t]he submarine cable industry does not support the imposition of any requirement for an Environmental Impact Assessment (EIA) for cable laying operations in the Sargasso Sea or any other area which is beyond national jurisdiction. In its view, it is not legally required, there is no clear benefit and the costs of conducting an EIA are potentially onerous").

11 T Davenport, 'Submarine Communications Cables and Law of the Sea: Problems in Law and Practice' (2012) 43(3) *Ocean Development & International Law* 201–242, at p. 223 (concluding that "[c]able operations ... have been subject to increasing coastal state regulation both in areas under sovereignty and areas outside of sovereignty to the detriment of international communications and the international community in general"); L Carter, D Burnett, and T Davenport, 'The Relationship Between Submarine Cables and the Marine Environment' in DR Burnett, RC Beckman and TL Davenport (eds), *Submarine Cables: The Handbook of Law and Policy* (Martinus Nijhoff Publishers, Leiden, 2013) (hereinafter "*Submarine Cable Handbook*") 179–212, at p. 212 (suggesting that "the marine environment can be sufficiently protected without the need to unduly restrict the freedom to lay and repair submarine cables").

PrepCom arguing that submarine cables should be "expressly excluded" from the scope of any new instrument,[12] a point reiterated during that session at an ICPC-sponsored side event.

The extent of coastal state jurisdiction over cable operations has been a matter of some discussion and debate.[13] But the ongoing negotiations are focused exclusively on ABNJ, including the "high seas"—the nearly two-thirds of the ocean that fall outside the jurisdiction of any one country.[14] These areas belong to none, but are of common interest and responsibility to all[15] and have been the subject of successive multilateral agreements addressing particular activities carried out upon them, specifically mining[16] and fishing.[17] These agreements have not, however, elaborated specifically upon states' duties with respect to marine biodiversity in ABNJ as a whole.[18] A new instrument will be expected to address this gap. Whereas it still remains anyone's guess as to the shape it will take,[19] it will have the potential to expand significantly the scope of global attention to and administration of activities in ABNJ.

---

12 Submission by the ICPC to the PrepCom: Submarine Cables and ABNJ (1 August 2016) (hereinafter "ICPC Submission"), available at http://www.un.org/depts/los/biodiversity/prepcom_files/ICC_Submarine_Cables_&_BBNJ_August_2016.pdf.

13 See (n 86) *infra*.

14 Pursuant to LOSC Article 86 (n 1), its provisions governing the high seas "apply to all parts of the sea that are not included in the exclusive economic zone, in the territorial sea or in the internal waters of a State, or in the archipelagic waters of an archipelagic State". For a general discussion of the LOSC provisions governing the high seas, see also RR Churchill and AV Lowe, *The Law of the Sea* (3rd ed., Manchester University Press, Manchester, 1999) 203–222. The seabed in ABNJ is governed under different provisions. See LOSC (n 1), Part XI and (n 16), *infra*.

15 A more specific international regime governs "the Area," those portions of "the seabed and ocean floor and subsoil thereof lying beyond the limits of national jurisdiction," LOSC (n 1), at Art. 1(1). Pursuant to LOSC Article 136, "[t]he Area and its resources are the common heritage of mankind".

16 Agreement Relating to the Implementation of Part XI of the United Nations Convention on the Law of the Sea of 10 December 1982 (New York, 28 July 1994, in force 28 July 1996) 1836 *UNTS* 42.

17 United Nations Agreement for the Implementation of the Provisions of the United Nations Convention on the Law of the Sea of 10 December 1982 relating to the Conservation and Management of Straddling Fish Stocks and Highly Migratory Fish Stocks (New York, 8 September 1995, in force 11 November 2001) 2167 *UNTS* 88.

18 E Druel and K Gjerde, 'Sustaining marine life beyond boundaries: Options for an implementing agreement for marine biodiversity beyond national jurisdiction under the United Nations Convention on the Law of the Sea' (2014) 49 *Marine Policy* 90–97, at p. 92 (cataloguing regulatory and governance gaps in the current high seas governance framework).

19 For a non-exhaustive catalogue of options, see *ibid.*, at pp. 92–97.

This potential is not unlimited. A focus on biodiversity means that the instrument will concern itself largely with activities affecting the marine environment and the living resources within it. Its drafters will have to navigate an intricate web of existing ocean governance agreements and institutions to ensure that they conform to the *Ad Hoc* Working Group's recommendation and the July 2015 Resolution's admonition not to "undermine existing relevant legal instruments and frameworks and relevant global, regional and sectoral bodies".[20]

Nevertheless, the instrument could have at least some overlap with submarine cable operations. The *Ad Hoc* Working Group's Recommendations and the July 2015 Resolution call for the preparatory committee to address a "package" of issues, among them the application in ABNJ of area-based management tools, including marine protected areas ("MPAs"), and environmental impact assessments ("EIAs") for activities with the potential to cause adverse impacts on the marine environment.[21] EIAs[22] and MPAs[23] are already employed to regulate submarine cable operations in national jurisdictions throughout the world, at

---

20 Recommendations (n 3), at para. 1(g); July 2015 Resolution (n 6) at para. 3.

21 In full, the recommendation calls for negotiations to address "the conservation and sustainable use of marine biological diversity in areas beyond national jurisdiction, in particular, together and as a whole, marine genetic resources, including questions on the sharing of benefits, measures such as area-based management tools, including marine protected areas, environmental impact assessments and capacity building and the transfer of marine technology". *Ibid.*, at para. 1(f).

22 Note that multilateral agreements already include requirements for EIAs. For example, Article 14 of the Convention on Biological Diversity (Rio de Janeiro, 5 June 1992, in force 29 December 1993) 1760 *UNTS* 79, requires its parties to "introduce appropriate procedures requiring environmental impact assessment of its proposed projects that are likely to have significant adverse effects on biological diversity". A new instrument can be expected either to provide uniform standards and/or greater specificity with respect to the high seas. L Kimball, *The International Regime of the High Seas and the Seabed Beyond the Limits of National Jurisdiction and Options for Cooperation for the Establishment of Marine Protected Areas (MPAs) in Marine Areas Beyond the Limits of National Jurisdiction* (Secretariat of the Convention on Biological Diversity, Montreal, Technical Series No. 19, 2005), at p. 43 (observing that "[c]ertain international instruments, considered above, already require environmental assessment before a particular activity may proceed" but "[a] more uniform approach could be developed among relevant bodies for advanced environmental assessment").

23 Similarly, regional management organizations have undertaken to establish protected areas, including on the high seas. BC O'Leary, RL Brown, DE Johnson, H von Nordheim, J Ardron, T Packeiser and CM Roberts, 'The first network of marine protected areas (MPAs) in the high seas: The process, the challenges and where next' (2012) 36 *Marine Policy* 598–605 (explaining the establishment and early-stage administration of the OSPAR MPA network in the North Atlantic).

times in questionable conformity with international law.[24] Additionally, UN Member States have suggested that cables fall among the "regulatory gaps" that could be addressed by a new agreement.[25] The relative significance of this "gap" is explored below.

Fortunately, this article is not the first analysis undertaken of submarine cable governance in ABNJ. A workshop (the "Sargasso Sea Workshop") convened in October 2014 by the ICPC and the Sargasso Sea Commission, among others, brought together government and industry representatives, scientists, academics, and lawyers to discuss legal and environmental aspects of submarine cables in the Sargasso Sea, an ocean region extending well beyond the exclusive economic zone ("EEZ")[26] of Bermuda into the high seas.[27] The Sargasso Sea encompasses critical habitat for many forms of marine life that take shelter in the *Sargassum* for which it is named. Although the Sargasso Sea Workshop focused on a particular region of ABNJ with unique characteristics,[28]

---

24 *Submarine Cable Handbook* (n 11), at p. 199 *et seq.*

25 International Institute for Sustainable Development (IISD) Reporting Services, 'Briefing Note on the WG on Marine Biodiversity: Summary of the Seventh Meeting of the Working Group on Marine Biodiversity Beyond Areas of National Jurisdiction 1–4 April 2014' (7 April 2014) available at http://www.iisd.ca/oceans/marinebiodiv7/ ("Costa Rica and Pakistan recalled that the report of the 2013 workshops held under the Working Group already specified regulatory gaps, including on fisheries, mining, submarine cables and climate-related geo-engineering".); see also K Gjerde, 'Challenges to Protecting the Marine Environment beyond National Jurisdiction' (2012) 27 *International Journal of Marine and Coastal Law* 839–847, at p. 844 (noting that a "reactionary approach" has left "many activities with a potential to cause significant adverse impacts in ABNJ unregulated or under-regulated [including] cable and pipeline laying").

26 The portion of ocean stretching not more than 200 nautical miles out from the baselines from which the breadth of the territorial sea is measured (LOSC (n 1), at Art. 57).

27 For a summary, see A Leonard de Juvigny, TM Davenport, DR Burnett and D Freestone, 'Submarine Telecommunication Cables in the Sargasso Sea' (2015) *30 International Journal of Marine and Coastal Law* (*IJMCL*) 371–378.

28 *Ibid.*, at p. 374. The Sargasso Sea "contains the world's only holopelagic seaweed ecosystem based upon floating *Sargassum*". Workshop Report (n 10), at p. 6. It is subject to a multi-sectoral and conservation-focused governance regime stemming from a non-binding political declaration. Specifically, the governments of Bermuda, the Azores, Monaco, the United States, and the United Kingdom adopted a declaration in 2014 (joined by the governments of the British Virgin Islands and the Bahamas in 2016) deciding to, among other things, "collaborate, to the extent possible, in pursuing conservation measures for the Sargasso Sea ecosystem through existing regional and international organisations with relevant competences". D Freestone and KK Morrison, 'The Signing of the Hamilton Declaration on Collaboration for the Conservation of the Sargasso Sea: A new paradigm for high seas conservation?' (2014) 29 *IJMCL* 345–362, at p. 355. A Commission was established through the declaration to "exercise a stewardship role for the Sargasso Sea and keep its health, productivity and resilience under continual review". *Ibid.* at p. 361.

its discussions and conclusions have general relevance and are a reference point throughout this article.

As explored below[29] and as emphasized in the ICPC's Submission,[30] submarine cables are likely to have low levels of interaction with the marine environment and are unlikely to pose a threat to the biodiversity it supports. Even so, the ICPC's position that submarine cables should be excluded entirely from the scope of the new instrument may be problematic, both for the instrument and for cable operations in ABNJ. An express exclusion poses a political challenge, particularly as it would open the door to exclusions for other activities that are less likely to be benign. It presumes, despite all indications to the contrary, that the new instrument will impose a burden on activities that are unlikely to have a significant impact on the marine environment in ABNJ, a category that arguably includes telecommunication cables. It also misses an opportunity to integrate into international decision-making the expertise and potentially important contribution of an industry consistently engaged in the exploration of the deep ocean floor.

Rather than exclude cables, a new instrument could instead formalize a flexible and cooperative approach with the cable industry to provide limited environmental management if and where necessary without restricting cable operations or network growth. This approach would be consistent with the LOSC and could also inform governance with respect to similar "low impact" activities in ABNJ.

This article aims to demonstrate that this outcome should be preferred by policymakers and industry representatives alike, proceeding in four parts. It first discusses the impacts of submarine cables on the marine environment, explaining why these are likely to be minimal in ABNJ. The second part explores the international legal regime governing the interactions between cables and the marine environment, contrasting the potential for multilateral environmental management in ABNJ with the restricted authority of coastal states to regulate cable operations within their areas of functional jurisdiction. The third part offers paths to address submarine cables in the new instrument that are consistent with their limited impact, but that also benchmark best regulatory practices and formalize industry cooperation. The final part discusses options for collaboration with the submarine cable industry that would go beyond pragmatic regulation to actively involve cable operations in marine environmental protection.

---

29 See *infra* (nn 56–61) and accompanying discussion.

30 ICPC Submission (n 12), at pp. 10–17.

2 Potential Impacts of Submarine Cables in ABNJ

2.1 *Physical Characteristics of Submarine Cables*

To understand why submarine cables are likely to have a limited environmental impact in ABNJ, a basic understanding of their physical characteristics and deployment methods is helpful. There are two types of submarine cables: telecommunication and power transmission. Telecommunication cables are relatively small—roughly the size of a garden hose—and at depths greater than 2000 meters are simply laid on the surface of the deep seabed.[31] At this depth, they are beyond the present limits of the deepest-reaching gear of the world's fishing fleets and thus require little physical protection.[32] At depths less than 2000 m, they are wrapped in protective layers of steel wire armor to prevent fouling damage from anchors or fishing. This armor makes them larger, but usually no more than 50 mm in diameter.[33] Even so-armored, the cables themselves have little or no impact on the seabed or marine life. However, in circumstances where cables are likely to encounter hazards that cannot be avoided, it may be necessary to both armor and bury cables in the seabed, a process described briefly below.[34] Power cables may be larger, but they are not yet a widespread fixture in ABNJ[35] and so are excluded from the scope of this analysis.

A cable's optimal route is determined before deployment through a series of steps. First, a desktop literature review identifies obstacles and human activities along a proposed route.[36] Bottom trawling and other fishing activities are the largest contributors to cable damage[37] and bottom features not only complicate cable-laying, but may also support marine ecosystems that in turn

31 *Submarine Cable Handbook* (n 11), at pp. 179–180; UNEP/ICPC Report (n 7), at pp. 18–19, 23–24.

32 *Submarine Cable Handbook* (n 11), at p. 179; UNEP/ICPC Report (n 7), at p. 19. Note, however, that "this depth limit is presently the extent of modern bottom trawlers, but their forays into deeper water may necessitate burial in even greater water depths". *Ibid.*, at p. 24.

33 *Submarine Cable Handbook* (n 11), at p. 179.

34 *Ibid.*, at p. 187; UNEP/ICPC Report (n 7), at pp. 23–24.

35 *Submarine Cable Handbook* (n 11), at p. 180. Submarine power cables at present are laid no deeper than about 1600 m, suggesting that they would not yet transit through ABNJ.

36 UNEP/ICPC Report (n 7), at pp. 21, 37; Leonard de Juvigny et al. (n 27), at p. 373.

37 JP Colonna and A Puech, 'State of the Art in Offshore Cable Route Surveys' (2005) *Geoline*, available at: http://www.geotech-fr.org/sites/default/files/congres/geoline/GEOLINE2005%20S2%20pp%201-15%20Colonna.pdf; UNEP/ICPC Report (n 7), at p. 45.

support fishing, increasing the probability of entanglement and damage.[38] They are avoided wherever possible. Next, a survey is conducted to obtain a detailed picture of the seabed along the intended route. A variety of tools, including multibeam echo-sounding systems, are used to detail the seafloor's relevant topography, sediment characteristics, and marine life.[39] A single multibeam track can provide a seabed map up to 20 km wide beneath the surveying vessel, depending on water depth,[40] and with decreasing resolution at increasing depth.[41] Seismic surveying and bottom and sub-bottom profiling are conducted only where depth and human activity require cable burial.[42]

Once the survey is complete, the cable can be deployed and buried if necessary. There are two techniques for burial. The most common is to use a rig with skids to tow a plow across the seabed and feed the cable into its furrow.[43] Where deep slopes or sediment conditions prevent plowing, or where cable has been laid and must be subsequently buried or repaired, a water jet is used to liquefy the sediment beneath the cable until it sinks to a specified depth.[44] Both methods disturb the seabed, including any marine fauna on it, but only along the ploughed strip and/or as a result of resuspended sediment.[45] This localized disturbance is generally less than 5 to 8 meters across and will only occur once in the life of the cable, absent a fault or an attempt at recovery and recycling.[46] Faults are infrequent, but do occur. For example, as of this

38 F Althus, A Williams, TA Schlacher, RJ Kloser, MA Green, BA Barker, NJ Bax, P Brodie and MA Schlacher-Hoenlinger, 'Impacts of bottom trawling on deep-coral ecosystems of seamounts are long-lasting' (2009) 397 *Marine Ecology Progress Series* 279–294, at p. 280 ("Several benthopelagic fish species aggregate for spawning or feeding over seamounts. Schools of these fish have increasingly become the target of commercial bottom-contact trawling during the last 3 decades as fishing fleets move from declining, traditional, shelf-based fisheries to exploit less accessible populations further offshore". (internal citations omitted)).

39 UNEP/ICPC Report (n 7), at p. 21.

40 *Ibid.*

41 See Presentation by G Evans to Center for International Law Workshop on Submarine Cables and the Law of the Sea, 'Overview of Submarine Cable Route Planning & Cable Route Survey Activities' (Singapore, 14 December 2009), at pp. 19–23, available at http://cil.nus.edu.sg/wp/wp-content/uploads/2009/10/CIL-Survey-Background-Presentation-Graham-Evans.pdf.

42 Workshop Report (n 10), at p. 10.

43 For detailed discussions of the cable burial process, see *ibid.*, at p. 18; UNEP/ICPC Report (n 7), at pp. 23–24; *Submarine Cable Handbook* (n 11), at p. 188.

44 UNEP/ICPC Report (n 7), at p. 34.

45 *Ibid.*, at pp. 33–34.

46 *Ibid.*

writing, eleven cables comprising eight systems now transit the Sargasso Sea.[47] Together, these experienced three faults requiring repair between 2008 and 2013.[48] Of the estimated 100 to 150 faults that occur worldwide each year,[49] an average of four occur on the high seas.[50] The cumulative environmental impacts of burial and repair do not appear to have been addressed in existing literature, but would seem to be similar to those incurred on initial deployment,[51] with the *caveat* that they are occurring for the second time or more in a cable's life. Cables have little to no chemical interaction with the ocean once deployed,[52] although they may displace sediment over their lifetime depending on environmental conditions like currents and wave action.[53]

Certain interactions between cables and the marine environment that raised concerns in the past are less relevant today. For example, whale entanglements once occurred with some regularity, but ceased entirely in 1959 following the transition from telegraph to coaxial and then fibre-optic cable systems.[54] Separately, cable surveys were at one point thought to be related to marine mammal beaching. Today, the high-frequency, low-energy acoustic systems used to survey the sea floor are thought to pose a relatively low risk to marine mammals in comparison to the high-energy naval sonar used by advanced militaries.[55]

At least three reasons have been put forward to believe that submarine cables and cable operations would have a limited impact on marine biodiversity in ABNJ. First, studies have confirmed that the presence of a submarine cable itself has no substantial impact on surrounding fauna.[56] These studies have

---

47 Leonard de Juvigny et al. (n 27); see also Map: International telecom cables in the Sargasso Sea Areas Beyond National Jurisdiction (ABNJ), available at http://www.sargassoalliance.org/storage/documents/International_Telecom_Cables_in_the_Sargasso_Sea_ABNJ.JPG (briefing material provided in connection with Sargasso Sea Workshop).

48 Presentation by RJ Rapp to the Sargasso Sea Workshop, 'Cable Laying and Repair—Cable Ship Operations' (Washington, D.C., 23 October 2014), at p. 19, available at: http://www.sargassoalliance.org/storage/documents/Cable_Installation_and_Maintenance_-_TE_SubCom_Sargasso_Sea_Final1.pdf.

49 UNEP/ICPC Report (n 7), at p. 44.

50 ICPC Submission (n 12), Annex B.

51 Rapp (n 48), at pp. 13–18 (detailing the process of cable repair).

52 *Submarine Cable Handbook* (n 11), at p. 186 ("[C]able grade, high density polyethylene sheathing is basically non-reactive with seawater").

53 *Ibid.*, at p. 182; UNEP/ICPC Report (n 7), at pp. 35–36.

54 UNEP/ICPC Report (n 7), at p. 31.

55 *Submarine Cable Handbook* (n 11), at p. 180.

56 *Ibid.*, at p. 183; UNEP/ICPC Report (n 7), at p. 9; Davenport (n 11), at p. 206.

compared marine communities spatially—near to and surrounding a cable,[57] and temporally—before and after cable deployment,[58] finding no evidence of environmental degradation. Second, cable deployment in ABNJ at present is unlikely to necessitate the precaution of burial. The ocean's average depth is over 4000 meters[59] and cable routes are planned to avoid shallow areas and bottom features. Finally, routes are also planned to avoid ecologically important areas, both to prevent environmental impacts and because they impose obstacles or correlate with conflicting human activity.[60] Existing routes are increasingly used to augment cable capacity, further narrowing the scope of potential impacts.[61] Industry experts consulted by the author in preparing this article were aware of no instances in which a cable was buried along any portion of its route beneath the high seas.

2.2 *The Marine Environment in ABNJ*

That cables may have limited interaction with marine life in ABNJ is not to say that such life does not exist. The high seas and seabed beyond the continental margin are not a flat, lifeless desert, but are geologically, topographically, and environmentally diverse. In recognition, the parties to the Convention on

---

57 *Submarine Cable Handbook, ibid.*, at pp. 182–183 (citing I Kogan, CK Paull, L Kuhnz, E Burton, S von Thun, HG Greene and JP Barry, 'ATOC/Pioneer Seamount Cable after 8 Years on the Seafloor: Observations, Environmental Impact' (2006) 26 *Continental Shelf Research* 771–787); BM Grannis, 'Impacts of Mobile Fishing Gear and a Buried Fiber-optic Cable on Soft-sediment Benthic Community Structure' (M. Sc. Thesis, University of Maine, 2001).

58 *Submarine Cable Handbook, ibid.*, at p. 183 (citing E Andrulewicz, D Napierskaa and Z Otremba, 'The Environmental Effects of the Installation and Functioning of the Submarine SwePol Link HVDC Transmission Line: A Case Study of the Polish Marine Area of the Baltic Sea' (2003) 49(4) *Journal of Sea Research* 337–345).

59 United States National Oceanic and Atmospheric Administration, 'How deep is the ocean?', available at http://oceanservice.noaa.gov/facts/oceandepth.html (Revised 14 March 2014).

60 Y Van Logchem, 'Submarine Telecommunication Cables in Disputed Maritime Areas' (2014) 45(1) *Ocean Development & International Law* 107–122, at p. 117 ("Whenever the circumstances allow, reefs or other sensitive natural areas will be avoided by the submarine cable industry because of the difficulties associated with environmental permitting and competing uses of other users of such areas".); UNEP/ICPC Report (n 7), at p. 37 ("[T]he submarine cable industry, together with environmental regulators, attempts to reduce or avoid any impact on vulnerable deep-water ecosystems by ... avoiding the deployment of cables on or through habitats such as seamounts, submarine canyons and hydrothermal vents, which are also unsuitable as cable routes due to the risk of natural hazards").

61 Presentation by B Wargo to the Sargasso Sea Workshop, 'Cable System Planning and Permitting: Business and Stakeholder Considerations (Washington, D.C., 23 October 2014), at p. 14, available at: http://www.sargassoalliance.org/storage/documents/Wargo_Sargasso_presentation.pdf.

Biological Diversity ("CBD"), a global agreement to protect biological diversity with a focus on components of biological diversity within areas under national jurisdiction,[62] have undertaken a decade-long effort to identify a global set of ecologically and biologically significant areas ("EBSAs") in ABNJ (an effort that has since expanded to include areas under national jurisdiction).[63] They have now assembled detailed information on 204 EBSAs through a series of regional workshops that have covered most of the globe.[64] Many of these areas fall within or incorporate some portion of ABNJ, and include biodiversity hotspots such as:

- Cold-water corals: Cold-water corals form reefs on seamounts and along continental slopes the world over.[65] Some are thousands of years old[66] and support diverse marine communities and form critical habitat for many species of commercially caught fish and other forms of marine life that do not, at least at present, appear to have "commercial" value as commonly understood.[67]
- Seamounts: These "islands" (usually defined as topographical rises from the seafloor that exceed 1000 meters in height) beneath the ocean surface are notable for, e.g., their high levels of endemism, unique marine communities, and facilitation of migratory movements and species dispersal.[68]

---

62 Convention on Biological Diversity (n 22), Art. 4 (for more information see the Convention's website at: http://www.cbd.int/).

63 DC Dunn, J Ardron, N Bax, P Bernal, J Cleary, I Cresswell, B Donnelly, P Dunstan, K Gjerde, D Johnson, K Kaschner, B Lascelles, J Rice, H von Nordheim, L Wood and PN Halpin, 'The Convention on Biological Diversity's Ecologically or Biologically Significant Areas: Origins, development, and current status' (2014) 49 *Marine Policy* 137–145.

64 See CBD, Decision XII/22, Marine and coastal biodiversity: ecologically or biologically significant marine areas (EBSAs) (17 October 2014), available at: https://www.cbd.int/doc/decisions/cop-12/cop-12-dec-22-en.pdf.

65 M Gianni, *High Seas Bottom Trawl Fisheries and Their Impacts on the Biodiversity of Vulnerable Deep-Sea Ecosystems: Options for International Action* (International Union for the Conservation of Nature (IUCN), Gland, Switzerland, 2004) 4; UNEP/ICPC Report (n 7), at p. 36.

66 Gianni (n 65), at p. 4.

67 *Ibid.*, at pp. 5–6; A Rogers, *The Biology, Ecology and Vulnerability of Deep-Water Coral Reefs* (IUCN, Gland, Switzerland, 2004), available at http://cmsdata.iucn.org/downloads/alexrogers_cbdcop7_deepwatercorals_complete.pdf.

68 Gianni (n 65), at pp. 7–8; G Pendleton, 'State Responsibility and the High Seas Marine Environment: A Legal Theory for the Protection of Seamounts in the Global Commons' (2005) 14 *Pacific Rim Law and Policy Journal* 485–514, at p. 487.

Certain characteristics of these features make them particularly sensitive to human impacts. For example, the marine communities they support are complex and interdependent, the development of local habitats (e.g., cold-water corals) is slow, and much of their supported fauna have long lifespans, low reproductive rates, and high endemism.[69] A submarine cable route would be planned to avoid these areas for the reasons discussed above. Only in the unlikely event that a proposed route did pass through such an ecosystem, and the decrease in depth and accompanying increase in human activity required the precaution of burial, would there be cause for further inquiry about the route's potential impacts.

3 High Seas Submarine Cables under the LOSC

The Recommendations and July 2015 Resolution specify that the new instrument is to be developed "under the [LOSC]".[70] Any elaboration of state rights or responsibilities inconsistent with those contemplated by the LOSC, including with respect to submarine cable activities on the high seas, would fall beyond the scope of the proposed negotiations. Under the LOSC, laying submarine cables, and attendant activities (e.g., surveying and repair by extension), are among the enumerated "freedoms" of the high seas.[71] The strength of the submarine cable network is thus treated, like robust shipping lanes, as a public good, and the circumstances under which cable-laying activities may be restricted are tightly circumscribed. Only a limited field of potential overlap remains between cables and the new instrument.

3.1 *The Freedom to Lay Submarine Cables*

The Convention for the Protection of Submarine Telegraph Cables[72] was the first agreement to address submarine cables directly and it continues to serve as the foundation for modern cable governance.[73] When it was adopted in 1884, submarine cables had already been in use for 60 years. This Convention makes no mention of the freedom to lay cables on the high seas, which was uncontested at the time of its drafting. Its focus falls instead on protecting cables

---

69 Gianni (n 65), at p. viii.

70 Recommendations (n 3), para. 1(e); July 2015 Resolution (n 6), para. 1.

71 See *infra* (n 76) and accompanying discussion.

72 Convention for the Protection of Submarine Telegraph Cables (Paris, 14 March 1884, in force 1 May 1888) *TS* 380 (the "1884 Convention").

73 UNEP/ICPC Report (n 7), at p. 26; Davenport (n 11), at pp. 203–204.

from competing uses or interference.[74] Indeed, the agreement assumes cable operations will take place on the high seas, noting that it applies "outside territorial waters to all legally established submarine cables".[75]

The modern system of spatially stratified ocean governance emerged alongside an increasing intensity and complexity of human activity on the ocean. With it came an explicit articulation of the freedoms of the high seas that included, *inter alia*, the freedom to lay submarine cables and pipelines,[76] codified in Part VII of the LOSC, specifically Article 87, providing in relevant part that:

> 1) The high seas are open to all States, whether coastal or land-locked. Freedom of the high seas is exercised under the conditions laid down by this Convention and by other rules of international law. It comprises, *inter alia*, both for coastal and land-locked States: (c) freedom to lay submarine cables and pipelines, subject to Part VI" [which vests a coastal state with 'sovereign rights for the purpose of exploring [its continental shelf] and exploiting its natural resources'].[77]
>
> 2) These freedoms shall be exercised by all States with due regard for the interests of other States in their exercise of the freedom of the high seas, and also with due regard for the rights under this Convention with respect to activities in the Area [of the seabed beyond national jurisdiction].

The above provisions are reinforced by LOSC Article 112, under which: "[a]ll States are entitled to lay submarine cables and pipelines on the bed of the high seas beyond the continental shelf" subject to an obligation under LOSC Article 79(5) to take "due regard of cables or pipelines already in position". In these provisions, cable activity is the focus, rather than the cables themselves. Cables, unlike vessels, do not carry a particular country's flag, nor are they viewed as an extension of a state. They are instead owned by one or more corporations that have invested in their deployment and generally lack a juridical personality under the LOSC. The freedom to lay cables applies not to a cable itself but to a vessel undertaking cable activities through the country of its flag

74 Davenport (n 11), at p. 227, n. 33 (2012) (citing M McDougal and W Burke, *The Public Order of the Oceans: A Contemporary International Law of the Sea* (Martinus Nijhoff Publishers, Leiden, 1962) 781).

75 1884 Convention (n 72), at Art. 1.

76 Convention on the High Seas (Geneva, 29 April 1958, in force 30 September 1962) 450 *UNTS* 11.

77 LOSC (n 1), at Art. 77(1).

or the nationalities of the cable owners.[78] The same would likely be true of any provisions adopted under a new instrument.

3.2 *Submarine Cables in Zones of Functional State Jurisdiction*

Many freedoms of the high seas, including the freedom to lay submarine cables, also extend to zones under the functional jurisdiction of coastal states, including the waters of their EEZ[79] and on their respective continental shelves.[80] In these zones the coastal state enjoys certain rights, including, *inter alia*, sovereign rights "for the purpose of exploring and exploiting, conserving and managing the natural resources, whether living or non-living" of the coastal state's EEZ and the seabed below it.[81] Similarly, if a state has a continental shelf within the meaning of LOSC Article 76 that extends beyond its EEZ, the waters above are considered "high seas," but the state has "sovereign rights for the purpose of exploring the shelf and exploiting its natural resources".[82] States have interpreted these rights to justify regulation of submarine cables, such as consent requirements for cable routes running through their EEZ, on their continental shelf beneath it, or—if applicable—on their continental shelf extending beyond the 200-nautical-mile EEZ limit.[83] Increasingly, coastal

78 Davenport (n 11), at p. 221 (noting that "[c]able companies ... are in fact exercising the rights of states, [but] are precluded from using the LOSC dispute settlement mechanisms because they are only open to states. Cable system owners are usually telecommunications carriers or a consortium of telecommunications carriers, which are either fully or partially privatized. Such owners would need to persuade the states in which they are incorporated to bring a claim under [the LOSC]".). But see also Van Logchem (n 60), at p. 117 ("Cable companies appear to operate under the assumption that the freedom to lay, maintain, and repair submarine cables applies to them directly and that they can invoke this right in connection with the conduct of submarine cable activities within areas of overlapping EEZ or continental shelf claims").

79 LOSC (n 1), at Art. 58 ("In the exclusive economic zone, all States, whether coastal or land-locked, enjoy, subject to the relevant provisions of this Convention, the freedoms referred to in article 87 of navigation and overflight and of the laying of submarine cables and pipelines, and other internationally lawful uses of the sea related to these freedoms").

80 The shelf is defined as "the seabed and subsoil of the submarine areas that extend beyond [a State's] territorial sea throughout the natural prolongation of its land territory to the outer edge of the continental margin, or to a distance of 200 nautical miles from the baselines from which the breadth of the territorial sea is measured where the outer edge of the continental margin does not extend up to that distance". *Ibid.*, at Art. 76(1).

81 *Ibid.*, at Art. 56(1)(a).

82 *Ibid.*, at Art. 77(1).

83 Davenport (n 11), at p. 212.

states have also designated areas of their EEZs as MPAs[84] with the potential to restrict cable routes.[85]

These measures have prompted some discussion about whether and to what extent coastal states are imbued with jurisdiction over submarine cable activities in the face of potentially conflicting rights.[86] In particular, there is the question over a state's ability to deploy cables for military applications on another coastal state's continental shelf without its consent. As the same regime applies to military and non-military cables alike, this question turns on a far larger debate about the permissibility of military activities by another state in a coastal state's EEZ or on its continental shelf in general, the scope of which lies beyond this article.[87]

With respect to environmental measures, however, several arguments have been advanced against restrictions on cable laying as an over-extension of coastal state authority. First, the LOSC vests coastal states with jurisdiction over seabed activities to prevent and control "pollution," among other things.[88] Submarine cables and related repair activities could constitute "pollution" as the LOSC defines that term, but only where they are "likely to result in such deleterious effects as harm to living resources or marine life, hazards to human health, hindrance to marine activities, including fishing and other legitimate uses of the sea, impairment of quality for use of sea water and reduction of amenities".[89] Second, Article 87(c) specifically subjects the freedom to lay

84 Defined in at least one context to be "any area of intertidal or subtidal terrain together with their overlying waters and associated flora, fauna, historical and cultural features, which has been reserved by law or other effective means to protect all or part of the enclosed environment". 17th General Assembly of the IUCN, Resolution 17.38.2(b) (1988), available at: data.iucn.org/dbtw-wpd/edocs/GA-17th-011.pdf.

85 Davenport (n 11), at p. 213; *Submarine Cable Handbook* (n 11), at p. 202; UNEP/ICPC Report (n 7), at p. 53.

86 Van Logchem (n 60), at p. 110 ("While it has been argued that the course of a submarine cable system is not subject to coastal state consent, the other view is that the route of a submarine cable system that passes through areas within functional coastal state jurisdiction can be subject to its approval".); Davenport (n 74), at p. 213 (noting that the LOSC arguably provides a basis for states to designate MPAs in their waters, but that "measures to protect the environment (including the designation of marine protected areas) should not include measures restricting the freedom to lay and repair cables outside of territorial waters").

87 See JA Roach, 'Military Cables' in *Submarine Cable Handbook* (n 11), at p. 344.

88 LOSC (n 1), at Art. 79(2); Art. 208.

89 *Ibid.*, at Art. 1(1)(4); see also Davenport (n 11), at p. 213; *Submarine Cable Handbook* (n 11), at p. 202.

cables to Part VI of the LOSC concerning the continental shelf[90] and whereas Article 79(2) of this section grants jurisdiction to the coastal state to control pollution from pipelines, it subjects cable operations only to "reasonable measures" related to exploration of the continental shelf and exploitation of natural resources.[91] Regarding MPAs specifically, it has been observed that the LOSC provisions relied upon for coastal state authority to establish MPAs in EEZs are non-jurisdictional, and so cannot be used to regulate cable deployment and repair.[92] Finally, it has also been suggested that there is no practical application for environmental measures concerning submarine cables because they have a minimal impact on the seabed.[93] As one commentator notes, "[t]here is no reason why cables and marine protected areas are mutually exclusive,"[94] but this presumes that the former does not unduly burden the latter.

3.3 *On the High Seas*

Under LOSC Article 58, the high seas freedom of laying submarine cables and internationally lawful uses of the sea related thereto applies in EEZs. Subject to LOSC Article 87(c) and Part VI, it also applies on the continental shelf within and, as applicable, beyond the limits of the EEZ. Yet the high seas themselves present a different question. The measures and arguments noted above concern unilateral action by a coastal state in a zone endowed with certain sovereign rights. On the high seas, ships, including those laying cables, are subject to the exclusive jurisdiction of their flag state, "save in exceptional cases expressly provided for in international treaties" or under the LOSC.[95] Action which might impede high seas freedoms must therefore flow from multilateral cooperation by flag states, including any measures affecting submarine cables. The LOSC provides the broad framework for this cooperation by imposing obligations attendant on the exercise of the freedoms of the high seas, including

90 This is in addition to the other conditions on all high seas freedoms under LOSC Article 87, as discussed in the following section.

91 *Submarine Cable Handbook* (n 11), at p. 198; Davenport (n 11), at p. 213.

92 *Submarine Cable Handbook* (n 11), at p. 204 (citing R Lagoni, 'Marine Protected Areas in the Exclusive Economic Zone' in A Kirchner (ed), *International Marine Environmental Law: Institutions, Implementation and Innovations* (Kluwer Law International, The Hague, 2003) 157–167, at p. 160).

93 Davenport (n 11), at p. 213; *Submarine Cable Handbook* (n 11), at pp. 205–207. Although most cable laying and repair activities may be unlikely to constitute pollution within the meaning of LOSC Article 1(1)(4), there may be exceptions. See UNEP/ICPC Report (n 7), at p. 35 (observing that specially designed ploughs were used and rehabilitative activities undertaken in particularly sensitive near-shore areas).

94 Davenport (n 11), at p. 213.

95 LOSC (n 1), at Art. 92; Churchill (n 14), at p. 208.

with respect to the marine environment. These are treated somewhat summarily in the submarine cable-related literature to date, perhaps because no specific guidance has yet been developed as to what these obligations might entail outside of the mining and fishing contexts. That stands likely to change in the face of a new instrument, and so these provisions are worth revisiting.

Section 2 of LOSC Part VII, concerning conservation and management of living resources of the high seas, reaches beyond "pollution" to impose a broader duty on states to cooperate in marine conservation. Much of the text in this section concerns rights and duties with respect to fishing on the high seas, but Article 117 provides more generally that "[a]ll States have the duty to take, or to cooperate with other States in taking, such measures for their respective nationals as may be necessary for the conservation of the living resources of the high seas". Under Article 118 "States shall cooperate with each other in the conservation and management of living resources in the areas of the high seas".

The "freedom to fish," is among the enumerated high seas freedoms laid out by Article 87, and it is explicitly made subject to Section 2. The freedom to lay cables is not similarly restricted, although Article 87(1) makes all high seas freedoms—including cable laying—subject to "the conditions laid down by this Convention and ... other rules of international law," as well as to the requirement that States exercise "due regard for the interests of other States" as set out in Article 87(2). These "conditions" would include those imposed under Section 2 as well Part XII of the LOSC, which deals exclusively with the protection of the marine environment and applies to all activities in all maritime zones. Beyond imposing on states an obligation to prevent, reduce, and control pollution,[96] Article 192 also imposes a more general obligation to "protect and preserve the marine environment" and, in Article 197, to cooperate in that regard.[97] Article 206 further requires that states having "reasonable grounds for believing that planned activities under their jurisdiction or control may cause substantial pollution of or significant and harmful changes to the marine environment" shall "assess the potential effects of [those] activities on the marine environment" and communicate the results of that assessment. This article has been interpreted as a general requirement to carry out EIAs in ABNJ, albeit with an implementation that has been "fragmented—and often

96 LOSC (n 1), at Art. 194.

97 *Ibid.*, Arts. 192, 197; see also Kimball (n 22), at pp. 7, 48; see also R Warner, 'Conserving marine biodiversity in areas beyond national jurisdiction: co-evolution and interaction with the law of the sea' (2014) 1 *Frontiers in Marine Science* art. 6, at p. 2, available at http://journal.frontiersin.org/article/10.3389/fmars.2014.00006/full ("[F]reedom of the high seas is exercised subject to the general obligation to protect and preserve the marine environment in Article 192 of the [LOSC]").

unsatisfying".[98] Furthermore, the LOSC anticipates that its parties may be subject already to "specific obligations ... under special conventions and agreements concluded previously which relate to the protection and preservation of the marine environment and to agreements which may be concluded in furtherance of the general principles set forth in this Convention".[99]

As noted above, Article 87 subjects the freedom of the high seas to "conditions" laid down by the LOSC and to "other rules of international law". Whether an instrument further elaborating the above-referenced provisions would be properly viewed as a "condition" under the LOSC or constitute "other rules," either would suggest that cooperative action by states that is necessary to conserve living marine resources under Article 118, protect and preserve the marine environment under Article 192, or gather information about potentially significant and harmful activities under Article 206, could address submarine cable operations through the new instrument without subverting the freedom to lay cables as reflected in the LOSC.

4 Options for a Path Forward

It is far from a foregone conclusion that the PrepCom will lead to a successful negotiating conference, which in turn will result in a new instrument. Indeed, one of the PrepCom's most intensely contested issues—the institutional framework for implementation—will likely determine much of the relationship between the instrument and submarine cables. It may be that the instrument goes no further than to articulate principles and common objectives, leaving implementation entirely in the hands of states and existing authorities. Or it may empower an international meeting or body to propose and adopt MPAs or carry out EIAs.[100] The framework adopted, and the many subsidiary decisions entailed, will have implications reaching far beyond cable operations, yet even tentative predictions about the structure of implementation can be useful to envision how cables might be addressed. As no formal report of the

98 E Druel, 'Towards a global agreement on environmental impact assessments in areas beyond national jurisdiction' (2013) *IDDRI Policy Briefs* N°01/2013, at p. 2, available at http://www.iddri.org/Publications/Towards-a-global-agreement-on-environmental-impact-assessments-in-areas-beyond-national-jurisdiction.

99 LOSC (n 1), at Art. 237(1).

100 Druel and Gjerde (n 18), at p. 93; J Ardron, E Druel, K Gjerde, K Houghton, J. Rochette and S Unger, 'Advancing Governance of the High Seas' (2013) *IASS Policy Brief* 1/2013, at p. 3, available at http://www.un.org/depts/los/biodiversityworkinggroup/documents/iass-iddri2013.pdf.

PrepCom's deliberations has been prepared, delegations' written submissions and statements in connection with the second session may provide a sense as to where the discussion is headed.

As noted above, two key elements of the package to be negotiated might affect cable operations: (i) the use of area-based management tools (ABMTs), including MPAs; and (ii) EIAs.[101] With respect to ABMTs, including MPAs, several delegations noted in their written submissions to the PrepCom that any measures undertaken to protect portions of the marine environment within ABNJ must be tied to specific conservation objectives,[102] a point also taken up on the floor of the PrepCom itself.[103] A collective understanding seems

101 The discussion of EIAs has extended to also include the potential role of strategic environmental assessments (SEAs) in framing EIAs. See Chair's indicative suggestions of clusters of issues and questions to assist further discussions in the Informal working groups at the second session of the Preparatory Committee (2016), at p. 4, available at http://www.un.org/depts/los/biodiversity/prepcom_files/IWGs_Indictive_Issues_and_Questions.pdf. SEAs are undertaken at a systemic or regional, rather than project, level in an attempt to integrate environmental concerns into "planning and programmatic decisions". N Craik, *The International Law of Environmental Impact Assessment Process, Substance and Integration* (Cambridge University Press, Cambridge, 2008) 156. Because this discussion remains in its early stages and is only a component of the broader discussion concerning EIAs, it is not addressed separately in this article.

102 See Views Expressed by the United States Delegation Related to Certain Key Issues under Discussion at the Second Session of the Preparatory Committee on the Development of an International Legally Binding Instrument under the United Nations Convention on the Law of the Sea on the Conservation and Sustainable Use of Marine Biological Diversity (9 September 2016) (hereinafter "US Submission"), at pp. 3–4, available at http://www.un.org/depts/los/biodiversity/prepcom_files/USA_Submission_of_Views_Expressed.pdf; Costa Rica and Monaco Joint Submission on Marine Protected Areas (31 August 2016), at p. 3, available at http://www.un.org/depts/los/biodiversity/prepcom_files/Costa_Rica_Monaco_BBNJ_Submission_MPAs.pdf; [Pacific Small Island Developing States] Submission to the Second Meeting of the Preparatory Committee for the Development of an international legally binding instrument under the United Nations Convention on the Law of the Sea on the conservation and sustainable use of marine biological diversity of areas beyond national jurisdiction (BBNJ PrepCom) (August 2016) (hereinafter "PSIDS Submission"), at p. 9, available at http://www.un.org/depts/los/biodiversity/prepcom_files/PSIDS_Submission_BBNJ.pdf; Development of an International Legally-Binding Instrument Under the [LOSC] on the Conservation and Sustainable Use of Marine Biological Diversity of Areas Beyond National Jurisdiction (BBNJ Process): Written Submission of the EU and its Member States (25 July 2016) (hereinafter "EU Submission"), at p. 3, available at http://www.un.org/depts/los/biodiversity/prepcom_files/EU&MS_Written_Submission_BBNJ.pdf.

103 IISD, 'Summary of the Second Session of the Preparatory Committee on Marine Biodiversity Beyond Areas of National Jurisdiction: 26 August–9 September 2016' (2016) 25 *Earth Negotiations Bulletin* 118, at pp. 7–8, available at: http://www.iisd.ca/oceans/bbnj/prepcom2/.

to be emerging that such measures must be non-arbitrary and based around demonstrated, or likely values and impacts within the particular area to be protected. Regarding EIAs, divergence remains as to who will be responsible for evaluating an EIA and making decisions about whether proposed activities can proceed. Some delegations have suggested that the instrument could include a list of activities that would be assumed to require an EIA *prima facie*,[104] with others suggesting that certain categories of activities could be excluded in their entirety.[105] However, participants appear to agree that an activity must meet at least some threshold of likely harm before a preceding EIA would be required.[106]

Given what is known about likely submarine cable interactions with the marine environment in ABNJ, it seems quite unlikely that the instrument will become a vehicle for imposing regulatory burdens that could inhibit cable operations on the high seas. Assessments required for activities that do not create "reasonable grounds for believing that" they "may cause substantial pollution of or significant and harmful changes to the marine environment" would nevertheless fall outside the scope of Article 206.[107] Meanwhile, cable regulations within MPAs would be required in the seemingly unusual circumstance that they were needed to fulfil the objectives of a particular MPA. To the extent that such regulations would not be required to protect and preserve the marine environment or to conserve and manage living marine resources in ABNJ, they would fall outside the scope for regulation of cable activities permitted by the LOSC. A pragmatic approach is needed, one balancing the freedom to lay submarine cables and their status as critical infrastructure with due regard for the environment and the broader context of the instrument. The following subsections evaluate three alternatives: (i) an explicit exclusion of cables from the scope of the instrument; (ii) silence in the instrument with respect to cables; and (iii) a cooperative approach whereby cable operations are treated as *prima facie* compliant with the instrument's environmental protections.

---

104 *Ibid.*, p. 9; PSIDS Submission (n 102), at p. 11.

105 The United States suggested in its written submission that certain categories of low-impact activities "may be identified by States ahead of time so that a State can simply confirm that the action is not likely to have a significant impact and does not involve extraordinary circumstances that would make environmental review necessary". US Submission (n 102), at p. 6.

106 IISD (n 103), at p. 10.

107 *Submarine Cable Handbook* (n 11), at p. 201 ("Given the relatively benign nature of submarine cables and cable operations, including the fact that they do not cause significant harm to the marine environment, there are grounds for arguing that there is no obligation to require an EIA [under LOSC Article 206]").

4.1 *Specific Exclusion*

Given the discussion above, an explicit exclusion of submarine cables from the scope of the instrument must be given serious consideration. Cable operations under this option would not be subject to the instrument in any respect, regardless of any significance thresholds, lists, or categories of activities that may be reflected therein. Instead, they would be bound only by the terms of the LOSC. If adopted, this exclusion would provide the cleanest delineation of the relationship between submarine cables and the new instrument, obviating any concern as to how the instrument might be applied to cable operations by states or a multilateral implementing authority. This option has likely attracted the support of industry members for this very reason.[108] But practically and politically, it is an unlikely outcome. First, opening the instrument to the exclusion of any particular activity will open the door to arguments in favour of additional sectoral carve-outs. Although a discussion around submarine cables might be straightforward, negotiators of an overarching agreement are unlikely to be able or willing to evaluate marine environmental impacts across a variety of activities in ABNJ on an industry-wide basis, a complication that can be avoided by refusing to entertain any discussions about specific exclusions. Second, past multilateral decisions concerning submarine cables have resulted in overly restrictive guidance,[109] promulgated without consultation of industry experts. If, as has been argued, these rules indeed provide evidence of a general misunderstanding of the environmental impacts of cable operations, that misunderstanding may extend to the discussions over the instrument. Delegates may be suspicious of any proposed exclusion and industry representatives will be forced to engage throughout the negotiations, identifying states willing to introduce exclusionary text and defend it through to the instrument's conclusion. The ICPC's side event at the second session of the PrepCom may have been intended to lay the groundwork for just such a campaign, but other options considered below may offer paths of less resistance.

Finally, a specific exclusion may appear as a desirable outcome for the submarine cable industry, but a new instrument presents a unique opportunity

108 *See* ICPC Submission note (n 12); The Sargasso Sea Workshop Report (n 10) at p. 4 also makes clear the cable industry's opposition to regulation in ABNJ, noting that "[t]he submarine cable industry does not support the imposition of any requirement for an Environmental Impact Assessment (EIA) for cable laying operations in the Sargasso Sea or any other area which is beyond national jurisdiction. In its view, it is not legally required, there is no clear benefit and the costs of conducting an EIA are potentially onerous". See also Leonard de Juvigny et al. (n 27), at pp. 375–376.

109 See *infra* notes 127–131 and accompanying discussion (regarding the complications surrounding submarine cable guidelines introduced by OSPAR in 2012).

for cooperation that should not be ignored. A governance regime established by the instrument that pragmatically incorporates submarine cables could serve as a standardizing function across jurisdictions, particularly those with overly restrictive regulations.[110] Rather than explicitly disclaim any relationship, the pending negotiations could instead produce consensus around a more flexible approach that could serve as a global model.

4.2 *Silence Regarding Cables*

Another option would have the instrument make no mention of submarine cables at all. This would ensure that submarine cable operations would not be subjected to unnecessary regulation at the instrument's outset and that no immediate action would be required on the part of policymakers. If necessary, industry representatives could encourage negotiators to keep the instrument's text silent in this regard, a task that should not be too difficult if that text only offered general rules or standards rather lists of specific activities as described above. The *status quo* would be preserved unless and until some likelihood of environmental harm from cable operations became apparent.

But there are drawbacks to this approach as well. It would do nothing to address the information gap surrounding cables in ABNJ. Although the data so far suggest that cables are having a limited impact on the marine environment, the lack of knowledge about deep sea ecosystems makes it difficult to say for certain,[111] particularly because efforts to understand the deep sea and identify vulnerable ecosystems in ABNJ are only just beginning to bear fruit. Policymakers waiting for a likelihood of environmental damage to manifest, rather than taking steps to understand and prevent it beforehand, may be leaving both ecosystems and industry at risk—ecosystems from the unknown effects of deep sea activities and industry from a regulatory backlash in the event of an incident. They would also be failing their obligations under the LOSC to be proactive in assessing and preventing likely harm to the marine environment.[112] Furthermore, and as noted, the cable industry will lose the

110 See (nn 83–85); see also *Submarine Cable Handbook*, (n 11), at p. 200 (noting that "the nature of the required information can vary between States and even within a single State" and that particularly onerous requirements can take up to a year to satisfy).

111 Workshop Report, (n 10), at pp. 20–21 (noting "general consensus that the impact of submarine communications cables in the Sargasso Sea was minimal," but "it was also pointed out that it could not be said with certainty that there was no impact, particularly given the data-poor environment in the Sargasso Sea").

112 Not only their obligation to assess activities under LOSC Article 206, but also the requirement in LOSC Article 196 to "take all measures necessary to prevent, reduce and control pollution of the marine environment resulting from the use of technologies under their jurisdiction or control ... to a particular part of the marine environment, which may

opportunity to implement a globally accepted, cooperative framework in ABNJ that could serve as a benchmark for national jurisdictions.

4.3 Prima Facie *Compliance*

A preferred approach would constructively engage the submarine cable industry in the instrument's regime without unduly restricting its operation and growth. One of the participants in the Sargasso Sea workshop, perhaps reaching toward that end, wondered whether it might be helpful for the submarine cable industry to carry out a scientific study on the impact of cables, "which would lay enough groundwork so that further assessments would not be necessary".[113] It was pointed out in response that an industry-sponsored study might not be credible given its source, and that peer-reviewed scientific studies already demonstrate minimal impacts.[114] Yet the underlying idea—that an instructive dialogue with the cable industry could preempt restrictive regulation—could integrate well along the full spectrum of outcomes that now seem possible for the instrument.

This approach would require industry representatives to continue providing information to the PrepCom throughout its work in 2017 and to any negotiating conference convened thereafter. Rather than exclusion, however, their ongoing engagement should aim for recognition that submarine cable activities are in *prima facie* compliance with the instrument's environmental protections, subject to specifically defined exceptions. If the instrument remains silent with respect to cables, those representatives should take the earliest opportunity following its adoption to encourage any implementing authority to issue guidance or a decision recognizing this *prima facie* compliance.[115] Exceptions

---

cause significant and harmful changes thereto" and LOSC Article 198 that "[w]hen a State becomes aware of cases in which the marine environment is in imminent danger of being damaged or has been damaged by pollution, it shall immediately notify other States it deems likely to be affected by such damage, as well as the competent international organizations".

113 Workshop Report (n 10), at p. 23.

114 *Submarine Cable Handbook* (n 11), at pp. 182–183.

115 This scenario presumes that the implementing authority would develop a mechanism for issuing regulatory guidance with respect to particular activities akin to those employed by national, regional, or sectoral administrative organizations. Regional fishery management organizations implement this kind of regulatory oversight over fishing activities. See M Engler Palma, 'Managing Fishing Capacity in International Fisheries: Approaches and Practices in Tuna Regional Fisheries Management Organizations (RFMOs)—Final Report' (2011), *ISSF Technical Report* 2011–06, at pp. 39–42, available at http://www.economistinsights.com/sites/default/files/legacy/ecasia/ISSF-2011-06-Fishing-Capacity-Intl-Fisheries-Aug-2011_combined_0.pdf (collecting and comparing vessel restrictions imposed by tuna RFMOs). There is a broad literature concerning the general growth and

would be those circumstances in which cable activities do create a likelihood of significant harm, perhaps if a cable route were intended to transit a known or likely-to-be vulnerable ecosystem in ABNJ or a route survey encountered such an ecosystem.

Treating an activity as *prima facie* compliant with environmental governance is not without precedent. The International Seabed Authority ("ISA"), the body responsible for regulating mining in ABNJ, has issued regulations adopting a similar approach with respect to mineral prospecting—the search for resource deposits, including estimation of their size, distribution and location. It is less invasive than the subsequent steps of a mining operation, namely "exploration," which includes deposit analysis, equipment testing, and impact and feasibility studies, and "exploitation," or the recovery of resources for commercial purposes.[116] Before exploration can commence, it must be approved through an application to the ISA that includes a "preliminary assessment of the possible impact of the proposed exploration activities on the marine environment" and a "description of proposed measures for the prevention, reduction and control of pollution and other hazards, as well as possible impacts, to the marine environment".[117] The requirements are likely to be even more stringent for exploitation once regulations are finalized.[118] For prospecting, however, the ISA need only receive notice of the identity of the prospecting party and the broad coordinates of the prospecting area.[119] The prospector has a duty to protect the marine environment during its operations and to notify the ISA of any incident "which has caused, is causing or poses a threat of serious

---

acceptance of international administrative rulemaking. For a seminal discussion, see B Kingsbury, N Kirsch and R Steward, 'The Emergence of Global Administrative Law' (2005) 68 *Law and Contemporary Problems* 15–62; see also R Wessell, 'Informal International Law-Making as a New Form of World Legislation?' (2011) 8 *International Organizations Law Review* 253–265.

116 ISBA/18/A/11, Decision of the Assembly of the International Seabed Authority relating to the Regulations on Prospecting and Exploration for Cobalt-rich Ferromanganese Crusts in the Area (27 July 2012) (hereinafter the "Regulations"), Annex, Regulation 1.3 (defining the steps in mining for purposes of cobalt crust exploration—these definitions are carried over to the regulations for other types of mining).

117 *Ibid.*, Regulation 20 (concerning applications for approval of plans of work for exploration in the form of contracts).

118 *Ibid.*, Part IV; R Warner, *Protecting the Oceans Beyond National Jurisdiction: Strengthening the International Law Framework* (Martinus Nijhoff Publishers, Leiden, 2009) 160 ("If a contractor moves to the exploitation stage, the environmental monitoring requirements become even more exacting, obligating the contractor to propose areas to be set aside and used exclusively as impact reference zones and preservation reference zones").

119 Regulations (n 116), at Regulation 3.

harm to the marine environment".[120] The ISA Secretary-General can inform the prospector if its application is deficient or if any portion of its notification includes areas that have been disapproved for exploitation because of the risk of serious environmental harm, but the notification otherwise discharges the prospector's regulatory burden, subject to ongoing reporting requirements.[121]

To facilitate a robust exchange of information, the instrument could adopt a similar framework for submarine cables, with a few important *caveats*. First, cable operations could generally be presumed as permitted without further action by an implementing authority. This is particularly necessary with respect to repairs. Under the ISA's regulations, its Secretary-General has 45 days to act on a prospecting notification,[122] but cable repairs are made on an emergency basis, usually within days or weeks.[123] A delay pending further assessment by an implementing authority would only be needed, where there was a likelihood of substantial pollution or significant harm to the marine environment. Second, in the absence of a direct regulatory *imprimatur*, the implementing authority would rely upon the submarine cable industry to provide ongoing information about its activities, particularly regarding any vulnerable marine areas it encountered. Notification and reporting could be facilitated by a standardized process for sharing the results of surveys, as elaborated below. Finally, the handful of above-referenced studies[124] demonstrating the limited impact of cable operations could be expanded to cover cable exhumation, repair, and recovery. Cables usually require little repair over their lifetime and most cable failures are associated with more intensive activities like fishing or anchoring.[125] It stands to reason that the cumulative environmental impacts of cable repair would either be limited or best viewed as a collateral impact of these other activities. Nevertheless, a better understanding of the impacts of cable maintenance would help to complete the picture of the relationship between cable operations and the marine environment and would be necessary to integrate submarine cables into cumulative impact assessments of all activities and strategic marine planning exercises.

---

120 *Ibid.*, at Regulation 5(3).

121 *Ibid.*, at Regulation 4.

122 *Ibid.*

123 Workshop Report (n 10), at p. 11 ("It is imperative that cable faults are repaired as soon as possible, not only because of the impact of lost service but because each cable acts as a restoration path for traffic on any damaged cable. Repairs are generally considered an emergency situation and are undertaken as expeditiously as possible").

124 See (nn 57, 58).

125 UNEP/ICPC Report (n 7), at p. 45.

In any event, ongoing communication would avoid a controversy similar to the one that enveloped the OSPAR Commission's 2012 Guidelines on Best Environmental Practice in Cable Laying and Operation (the "Guidelines").[126] Through the Convention for the Protection of the Marine Environment of the Northeast Atlantic (the "OSPAR Convention"), fifteen governments cooperate to protect five regions of the Northeast Atlantic, including portions of the high seas.[127] The OSPAR Commission is the regional body established to implement the Convention. Its Guidelines, albeit non-binding, represent a first attempt at multilateral action to address the environmental impacts of cables. Yet they have been critiqued by industry representatives for exaggerating the potential environmental impacts of cables and for proposing formal "Environmental Impact Statements (EIS)" for cable operations in ABNJ.[128] Perhaps most importantly, critics have observed that the Guidelines "were conceived and issued without input from stakeholders in the telecommunication and power cable industries".[129] Instead, they were developed by country representatives to the Commission's Environmental Impact of Human Activities Committee based on a pair of written reports regarding cables' environmental impacts.[130] The result was clearly unsatisfactory from an industry perspective[131] and its value added from an environmental perspective remains to be seen. It highlights, however, the need for a more effective dialogue, one the new instrument is well positioned to facilitate.

126 OSPAR Agreement 2012–2, Guidelines on Best Environmental Practice (BEP) in Cable Laying and Operation (2012) available for download at http://www.ospar.org/documents?d=32910.

127 Convention for the Protection of the Marine Environment of the Northeast Atlantic (Paris, 22 September 1992, in force 25 March 1998) 2354 *UNTS* 67.

128 *Submarine Cable Handbook* (n 11), at p. 210.

129 *Ibid.*, at pp. 210–211.

130 Submarine Cable Handbook (n 11), at p. 208; OSPAR Commission, 'Background Document on Potential Problems Associated with Cables other than those for Oil and Gas Activities' (2008), Pub. No. 370/2008, available at http://www.ospar.org/documents?v=7128; (concluding that in "environmentally sensitive areas physical disturbance, damage, displacement and removal of flora and fauna might turn out to be a significant impact"); OSPAR Commission, 'Assessment of the Environmental Impact of Cables' (2009), Pub. No. 437/2009, available at http://qsr2010.ospar.org/media/assessments/p00437_Cables.pdf (concluding that "[s]ince there is sufficient evidence that the placement and operation of submarine cables may affect the marine environment, the precautionary principle should be applied and appropriate mitigation measures should be taken").

131 *Ibid.*, at pp. 211–212 (noting that while the Guidelines may have been adopted pursuant to the precautionary principle, they "include no cost versus benefit analysis of [OSPAR's] controversial measures".).

4.4 *Options for Industry Collaboration*

Presuming that submarine cable operations are not excluded in their entirety from the scope of a new instrument, cooperation between the industry and an implementing authority can only improve the latter's understanding of cable impacts and enhance its effectiveness. Beyond conversations about regulation, this cooperation can be carried forward in at least two ways: (A) the use of survey data in the management of the marine environment; and (B) collecting data through sensors deployed on cables. It must be noted that these options do not fall strictly within the scope of negotiations contemplated for the new instrument and no provisions of the LOSC would permit imposing them upon the cable industry as a condition of its operations. Yet "a remarkably small portion of the deep sea has been investigated in detail"[132] and the cable industry is part of a very small cadre that is consistently engaged in collecting information about it, even if only for its own purposes. It would be a shame not to leverage this expertise toward a deeper understanding of the marine environment in ABNJ.

4.4.1 Use of Survey Data

Although cable route surveys cover only a narrow portion of the seabed and are not designed for systematic investigation of the marine environment, survey images and data have been used to successfully identify and map benthic habitats.[133] Route survey data do not have sufficient resolution to identify specific biological features, but they can identify larger topographical ones.[134] They may constitute important data points in the sparse universe of information about the seabed in ABNJ and could help in identifying marine areas that could benefit from more focused scientific investigation.

In practice, one approach might be for submarine cable providers or the states flagging their vessels to provide survey data prepared for ABNJ to a global database that could be used to identify potential vulnerable marine ecosystems (VMEs) as they are encountered. For example, the United Nations Food

---

132 J Ingels, MR Clark, M Vecchione, JAA Perez, LA Levin, IG Priede, T Sutton, AA Rowden, CR Smith, M Yasuhara, AK Sweetman, T Soltwedel, R Santos, BE Narayanaswamy, HA Ruhl, K Fujikura, L Amaral Zettler, DOB Jones, AR Gates, P Snelgrove, P Bernal, S Van Gaever, 'Chapter 34F: Open Ocean Deep Sea' in *The First Global Integrated Marine Assessment (First World Ocean Assessment)* (United Nations, New York, 2016), at p. 1, available at http://www.un.org/depts/los/global_reporting/WOA_RPROC/Chapter_36F.pdf.

133 UNEP/ICPC Report (n 7), at p. 21.

134 Personal communication with representatives from the submarine cable industry.

and Agriculture Organization (FAO) VME database,[135] which serves as a global inventory of protective fishing measures, could be expanded to serve as a repository for survey data to assist in the scientific identification of VMEs. In a reciprocal exchange, the implementing authority could notify industry participants of the existence of VMEs identified through other means so that they can be avoided in future desktop surveys. These relationships need not be created pursuant to the instrument itself, but could instead evolve through letters of agreement between an implementing authority and industry representatives, the flag states of industry vessels, or the states of nationality of the cable owners. Such correspondence could set forth the method and timing for providing data, the parties with access to the database, and rules concerning public disclosure. In this way, survey data would be communicated in the ordinary course of business to a single entity, avoiding the need to reach an accommodation with multiple management bodies.

A challenge would be to protect the proprietary interests of submarine cable companies in their survey data. Industry representatives have expressed their reluctance to release such data publicly,[136] but survey data are unlike fishery data, which retain their relevance season after season and so are closely guarded by competitive fishermen. In contrast, a deployed cable will be marked on publicly available charts, diminishing confidentiality concerns surrounding its associated survey.[137] It may be appropriate, to incorporate a delay into either the submission of any survey data to the implementing authority or their broader publication in order to ensure that the interests of cable owners are accommodated.

Several other approaches used to address confidentiality in multilateral fora might also be employed. The first is reducing data resolution. For example, among regional fishery management organizations (RFMOs), the international entities responsible for regulating fishing for shared fish stocks, data on catch amounts and locations are critical to the effective management of the fishery.

---

135 FAO, Vulnerable Marine Ecosystems Database, http://www.fao.org/in-action/vulnerable-marine-ecosystems/vme-database/en/; see also FAO Doc. FIPS/R1093, Report of the FAO Workshop on the Global Database for Vulnerable Marine Ecosystems, Rome, 7–9 May 2014, at p. 25 (noting a proposal that the FAO database could extend "to identifying areas of overlap between deep-sea bottom fisheries and predicted distributions of corals and sponges" but that this would "move the VME DataBase into a rather speculative area, especially as predicted distributions are currently approximate and at rather coarse resolutions").

136 See Evans (n 41), at pp. 32–33.

137 Personal communication with representatives from the submarine cable industry. These conversations have, however, generated conflicting views on the ongoing need for confidentiality once a cable is deployed.

But because they are a closely guarded secret, certain RFMOs have determined that any operational data on catch and effort that they receive will only be released to the public once aggregated to, for example, a level of three vessels or more.[138] With respect to submarine cable surveys, combining survey data would not be useful, but reducing its resolution might be. Further discussion between industry representatives and experts may determine whether a particular resolution will provide useful management information and be suitable for public disclosure. An alternative might be to provide only a survey's relevant portions showing areas of interest. An implementing authority could then take any precautionary management action that it deemed necessary, including initiating further study.

Whether a survey is published at a lower resolution, in portions, or while it is retained for a period by an implementing authority, confidentiality protections adopted within the instrument's implementing framework could protect the data received. RFMOs may again provide a useful signpost, as many have adopted detailed confidentiality requirements and imposed strict data control rules on their secretariats and participants, including for civil society observers.[139] Similarly, the ISA's regulations on prospecting require the Secretary-General to "ensure the confidentiality of all data and information" received, although "data and information relating to the protection and preservation of the marine environment, in particular those from environmental monitoring programmes," are not considered confidential.[140]

Survey data provided to an implementing authority would assist in the execution of its duty to facilitate cooperation in the protection and preservation of the marine environment and should not constitute "marine scientific research" subject to a public disclosure requirement under the LOSC.[141] As others have noted, cable surveys are undertaken for the sole purpose of identifying

138 See, e.g., Inter-American Tropical Tuna Commission (IATTC) Resolution C-13-05, Data confidentiality policy and procedures (June 2013) available at http://www.iattc.org/PDFFiles2/Resolutions/C-13-05-Procedures-for-confidential-data.pdf (hereinafter "IATTC Rules"); IATTC Secretariat, 'Progress made in respect of the Course of Actions for RFMOs from the Joint Meeting of Tuna RFMOs in Kobe' available at http://www.tuna-org.org/Documents/TRFMO2/10%20ANNEX%205.3.1%20eng.pdf (explaining that "[c]atch and effort data in the public domain must be aggregated to a level of three vessels or more").

139 See, e.g., *ibid.*; see also Indian Ocean Tuna Commission Resolution 12/02, Data confidentiality policies and procedures (2012) available at: file:///C:/Users/acf280/Downloads/iotc_cmm_12-02_en.pdf.

140 Regulations, (n 116), at Regulation 7(1).

141 LOSC (n 1), at Art. 249(1)(e) ("States and competent international organizations when undertaking marine scientific research in the exclusive economic zone or on the continental shelf of a coastal State shall ... [ensure] that the research results are made

a cable route.[142] That a cable route's survey data may have value beyond this initial purpose would not change the fact that the data were collected incidentally to the exercise of a high seas freedom. Any survey data transmitted to the implementing authority should consequently remain confidential unless or until public disclosure would not jeopardize the cable project.

4.4.2 Cables as Platforms for Ocean Observation

The International Telecommunication Union (ITU), the Intergovernmental Oceanographic Commission of the United Nations Educational, Scientific and Cultural Organization (UNESCO/IOC), and the World Meteorological Organization (WMO) have together established a Joint Task Force (JTF) to investigate the use of submarine telecommunications cables for ocean and climate monitoring and disaster warning.[143] As envisioned by the JTF, these sensors would have two uses: the first would be to monitor seismic activity in real time to provide early warnings of natural disasters like tsunamis. They could also be adapted to provide data about the ocean climate, including temperature, salinity, and pressure, observations which could be used to better understand and respond to environmental threats resulting from climate change. As the JTF noted in its report, "none of the world's telecommunication cable systems possess even the simplest sensory instrumentation to monitor anything other than their own internal state-of-health".[144] According to the same report "[t]echnological advances have made it possible to integrate basic sensors with repeaters on submarine telecommunication cables at intervals of about 50–70 km, at an estimated installation cost of 5–10% of the total cost of system deployment".[145] Importantly, however, these estimates assume that such sensors will be deployed along the entire length of a cable. Although companies have been exploring the inclusion of sensor ports as part of a cable's

internationally available through appropriate national or international channels, as soon as practicable").

142 U Leanza, 'Marine Scientific Research and the Right to Lay Submarine Cables and Pipelines' in N Martínez Gutiérrez (ed), *Serving the Rule of International Maritime Law: Essays in Honour of Professor David Joseph Attard* (Routledge, Abingdon, 2010) 129–135, at p. 134; Davenport (n 11), at p. 210.

143 ITU/WMO/UNESCO, IOC Joint Task Force, http://www.itu.int/en/ITU-T/climatechange/task-force-sc/Pages/default.aspx.

144 JTF, *The scientific and societal case for the integration of environmental sensors into new submarine telecommunication cables* (2014) 1, available at http://www.itu.int/dms_pub/itu-t/opb/tut/T-TUT-ICT-2014-03-PDF-E.pdf.

145 *Ibid.*

proposed business case,[146] at this stage, the critical barrier to their deployment in scientific studies has been securing funding for pilot projects.[147]

The possibility of incorporating environmental sensors into submarine cables was raised at the Sargasso Sea Workshop, where participants cited cost concerns and technical challenges to suggest that that the decision to deploy sensors on commercial cables should remain "subject to the business models and decisions of the cable owners".[148] They also noted "that in areas under national jurisdiction such as the EEZ/continental shelf, submarine communications cables which also have marine data collection capabilities could be regulated as Marine Scientific Research and thus subject to coastal State and landlocked State consent".[149] As was acknowledged in the Workshop, however, marine scientific research in ABNJ is among the freedoms of the high seas enshrined in Article 87.[150] Although research in the seabed in ABNJ must be carried out "exclusively for peaceful purposes and for the benefit of mankind as a whole" pursuant to Article 143 of the LOSC, that article suggests that there might be public disclosure requirements associated with the data obtained,[151] but not grounds to regulate cable deployment.[152] Nor should the conduct of research in ABNJ subject a cable to regulation in other jurisdictions

146 See P Wilton, 'SubPartners to build sensor overlay on Pacific Ocean cable' (28 October 2013) *COMMSDAY.COM*, http://www.commsday.com/commsday-australasia/subpartners-to-build-sensor-overlay-on-pacific-ocean-cable. An industry executive explains that "this isn't so much a leasing play or [something] to make money out of for general consumption" but will instead make a system "more attractive to educational and research institutions, and particularly government entities as well—who see … this added side benefit of monitoring of the Pacific and the region in general".). No such effort has yet gone forward.

147 Personal communication with representatives from the submarine cable industry.

148 Workshop Report (n 10) at p. 29.

149 *Ibid.*, at p. 25.

150 See also LOSC (n 1), Art. 257 ("All States, irrespective of their geographical location, and competent international organizations have the right, in conformity with this Convention, to conduct marine scientific research in the water column beyond the limits of the exclusive economic zone").

151 *Ibid.*, Art. 143(3)(c) (calling on States to promote international cooperation in marine scientific research in the Area by "effectively disseminating the results of research and analysis when available, through the Authority or other international channels when appropriate") and Art. 244 (pursuant to which states are required to "make available … knowledge resulting from marine scientific research").

152 This presumes that the cables are indeed being deployed for environmental research and not for military applications, in which case they would raise much deeper questions about whether they were being used for "peaceful purposes" or whether they could indeed be classified as "marine scientific research".

where it might fall. After all, it is the instrumentation deployed with the cable that is carrying out the research, not the cable itself.[153]

Even absent the cost and technical issues associated with cable-based sensors, it is reasonable that cable owners should continue to make decisions about using their cables for research. Meanwhile, the instrument and its implementing framework could provide global coordination to collect and aggregate the data needed for successful environmental management in ABNJ. It could establish a centralized repository for data to facilitate cooperative identification of research opportunities and monitoring and analysis of ecosystems.[154] It could leverage existing collaborative tools for pooling data like the Intergovernmental Oceanographic Commission's Global Ocean Observing System[155] or the Ocean Biogeographic Information System,[156] or create new ones as needed. Facilitating cooperation would not only foster the collection of more useful data from ABNJ, it could also pave the way toward collaborative funding and research. Creating "common pools" of resources and results has already been contemplated with respect to another element of the "package" of issues to be negotiated, namely access and benefit sharing of marine genetic resources.[157] It is a concept that could be usefully extended here.

---

153 Compare Leonard de Juvigny et al. (n 27), at p. 377 (suggesting that the installation of environmental sensors would "deprive submarine cables of their priority status in non-ABNJ waters, because the Marine Scientific Research regime under the LOSC is significantly more restricted than cable operations").

154 NC Ban, SM Maxwell, DC Dunn, AJ Hobday, NJ Bax, J Ardron, KM Gjerde, ET Game, R Devillers, DM Kaplan, PK Dunstan, PN Halpin and RL Pressey, 'Better integration of sectoral planning and management approaches for the interlinked ecology of the open oceans' (2014) 49 *Marine Policy* 127–136, at p. 133.

155 "IOC-GOOS" is "a permanent global system for observations, modelling and analysis of marine and ocean variables to support operational ocean services worldwide. GOOS provides accurate descriptions of the present state of the oceans, including living resources; continuous forecasts of the future conditions of the sea for as far ahead as possible, and the basis for forecasts of climate change". GOOS, 'What is GOOS?', http://www.ioc-goos.org/index.php?option=com_content&view=article&id=12&Itemid=26&lang=en.

156 "OBIS" provides a "portal or gateway to many datasets containing information on where and when marine species have been recorded. The datasets are integrated so you can search them all seamlessly by species name, higher taxonomic level, geographic area, depth, and time; and then map and find environmental data related to the locations". OBIS, About OBIS, http://www.iobis.org/about/index.

157 A Broggiato, 'Fair and equitable sharing of benefits from the utilization of marine genetic resources in areas beyond national jurisdiction: Bridging the gaps between science and policy' (2014) 49 *Marine Policy* 176–185.

5 Conclusions

With the PrepCom slated to convene twice again in 2017, it remains far too soon to say how the negotiations will play out. But it is conceivable that a negotiating conference could be convened to conclude an instrument as early as 2018. Once negotiations are underway, submarine cable operations will be only one of many activities in ABNJ facing implications. In addition to a raft of existing activities, the instrument will also need to address emerging activities, like high seas aquaculture[158] and offshore power generation,[159] with varying degrees of potential to affect biodiversity and the marine environment. How the instrument responds to submarine cables will chart a pathway for these other activities, particularly those that are likely to be similarly benign. In this way, the submarine cable industry can act as a critical first-mover in developing an efficient and effective regulatory regime. It has every incentive to do so. By setting a cooperative precedent, it can ensure that any overlap between the instrument and cable operations is fair and consistent with the principles of the LOSC, including the freedom to lay cables in ABNJ.

158 Presentation by C Goudey, SH Page and B O'Hanlon to World Aquaculture Society—Aquaculture America 2009, 'Sea Trials of a Self-Propelled Offshore Sea Cage' (Seattle, 18 February 2009) at p. 3, available at https://www.was.org/documents/MeetingPresentations/AA2009/AA2009_0311.pdf (explaining reasons for advancing aquaculture "into the high seas").

159 M Kanellos, 'FAQ: Energy on the high seas' (15 August 2009) *CNET*, available at http://news.cnet.com/FAQ-Energy-on-the-high-seas/2100-11392_3-6202562.html.

CHAPTER 8

International Legal Obligations for Environmental Impact Assessment and Strategic Environmental Assessment in the Arctic Ocean

Gunnar Sander
The Norwegian College of Fishery Science, University of Tromsø, Norway

Abstract

Environmental impact assessment (EIA) and strategic environmental assessment (SEA) are procedures for the prior assessment of impacts of proposed developments before decisions are taken. Customary law and most international agreements relevant for the Arctic Ocean are unspecific about assessment tools and content. The Espoo Convention and its SEA Protocol are the only specialised instruments available. They do not cover marine activities well, and not all the Arctic Ocean coastal states are parties. Other problems in the assessment regime are related to uneven geographical and sectoral coverage. Weaknesses may be addressed both globally in the negotiations on a new instrument under the Law of the Sea Convention (LOSC) on biodiversity beyond national jurisdiction, and in a regional process under the Arctic Council. Important improvements would be the creation of a more specific default mechanism for prior assessment of marine activities and closer linkage of assessments with substantive goals.

Keywords

environmental assessment – environmental impact assessment (EIA) – strategic environmental assessment (SEA) – law of the sea – Arctic Ocean – Arctic governance

1 Introduction

The expansion of human activities in the oceans has led to an increased focus on the use of assessments as tools for protecting the environment. This article examines what obligations exist for states under international law to conduct environmental impact assessment (EIA) and strategic environmental

 | DOI:10.1163/9789004391703_010

assessment (SEA) in the Arctic Ocean (AO).* The analysis considers the degree to which obligations are legally binding and how specific they are in designating EIA or SEA, with definite requirements for the assessment process and content. The second issue raised is the identification of weaknesses in the legal framework. Analysing the obligations for a specific ocean reveals the interplay between different agreements. This is also relevant for discussions regarding other oceans, although the constellation of regional instruments will differ. The status of EIA and SEA is relevant for the processes that may lead to a draft implementation agreement under the Law of the Sea Convention (LOSC)[1] and for a regional Arctic initiative. The global process is the result of a decades-long discussion about marine biodiversity in areas beyond national jurisdiction (ABNJ).[2] In June 2015, the UN General Assembly (UNGA) adopted a resolution setting out a decision to develop an international legally binding instrument under the LOSC on this issue.[3] It established a preparatory committee to make recommendations on the elements of a draft text, which is to address a package of topics including "environmental impact assessments". Regionally, the Arctic Council ministerial meeting in April 2015 decided to establish a task force to "assess future needs for a regional seas programme or other mechanism, as appropriate, for increased collaboration in Arctic marine areas".[4] Assessments are vital for regional ocean collaboration, and most Regional Seas

* Acknowledgements: I delivered a first analysis of this topic in 2009 as a master's thesis to the LL.M. programme in the law of the sea at the University of Tromsø (UiT). My employer at that time, the Norwegian Polar Institute, generously gave me time to write the thesis. I am grateful to Erik Molenaar for good supervision during that process, and for comments on this updated and revised version. Aline Jaeckel was helpful in correcting my misunderstandings about the ISA. I also thank colleagues at UiT for good discussions and several reviewers who have helped me to improve the language.

1 United Nations Convention on the Law of the Sea (Montego Bay, 10 December 1982, in force 16 November 1994) 1833 *UNTS* 396.

2 Documents from the UN Working Group that was the main forum for the discussions are available at http://www.un.org/depts/los/biodiversityworkinggroup/biodiversityworking group.htm.

3 UNGA A/RES/69/292: Development of an international legally-binding instrument under the United Nations Convention on the Law of the Sea on the conservation and sustainable use of marine biological diversity of areas beyond national jurisdiction. Available at http://www .un.org/depts/los/general_assembly/general_assembly_resolutions.htm.

4 Iqaluit Declaration 2015, made on the occasion of the Ninth Ministerial meeting of the Arctic Council, para. 53 and Senior Arctic Officials' Report to Ministers, pp. 77–78. Available at http://www.arctic-council.org/index.php/en/document-archive/category/604-decla ration-sao-report.

Conventions have special provisions for EIA.[5] The Arctic Council previously has urged that any future exploitation of natural resources in the Arctic must be based on thorough impact assessments and has identified the need to consider a set of operational guidelines for assessing the impact of projects, plans and programmes in the Arctic.[6]

The AO, as discussed here, will be the central AO and its nearest adjacent seas. It comprises the maritime zones of five coastal states (Areas within National Jurisdiction—AWNJ), as well as the deep seabed and a high seas area (i.e., ABNJ). The discussion is restricted to assessments of activities *within* the AO. This excludes transboundary assessments of activities located *outside*, even when they cause important impacts on the AO.[7] For the same reason, the focus is on the AO coastal states.

When EIA and SEA are jointly discussed, they are collectively referred to as environmental assessment (EA). The first section provides an overview of EA, their generic structure and what these tools may realistically achieve. The second reviews the EA provisions in international law that are relevant to the AO. The third provides an interpretation across these instruments. This is followed by an analysis of what may be perceived as legal weaknesses. Finally, a conclusion that also contains some reflections for further deliberation in the ongoing processes is offered.

2 Environmental Assessments and Their Roles

2.1 *Types of Assessments and Terminology*

Since the introduction of EIA in the US in 1969, related tools have proliferated globally. A common characteristic is the anticipation of the future impacts of proposed developments. For this discussion, it is useful to distinguish between:

- The values and hence the types of impacts that are in focus.
- The level of development assessed: projects or strategies.
- Whether the process accounts for impacts beyond the national territory.

5 See texts in appendix 1 in N. Craik, *The International Law of Environmental Impact Assessment. Process, Substance and Integration* (Cambridge University Press, Cambridge, 2008). The assessment obligations in most Regional Seas Conventions are restricted to AWNJ because of the geographical scope of the Conventions.

6 Senior Arctic Officials' Report to Ministers, April 2009, section 3.2 (adopted by the Ministers). Available at http://www.arctic-council.org/index.php/en/document-archive/category/53-final-reports-and-statements.

7 Especially activities leading to climate change and long-range transport of pollutants; please refer to the Arctic Council's assessments addressing these topics, available at http://www.amap.no/.

Environmental assessment focuses on the "environment", usually understood as covering at least biophysical conditions. However, it is also common to incorporate human health, cultural heritage and, sometimes, social or economic issues related to changes in biophysical conditions. It is therefore necessary to identify carefully what each instrument covers.

Impact assessment is a generic term for assessments covering any type of impact. It includes a variety of specialised tools, for example, focusing on health, social issues or risks, and integrated assessments incorporating all relevant impacts in the same process. Each may have its own tradition and even legal basis. However, all share the same basic traits and represent further development and application of EIA to a wider set of issues and concerns.[8]

In the US and elsewhere, assessments first took the form of EIAs focused on concrete projects. This revealed shortcomings. At the project level, the discussion is about how to develop. The possibilities for better solutions can be severely restricted if decisions already have been made on the more fundamental questions of why, what and where to develop. This led to a call for the "up-streaming" of environmental considerations into strategic initiatives. Furthermore, it was pointed out that it is inappropriate to assess cumulative or larger-scale impacts based on piecemeal project-based assessments. These issues were important motives for the introduction of *SEA of policies, plans and programmes*[9] as a separate tool, gradually with its own legal base.[10] Together, SEA and EIA can ensure a tier of assessments throughout all stages of development.

A new development initiative may lead to extraterritorial impacts beyond the state of origin. The assessment of impacts abroad requires knowledge about the affected environment and extensive collaboration across borders. To ensure that affected states have a right to be involved in a satisfactory manner, special tools for *transboundary EA* have been elaborated, mostly at the project

8 *Impact Assessment and Project Appraisal* (vol. 30(1), 2012) contains review articles regarding EIA, SEA, policy assessment, social impact assessment, health impact assessment and sustainability assessment. See particularly RK Morgan, 'Environmental impact assessment: the state of the art' at pp. 5–14; M Tetlow and M Hanusch, 'Strategic environmental assessment: the state of the art' at pp. 15–24. These reviews are discussed further in J Pope, A Bond, A Morrison-Saunders and F Retief, 'Advancing the theory and practice of impact assessment: Setting the research agenda' (2013) 41 *Environmental Impact Assessment Review* 1–9.

9 There is no uniform definition of these terms, although policies are commonly regarded as the highest and most politicized level.

10 S Marsden, *Strategic Environmental Assessment in International and European Law. A Practitioner's Guide* (Earthscan, London, 2008).

level. These are domestic processes that lead to decisions in the states of origin, but are conducted in collaboration with affected states and, sometimes, non-state parties. Transboundary assessments may also account for impacts on global commons.[11]

Most legal instruments only require an assessment of the final proposal for a policy, plan, programme or project. I will refer to this as EA in a strict legal sense. This is different from planning, where continuous consideration of impacts is common in order to develop the best final proposal. It also distinguishes EA from state-of-the-environment reports. As long as such reports do not end up with concrete proposals for actions, they are not covered by legal EA requirements. However, proposals for action plans may require SEA, or eventually EIA.

2.2 *Process and Content*

When the United Nations Environment Programme (UNEP) adopted "Goals and Principles of EIA" in 1987,[12] it could build on extensive national experience and thus became the first elaborate international instrument on this subject. In a concise and generic fashion, it summarised what had become a common understanding of EIA (Fig. 1):

- Screening: The determination of whether an activity is likely to significantly affect the environment and, therefore, is subject to an EIA. Lists of activities, areas or resources with guiding criteria can assist such decisions. An initial examination may also be used.
- Scoping: The determination of the content of the assessment. UNEP only specified the identification of the environmental topics that should be studied. However, it is common for scoping to address a broad range of issues about the assessment process, often with input from stakeholders, and to conclude with terms of reference for the assessment.
- Assessment of impacts and reporting: The report should contain a description of the proposed activity and practical alternatives to it, the baseline of environmental conditions and the likely impacts of the alternatives (*ex ante* prediction). It should address uncertainties and knowledge gaps, and measures to mitigate adverse impacts. A non-technical summary should communicate the findings.

11 K Bastmeijer and T. Koivurova (eds.), *Theory and Practice of Transboundary Environmental Impact Assessment* (Martinus Nijhoff Publishers, Leiden, 2008).

12 UNEP Council Decision 14/25, Environmental Impact Assessment, 17 June 1987; available at http://www.unep.org/Documents.Multilingual/Default.asp?DocumentID=100&ArticleID=1658.

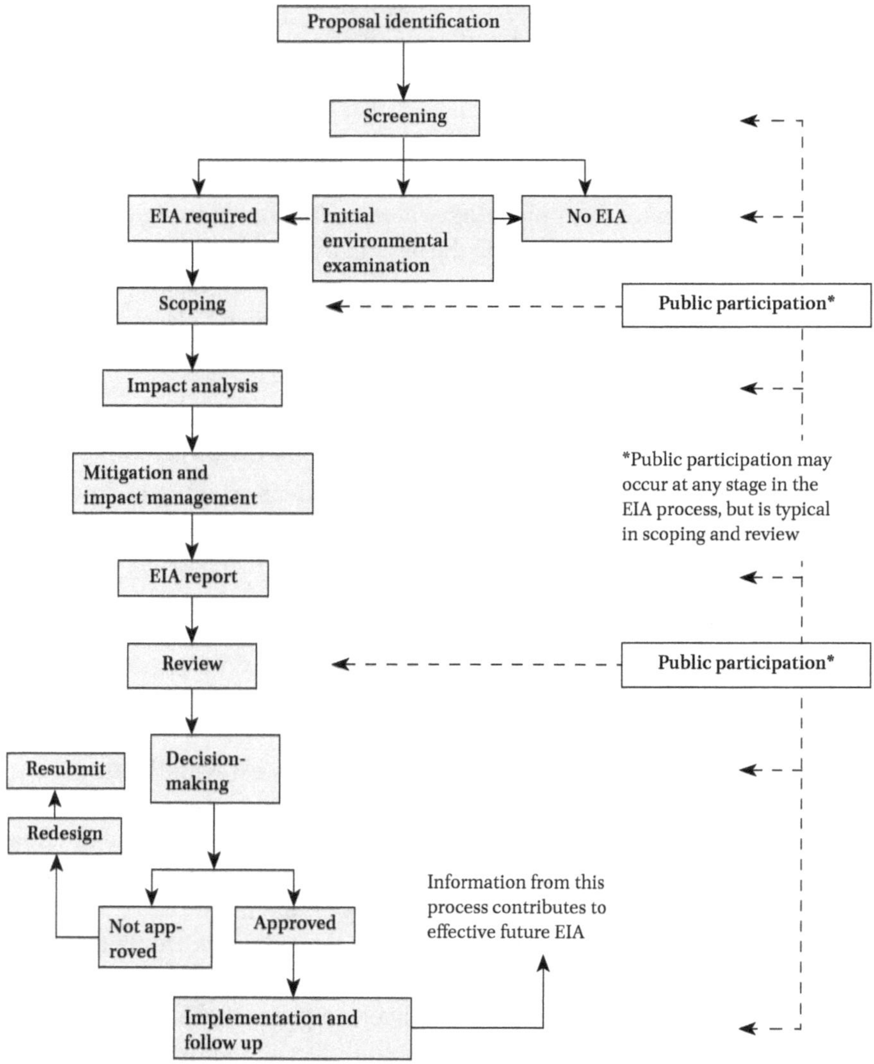

FIGURE 1 The EIA process (based on UNEP)

- Review and public participation: An impartial examination of the information should be undertaken prior to the decision. Government agencies, the public, experts and interest groups should have an appropriate opportunity to comment.
- Final decision: Decisions authorising a potentially harmful activity should not be taken before the EIA allows the effects to be fully taken into account. The decision should be in writing, be reasoned and explain how it would try

to prevent, reduce or mitigate damage to the environment. Interest groups should have access to the documents.

- Follow-up: The activity and its effects on the environment should also be monitored appropriately after the decision (*ex post* evaluation).

SEA is more diverse. It can have different roles and can be seen as an overarching concept for a family of related tools. The traditional approach was to extend the EIA methods to strategic initiatives. Later developments focused on the strategic role of SEA in shaping and formulating strategic initiatives as a part of the planning process. With its ability to integrate environmental, social and economic considerations, SEA has broad potential as a tool for sustainable development.[13]

2.3 *What May Environmental Assessment Achieve?*

There are different theoretical assumptions about the purpose and role of EA and thus different views on what to look for in research on the performance of EA systems.[14] At least three perspectives can be distinguished.

One reason for the introduction of EIA in the 1970s was to ensure that environmental impacts are considered on a par with other types of impacts before decisions are made. With EIA systems in place in almost all UN member states, the situation today is radically different. Environmental data are sampled, and assessments are routinely made and brought to the attention of decision-makers. This has been characterised as a wide-ranging environmental reform.[15]

The immediate "so what" question is whether this mainstreaming of environmental information has changed the outcome of decisions in a more sustainable direction. The rationalistic assumption was that it would do so by providing neutral facts to decision-makers. However, assessments may be conducted in separate processes that do not necessarily feed well into planning and decision-making, and facts are just a part of what influences decisions. Even though there may be a legal requirement to review the EA results, there is usually no obligation on decision-makers to give specific weight to the environmental information or to restrain decisions so that harmful effects are

---

13 Tetlow and Hanusch (n 8); B Sadler, R Aschemann, J Dusik, T Fischer, MR Partidario and R Vereem (eds.), *Handbook of Strategic Environmental Assessment* (Earthscan, London, 2010).

14 Usually, the term "EA effectiveness" is used. See particularly Morgan in (n 8) for an overview.

15 J Holder, *Environmental Assessment. The Regulation of Decision Making* (Oxford University Press, Oxford, 2004).

avoided.[16] Thus, EA is a procedural legal requirement; EA laws can prohibit uninformed, but not unwise, decisions.[17] This is different from substantive and prescriptive regulations setting environmental standards. Therefore, it should be no surprise that studies of different EA systems find very mixed results regarding the extent to which assessments lead to rejection or modification of potentially harmful developments.[18]

EA may also exert influence more indirectly. Requiring the collection and consideration of environmental information can increase environmental awareness and learning. This can create more subtle changes, such as a new understanding of environmental issues, as well as changes in values and norms and in organisational structures and routines. Public participation is crucial in such an understanding of EA, as it can open up a field for debate and collective reflection. In the longer run, this may create the support needed to address severe environmental problems and have a gradual, transformative effect on society and decisions.

3 International Environmental Assessment Obligations Relevant for the Arctic Ocean

EA is contained in all sources of international law. This section reviews these sources as a basis for analysing the legal status across the instruments in the next section. The focus on the AO implies my exclusion of several instruments that appear in general discussions of EA in international law.[19]

16 S Jay, C Jones, P Slinn and C Wood, 'Environmental Impact Assessment: Retrospect and Prospect' (2007) 27 (4) *Environmental Impact Assessment Review* 287–300.

17 US Supreme Court decision, referred to in Craik (n 5), at pp. 4–8.

18 Jay *et al.* (n 16) at pp. 290–294; Tetlow and Hanusch (n 8) at pp. 18–20; Pope *et al.* (n 8) at pp. 5–6.

19 Compared to T Koivurova, *Environmental Impact Assessment in the Arctic: A Study of International Legal Norms* (Ashgate, Aldershot, 2002) at pp. 374–92, I have excluded treaties on land and watersheds and those applicable only in Arctic sub-regions. European Union (EU) law has limited relevance because Greenland is not a member, and Svalbard is excepted from the European Economic Area. Instruments on climate change and the Madrid Protocol to the Antarctic Treaty are excluded because of their geographical scope, although the latter is a detailed regulation with several provisions highly relevant for ABNJ.

The review considers the degree to which assessment obligations are legally binding and identifies the specific processes and content they require. Building on Craik,[20] I distinguish between three levels of specificity:

1. *Explicit provisions of EIA or SEA*: These can either contain elaborate requirements for assessment procedures and content or be less elaborate, although still explicitly designating EIA or SEA.
2. *Assessment obligations*: There is a requirement to "assess" or similar wording, but the tool is open towards EIA, SEA or other approaches.
3. *Implicit or indirect assessment obligations*: The obligation cannot be met without some sort of prior examination, although this is not explicitly required.

3.1 *Legal Sources with Low Specificity*

3.1.1 General Principles

Several principles of international environmental law are relevant for understanding the role and structure of EA.[21] They provide basic norms that also can support interpretation, but need further codification in law in order to be operational.

The most fundamental is the *no-harm principle*, which is a rule of customary international law.[22] It implies an obligation on states to act with due diligence by introducing policies and legislation that prevent or reduce the risk of significant transboundary harm to other states and ABNJ. Such instruments must have the ability to anticipate and evaluate harm at an early stage. The duty of due diligence also entails an evolving standard of regulations, often referred to as "best practical means" or "best environmental practices".

States have a well-established *duty to cooperate*. This includes notifying potentially affected States of relevant information in case of significant transboundary harm and consulting with them.[23] Together with the no-harm principle, this provides the fundamental rationale for transboundary assessments. Norms for transboundary conduct can also be deduced from

20 Craik (n 5).

21 General principles of law and EA are discussed in Koivurova (n 19); Craik (n 5); SA Atapattu, *Emerging Principles of International Environmental Law* (Transnational Publishers, Ardsley, 2006); P Birnie, A Boyle and C Redgewell, *International Law and the Environment* (Oxford University Press, Oxford, 2009).

22 Birnie *et al.* (n 21) at pp. 137–52; Atapattu (n 21) at pp. 273–7 and 290–300; Craik (n 5) at pp. 59–68.

23 Rio Declaration on Environment and Development, Principle 19. Available at http://www.unep.org/Documents.Multilingual/Default.asp?documentid=78&articleid=1163.

the *principle of non-discrimination* between domestic and external harm, and the *principle of equal access* to information and public participation in other states.

The no-harm principle is also an indirect rationale for domestic EA: a state acting with due diligence must have a general system for prior assessment that screens all developments for potential transboundary harm. Domestic commitments are also supported by states' wider duties to protect environmental values that used to be seen as internal affairs, at least regarding issues of "common concern".[24] However, EIA itself has gradually evolved as a principle in international law, expressed in unqualified and wide terms in Rio Principle 17: "Environmental impact assessment, as a national instrument, shall be undertaken for proposed activities that are likely to have a significant adverse impact on the environment and are subject to a decision of a competent national authority".

The increased emphasis on *public participation* in environmental decision-making as found, for example, in Rio Principle 10, also has a bearing on EA systems. So does the *precautionary approach or principle*. Its implication for EAs is more straightforward than the widely debated topic of precautionary decision-making: the EA must provide information about the degree of uncertainty in its predictions of impacts. This is a basis for deliberations on the need for precaution in later decisions. Finally, it should be mentioned that *the principle of integration* between environmental protection and the development process has been used particularly as a mandate for SEA.[25]

3.1.2 Customary Law

SEA has not attained the status of customary law, but there has been considerable support for the view that EIA is required, at least when impacts are transboundary.[26] In 2010, the International Court of Justice (ICJ) confirmed that "it may now be considered a requirement under general international law to undertake an environmental impact assessment where there is a risk that the proposed industrial activity may have a significant adverse impact in a transboundary context, in particular, on a shared resource".[27] In 2011, an advisory opinion of the International Tribunal of the Law of the Sea (ITLOS)

24 Atapattu (n 21) at p. 7; Birnie *et al.* (n 21) at pp. 128–30.

25 Craik (n 5) at p. 156.

26 Atapattu (n 21) at p. 347; Birnie *et al.* (n 21) at pp. 166–70.

27 *Pulp Mills on the River Uruguay* (*Argentina* v. *Uruguay*), International Court of Justice (ICJ), 20 April 2010, para. 204. Available at http://www.icj-cij.org/docket/index.php?p1=3&p2=3&case=135&p3=4.

interpreted this as also including ABNJ.[28] However, the duty to assess when the impacts are purely domestic was not an issue in these cases. Opinions differ about whether this is also a customary obligation.[29]

The ICJ also stated that "it is for each State to determine (...) the specific content of the EIA required in each case (...)".[30] This illustrates the problem with defining customary EA obligations: "Whether the norm has achieved customary status is of secondary importance where the norm itself lacks the necessary detail to influence behaviour."[31] It is therefore better to scrutinise treaty obligations in search for more specific content.

3.2 *Environmental Assessment Provisions in International Treaties*

The review begins with specialised EA instruments before turning to the law of the sea, biodiversity and sectoral applications.

3.2.1 The 1991 Espoo Convention[32]

The Espoo Convention is the only international convention that has EA as its primary purpose, and it has set the standard for numerous other instruments. Its objective is to "prevent, reduce and control significant adverse transboundary environmental impact from proposed activities".[33] States must establish a national EIA system for implementation.[34] In this way, the minimum requirements for domestic EIA are also defined. The Espoo Convention covers the classical transboundary situation between state parties.[35] This excludes ABNJ, both as affected areas and as the origin of harm. All the Arctic coastal states have signed the treaty, but Russia and the US are not parties.

---

28 Responsibilities and Obligations of States Sponsoring Persons and Entities With Respect to Activities in the Area, Advisory Opinion, 1 February 2011, ITLOS Reports 2011, para. 148. Available at https://www.itlos.org/cases/list-of-cases/case-no-17/.

29 Compare Birnie *et al.* (n 21) at p. 167 and Atapattu (n 21) at p. 308.

30 ICJ (n 27) at para 205. The Court also added some very general statements about EIA content, with one exception: it confirmed that monitoring of effects throughout the life of the project must be undertaken. This had previously been expressed only in separate opinions; see Craik (n 5) at pp. 114–115.

31 Craik (n 5) at p. 124.

32 Convention on Environmental Impact Assessment in a Transboundary Context (Espoo, 25 February 1991, in force 10 September 1997) 1989 *UNTS* 310.

33 *Ibid.*, Art. 2(1).

34 *Ibid.*, Art. 2(2).

35 *Ibid.*, Art. 1(viii). States do not have to be adjacent, although the discussion here may leave that impression.

The impacts to consider are environmental, meaning primarily changes in biophysical factors and human health. Impacts on socio-economic conditions and cultural heritage are only to be included when caused by initial biophysical changes.[36] The procedural steps, summarised in Fig. 2, are:

- Screening: The list of activities in Annex I contains the first criterion for requiring a transboundary EIA. This mostly refers to land-based activities. However, activities are only subject to transboundary EIA if it is likely that significant adverse impacts may occur in other states. States may also agree to include activities other than those listed in Annex I.[37]
- Scoping: There are no explicit references to scoping or decisions about the content of the EIA. This is left open to the national systems to determine.
- Environmental Impact Report: The minimum content[38] is very similar to the UNEP principles, but differs by not requiring indirect, cumulative and long-term impacts to be addressed.
- Transboundary collaboration: States are the primary actors in the procedures for notification and consultation.[39] However, the public in the affected state shall be involved, both in the preparatory phase and in the review of the final report.[40]
- Final decision: States shall enter into consultation before a final decision. The state of origin shall take due account of the outcome of the EIA and the comments. Afterwards, the affected state(s) shall receive reasoned information about the final decision.[41]
- Follow-up: The parties shall determine whether a post-project analysis is needed. If they decide it is, monitoring is recommended to identify any adverse transboundary impacts, which may lead to new consultations.[42]

It is relevant for the situation in the Arctic that the Espoo Convention encourages bi- and multi-lateral agreements between states.[43] States also collaborate in sub-regions.

---

36 *Ibid.*, Art. 1(vii).

37 *Ibid.*, Art. 2(2). Activities beyond Annex I can be included on a case-by-case basis (Art. 2(5) and Appendix III), or by an agreement based on an additional set of criteria (Arts. 2(9) and 8).

38 *Ibid.*, Appendix II.

39 *Ibid.*, Arts. 3–7.

40 *Ibid.*, Arts. 2(6), 3(8) and 4(2).

41 *Ibid.*, Arts. 5 and 6.

42 *Ibid.*, Art. 7.

43 *Ibid.*, Arts. 2(9) and 8.

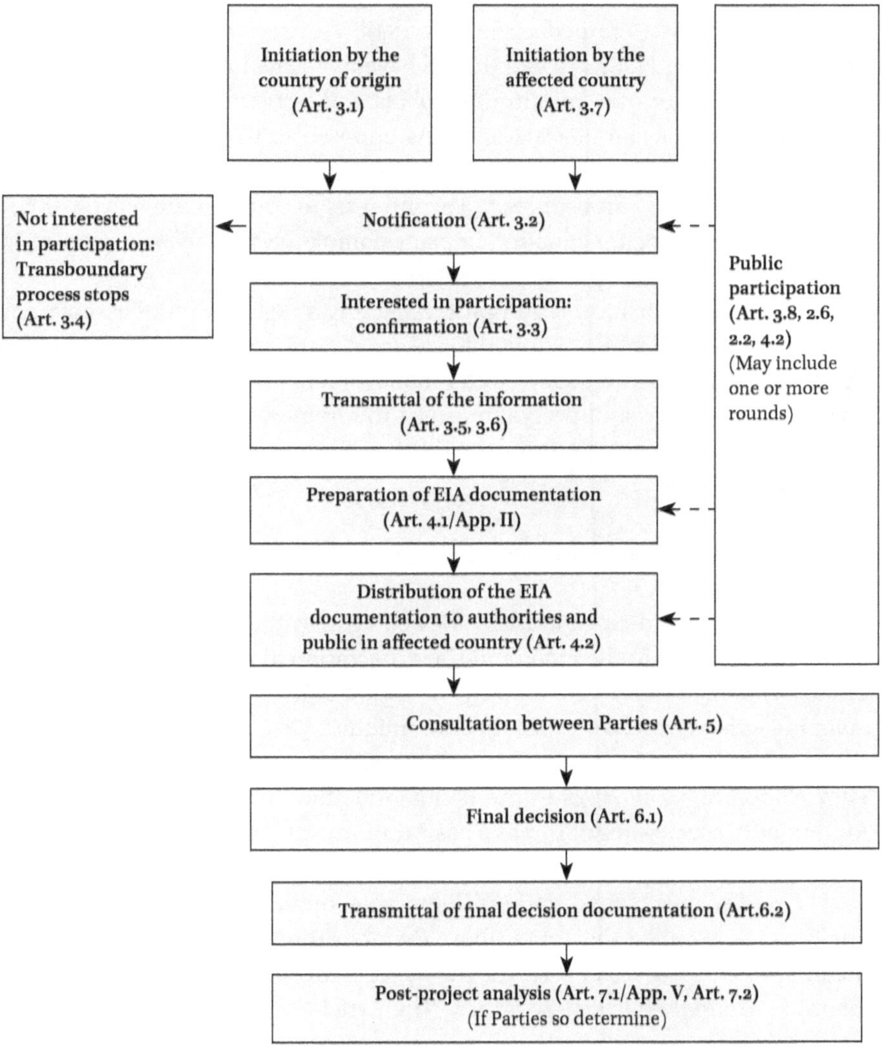

FIGURE 2 Main procedural steps in the Espoo Convention (based on UNECE)

The 2003 Kiev Protocol on Strategic Environmental Assessment[44]

The Kiev Protocol on SEA (SEA Protocol) introduced a legally binding instrument with content that is more appropriate for strategic assessment than

44 Protocol on Strategic Environmental Assessment (Kiev, 21 May 2003, in force 11 July 2010) 2685 *UNTS*.

the weak commitment to SEA in the Espoo Convention.[45] Like the Espoo Convention, the SEA Protocol excludes ABNJ.[46] Norway and Denmark are parties, whereas Canada, Russia and the US have not signed it.

SEA is mandatory for certain draft plans and programmes and is recommended for policies and legislation.[47] As opposed to the Espoo Convention, the SEA Protocol focuses on national systems, with additional considerations about transboundary procedures.[48] The interests to consider are narrower because it excludes socio-economic impacts completely.[49] However, scoping is included, with optional public participation.[50]

The field of application is complex, reflecting a higher level of assessment and many criteria.[51] SEA is required for sectoral plans and programmes within, e.g., fisheries, mining, transport, water management and tourism. This applies only when the plans and programmes set the framework for future development consent for projects listed in the Espoo Convention or according to national legislation.

3.2.2 The 1997 Guidelines for Environmental Impact Assessment in the Arctic

The Arctic EIA Guidelines must be viewed against the commitments to EIA by the Arctic states in the 1990s and the expectation of obtaining a pan-Arctic EIA treaty if all of them were to ratify the Espoo Convention.[52] The Guidelines' main objective is to raise issues that are unique to Arctic assessments, for example, Arctic-specific environmental thresholds and significance criteria. They elaborate on all steps in the UNEP guidelines, thereby underlining the Arctic states' acceptance of this as a basic uniform structure of the EIA process.

3.2.3 The 1982 United Nations Convention on the Law of the Sea

The LOSC established that "states have the obligation to protect and preserve the marine environment".[53] This is the context for Article 206 on the "assessment of potential effects of activities." The Article has a broad scope: first, by

45 Espoo Convention, Art. 2(7).

46 SEA Protocol, Preamble, Arts. 15, 2(3) and 2(4).

47 *Ibid.*, Preamble, Arts. 4 and 13.

48 *Ibid.*, Art. 10.

49 *Ibid.*, Art. 2(7).

50 *Ibid.*, Art. 6.

51 *Ibid.*, Art. 4.

52 T Koivurova, 'Implementing guidelines for environmental impact assessment in the Arctic' in Bastmeijer and Koivurova (n 11) at pp. 165–7.

53 LOSC Article 192, further developed in Arts. 193 and 194.

establishing that the obligation applies to all maritime zones, and second, by referring to "planned activities" in general terms, thereby allowing assessments of both strategic and project-oriented initiatives of all kinds. All the Arctic coastal states, except the US, are parties to the LOSC.

The duty to assess comes into operation when there are "reasonable grounds" to believe that substantial pollution or significant harm will occur. When this threshold is met, states shall carry out an assessment "as far as practicable". This most likely refers to states' differentiated responsibilities often found in the LOSC and gives leeway in determining the level of detail and depth in the assessment.[54] Additional leeway is given by the duty to "assess", instead of conducting an EIA. However, the reference to "planned" activities demonstrates that there is a requirement for prior assessment. The only specified procedure is the duty to notify "all States" about the results. After permitting an activity, states must monitor the effects and continue to notify other states.[55]

3.2.4 The Convention for the Protection of the Marine Environment of the North-East Atlantic[56]

The geographical scope of the Convention for the Protection of the Marine Environment of the North-East Atlantic (OSPAR) includes a sector of the AO, including ABNJ. Denmark and Norway are the only parties among the AO coastal states. Unlike most Regional Seas Conventions, OSPAR contains no explicit EA provisions so as to not to interfere with EU legislation.[57] OSPAR requires the parties to assess the status and trends of the marine environment, supported by collaborative monitoring and research.[58] This has resulted in comprehensive monitoring programmes and state-of-the-environment assessments. The assessments shall include evaluations of the effectiveness of measures taken and planned, and identification of priorities for action. One may argue that the evaluation of actions planned is an EA in a strict legal sense. OSPAR also requires the adoption of programmes and measures to prevent pollution or to safeguard ecosystems and biodiversity.[59] Their "nature and extent" (not

54 See the common and differentiated responsibility principle (Atapattu (n 21), ch. 5).

55 LOSC Arts. 204(2) and 205.

56 Convention for the Protection of the Marine Environment of the North-East Atlantic (Paris, 22 September 1992, in force 25 March 1998) 32 *ILM* 1072 (1993).

57 Former OSPAR Chairman and Executive Secretary Alan Simcock, personal communication.

58 OSPAR Convention, Arts. 6, 8 and Annex IV.

59 *Ibid.*, Art. 2(3)1, Annex I, III and V. Appendices 2 and 3 contain criteria for screening and evaluation.

impacts) must be assessed. Furthermore, OSPAR contains implicit assessment obligations related to transboundary pollution[60] and to derogations from the general ban on dumping waste and petroleum installations.[61]

3.2.5 The 1992 Convention on Biological Diversity[62]

The Convention on Biological Diversity (CBD) covers both AWNJ and ABNJ.[63] All Arctic coastal states are parties, except the US. According to Article 14 on "impact assessment", parties must introduce appropriate procedures for EIA of plans and SEA of programmes and policies that are likely to have significant adverse effects on biodiversity. The Article may seem to be highly qualified. However, the underlying assumption is that "the actual modalities of conducting the EIA will be addressed in domestic legislation and through bilateral, regional and multilateral instruments". As long as a state has an existing EA system and a demonstrated capacity to conduct EAs, the obligation to incorporate biodiversity concerns is strengthened.[64]

In 2006, the CBD adopted voluntary guidelines on how to incorporate biodiversity concerns into existing EA procedures.[65] The EIA guidelines link the advice to internationally accepted procedural steps with particular attention to screening and scoping. The SEA guidelines are more open towards different approaches. However, both mainly refer to terrestrial and coastal experiences. The CBD therefore annotated the original guidelines to incorporate marine issues.[66] The limited knowledge leading to greater uncertainty in marine assessments and the differences in governance structure and organisational settings are recurrent topics in the annotations.

---

60 *Ibid.*, Art. 21.

61 *Ibid.*, Annex II, Art. 4; Annex III, Art. 5. There are assessment obligations (also explicit) in OSPAR decisions, e.g., on the disposal of used offshore installations and on marine research.

62 Convention on Biological Diversity (Nairobi, 22 May 1992, in force 29 December 1993) 31 *ILM* 822.

63 *Ibid.*, Art. 4.

64 Craik (n 5) at p. 100.

65 COP Decision VIII/28, Voluntary guidelines on biodiversity-inclusive impact assessment, March 2006. Available at https://www.cbd.int/decision/cop/?id=11042.

66 COP Decision XI/18, Marine and coastal biodiversity: sustainable fisheries and addressing adverse impacts of human activities, voluntary guidelines for environmental assessment, and marine spatial planning, October 2012. Available at https://www.cbd.int/decision/cop/?id=13179.

3.2.6 Conventions on Conservation of Nature

Several conservation Conventions have indirect requirements for EAs or related tools. The *Convention on Migratory Species* (CMS)[67] is particularly relevant in the AO, where many species of fish, mammals and birds use the area only in summer. It can apply to the whole geographic range of a species,[68] but its importance in the AO is reduced because only Denmark and Norway are full parties, and there are no subsidiary agreements with assessment obligations for Arctic species. The parties have emphasised "the importance of good quality EIA and SEA" in implementing several articles that imply a need to anticipate and predict effects.[69] The *Ramsar Convention*[70] on wetlands has been ratified by all of the Arctic coastal states, and thus applies to their coastal areas.[71] The Ramsar parties have agreed to "ensure that any projects, plans, programmes and policies with the potential to alter the ecological character of wetlands on the Ramsar list or impact negatively on other wetlands in their territory, are subjected to rigorous impact assessment procedures and to formalize such procedures [...]."[72] The parties to both of these Conventions took part in the elaboration of the biodiversity guidelines under the CBD and recommended their use. The *Polar Bear Agreement*[73] implicitly requires the parties to establish a prior evaluation procedure for proposed activities that may affect "ecosystems of which polar bears are a part".[74]

67 Convention on the Conservation of Migratory Species of Wild Animals (Bonn, 23 June 1979, in force 1 November 1983) 1651 *UNTS* 333.

68 *Ibid.*, Arts. 1(f) and 1(h).

69 Resolution 7.2, Impact assessment and migratory species, COP7, September 2002. Available at http://www.cms.int/en/meeting/seventh-meeting-conference-parties-cms It identifies assessments as relevant for Arts. II(2) on avoiding species becoming endangered, III(4) on the protection of Appendix I species, Arts. IV(3) and (4) on Agreements concerning certain species and the interpretation of conservation status.

70 Convention on Wetlands of International Importance especially as Waterfowl Habitat (Ramsar, 2 February 1971, in force 21 December 1975), 996 *UNTS 245*.

71 *Ibid.*, Art. 2(1) restricts its jurisdiction to wetlands within the territory of a party.

72 Resolution VII.16, The Ramsar Convention and impact assessment: strategic, environmental and social, May 1999. Available at http://www.ramsar.org/library/field_tag_body_event/conference-of-contracting-parties-366/field_tag_body_event/cop7-san-jos%C3%A9-1999-454.

73 Agreement on the Conservation of Polar Bears and Their Habitat (Oslo, 15 November 1973, in force 26 May 1976) 13 *ILM* 3 (1974).

74 *Ibid.*, Art. II; Koivurova (n 19), at p. 158.

3.2.7 Fisheries

The general principles in the LOSC are further developed in the UN Fish Stock Agreement (UNFSA),[75] several Food and Agriculture Organization (FAO)-related instruments and by regional fisheries bodies, such as the North-East Atlantic Fisheries Commission (NEAFC).[76] They contain no explicit references to EA. Even the words "assess/assessment" are hardly used. Nevertheless, some types of assessments are needed for vital parts of the fisheries regime, such as setting the total allowable catch, establishing selective regulations and evaluating their effects on fish stocks.[77] The UNFSA is an exception. It requires assessments (not EA) of how fisheries and other activities affect fish stocks and the marine ecosystem, and for managing new and exploratory fisheries.[78]

The UNGA has addressed destructive fishing practices in ABNJ in its annual resolution on fisheries every year since 2004.[79] This led the FAO to develop "International guidelines for the management of deep-sea fisheries in the high seas" in 2009.[80] They apply to experimental, exploratory and established fisheries in the high seas that may affect the seafloor.[81] Sequences of impact assessments play a prominent role in this framework for adaptive management, which aims at preventing significant adverse impacts on vulnerable marine ecosystems (VMEs) and encouraging sustainable use. The assessments should evaluate whether deep-sea fishing activities cause significant adverse impacts on VMEs through an approach that shares the main characteristics of an EA.[82] The results should guide the designation of interim measures, such as the closing of areas, and precautionary, later permanent, conservation and

75 Agreement for the Implementation of the Provisions of the United Nations Convention on the Law of the Sea of 10 December 1982 relating to the Conservation and Management of Straddling Fish Stocks and Highly Migratory Fish Stocks (New York, 4 August 1995, in force 11 December 2001) 34 *ILM* 1542 (1995).

76 Convention on Future Multilateral Cooperation in the North-East Atlantic Fisheries (London, 18 November 1980, in force 17 March 1982) 1285 *UNTS* 129.

77 LOSC Arts. 61(1–3), 62 and 119(1)a; UNFSA Art. 5(a–b).

78 UNFSA Arts. 5(d), 6(3)d, 6(6) and 7(2)d.

79 See particularly UNGA A/RES/61/105 (2006) Arts. 83–87, A/RES/64/72 (2009) Arts. 119–122, A/RES/66/68 (2011) Arts. 129–130 and 135–137. Available at: http://www.un.org/depts/los/general_assembly/general_assembly_resolutions.htm.

80 Available at http://www.fao.org/docrep/011/i0816t/i0816t00.HTM.

81 They may also be applied to other fisheries and in AWNJ (*ibid.*, paras. 8 and 10; see also UNFSA Art. 6(6), which applies to all maritime zones).

82 *Ibid.*, paras. 17–20, 47–53 and 81–83.

management measures.[83] In the assessment provisions, references to areas and cumulative impacts point in the direction of SEA. However, final management measures should be specific and tailored to the characteristics of individual fisheries. Thus, one can interpret the guidelines as a flexible framework for both SEA- and EIA-like assessments.

The NEAFC has a regulatory area that covers a sector of the AO high seas. The NEAFC has implemented the UNGA Resolutions in recommendations that designate "existing bottom fishing areas" and "area closures for the protection of VMES".[84] Bottom fisheries outside of these areas are defined as exploratory and can only proceed according to prior notification, a preliminary assessment along the lines of the FAO guidelines and permission from the NEAFC. The criteria for notification show that the scope covers individual fishery activities. These rules apply to fisheries in the high seas sector covered by the NEAF Convention, because no fishing areas are designated there.[85]

3.2.8 Shipping

The general nature of LOSC Art. 206 also establishes a duty to assess potentially harmful effects of shipping. However, the Conventions of the International Maritime Organization (IMO) seem to contain no provisions explicitly requiring EA of shipping activities.[86]

83 *Ibid.*, paras. 63, 65 and 70–72.

84 NEAFC Recommendation on the protection of vulnerable marine ecosystems in the NEAFC Regulatory Area, as amended by Recommendation 09:2015. Available at http://www.neafc.org/rec/2014/19.

85 The July 2015 declaration by the AO coastal states closes the AO high seas for commercial fishing by their own vessels until an international instrument is in place. Thus, the AO high seas are open for their non-commercial fishing and fishing by other states. Available at https://www.regjeringen.no/en/aktuelt/fishing-arctic-ocean/id2427705/.

86 Regarding assessment obligations, there is at least one, requiring "case-by-case evaluation" to permit dumping (IMO Res. A.672(16) Guidelines for removal of offshore installations). Available at http://cil.nus.edu.sg/1989/1989-guidelines-and-standards-for-the-removal-of-offshore-installations-and-structures-on-the-continental-shelf-and-in-the-exclusive-economic-zone-imo-resolution-a-672-16-adopted-on-19-october-198/.

3.2.9 The 1996 London Protocol to the 1972 London Convention on Prevention of Marine Pollution by Dumping of Wastes and Other Matter[87]

The 1996 London Protocol to the 1972 London Convention introduced a global ban on the dumping of wastes and other matter.[88] It lists possible exceptions, but parties may only permit dumping based on a series of assessments:[89] An initial *audit* should consider waste reduction and waste management as alternatives to dumping. An *assessment* should consider alternative options for the disposal of residual waste and its effects on human health, living resources, hazards, economics and the exclusion of future uses, concluding with a recommendation to issue or refuse a dumping permit. Subsequent *monitoring* may lead to the modification or revocation of a permit. There are no requirements for the assessment processes, leaving it up to states to apply EIA or other approaches. Canada, Norway and Denmark are parties to the London Protocol, whereas Russia and the US are parties only to the London Convention.

The parties have also introduced a separate two-step assessment procedure for ocean fertilisation in order to determine whether applications constitute legitimate scientific research that can be permitted.[90]

3.2.10 The International Seabed Authority Regulations on Deep Seabed Mining

The deep seabed beyond national jurisdiction ("the Area") and its mineral resources are the common heritage of mankind and are managed by the International Seabed Authority (ISA).[91] The ISA shall contribute to the development of mineral resources, but it also has a sectoral mandate to protect the marine environment from mining activities.[92] This includes preparing "assessments of the environmental implications of activities in the Area".[93] The Article should mandate SEA, but no regulations or strategic assessments have

87 1996 Protocol to the Convention on the Prevention of Marine Pollution by Dumping of Wastes and Other Matter (London, 7 November 1996, in force 24 May 2006) 36 *ILM* 1.

88 *Ibid.*, Art. 23. The London Convention does not apply to internal waters, but Art. 7 of the London Protocol conditionally includes this zone.

89 *Ibid.*, Art. 4 with annexes.

90 R Warner, 'Oceans beyond Boundaries: Environmental Assessment Frameworks' (2012) 27 *The International Journal of Marine and Coastal Law* 481–499, at pp. 494–497.

91 LOSC Arts. 1(1), 133, 136, 137(2) and 156.

92 LOSC Arts. 150(a), 145 and 209. Note the corresponding flag states' responsibility.

93 LOSC Arts. 165(2)d and f.

yet emerged, despite a growing need.[94] When it comes to EIA, the regulations for the prospecting and exploration of three types of mineral resources include EIA for individual mining sites.[95]

The limited knowledge about the deep oceans makes assessments in the Area highly uncertain. The ISA tries to gradually improve the knowledge base and to develop regulations incrementally. When applying for an exploration contract, applicants must submit a plan of work,[96] accompanied by a preliminary EIA and a programme for environmental baseline studies.[97] Before commencing certain exploratory activities that may provoke serious environmental harm, the contractor must submit an EIA, together with a proposal for a monitoring programme to reveal actual impacts. Regular revisions of the programme of work and the obligation to conduct EIA for the listed activities mandate sequences of EIAs. A regulatory framework that is under preparation will also include rules concerning EIA for exploitation.

The ISA regulations are unclear on the differences between the preliminary EIA, which is probably meant to be a first screening, and the EIA. There are detailed screening criteria, but weak descriptions of scoping and review mechanisms, and no rules for public participation.

3.2.11 Offshore Hydrocarbon Activities

There are no comprehensive global regulations for offshore hydrocarbon activities and, therefore, no EA obligations covering the whole sector. Parts of the activities are regulated by Conventions requiring EAs (OSPAR, Espoo and London Conventions). Regionally, the Arctic Council has adopted non-binding guidelines for the offshore sector.[98] Their recommendation to apply

94 A Jaeckel, 'An Environmental Management Strategy for the International Seabed Authority? The Legal Basis' (2015) 30 (1) *The International Journal of Marine and Coastal Law* 93–119, at pp. 112–113.

95 Polymetallic nodules, polymetallic sulphides and cobalt-rich ferromanganese crusts. See G Le Gurun, 'Environmental Impact Assessment and the International Seabed Authority' in Bastmeijer and Koivurova (n 11), at pp. 221–264 and Jaeckel (n 94).

96 LOSC Art. 153(2) and Agreement Relating to the Implementation of Part XI of the United Nations Convention on the Law of the Sea of 10 December 1982 (adopted 28 July 1994, entered into force 28 July 1996) 33 *ILM* 1309; Annex, section 1(7) and (9).

97 ISBA/19/LTC/8, Recommendations for the guidance of contractors for the assessment of the possible environmental impacts arising from exploration for marine minerals in the Area, paras. 1, 8 and 18–25. Available at https://www.isa.org.jm/documents/isba19ltc8.

98 Arctic Council 2009, Arctic offshore oil and gas guidelines. Available at http://www.pame.is/index.php/projects/offshore-oil-and-gas.

SEA particularly for addressing cumulative effects is the most interesting in this context. However, there is no guidance on how to conduct an SEA.

4 The Status of Environmental Assessments in the Arctic Ocean

Based on the legal sources examined above and the Arctic coastal states' treaty obligations, I now discuss to what extent states are compelled to conduct EAs for activities in the AO. This is relatively easy to answer for basic issues like where, when and for what purposes EAs are required, but more complex for how assessments should be undertaken.

4.1 *Where and When Are Environmental Assessments Required?*

4.1.1 Geographical Scope

Customary law applies to the whole AO, regardless of jurisdiction. LOSC Art. 206 is also a transnational obligation, requiring parties to "assess" the potential effects of planned activities. Even though assessment practices have evolved since 1982, one should be cautious in reinterpreting this to mean EIA and SEA because that may not have been the intention of the parties. However, the duty to apply "best environmental practices" means that this evolution influences what may be considered reasonable. The assessment capabilities of a state will be judged from its national practices and other treaty obligations.[99] It is reasonable to assume that the highly developed AO coastal states have the capacity to conduct EIA and SEA according to a basic understanding of the tools, such as the UNEP Guidelines. With this interpretation, the LOSC contains a binding transnational EA obligation in the AO. The CBD contains an explicit EA obligation applicable across all maritime zones. Other explicit, binding EA provisions apply only to parts of the maritime zones, as illustrated in figure 3. However, incomplete ratification of the Conventions limits their geographical scope in the AO.

With regard to treaty-based obligations with less explicit EA provisions, the Ramsar Convention will mostly cover domestic assessments (Fig. 3: upper left cell). Assessments according to the LOSC, OSPAR, the London Protocol and the CMS may apply across all zones. The NEAFC's rules for bottom fisheries apply only to the high seas (Fig. 3: lower right cell). The UNFSA has the same high seas focus, although there is also a mandate to assess across zones.[100]

---

99 Craik (n 5), at pp. 128–129.

100 UNFSA Arts. 3(1) and 7.

		Areas affected by the impact	
		Coastal state zones	**High Seas and the Area**
Location of activity	**Coastal state zones**	SEA-protocol; SEA-protocol; Espoo convention; CBD	CBD
	High Seas and the Area	CBD; ISA deep seabed mining	CBD; ISA deep seabed mining

FIGURE 3 The scope of explicit EA obligations in international Conventions according to where an activity takes place (rows) and where the impacts occur (columns). The area indicated by a dotted line illustrates domestic EA. All other combinations of activities and impacts will lead to transboundary assessments. The *CBD* is transnational and is thus applicable to all locations of activity and affected areas.

4.1.2 Threshold and Values

It is a rather uniform understanding that the likelihood of significant environmental harm to certain values is the trigger for EAs. Provisions applying this threshold can be found in the UNEP Guidelines, the CBD and the Espoo Convention, and in practice also in the LOSC.[101] The criterion contains elements of both the probability that the harm will occur and of significance criteria, such as magnitude, extent, duration and irreversibility. It requires some form of legal test and is not trivial, either from a legal or practical point of view.[102]

The Conventions aim at protecting different values from significant harm. The LOSC and the ISA are concerned about pollution or other potentially harmful changes to the marine environment. This open formulation should capture all environmental harm. The question is to what degree it also encompasses socio-economic impacts. When they occur as an indirect result of changes to the marine environment, it will be reasonable to answer yes; if

101 Craik (n 5), at p. 133.

102 Holder (n 15), ch. 4; DP Lawrence, 'Impact significance determination—Back to basics' (2007) 27 (8) *Environmental Impact Assessment Review* 755–769.

not, the better view probably is no. The CBD is concerned with impacts on biological diversity, which provides a comprehensive scope for assessing the biological environment. The Espoo Convention adds human health and is explicit with respect to indirect impacts on socio-economic conditions and cultural heritage. Other values that are not so clearly linked to a significance threshold are migratory species, Ramsar sites, fish stocks, VMEs, hazards, the economy and other uses of the sea. Beyond that, states can assess whatever values or interests they wish.

4.2 *How Should Environmental Assessments Be Conducted?*

With the many unspecific treaty obligations, it is unclear whether it is possible to interpret reasonably the requirements for the content and process of EAs.

4.2.1 Relationship between Treaties

Whereas the LOSC and the CBD mostly operate at the same level of generality, the CBD is more specific than the LOSC in that it explicitly requires EIA and SEA, supported by guidelines. Because the EA provisions of the CBD are in accordance with the principles of the LOSC, specific biodiversity-related assessments could be considered sufficient under both Conventions.[103]

Correspondingly, the more specific Espoo instruments can fill in when assessments under the LOSC are transboundary or strategic (or both); they also can do so under the CBD.[104] The Espoo procedures therefore must be followed in transboundary EIAs addressing "pollution/environmental harm" and "biological diversity" between the maritime zones of Canada, Norway and Denmark, and to a certain degree, those of Russia and the US, which are signatories to the Espoo Convention. Similarly, the London Protocol, the ISA regulations and regulations building on the FAO guidelines provide some direction regarding the content of assessments for their specific purposes. In theory, the Espoo instruments could have covered the assessment obligations under these Conventions with more specific procedures as well. However, several gaps in the Espoo instruments limit this possibility (see below).

4.2.2 Environmental Assessment as a Special Legal Term

Above, I have referred to several characteristics of the role, process and content of EA. To what degree does this have legal implications? Have "EIA" and "SEA" developed special meanings according to Art. 31(4) of the Vienna

103 LOSC Arts. 237(1) and 311(2).

104 CBD Arts. 22(1) and 14(1)c.

Convention,[105] so that it is possible to add, by interpretation, more flesh to these conceptual bones?

Craik argues that this is the case for EIA.[106] During the 1980s, the use of EIA proliferated. Specialised regimes developed both nationally and internationally. We therefore can assume that negotiating parties were conscious of their use of the terms "assess" or "EIA". He concludes that "for those treaties negotiated after the mid-1980s, where the term "EIA" is used, it should be interpreted to include the minimum core of procedural requirements in the UNEP EIA principles, unless some contrary intentions can be shown."

Holder argues in the same direction for both EIA and SEA.[107] "Even accounting for substantial variations between definitions of assessment and correspondingly different laws on EA, a generic legal form may be identified," which is characterised by:

- Ability to predict environmental effects.
- Judgments of how significant the effects are.
- Consideration of alternatives.
- Participation by experts and non-experts in the assessment process and discussions of the design of the project or strategy under consideration.
- Regulation of decision-making by requiring the results of the EA to be taken into account before granting consent.

However, only four of the treaties examined have explicit references to "EIA" or "SEA". The special meaning of EIA could be an argument for improving certain aspects of the ISA regulations. For the CBD and the two Espoo instruments, the special meanings suggested here will mostly bolster their existing content.

4.2.3 Conclusion on EIA

The UNEP principles can be seen as a minimum requirement for how to conduct EIA in all zones of the AO. This is based on an interpretation of what amounts to due diligence for the Arctic coastal states when discharging their obligation to "assess" under the LOSC. For biodiversity assessments according to the CBD, it is a clear conclusion.[108] Because of the wide participation in the CBD and the great likelihood that expanding activities in the AO will affect biological resources, the CBD may be the most important transnational instrument defining the content of EIAs in the AO.

105 Vienna Convention on the Law of Treaties (Vienna, 23 May 1969, in force 27 January 1980) 1155 *UNTS* 331.

106 Craik (n 5) at pp. 126–7. It is clear from the context that only EIA is meant here (see p. 3).

107 Holder (n 15), ch. 1.

108 See the CBD biodiversity guidelines and the "special meaning" of EIA.

4.2.4 Conclusion on SEA

The SEA Protocol has little influence in the AO, because Canada, Russia and the US have not signed it. Norway and Denmark,[109] as the only parties among the AO coastal states, are obliged to apply its specialised provisions to both domestic and transboundary SEA. For transboundary SEA between Canada, Norway and Denmark, there is also a qualified obligation to extend the Espoo Convention's procedures also to SEA.[110] Beyond that, the CBD provisions, with the guidelines, is the only international SEA instrument accepted by all coastal states, apart from the US.

5 Weaknesses in the Legal Assessment Regime

Based on the above interpretation across instruments, I suggest that the legal regime for the AO contains the following weaknesses:

- Insufficient acceptance of existing instruments.
  Incomplete acceptance of existing treaties is an obstacle to a uniform EA regime. The US, where EIA originated, is in a very peculiar position, as it is not a party to, i.a., the LOSC, the CBD and the two Espoo instruments. Russia is not a party to the Espoo instruments, and Canada is not a party to the SEA Protocol. This may undermine the legitimacy of the Arctic coastal states' self-declared stewardship role in protecting the unique AO ecosystem.[111]
- Major sectors have no or uneven assessment obligations.
  There is no regional fisheries management organisation with EA provisions outside of the NEAFC sector of the AO. With the coastal states' interim measures on commercial high seas fisheries,[112] the most pressing need is to ensure general acceptance of the duty to assess new and exploratory fisheries. The EA-like assessments in the FAO guidelines and their implementation by the NEAFC do not cover pelagic fisheries and are only voluntary for AWNJ. Furthermore, there are no specific assessment obligations for the environmental impacts of shipping and marine tourism, and only patchy coverage for the oil industry. Other activities could have been captured by EA requirements in a regional seas organisation, but OSPAR only covers a sector of the

109 Danish ratification does not necessarily include Greenland, due to the Greenlandic home rule.

110 Espoo Convention, Art. 2(7).

111 The Illulisat Declaration (Arctic Ocean Conference, Illulisat, Greenland 27–29 May 2008). Available at http://www.arcticgovernance.org/the-ilulissat-declaration.4872424.html.

112 See (n 85).

AO and does not contain explicit EA provisions. Nor are there more specific, default EA mechanisms in other instruments, primarily the LOSC.[113]

- Weak obligations for domestic EA.
  Domestic EA is subject to the weakest obligations in general principles and international customary law. After all, the no-harm principle also gives states "the sovereign right to exploit their own resources pursuant to their own environmental and developmental policies".[114] The strongest commitments are for issues of common concern like biodiversity and climate change. In treaty law, one may interpret the LOSC to mandate state parties to conduct domestic SEA and EIA for any type of activity and any type of environmental harm in the AO, if it is seen as a due diligence obligation according to their capabilities. Unless this is confirmed in a more binding form, there will be doubt with regard to the extent to which these states see themselves as committed to more specific assessment procedures.
- Weak coverage of ABNJ.
  Given the strong status of transboundary obligations, it is striking to note the lack of more specific rules for the assessment of impacts on ABNJ originating from activities in AWNJ, as the commons are excluded from the Espoo instruments. Regarding activities occurring in the Area, the ISA has a mandate to establish assessment procedures only for mineral activities. Their EIA system could be improved to ensure better transparency, participation and review. There is also a need for SEA in areas with many mining licences. New mineral, hydrocarbon and non-mineral developments[115] that may emerge in the Area are not covered by specific assessment obligations. In and on the high seas, there are no specific assessment obligations for activities other than deep-sea fisheries, dumping and ocean fertilisation. There is an institutional challenge regarding the responsibility to develop and manage more specific assessment obligations in ABNJ. This includes the responsibility for strategic assessments that cover all human impacts on these areas.
- Low marine relevance of the Espoo instruments.
  The applicability of the Espoo instruments to marine areas is limited by their listing of sectors[116] and activities[117] that in combination define when

113 Warner (n 90), at p. 482.

114 Rio Principle 2 (n 23).

115 For instance, cables and pipelines (LOSC Art. 112), scientific research (LOSC Art. 143(3)), bioprospecting and energy production.

116 SEA Protocol, Art. 4(2).

117 *Ibid.*, Annex I and II; Espoo Convention, Annex I.

assessments are required. Fisheries may be subject to SEA, but because catching fish is not on any of the subsequent lists (although fish farming, fish-meal and fish-oil factories are), neither SEA nor transboundary EIA are required for fisheries. One implication is that the Espoo procedures, by legal interpretation, cannot fill in to require EIA or SEA in fishery assessments. Shipping activities could be subject to SEA under "transport", but the next list establishes an assessment obligation only for "trading ports". Tourism, in principle, may be subject to SEA, but the tourist developments on the following lists are of little relevance for marine tourist activities. Offshore oil and gas is the only maritime activity that is covered well, as it is explicitly mentioned, together with pipelines, major storage facilities and terminals.

– Strategic level not covered well.
  Because of the low accession to the SEA Protocol, relevant international law contains only weak and/or unelaborated SEA obligations. This is a mismatch to a situation where economic activities are expected to expand into completely new areas. A cautious approach consonant with the high environmental ambitions for the Arctic would be to apply strategic assessments to capture the larger-scale impacts of new developments and to agree on the necessary measures before individual projects start. The rapid environmental changes in the AO also make strategic assessments more important in updating knowledge about marine ecosystems as a basis for better predictions in impact assessments. Other strategic assessment needs arise from the Arctic Council's commitment to ecosystem-based management[118] and the UN World Ocean Assessment.[119] These processes will need several forms of strategic assessments, in addition to SEA in a strict legal sense.

6 Conclusions

EIA is a tool that implements several principles of environmental law. It is a customary obligation according to international law to undertake EIA when projects may cause transboundary harm, also to ABNJ. Despite almost 50 years of existence, widespread practice globally and agreement on the basic characteristics and quality criteria, international courts have not decided what this implies for the content and process of EIA; this is up to each state to determine.

118 Expert Group on Ecosystem-Based Management (2013): *Ecosystem-based Management in the Arctic*, Arctic Council, Tromsø. Available at http://www.arctic-council.org/index.php/en/expert-groups/340-egebm.

119 Home page: http://www.worldoceanassessment.org/.

SEA developed later for the assessment of policies, plans and programmes. It is a more diverse collection of various approaches, and a duty to undertake SEA has not yet attained the status of customary international law.

A review of assessment obligations under international treaty law demonstrates that only four instruments relevant for the AO explicitly require EIA or SEA: the CBD and the Espoo Convention with its SEA Protocol require both, whereas the ISA regulations only require EIA. Apart from the CBD, which applies across all maritime zones, the geographical coverage of the others is restricted, as illustrated in figure 3. The LOSC and the other agreements reviewed contain assessment obligations that are less specific.

It is a rather uniform requirement across instruments that assessments must be undertaken when new developments are likely to cause significant harm to certain values; most comprehensively to the marine environment (LOSC) and to biodiversity (CBD), or to other values specified in each Convention. Based on an interpretation of what may be seen as a due diligence obligation for the AO coastal states, it is suggested that the content and process of EIA should at least conform to the UNEP principles, regardless of maritime zones and assessment purposes. The transboundary EIA procedures in the Espoo Convention mostly apply to assessments of offshore oil and gas production between Canada, Norway and Denmark/Greenland. Regarding SEA, the detailed provisions of the SEA Protocol only apply to the two parties, Denmark and Norway.

I suggest that the international legal regime on assessments contains several weaknesses. Incomplete acceptance of existing treaties is an obstacle to a uniform EA regime in the AO. The lack of default and specific requirements for EIA and SEA, primarily in the LOSC, creates a patchwork of areas and activities that are covered by more specific assessment obligations. Regarding sectors that are particularly relevant for the Arctic Ocean, there are no specific assessment obligations for shipping, pelagic fisheries and tourism, and uneven coverage of oil and gas activities. One reason for this is the low coverage of marine activities in the Espoo instruments. Geographical gaps occur due to the lack of a regional fisheries management organisation outside of the NEAFC sector of the AO and, correspondingly, the lack of a regional seas organisation outside of the OSPAR area. Other geographical gaps arise from the weak obligations to assess for harm to ABNJ, regardless of the geographic origin of the harmful activities, and when only domestic areas are affected. Finally, there is a mismatch between the urgent need for various types of strategic marine assessments and the weak coverage of SEA in international instruments.

The major problem identified here is the predominance of unspecific assessment obligations, primarily in the LOSC. A natural response would be to define more specific obligations and minimum standards for EIA and SEA in the new LOSC instrument. This could create a default mechanism for activities not covered by specialised instruments and serve as the legal minimum that such instruments could further build upon as *lex specialis*. However, only instruments that explicitly require EIA and SEA will automatically be legally affected (the CBD, the ISA, the Espoo instruments, and most Regional Seas Conventions). This is not necessarily the case for instruments with unspecific assessment obligations (e.g., the FAO guidelines and the London Protocol), and even less for those containing only indirect assessment obligations.

A related issue is how specific a new instrument under the LOSC should be with respect to the wider set of impact assessments. Introducing separate provisions for several of them runs the risk of causing confusion and overlaps, and jeopardising cost-effectiveness.[120] It would be a better option to formulate generic rules for EIA and SEA that are open to a broader set of tools and other values than the biophysical environment. This would capture the desire of the UNGA to protect biodiversity and also correspond with the call for integration that has echoed both in the assessment community and in marine policy documents.

The relationship to the Espoo Convention, with its SEA Protocol, deserves particular attention in the ongoing processes. The Espoo Convention will become a global treaty if enough member states approve the amendment that opens up formal adherence to all UN member states,[121] as the SEA Protocol already does. The UN preparatory committee would benefit from using them as a starting point in discussions about transboundary procedures. Depending on the content of the new LOSC instrument, the parties to the Espoo Convention could eventually amend the treaty to increase its marine relevance. However, the AO coastal states, all of which are signatories to the Espoo Convention, may also adopt a regional instrument on transboundary EA, building on the Espoo instruments and the CBD.[122] This could allow non-parties to modify the Espoo obligations that are unacceptable to them, expand the marine activities that are covered and provide more detailed transboundary

120 Pope *et al.* (n 8).

121 Espoo Convention, 1st amendment. Available at http://www.unece.org/env/eia/about/amendment.html.

122 Relevant Espoo provisions are referred to in (n 37) and (n 43). CBD Art. 14(1)c also encourages more detailed assessment arrangements between states.

procedures between these five states. The EIA Protocol negotiated under the Caspian Seas Convention, which involves Russia, is an example.[123]

It is important for the development of marine assessments to use the lessons learned from five decades of EA, as experienced by states and the professional and academic assessment community.[124] Complaints about low quality assessments have been a persistent issue, but recently there is positive progress, especially concerning procedural and institutional developments.[125] The legal and institutional frameworks at best can enable conditions for good practice, and both skills and institutions need time to develop and mature.[126] The UN preparatory committee therefore should include EA when addressing its mandate on capacity-building and consider this in connection with the initiatives to build up the assessment capacities for the World Ocean Assessment. Regionally, the Arctic Council has a long tradition of sharing experiences. The Nordic collaboration on EIA (1991–2006) could serve as a good model for new activities on EA.[127]

Conducting an EA is not a safeguard against the approval of developments with significant harmful effects because EA is a procedural requirement, not a substantive regulation. One line of thought to address this has been to link EA systems more closely with substantive goals of environmental sustainability and reduce the discretion in decision-making.[128] The FAO guidelines on deep-sea fisheries and their implementation by NEAFC and other regional fisheries bodies are interesting attempts to close the procedure-vs.-substance divide by the coupling of assessments to the designation of measures to protect VMEs.

123 R Tsutsumi and K Robinson, 'Environmental impact assessment and the Framework Convention for the Protection of the Marine Environment of the Caspian Sea' in Bastmeijer and Koivurova (n 11), at pp. 53–70.

124 The International Association for Impact Assessment (IAIA) is an important organisation in this respect and has, e.g., analysed best practice, issued guidelines and promoted education. See <www.iaia.org>.

125 Personal communication from Barry Sadler, who is preparing a new IAIA effectiveness study.

126 Pope *et al.* (n 8).

127 The responsible authorities in each country led the programme, which also involved researchers and practitioners. Studies comparing assessment systems and practices were undertaken and presented in conferences, reports and scientific papers.

128 Jay *et al.* (n 16); E Druel and KM Gjerde, 'Sustaining marine life beyond boundaries: Options for an implementing agreement for marine biodiversity beyond national jurisdiction under the United Nations Convention on the Law of the Sea' (2014) 49 (0) *Marine Policy* 90–97.

The UN preparatory committee has interesting options to advance such developments, as its mandate also includes area-based management and marine protected areas.

A final lesson concerns the relationship to planning. What I have called the strict legal form of EA puts assessments in a reactive role, as an extra add-on after the final elaboration of a development proposal; it is comparable to an end-of-pipe approach in pollution control. The assessment community, by contrast, advocates the use of assessments from the very beginning of the planning process. When better integration with planning is achieved, EA has demonstrated that it is not only able to avoid harm, but can contribute to better solutions. Promoting this in the marine environment would be a significant step forward in the evolution of EA.

CHAPTER 9

Current 'Light' and 'Heavy' Options for Benefit-sharing in the Context of the United Nations Convention on the Law of the Sea

Gaute Voigt-Hanssen
Senior Legal Adviser, Norwegian Ministry of Climate and the Environment, Oslo, Norway

Abstract

An international legally binding instrument under the United Nations Convention on the Law of the Sea (LOSC) will need to address "Marine Genetic Resources (MGRs), including questions on the sharing of benefits" from areas outside national jurisdiction (ABNJ). Existing international models of benefit-sharing have all evolved in the context of national jurisdiction and cannot readily be put to use in ABNJ. Current use of MGRs from ABNJ is practically non-existent, although any instrument or model would have to both cater for this situation and provide for any potential technological development and increase in use. The aim of this paper is to provide a simplified overview of options for access and benefit-sharing, drawing on existing models from international and national instruments. Existing options could be analysed through separating access from benefit-sharing and assessing them factually in terms of how 'light' and 'heavy' they are.

Keywords

marine genetic resources (MGRs) – biological diversity of areas beyond national jurisdiction (BBNJ) – access and benefit-sharing (ABS) – benefit-sharing – United Nations Convention on the Law of the Sea (LOSC)

 | DOI:10.1163/9789004391703_011

1 Introduction

The protection of the marine environment in areas beyond national jurisdiction (ABNJ) is rising up the political agenda. In A/RES/69/292 of 19 June 2015,[1] the UN General Assembly decided to develop an international legally binding instrument (ILBI) under the United Nations Convention on the Law of the Sea (LOSC) on the conservation and sustainable use of marine biological diversity of areas beyond national jurisdiction (BBNJ) and mandated a Preparatory Committee (PrepCom) to meet four times between 2016 and 2017.[2] An important part of the negotiations concerns access to marine genetic resources (MGRs) from ABNJ, including questions of benefit-sharing. Other issues being debated include measures such as area-based management tools, including marine protected areas (MPAs), environmental impact assessments (EIAs), capacity-building, and the transfer of marine technology.[3] Following the four sessions of the PrepCom, the General Assembly adopted A/RES/72/249 on 24 December 2017.[4] An organisational session was held 16–18 April 2018, in New York.[5] The first session of the Intergovernmental Conference will be held

1 I would like to express my very great appreciation to Special Adviser Kjell Kristian Egge, Norwegian Ministry of Foreign Affairs, Prof. Dr. Christina Voigt, University of Oslo, Dr. Thomas Vanagt, ABS-int, and Julian Jackson, former UK CBD, NP and ITPGRFA focal point, for their very valuable and constructive suggestions. Available at http://www.un.org/en/ga/search/view_doc.asp?symbol=A/RES/69/292; accessed 6 June 2018.

2 *Ibid.*

3 The mandate does not explicitly mention access, but rather MGRs, including questions on the sharing of benefits: "that negotiations shall address the topics identified in the package agreed in 2011, namely, the conservation and sustainable use of marine biological diversity of areas beyond national jurisdiction, in particular, together and as a whole, marine genetic resources, including questions on the sharing of benefits, measures such as area-based management tools, including marine protected areas, environmental impact assessments and capacity-building and the transfer of marine technology"; available at http://www.un.org/depts/los/general_assembly/general_assembly_resolutions.htm; accessed 6 June 2018.

4 The UN General Assembly decided to convene an intergovernmental conference, under the auspices of the United Nations, to consider the recommendations of the preparatory committee on the elements and to elaborate the text of an internationally legally binding instrument under the United Nations Convention on the Law of the Sea on the conservation and sustainable use of marine biological diversity of areas beyond national jurisdiction, with a view to developing the instrument as soon as possible; available at http://www.un.org/depts/los/general_assembly/general_assembly_resolutions.htm; accessed 6 June 2018.

5 A/RES/72/249, International legally binding instrument under the United Nations Convention on the Law of the Sea on the conservation and sustainable use of marine biological diversity of areas beyond national jurisdiction, nr 4; available at http://www.un.org/depts/los/general_assembly/general_assembly_resolutions.htm; accessed 6 June 2018.

4–17 September 2018, in New York.[6] To assist delegations in their preparations, the President issued the document 'President`s Aid to Discussions'.[7]

The question of access to, and benefit-sharing of, MGRs from ABNJ, which could also contribute to conservation and sustainable use of marine biodiversity, remains the most complicated and least developed element in the package and few propositions have been fleshed out. All existing access and benefit-sharing (ABS) mechanisms are developed in the context of state sovereignty. However, in ABNJ no State has sovereignty. The genetic and biochemical diversity of the species found in deep-sea habitats, for example hydrothermal vents, deep water coral ecosystems and cold seeps, some of which are new to science, is attractive in particular for the development of medicines for human use. Only a few countries have the economic and technical resources to access and utilise these natural resources; the need for capacity-building and transfer of marine technology to level the playing field with regard to scientific research related to MGRs has been highlighted.[8] There is no universal definition of "MGRs" and the term is not used in the LOSC. The Convention on Biological Diversity (CBD)[9] defines genetic resources as "genetic material of actual or potential value" and genetic material as "any material of plant, animal, microbial or other origin containing functional units of heredity".[10] The definitions in the CBD will possibly be used as a starting point when crafting a definition of MGRs in the context of the ILBI. The possible definition of MGRs is closely linked to the scope of the ILBI.[11] Derivatives such as enzymes and

6 Calendar of meetings for 2018, available at http://www.un.org/Depts/los/reference_files/calendar_of_meetings.htm; accessed 6 June 2018.

7 Available at http://undocs.org/en/A/CONF.232/2018/3; accessed 3 August 2018.

8 See 'Intersessional Workshops aimed at improving understanding of the issues and clarifying key questions as an input to the work of the Working Group in accordance with the terms of reference annexed to General Assembly Resolution 67/78, summary of proceedings prepared by the co-Chairs of the Working Group 1, section 13 (ADVANCED [*sic*], UNEDITED VERSION)'; available at http://www.un.org/Depts/los/biodiversityworkinggroup/documents/BBNJ_Worshops.pdf; accessed 6 August 2018.

9 Convention on Biological Diversity (Rio de Janeiro, 5 June 1992, in force 29 December 1993) 1760 UNTS 79.

10 *Ibid.*, Article 2.

11 When we look at patents from the marine environment, quite a few are awarded on proteins, nucleic acid encoding and enzymes which are derivatives and do not contain functional units of heredity; see M Vierros, 'Marine Genetic Resources—Current uses and schemes for benefit-sharing'; available at www.globaloceanforumdotcom.files.wordpress.com; accessed 28 August 2017. Hence the question of scope is of practical and possibly economic importance.

proteins do not contain functional units of heredity.[12] The CBD definition of genetic resources does not mention derivatives. A dynamic interpretation of the CBD definition, based on the notion that types of uses of genetic material will develop over time, would capture derivatives. Whether the CBD applies to derivatives is therefore open for interpretation.[13] One of the main issues to address is the material scope: whether the ILBI should be limited to MGRs that contain functional units of heredity as in the CBD, or whether it should more broadly cover the utilisation of other parts of biological resources, such as derivatives including enzymes and proteins, and possibly also the utilisation of information, including genetic sequence data.[14]

States have the right to conduct marine scientific research (MSR) in the ABNJ,[15] and in a broad sense this freedom also covers bioprospecting.[16] Drawing from existing models in international, regional and national instruments, many options are available for possible inclusion in the ILBI, but there are, as yet, not many concrete proposals on the table to address the ABS system of the future ILBI. It is suggested here that the introduction and use of the concepts of 'light' and 'heavy' in terms of ABS offer a practical way of grouping various alternatives and provide guidance at a broad level. What will be decisive in characterising an instrument or alternative as 'light' or 'heavy' is normally

12 The Nagoya Protocol on Access to Genetic Resources and the Fair and Equitable Sharing of Benefits Arising from their Utilization to the Convention on Biological Diversity (Nagoya, 29 December 2010, in force 12 October 2014) UNEP/CBD/COP/DEC/X/1, Annex 1 (2010); C.N.782.2010.TREATIES-1(2010 Nagoya Protocol). Article 2 e) defines 'Derivative' as "a naturally occurring biochemical compound resulting from the genetic expression or metabolism of biological or genetic resources, even if it does not contain functional units of heredity".

13 For a thorough discussion on these issues, see PJ Schei and MW Tvedt, 'Genetic Resources in the CBD: The Wording, the Past, the Present and the Future', FNI *Report* 4/2010, 1–24, at p. 7; available at https://www.fni.no/getfile.php/131744-1469869059/Filer/Publikasjoner/FNI-R0410.pdf; accessed 6 June 2018.

14 The full range of views is reflected in the Chair's "non-paper on elements of a draft text of an international legally-binding [*sic*] instrument under the United Nations Convention on the Law of the Sea on the conservation and sustainable use of marine biological diversity of areas beyond national jurisdiction" at p. 6; available at http://www.un.org/depts/los/biodiversity/prepcom_files/Chair_non_paper.pdf; accessed 11 June 2018.

15 United Nations Convention on the Law of the Sea (Montego Bay, 10 December 1982, in force 16 November 1994) 1833 *UNTS* 396, Article 238: "All States, irrespective of their geographical location, and competent international organizations have the right to conduct marine scientific research subject to the rights and duties of other States as provided for in this Convention".

16 According to the *Oxford Dictionary*, 'bioprospecting' means: "The search for plant and animal species from which medicinal drugs and other commercially valuable compounds can be obtained"; available at http://www.en.oxforddictionaires.com; accessed 28 August 2017.

the inclusion of monetary benefit-sharing provisions, especially where these are linked to a genetic resource. The reason is the substantial administrative costs that are associated with monetary benefit-sharing provisions in terms of tracking, monitoring, reporting and enforcement. In general terms it is the view of the author that the ratio of administrative and enforcement costs to gains could probably best be compared with the situations that States encounter in domestic tax enforcement.[17] Monetary instruments may also require a fund to administer earnings. As a consequence, instruments that rely on non-monetary benefit-sharing are characterised as 'light'. It is important, however, to remember that costs are also associated with non-monetary benefit-sharing, but as a starting point these costs are probably substantially lower in comparison with monetary benefit-sharing models.[18]

When designing a full benefit-sharing system for the ILBI, negotiators will also need to address some other questions, which are not dealt with in this paper, such as:

Does the model foster scientific research? How does the model fare in a cost-benefit analysis? What model best addresses the predictions for the future commercial use of genetic material from ABNJ? What model contributes best to conservation and sustainable use of biodiversity? What model stimulates fair and equitable sharing of benefits, also for developing countries? Does the preferred ABS-model have to relate to other elements in the package, such as area-based management tools, and if so, which ABS model fits into a global, hybrid or regional governance system?

2 The LOSC and Concepts Related to Access and Benefit-sharing for the Conservation and Sustainable Use of Biodiversity

Article 193 of the LOSC provides that States have the sovereign right to exploit their natural resources.[19] This principle is also embedded in CBD Article 3 and the Nagoya Protocol on Access to Genetic Resources and the Fair and

17 This depends on how costs are defined. One example where non-monetary benefit-sharing could be more 'costly' than monetary benefit-sharing, is if non-monetary benefit-sharing requirements do not guarantee legal certainty. This then comes with a high 'cost', at least to industrial users. This would be considered a much higher cost than having to pay a reasonable monetary fee in a system that is very simple, clear, transparent and predictable.

18 Non-monetary measures, such as technology transfer and capacity-building, can also be costly and burdensome, depending on the circumstances.

19 LOSC Article 193: "States have the sovereign right to exploit their natural resources pursuant to their environmental policies and in accordance with their duty to protect and preserve the marine environment".

Equitable Sharing of Benefits Arising From Their Utilization to the Convention of Biological Diversity (the Nagoya Protocol).[20] Article 3 of the CBD spells out that "States have, in accordance with the Charter of the United Nations and the principles of international law, the sovereign right to exploit their own resources pursuant to their own environmental policies, and the responsibility to ensure that activities within their jurisdiction or control do not cause damage to the environment of other States or of areas beyond the limits of national jurisdiction". Benefit-sharing is not part of the general obligation states have to "protect and preserve the marine environment" in Article 192 LOSC, although measures that states take to fulfil their environmental obligations under the LOSC might benefit the environment and human society as a whole. The LOSC does not address ABS for the conservation and sustainable use of biodiversity in ABNJ, but some Articles touch upon issues associated with benefit-sharing. LOSC Part XIII on MSR establishes the right to conduct MSR. Scientific research on material of plant, animal, microbial or other origin containing functional units of heredity may be one of the aims of accessing biological resources from ABNJ, but there are no benefit-sharing requirements in Part XIII. There are merely provisions on MSR in the Area in Article 256, and in the water column beyond the exclusive economic zone (EEZ) in Article 257, which provide that states have the right to conduct MSR in these areas. The LOSC has general obligations for Parties on the transfer of marine science and technology on fair and reasonable terms and conditions in Part XIV on Development and Transfer of Marine Technology, which would also cover development and transfer of technology on utilisation of MGRs.[21] However, the transfer of marine technology as set out in LOSC Part XIV is conceptually not regarded as benefit-sharing. Nonetheless, Parties have a duty to promote the establishment of regional marine scientific and technological research centres, particularly in developing states, and foster the transfer of marine technology.[22] Parties' efforts in implementing Part XIII and XIV are assisted by the Intergovernmental Oceanographic Commission of UNESCO

20 See (n 12).

21 LOSC Articles 266, 267, 268 and 269.

22 LOSC Article 276:

> 1. States, in coordination with the competent international organizations, the Authority and national marine scientific and technological research institutions, shall promote the establishment of regional marine scientific and technological research centres, particularly in developing States, in order to stimulate and advance the conduct of marine scientific research by developing States and foster the transfer of marine technology.
>
> 2. All States of a region shall cooperate with the regional centres therein to ensure the more effective achievement of their objectives.

(IOC-UNESCO; hereinafter referred to as the IOC), which is recognised through the LOSC as the competent international organisation in the fields of Marine Scientific Research and Transfer of Marine Technology.[23] The purpose of the IOC is, inter alia, to promote international cooperation and to coordinate programmes in research, services and capacity-building. Criteria and guidelines for the transfer of marine technology have been developed by the IOC.[24] For MSR the Division of Ocean Affairs and Law of the Sea (DOALOS) has developed guidance.[25] However, guidance on genetic resources is not explicitly a part of the work stream of the IOC through its Advisory Body on Experts on the Law of the Sea (ABE-LOS).

The "Area"[26] has the status of "the Common Heritage of Mankind" (CHM) and the International Seabed Authority (ISA) manages the resources on behalf of the international community and is given the responsibility to assist Parties in fleshing out the concrete content and application of the CHM regarding minerals.[27] The ISA does not have the competence to deal with biodiversity ABS and in legal terms there is no demand for prior informed consent to explore or to exploit MGRs in the deep seabed. As a consequence, the Agreement relating to the Implementation of Part XI of the LOSC does not establish a demand for prior informed consent to access MGRs on the seabed.[28] It covers mineral resources which are non-renewable bulk commodities and differ greatly from

23 The IOC's particular role within the framework of Part XIV of the LOSC on Development and Transfer of Marine Technology is reflected in 'Draft IOC Principles on Transfer of Marine Technology, IOC/ABE-LOS I/3 Annex V', at p. 3; available at http://unesdoc.unesco.org/images/0012/001251/125123e.pdf; accessed 11 June 2018.

24 The XXII Session of the Assembly of the Intergovernmental Oceanographic Commission in Resolution XXII-12 adopted 'The IOC Criteria and Guidelines on Transfer of Marine Technology' following the mandate established in Article 271 of the Convention, see IOC-XXII/3 Annex II, at p. 17; available at http://ioc-unesco.org/index.php?option=com_oe&task=viewDocumentRecord&docID=2052; accessed 13 June 2018.

25 DOALOS, 'The Law of the Sea—Marine Scientific Research—A revised guide to the implementation of the relevant provisions of the United Nations Convention on the Law of the Sea'; available at http://www.un.org/depts/los/doalos_publications/publicationstexts/msr_guide%202010_final.pdf; accessed 30 May 2018.

26 LOSC Article 1(1): "Area" means the seabed and ocean floor and subsoil thereof, beyond the limits of national jurisdiction.

27 LOSC Article 153: "Activities in the Area shall be organized, carried out and controlled by the Authority on behalf of the mankind as a whole in accordance with this article as well as other relevant provisions of this Part and the relevant Annexes, and the rules, regulations and procedures of the Authority".

28 Agreement relating to the Implementation of Part XI of the United Nations Convention on the Law of the Sea of 10 December 1982 (New York, 28 July 1994, in force 28 July 1996) 1836 *UNTS* 3.

genetic resources.[29] Thus, the management of minerals from the Area as spelled out in the LOSC should not be regarded as "access and benefit-sharing for the conservation and sustainable use of biodiversity", but rather as distribution of benefits related to the exploitation of mineral commodities. Although the regime for exploitation of minerals is different, there are potential similarities in ways of thinking in terms of benefit-sharing. Article 140 says that:

> Activities in the Area shall … be carried out for the benefit of mankind as a whole and that the Authority shall provide for the equitable sharing of financial and other economic benefits derived from the activities in the Area through any appropriate mechanism.

Thus the 1994 Part XI Implementing Agreement solely deals with benefit-sharing from exploitation of minerals and not genetic resources.

As an innovative financing tool for the conservation and sustainable use of the environment, ABS is characterised by an ambition to direct benefits arising from the utilisation of genetic resources towards the conservation of biological diversity and the sustainable use of its components.[30] On land, benefit-sharing resulting from the utilisation of genetic resources can incentivise the conservation of the ecosystem by the inhabitants or owners of the area from which the genetic resources are sourced. However, the approach does not work in ABNJ or on the seabed. There is no obligation to direct benefits arising from the exploitation of minerals towards the conservation of biological diversity and the sustainability of its components within the CHM regime of Part XI LOSC. This is not an obstacle to using the existing minerals system as a starting point for a model for the management of ABS of MGRs for the conservation and sustainable use of biodiversity as long as proper attention is given to the fundamental differences between managing a commodity such as minerals and managing genetic material.[31]

---

29 "The important difference between genetic resources and biological resources (commodities) lies in a key attribute—replication ability", see Secretariat of the Convention on Biological Diversity, 'The Nagoya Protocol on Access to Genetic Resources and the Fair and Equitable Sharing of Benefits arising from Their Utilization'; available at https://www.cbd.int/doc/nbsap/nbsapcbw-casi-02/nbsap-istanbul-scbd-abs-protocol.pdf; accessed 7 June 2018.

30 Nagoya Protocol Article 9: "The Parties shall encourage users and providers to direct benefits arising from the utilization of genetic resources towards the conservation of biological diversity and the sustainable use of its components".

31 The Royal Society, *'Future Ocean Resources, Metal-Rich Minerals and Genetics' Evidence Pack* (The Royal Society, London, 2017). The Royal Society states: "These two resources differ, in that exploitation of genetic information is likely to have minimal environmental

3 The Nagoya Protocol and the Concept of Prior and Informed Consent

The Nagoya Protocol applies to genetic resources within the scope of Article 15 of the CBD. Article 15 recognises the sovereign rights of states over their natural resources, and further states that the authority to determine access to genetic resources rests with the national governments and is subject to national legislation.

The bilateral default system under the Nagoya Protocol is based on an assumption that biodiversity-rich provider countries will regulate access to genetic resources by making access by the user subject to prior informed consent. Requirements for benefit-sharing may be included in the access provisions and/or in a contract. In a historical context the user is usually a private entity seeking access to genetic resources in a foreign biodiversity-rich country. The State Party where the genetic resources are being utilised has to prove that the genetic resources utilised within its jurisdiction have been accessed in accordance with prior informed consent and that mutually agreed terms have been established, as required by the other State Party. The State Party where the genetic resource is being utilised also has to monitor the utilisation of genetic resources, by setting up at least one checkpoint. Hence, in the Nagoya Protocol context, the utilisation of genetic resources is a matter between two State Parties, possibly also with a third State Party where the same genetic resource is found in situ within the territory of more than one State Party.[32]

Although the Protocol heavily relies on the principle of state sovereignty and bilateral negotiations, it foresees the possibility of a global multilateral benefit-sharing mechanism in its Article 10, but that Article only states that "Parties shall consider the need for and modalities of a global multilateral benefit-sharing mechanism", and so far, Parties to the Nagoya Protocol disagree on the need for such a mechanism.[33]

---

impact, whereas mining may have substantial environmental consequences. But these resources are also environmentally linked; any loss of marine biodiversity imposed by mining will decrease the potential for discovery of useful biological materials".

32 Nagoya Protocol, Article 11.

33 See Decision CBD/NP/MOP/DEC/2/10, where the Subsidiary Body on Implementation is requested to explore the need for a global multilateral benefit-sharing mechanism and make recommendations for consideration by the Conference of the Parties serving as the meeting of the Parties to the Nagoya Protocol at its third meeting in November 2018; available at https://www.cbd.int/doc/decisions/np-mop-02/np-mop-02-dec-10-en.pdf; accessed 13 June 2018.

The concept of prior and informed consent is also at the core of the Nagoya Protocol and appears in Article 6:

> In the exercise of sovereign rights over natural resources, and subject to domestic access and benefit-sharing legislation or regulatory requirements, access to genetic resources for their utilisation shall be subject to the prior informed consent of the Party providing such resources that is the country of origin of such resources or a Party that has acquired the genetic resources in accordance with the CBD, unless otherwise determined by that Party.[34]

The aim is that benefits arising from the utilisation of the accessed resource should flow from users to the Party that provided the resource. Crucial for this "bilateral approach" is that the Party with jurisdiction where the resource is being utilised has a duty to "take appropriate, effective and proportionate legislative, administrative or policy measures to provide that genetic resources utilised within its jurisdiction have been accessed in accordance with prior informed consent and that mutually agreed terms have been established, as required by domestic ABS legislation or regulatory requirements of the other Party".[35] Items such as strengthening capacity for technology transfer are listed as non-monetary benefits in the Annex to the Nagoya Protocol.[36]

The Parties shall encourage users and providers to direct benefits arising from the utilisation of genetic resources towards the conservation of biological diversity.[37] Some countries, mainly developing countries, are developing permit requirements for access to genetic resources within their territories, whereas other, mainly developed countries, either leave access unrestricted or with few restrictions.

4 The International Treaty on Plant Genetic Resources for Food and Agriculture

The most relevant model to draw upon in a BBNJ-context is, in my view, perhaps the International Treaty on Plant Genetic Resources for Food and Agriculture

34 Nagoya Protocol, Article 6, nr. 1.
35 *Ibid.*, Article 15 nr. 1.
36 Nagoya Protocol, Annex nr. 1 f and g.
37 *Ibid.*, Article 9.

(ITPGRFA).[38] At its core is the assumption that genetic resources for food and agriculture are widespread and that a multilateral approach is suitable for such resources. The ITPGRFA revolves around a system of facilitated access. To obtain access to a sample of one of the 64 genera of food and feed crops listed in the annex of the ITPGRFA, a standard material transfer agreement (SMTA) has to be signed. The SMTA has fixed terms and conditions on access to and utilisation of these crops. This system is referred to as a multilateral system of access and benefit-sharing (MLS). The attractiveness of the system is its simplicity: the absence of a need to negotiate terms, which lowers administrative burdens and costs to both the Provider and the User. If products are developed that are derived from the accessed material and the developer decides to restrict others from accessing the products through intellectual property restrictions, then the developer is obliged to pay a percentage of the sales of the product to the Benefit-Sharing Fund. This obligation to pay persists even if only a small quantity of accessed material has been included in the product.[39] The obligation to pay will only end if facilitated access to the product that makes use of the accessed material is restored, or, in other words: put back into the public domain. This is the case for most crop varieties that are available under the Plant Breeder's Rights System. The Fund is to be used to support conservation and further development of agriculture in developing countries.[40]

Questions have been raised about the effectiveness of the MLS and the Benefit-Sharing Fund.[41] On the one hand, no significant mandatory payments have been made to the Fund, which was established in 2008, only voluntary payments.[42] On the other hand, one could argue that the main benefit of the system is to facilitate access to crops and encourage sharing, with millions of accessions being transferred annually using the SMTA and thereby contributing to conservation and sustainable use. Stimulating mandatory payments to the

38 The International Treaty on Plant Genetic Resources for Food and Agriculture (Rome, 3 November 2001, in force 29 June 2004) 2400 *UNTS* 303.

39 ITPGRFA, Article 13.2 d) ii.

40 FAO, *The Multilateral System*; available at http://www.fao.org/plant-treaty/areas-of-work/the-multilateral-system/overview/en/; accessed 7 June 2018.

41 F Rabitz, 'Access without benefit-sharing: Design, effectiveness and reform of the FAO Seed Treaty' (2017) 11(2) *International Journal of the Commons* 621–640; available at http://doi.org/10.18352/ijc.736; accessed 7 June 2018.

42 By 8 March 2017, Italy, Australia, The European Seed Association, Sweden, Indonesia, The International Seed Federation, Austria and Norway had contributed funds that will be used in preparation of the Fourth Call for project proposals; see FAO news release "Norway supports farmers' active use of plant genetic resources"; available at http://www.fao.org/plant-treaty/news/news-detail/en/c/522317/; accessed 9 June 2018.

Benefit-sharing Fund would restrict access as the main benefit.[43] Funds are accessed through a Grant system. However, the resulting paucity of payments to the Fund has led to an establishment of an Ad-Hoc Open-ended Working Group to Enhance the Functioning of the Multilateral System of Access and Benefit-sharing. The purpose of this Working Group is to increase user-based payments and contributions to the benefit-sharing Fund in a sustainable and predictable long-term manner, and enhance the functioning of the MLS by additional measures.[44] The Working Group has, inter alia, been requested to elaborate a full draft of a revised SMTA focusing especially on the development of a Subscription System that would aim to avoid the necessity of any other legal instrument, primarily through a revision of Article 6.11 of the SMTA.[45] The mandate of the Working Group has been extended for the 2018–2019 Biennium.[46]

5 The Special Factors in ABNJ

A number of factors particular to MGRs from the ABNJ have to be borne in mind when developing alternatives for benefit-sharing systems in an agreement such as the proposed ILBI:

- The knowledge base for marine ecosystems in ABNJ, even more than for areas within national jurisdiction, is poorer than for terrestrial ecosystems. ABNJ are the remotest, often deepest, and the most poorly explored parts of the ocean. In effect the collection of genetic material is more likely to be exploratory or speculative in nature than collecting samples of known or anticipated species.
- The geographical distances from ports also means that any authority will be far away from the collection area.
- There is no sovereignty over ABNJ and therefore no basis for access subject to prior informed consent as envisaged by the CBD and the Nagoya Protocol.

43 FAO, *'Second report on the world's plant genetic resources for food and agriculture'* (2010), at p. 99; available at http://www.fao.org/docrep/013/i1500e/i1500e.pdf; accessed 14 August 2018.

44 FAO Resolutions 1/2015(IT/GB-6/15/Res1).
Measures to Enhance the Functioning of the Multilateral System of Access and Benefit-Sharing"; available at http://www.fao.org/3/a-bl138e.pdf, and 2/2015(IT/GB-6/15/Res 2) "Implementation of the Funding Strategy of the International Treaty available at www.fao.org/3/a-bl139e.pdf; accessed 7 June 2018.

45 *Ibid.*

46 IT/GB-7/17/Res 2; available at http://www.fao.org/3/a-mv104e.pdf; accessed 7 June 2018.

- In general, few environmental concerns are associated with the collection of genetic material.[47] However, this would depend on the appropriate collection gear being used, the scarcity of the genetic material and the volume of material collected.
- Only seven pharmaceutical products derived from marine organisms are currently on the market, of which six are based on genetic material from within national jurisdiction and the seventh from a species found both inside national jurisdiction and outside national jurisdiction;[48] and, perhaps most importantly,
- the chances of developing a commercial product from any one sample of a genetic resource are relatively slim.[49]
- There is currently little evidence of systematic commercial-scale development of MGRs from ABNJ.[50] Still, one cannot entirely rule out the possibility that this might change, and the new regime would need to anticipate in some way future technologies and put in place safeguards to ensure conservation and sustainable use.

These factors have some implications for the practical set-up of the various benefit-sharing alternatives, especially for the implementation of prior informed consent and its feasibility in a potential benefit-sharing system.[51]

---

47 The Royal Society (n 31).

48 A Broggiato, T Vanagt, L E Lallier, M Jaspars, G Burton and D Muyldermans, 'Mare Geneticum: Balancing Governance of Marine Genetic Resources in International Waters' (2018) 33(1) *International Journal of Marine and Coastal Law* (*IJMCL*) 3–33, at p. 23. It is difficult to establish whether products and patents which include MGRs are based on genetic material found in ABNJ. R Blasiak *et al.* have identified more than "1600 sequences from 91 species associated with deep-sea and hydrothermal vent systems, reflecting commercial interest in organisms from remote ocean areas, as well as a capacity to collect and use the genes of such species", but admit that "the extent to which organisms collected in the ABNJ are the subject of gene patents will remain unclear until patent authorities require and verify the MGR origin or until voluntary disclosure becomes an industry norm". See R. Blasiak, J-B Jouffray, C Wabnitz, E Sundström and W Österblom, 'Corporate control and global governance of marine genetic resources' (2018) *Sciences Advances* 4(6) eaar 5237, DOI: 10.1126/sciadv.aar5237, at p. 1; available at www.advances.sciencemag.org; accessed 23 June 2018. The author assumes that most of the genetic material referred to in the article is collected from organisms within areas of national jurisdiction, simply because these areas are more accessible than areas outside national jurisdiction and also cheaper to access.

49 Broggiato *et al.*, *ibid.*

50 *Ibid.*, at p. 13.

51 The revised proposal on access to genetic material in Norway was given a public hearing by the Norwegian Government on 3 July 2017. It has a provision in chapter 2, section 9 tailored for the marine environment which gives the permit holder the obligation to, within a reasonable period of time, update the inventory of species collected from

6 Grouping of Approaches Based on Assessment of Existing Instruments

6.1 *Model A: Double Heavy Approach, Heavy on the Access Side, Heavy on the Benefit-sharing Side—The Nagoya Protocol Model*

6.1.1 'Heavy' Access—the Nagoya Model

This model—based on the Nagoya approach—could also be referred to as the "national" model or the "bilateral" model. It would entail the establishment of fully-fledged access regulations or provisions to pave the way for prior and informed consent. Although the Nagoya Protocol does not oblige states to develop access requirements, the Protocol was crafted on the assumption that biodiversity-rich countries will take an interest in developing such requirements. The purpose of access requirements will usually be to set conditions of future benefit-sharing stemming from the utilisation of the resources as foreseen in the Annex to the Nagoya Protocol. States that decide to demand prior informed consent would have to design their measures in accordance with Article 6 (3) of the Protocol to, inter alia, "provide for legal certainty, clarity and transparency of their domestic ABS legislation or regulatory requirements"[52] and "provide for fair and non-arbitrary rules and procedures on accessing genetic resources".[53] Most national access regulations establish a requirement to apply for an access permit to obtain legal access to that country's genetic resources. This requires an institutional set-up: some type of body or authority that can process applications and/or negotiate mutually agreed terms. That authority then decides on permits according to given criteria. To assist with international transparency, in the Nagoya Protocol system, permits constitute

---

the environment; available at https://www.regjeringen.no/no/dokumenter/forskrift-bioprospekteringsforskriften/id711181/; accessed 27 July 2017.

52 Nagoya Protocol, Article 6(3).

53 Nagoya Protocol Article 6 (3b); T Greiber, S Peña Moreno, M Åhrén, J Nieto Carrasco, E Chege Kamau, J Cabrera Medaglia, M Julia Oliva and F Perron-Welch, in cooperation with N Ali and C Williams, *'An Explanatory Guide to the Nagoya Protocol on Access and Benefit-sharing'* (IUCN Environmental Law and Policy Paper No. 83) (IUCN, Gland, 2012) at p. 103 states: "According to Subparagraph (b), a provider State's rules and procedures on accessing genetic resources must be 'fair' and 'non-arbitrary'". Both address the treatment the providing Party accords to parties that request access to its genetic resources. "Fairness" means that equal treatment in applications for access to genetic resources is accorded to similar domestic and foreign applicants and to similar foreign applicants of different Parties. "Non-arbitrariness" is the non-dependence on arbitrary (that is, individual or one-sided) discretion. It is rather fixed on standards and/or rules of law. It also means restrained exercise of power.

internationally recognised certificates of compliance when registered at the ABS Clearing House Mechanism (ABSCH).[54]

6.1.2 'Heavy' Benefit-sharing—the Nagoya Model

Benefit-sharing according to the terms included in individually negotiated contracts is the backbone of the Nagoya Protocol. Contracts, if drafted correctly, would be enforceable through the courts, and possibly through arbitration, depending on the terms.[55] The terms would usually concern themselves with monetary benefit-sharing from revenue from sales from a product that is based on genetic resources, but could also entail obligations of non-monetary benefit-sharing, such as technology transfer. The State authority will negotiate terms up front with the proposed user on a case-by-case basis, or the user signs a standard contract (to lower administrative costs), which could compel them to renegotiate terms once development of a product becomes more certain, or if there is a change in permitted use, e.g., from non-commercial to commercial utilisation. These issues would be entirely up to the Provider Country and the User to agree—although model terms could be available. One of many options would be the requirement for progressive milestone payments based on gross revenue. To be effective, such a system would rely on an efficient tracking and monitoring system and a duty to report back on utilisation.

6.1.3 What Could a 'Heavy-Heavy' Benefit-sharing Model Look Like?

If the ILBI were to reflect both the "heavy" access and the 'heavy" benefit-sharing provisions, then it could state directly that access to MGRs in ABNJ demands a permit enabling prior informed consent as a condition for access to genetic resources in ABNJ. The modalities of the permit system could either be set out in the ILBI or finalised at a later stage. It would need to designate a body to handle applications. In practical terms, an open permit to bioprospect could be awarded by an appropriately authorised body, and details about the genetic material collected would have to be reported to that body at a later stage to enable contract negotiations between the party seeking access to genetic material and the authorised body. Alternatively, to simplify the process, a lump sum could be paid in advance for access, and placed into a fund. A more

54 Nagoya Protocol, Article 17 nr. 2: "A permit or its equivalent issued in accordance with Article 6, paragraph 3(e) and made available to the Access and Benefit-Sharing Clearing-House, shall constitute an internationally recognised certificate of compliance".

55 On the importance of well-drafted contracts, see T Rosanne Young and M Tvedt, *Drafting Successful Access and Benefit-sharing Contracts* (Brill, Leiden, 2017).

advanced version of this alternative could be to pair the lump-sum access condition with "earn-out" provisions in case of commercialisation.[56]

Regarding the choice of organisations to serve as the authorised body, the options available range from making use of existing organisations, such as the ISA which already handles access applications for exploration for mineral resources in the Area, to integrating these functions into the role of the ILBI Secretariat, or the establishment of a separate Marine Genetic Resources Body. A potential argument for giving this role to the ISA is that valuable mineral resources and genetic resources often are found in the same ecosystem in the Area. It can therefore be argued that there should be some coherence between the ISA regulatory regime of deep sea mining and the potential regime in the ILBI for MGRs, both to avoid regulatory conflicts and (in the case of the operation of deep sea mining) to make sure that MGRs are properly collected and stored ex situ if deep sea mining is likely to have adverse effects on the genetic potential of the biological resources in the sites where deep sea mining is planned. The authorised body would have to be well staffed and competent in order to handle negotiations and enforcement issues. The permit could depend on the successful contract negotiation between the authorised body on the one side and the entity seeking the MGRs on the other on a case-by-case basis. The contract would have to be enforceable before courts and spell out the various benefit-sharing elements, which could be of both a monetary and a non-monetary character. Payments could be made to a benefit-sharing fund.

6.2 *Model B: Double 'Light' Approach, 'Light' on the Access Side, 'Light' on the Benefit-Sharing Side—Share the Science Model*

6.2.1 'Light' Approach to Access

The absence of sovereignty over ABNJ can possibly pave the way for an arrangement that differs from the prior informed consent and permit system that is the hallmark of the Nagoya Protocol approach. An alternative approach might establish a duty to notify or report to a body such as DOALOS, IOC or the ISA on MGRs collected in ABNJ. Detailed cruise reports could satisfy the need for information of who accessed what, where and when, in what way and

56 "An earnout is a contractual provision stating that the seller of a business is to obtain additional compensation in the future if the business achieves certain financial goals, which are usually stated as a percentage of gross sales or earnings. If an entrepreneur seeking to sell a business is asking for a higher price than a buyer is willing to pay, an earnout provision can be utilized. In a simplified example, there could be a purchase price of $1,000,000 plus 5% of gross sales over the next three years". See: https://www.investopedia.com; available at https://www.investopedia.com/terms/e/earnout.asp; accessed 9 June 2018.

in what quantity. Because of uncertainties about the exact nature of material gathered at sea the reporting requirements could apply post-cruise. The data could be fed into a data base to increase the knowledge base of ABNJ ecosystems. The ecosystem and scientific information gathered could be shared in an open-access system, possibly linked to a repository or a clearing house. Many states already demand that results from publicly funded research are made available and accessible to all.[57] However, companies accessing MGRs in ABNJ that fund their own research consider information such as genetic sequence data as business-sensitive and may be reluctant to share such information. A way to circumvent this problem could be to have an embargo period before the data become public, to secure the interests of the business community.[58] The approach could be combined with a duty of care when collecting MGRs, which in practical terms translates into a duty to use the appropriate gear or possibly even refrain from collecting samples in sensitive areas, such as ecologically or biologically significant marine areas (EBSAs) under the CBD. Furthermore, even stricter criteria for access could apply in MPAs.

A variation of this 'light' approach would be to have no access regulations at all, but simply non-monetary benefit-sharing requirements according to criteria set out in the ILBI, possibly with a duty of care when collecting genetic material. This 'light' approach would then rely heavily on capacity-building on the benefit-sharing side.

6.2.2 'Light' Approach to Benefit-sharing

This model would imply some non-monetary benefit-sharing requirements in the ILBI. These could possibly be the requirement to share genetic sequence data after access, or to share also information on derivatives, such as information on biochemical components. Central to such a 'light' approach would be a duty to deposit a sample in public collections in the flag state or in the port state, or alternatively in a collection with regional responsibility under the ILBI. The public collections could provide easy access for all and network with public collections in developing countries. One possibility would be to build on the existing *ex-situ* science networks between north-south and south-south and let interested State Parties participate in those networks. This structure can be found in the ITPGRFA which links *ex-situ* collections at a national, regional and international level. The IOC Criteria and Guidelines on Transfer of Marine Technology (CGTMT), drawn up by the ABE-LOS following the mandate established in Article 271 of the LOSC, has elements that

57 Broggiato *et al.* (n 48), at p. 22.
58 *Ibid.*

can possibly be expanded to cover MGRs.[59] This 'light' approach puts emphasis on the role of private companies in innovation and product development and acknowledges that this is a benefit for society in itself. It excludes mandatory monetary benefit-sharing and relies on a mix of enabling benefit-sharing measures in the ILBI, such as cooperation and technology transfer, and some capacity-building measures. A benefit-sharing fund, or an existing fund, could be open to voluntary contributions.

6.2.3 What Could a 'Light-Light' Benefit-sharing Model Look Like?

The ILBI could either state directly that collection of MGRs in ABNJ is free or that the collection of genetic resources depends on notification either pre-collection or post-collection when the genetic material is placed in an ex-situ collection.[60] Both alternatives would correspond well with Article 238 LOSC, which states that all States and competent international organisations have a right to conduct MSR subject to the requirements set forth in the LOSC. A 'light-light' approach would then need to work within the boundaries of the LOSC to address the benefit-sharing gaps at the same time as maintaining the freedom of scientific research. To address environmental concerns, access could depend on a duty of care combined with a duty to use best available techniques and methods of operation.

There could also be a duty to share information, and here the options range from the sharing of information on the ecosystem where the sample was collected, the sharing of information on the genetic properties of the sample, the sharing of the genetic sequence data of the organism and the sharing of information on derivatives such as proteins and enzymes. The ILBI could have all of the above or only some of them.[61] There would also be capacity-building elements.

---

59 IOC/ABE-LOS, 'IOC Criteria and Guidelines on Transfer of Marine Technology'; available at https://classroom.oceanteacher.org/pluginfile.php/14356/mod_label/intro/IOC%20TMT%20Criteria%20and%20Guidelines.pdf; accessed 11 June 2018.

60 On a possible prior notification system see Broggiato *et al.* (n 48), at p. 18.

61 Both the CBD and ITPGRFA are currently discussing the implications of genetic sequence data for ABS which are not addressed in a clear way in either instrument; see Recommendation SBSTTA-22/1, Digital sequence information (DSI) on genetic resources; available at https://www.cbd.int/meetings/SBSTTA-22; accessed 6 August 2018; see also FAO Resolution 2/2017, 'Measures to enhance the functioning of the multilateral system of Access and Benefit-sharing':

> 13. The Co-Chairs explained how their proposed consolidated text for the revised SMTA made provision for the concept of DSI to be reflected in the revised SMTA through a new definition of "genetic parts and components.

6.3 *Model C: Light Access with Heavy Benefit-sharing Elements in Case of Commercialisation—Monetary Model*

6.3.1 'Light' Access

This model would have many of the same features on the access side as Model B. Notification or reporting requirements would be the basis for the mandatory monetary benefit-sharing requirements in the ILBI. A system of facilitated access like that under the ITPGRFA would mean that it would be possible to access genetic material through gene banks in the public domain and under the direct control of the ILBI Contracting Parties by creating a common pool of sampled MGRs.[62] The access to the material would be meant to be free of charge and swift. A potential fee could only cover the actual processing and posting costs of accessing the *ex-situ* sample. The main obligations on the user/recipient side, according to the SMTA of the ITPGRFA, is to undertake that "the Material shall be used or conserved only for the purposes of research, breeding and training for food and agriculture. Such purposes shall not include chemical, pharmaceutical and/or other non-food/feed industrial uses".[63] Similar limitations on use could potentially be introduced in the ILBI.

6.3.2 'Heavy' Benefit-sharing

The core of this model would be detailed monetary benefit-sharing requirements in the ILBI itself or in a SMTA or other type of standard contract. Variations of this approach have been implemented within national jurisdiction either as part of the implementation of the CBD or the Nagoya Protocol, notably in the Australian regulations that state:

> Where an application is made for a permit to access genetic resources in Commonwealth Areas for commercial or potential commercial purposes, the applicant will enter into a benefit-sharing agreement with each Access Provider before the permit can be issued.[64] Where the Gross Exploitation Revenue received by the Access Party in a calendar year falls within a

14. There was no consensus at this meeting on if and how to reflect issues related to DSI in the text of the revised SMTA

available at http://www.fao.org/3/a-mv104e.pdf; accessed 8 June 2018.

62 M Tvedt and E Jørem, 'Bioprospecting in the High Seas: Regulatory Options for Benefit Sharing' (2013) (16)(4–5) *The Journal of Intellectual Property* 150–167, at p. 155; Doi: 10.1002/jwip.12010.

63 Standard Material Transfer Agreement Article 6.1; available at http://www.fao.org/3/a-bc083e.pdf; accessed 8 June 2018.

64 Part 8A of the Australian Environment Protection and Biodiversity Conservation Regulations 2000; available at https://www.legislation.gov.au/Details/F2016C00914; accessed 2 August 2018.

specified range, the Access Party will have pay to the Commonwealth the corresponding percentage of gross Exploitation Revenue specified in the table. This range is between 0–5 %.[65]

Hence, in the BBNJ context it could also be possible to have no monetary benefit-sharing obligations for materials used in basic science (i.e., non-commercial use), but rather have such provisions upon commercialisation. However, there is a question on how effective such a division is, because it could be easy to circumvent, and frequently the intention of the user is unclear or a 'grey area'.

The revised 2015 Brazilian regulation is also based on a division between commercial use and non-commercial use that does not lead to commercial uses and it has a mandatory notification requirement for commercial uses through an electronic system, SisGen.[66] However, in cases involving access to genetic heritage in maritime regions within Brazilian jurisdiction, prior government authorisation is required.[67] Benefit-sharing is triggered by economic exploitation; the manufacturer of the finished product is expected to share benefits.[68] A standard benefit-sharing agreement between the State of Brazil and the user establishes that up to 1% of the total income from sales of a product derived from Brazilian biodiversity will go to a government-managed fund, exclusively used for environmental preservation and valorisation of traditional

---

65 Australian Government, Department of the Environment, 'Deed of Agreement in relation to Access to Biological Resources in Commonwealth areas for commercial or potential commercial purposes and Benefit-Sharing, Schedule 3. Benefit-Sharing with the Commonwealth'; available at http://environment.gov.au/system/files/pages/e3584028-d083-4aec-acdd-c0aa635a529f/files/commonwealth-and-access-party-model-benefit-sharing-agreement-2012.pdf; accessed 6 August 2018.

66 Law 13,123 of 20 May 2015. Subsequent related regulations are: Decree 8,772 of 11 2016; available at http://www.planalto.gov.br/ccivil_03/_Ato2015-2018/2016/Decreto/D8772.htm; accessed 3 August 2018.

67 T Delille, B Luvizotto and T de Bessa Antunes, 'New Brazilian Law on Genetic Heritage gives one year to companies to report on their past activities having used Brazilian genetic heritage', *Mayer Brown Legal Update* (2017); available at https://www.mayerbrown.com/new-brazilian-law-on-genetic-heritage-gives-one-year-to-companies-to-report-on-their-past-activities-having-used-brazilian-genetic-heritage-12-07-2017/; accessed 23 April 2018.

68 K Davis, P Holanda, C Lyal, M Silva and E Fontes, 'Implementation of the Nagoya Protocol on Access and Benefit Sharing: Dialogue between Brazil and the European Union' (2016) at p. 39; available at https://www.researchgate.net/publication/312305543_Implementation_of_the_Nagoya_Protocol_on_Access_and_Benefit_Sharing_Dialogue_between_Brazil_and_the_European_Union; accessed 3 August 2018.

groups.[69] Benefit-sharing may also be non-monetary and is fixed at 75% of the monetary value, by agreement.[70] If the revenue comes from a product derived from traceable traditional knowledge, there must be a negotiation with the community which "owns" it in order to establish the amount to be reinvested in that community; it also must exempt small companies from entering into a benefit-sharing agreement.[71] The hallmark of this approach is that the price to pay for access is payment at the time of commercialisation of a product either based on turnover or revenue ("earn out" agreements).[72]

The reason for grouping these instruments as 'heavy' and not 'light' is not the monetary payment part as such, but the considerable administrative effort that follows the implementation of such monetary benefit-sharing regimes. The SMTA system, as spelled out in the ITPGRFA, does not require tracking and monitoring in itself, but some form of its reporting requirements would be necessary for effective enforcement. Also, in a BBNJ context a standard contractual approach requires some kind of interaction with a body other than the Provider and the User. In the context of the ITPGRFA the FAO performs these functions as 'Third Party Beneficiary' to make the obligations of the SMTA effective. This concept also responds to the need for an institutional mechanism to guarantee compliance with SMTA obligations.[73] The SMTA requires that a recipient who is obliged to make payments submit to the governing body an annual report on the sales of the product, the amount of the payment due and the information that allows the identification of any restrictions that have given rise to the benefit-sharing obligations.[74]

69 According to the *Merriam-Webster Dictionary*, "valorisation" is to assign value or merit to; available at www.merriam.webster.com; accessed 9 June 2018.

70 Davis *et al.* (n 68).

71 G Di Blasi and E Emrich, 'Brazilian biodiversity: Levelling the genetic resources playing field' (2016) *Life Sciences Intellectual Property Review* (*LSIPR*); available at https://www.lifesciencesipreview.com/contributed-article/brazilian-biodiversity-levelling-the-genetic-resources-playing-field; accessed 31 August 2017.

72 See (n 56): "An earnout is a contractual provision stating that the seller of a business is to obtain additional compensation in the future if the business achieves certain financial goals, which are usually stated as a percentage of gross sales or earnings".

73 G Moore, 'Protecting the Interests of the Multilateral System under the Standard Material Transfer Agreement the Third Party Beneficiary' in M Halewood, I López Noriega and S Louafi (eds), *Crop Genetic Resources as a Global Commons: Challenges in International Law and Governance* (Routledge, Abingdon, 2013) 164–176.

74 D Mancella, 'The Design and Mechanics of the Multilateral System of Access and Benefit Sharing' in Halewood *et al.* (eds), *ibid.*, 150–163.

6.3.3 What Would a 'Light-Heavy' Benefit-sharing Model Look Like?

The notification procedure on the access side could follow the same lines as in option B. The ILBI State Parties could enter into a multilateral system set out in the ILBI itself which links existing public *in-situ* collections into a network. When collecting genetic material from ABNJ, a standard contract could be signed by the entity seeking access to the genetic material, and related information could be made accessible to all parties. For private entities this could entail delivering a sample to a public collection which forms a part of the multilateral system where physical samples and related information could be accessed. There could also possibly be a Clearing House under the IOC or another body.

A system of open access is already being practised by many actors in the scientific community and could be combined with payments to a biodiversity fund. A key issue for the private sector would be the possibility of an extended embargo period, allowing samples and data to be kept confidential for a certain period against payment to the Fund.[75] In general, income from the commercialisation of genetic material collected in ABNJ could flow into a special fund set up for this purpose or into a repurposed existing fund. The private entities, and whoever accesses the samples, could sign a standard contract with the public collection on behalf of the body upon commercialisation (meaning that the obligation to pay commences when the product is placed on the market) of products that are based on the genetic properties of the samples. This means that elements of the Brazilian model to a certain extent is replicable in the ABNJ context. A body such as the ISA, the ILBI Secretariat, or some separate MGR body, could also have the mandate to oversee the signing of the standard agreement, which could be done electronically to lower the transaction costs. Here it is important to note that the SMTA system as implemented by the parties to the ITPGRFA does not require tracking and monitoring in itself, but some form of reporting requirements would be necessary for effective enforcement. Also, in an ABNJ context, a standard contractual approach requires some kind of interaction with a body other than the provider and the user.

7 Conclusion: the Road Ahead

There are many possible variations of the various models. So far, developed countries seem to favour 'light-light' approaches, whereas developing

75 Broggiato *et al.* (n 48).

countries prefer either a 'heavy-heavy' approach, or a 'light-heavy' approach.[76] At the same time, many delegations, whether from developed or developing countries, have explicitly stated that the ILBI should not impede scientific research.[77] The main ambition in the negotiations should be to tailor a model which works practically in the ABNJ context today and also paves the way for possible sharing of benefits in the future. In this context important lessons are to be learned from the ongoing developments in other international instruments, such as the CBD, the Nagoya Protocol and the ITPGRFA. The most important lesson learned is to sensibly clarify the material scope of the instrument, to avoid the ILBI ending up as an underwater battle-field between different groups of countries, similar to the situation with the CBD and the Nagoya Protocol.[78] The second lesson is that there are few success stories in the regulatory history of monetary access and benefit-sharing, apart from the Pandemic Influenza Preparedness (PIP) Framework under the World Health Organization (WHO) (which cannot be replicated in a BBNJ context).[79] It will be critical to build trust in any process and important to have some degree of international transparency in the collection and use of MGRs and derivatives from ABNJ. This could provide common ground as the backbone of the ILBI on benefit-sharing. After all, much scientific research is already being shared within the scientific community. This could also clarify the quantities of genetic material that are being accessed in ABNJ. The ABNJ do not comprise one ecosystem: there are many, and many are connected with areas within national

76 Personal observation based on interventions made from the floor at PrepCom 3. For a summary of views, see 'Preparatory Committee established by General Assembly resolution 69/292: Development of an international legally binding instrument under the United Nations Convention on the Law of the Sea on the conservation and sustainable use of marine biological diversity of areas beyond national jurisdiction, Chair's overview of the third session of the Preparatory Committee'; available at http://www.un.org/depts/los/biodiversity/prepcom_files/Chair_Overview.pdf; accessed 9 June 2018.

77 *Ibid.*, at p. 5.

78 *IISD Earth Negotiations Bulletin* (Monday, 1 November 2010) (9)(544), 'Summary of the tenth conference of the Parties to the Convention of Biological Diversity' 18–29 October 2010: "Final compromise text was characterized by many as a 'masterpiece in creative ambiguity.' Instead of resolving outstanding issues by crafting balanced compromise proposals—an endeavor that would have been doomed to fail—the contentious references were either deleted from the text or replaced by short and general provisions allowing flexible interpretation, but possibly also too wide a berth for implementation"; available at http://enb.iisd.org/vol09/enb09544e.html; accessed 3 August 2018.

79 World Health Organization, 'Pandemic Influenza Preparedness Framework for the sharing of influenza viruses and access to vaccines and other benefits' (2011); available at http://apps.who.int/iris/bitstream/handle/10665/44796/9789241503082_eng.pdf;jsessionid=5AF51BEDF5C6567545D60601AE604A0B?sequence=1; accessed 6 June 2018.

jurisdiction; information about ecological connectivity between ABNJ and coastal areas could usefully inform national and international marine regulations. Many developing countries are in need of capacity building to better conserve and sustainably use their own genetic resources before they commence utilising genetic material from ABNJ. Taking part in cruises, laboratory work, product development, etc., related to MGRs from ABNJ could prove beneficial for developing states in their utilisation of national genetic resources. It is important that the design of the ILBI should give appropriate attention to these cross-cutting issues.

CHAPTER 10

Mare Geneticum: towards an Implementing Agreement for Marine Genetic Resources in International Waters

Thomas Vanagt,[a,b] *Arianna Broggiato,*[a,b] *Laura E. Lallier,*[a,e] *Marcel Jaspars,*[c] *Geoff Burton,*[d] *and Dominic Muyldermans*[b]

[a] eCOAST Marine Research, 8400 Ostend, Belgium

[b] ABS-int, 9052 Zwijnaarde, Belgium

[c] Marine Biodiscovery Centre, Department of Chemistry, University of Aberdeen, Aberdeen AB24 3UE, UK

[d] United Nations University, Institute for the Advanced Study of Sustainability, Tokyo 150-8925, Japan

[e] Maritime Institute, Faculty of Law, University of Ghent, 9000 Ghent, Belgium

Abstract

A fair and effective regime regulating benefit-sharing of marine genetic resources (MGR) in areas beyond national jurisdiction (ABNJ) must consider the inclusion of developing states, support scientific research and safeguard investments of the private sector. The present innovative proposal ensures a delicate balance through an approach based on open access, albeit with limitations. Access to MGR in ABNJ is facilitated, but conditional on the public release of collected samples and raw data. Adoption of the open access principle guarantees a powerful form of non-monetary benefit-sharing. The balance is maintained by the option for an extended embargo period, allowing samples and data to be kept confidential for a certain period, against payment to a biodiversity contribution fund. Monetary benefit-sharing, as a sector-negotiated percentage on revenue, could be imposed at the point of product commercialisation, and would offer a tangible payment system with a low transaction cost.

DOI:10.1163/9789004391703_012

Keywords

marine genetic resources – areas beyond national jurisdiction – biodiversity – Law of the Sea – benefit-sharing – research – open access

1 Introduction

Mare Liberum.* Freedom of the seas. When Hugo Grotius wrote this piece—one of the foundations of contemporary maritime legal doctrine—in 1609,[1] the seas of this world had already been a *de facto* synonym for freedom for a number of centuries. In the context of naval conflicts in Europe, Grotius thought that the world's oceans should be freely accessible to all and shared amongst nations. This perspective was in direct response to the Portuguese maritime policy that claimed exclusivity of traffic to the East Indies for trade purposes.[2] Grotius's essay was not well received then. A further example of opposition to the freedom of the seas was provided by John Selden's *Mare Clausum*. This gives insight into the British point of view at the time, claiming a monopoly over fishing rights in the North Sea.[3]

Nevertheless, Grotius's *Mare Liberum* left us with a heritage of thoughts tending towards the consideration of the oceans as a common space and common resource to be "free and open to all".[4] Even though coastal states' creeping

---

* This chapter is an updated version of Broggiato, A., Vanagt, T., Lallier, L.E., Jaspars, M., Burton, G. and Muyldermans, D. Mare Geneticum: Balancing Governance of Marine Genetic Resources in International Waters. *International Journal of Marine and Coastal Law* vol. 3 issue 1 Pages 3–33 (2017).

Corresponding author: Thomas Vanagt (e-mail: thomas.vanagt@abs-int.eu). Arianna Broggiato and Thomas Vanagt are equally contributing first authors. Acknowledgements: This chapter is a background contribution to the PharmaSea project—Increasing Value and Flow in the Marine Biodiscovery Pipeline—supported by the European Union's FP7 Programme under grant agreement No 312184. The authors would like to thank Lyle Glowka, Meredith Evans-Lloyd, Matthias-Leonhard Mayer, Chris Lyal, Hiroko Muraki Gottlieb, Julian Jacksons and the referees for their comments on a preliminary draft of their article. Any comments expressed by the authors therein must not be attributed to any state, international body or non-governmental organization.

1 H Grotius, *Freedom of the Seas, or, the right which belongs to the Dutch to take part in the East Indian trade* (Oxford University Press, New York, 1916).

2 MB Vieira, '*Mare Liberum* vs. *Mare Clausum*: Grotius, Freitas, and Selden's debate on dominion over the seas' (2003) 64(3) *Journal of the History of Ideas* 361–377, at p. 361.

3 *Ibid.*, at p. 362.

4 H Grotius (n 1), at p. 32.

jurisdiction has continuously expanded into the ocean over the 20th century,[5] 40%[6] of the planet's surface (64% of the surface of the oceans) still lies in international areas of the High Seas[7] and the Area,[8] commonly referred to as areas beyond national jurisdiction (ABNJ).

The Freedom of the High Seas that all sailors knew and cherished slowly became a "relative" freedom as the international community cooperated to regulate certain activities that occur in ABNJ. The 1958 Geneva Convention on the High Seas[9] addresses what can and cannot be controlled in international waters, e.g., piracy, pollution, and the activity of warships.

In 1982, with the adoption of the United Nations Convention on the Law of the Sea (LOSC),[10] the jurisdiction of coastal states was further extended. The freedom of the High Seas, though recognised as a principle, was further restricted. In the Area, for example, mineral resources were designated as being the Common Heritage of Mankind.[11]

Despite appearances, however, Grotius's heritage has not been slowly erased but rather operationalized. The pillar of his argument for freedom relied on the idea of sharing a common domain: the sea.[12] The current tendency to regulate these traditionally unregulated areas is not occurring in a *Mare Clausum* type of policy, but is rather following the recognition that there is a further need for sharing the resources provided by our planet. This comes with realising the need for international cooperation and regulation in order to put the adequate frameworks in place within which such sharing can happen in a peaceful and harmonised way.

In the context of this ideology of global sharing, the international community is now in the process of negotiating a new international legally binding instrument (ILBI) under the LOSC. Launched by the UN General Assembly in 2004,[13] the purpose of the "biodiversity beyond national jurisdiction"

5 E Franckx, 'The 200-Mile Limit: Between Creeping Jurisdiction and Creeping Common Heritage? Some Law of the Sea Considerations from Professor Louis Sohn's Former LL.M. Student' (2007) 39(3) *The George Washington International Law Review* 467–498, at p. 469 et seq.

6 See the Global Environment Facility, available at http://www.thegef.org/topics/areas-beyond-national-jurisdiction; accessed 18 January 2017.

7 United Nations Convention on the Law of the Sea (Montego Bay, 10 December 1982, in force 16 November 1994), 1833 *UNTS* 396, Art. 87.

8 *Ibid.*, Art. 1(1).

9 Convention on the High Seas (Geneva, 29 April 1958, in force 30 September 1962), 450 *UNTS* 11.

10 LOSC (n 7).

11 *Ibid.*, Art. 136.

12 Grotius (n 1), at p. 22 *et seq.*

13 UNGA Res. 59/24, UN Doc. A/RES/59/24, 17 November 2004, para. 73.

(BBNJ) process was to assess the status of conservation and sustainable use of marine biodiversity in ABNJ and to investigate the potential need for further international cooperation. The BBNJ process led the General Assembly to launch the development of the aforementioned ILBI in 2015, establishing a Preparatory Committee for the purpose of providing recommendations on the elaboration of a draft text.[14] The Preparatory Committee "shall address the conservation and sustainable use of marine biological diversity of areas beyond national jurisdiction, in particular, together and as a whole, marine genetic resources, including questions on the sharing of benefits [...]".[15] In July 2017, at the end of the fourth meeting of the Preparatory Committee, a recommendation to the UN General Assembly was adopted by consensus, even though many items remain unresolved, amongst other many aspects related to marine genetic resources (MGR), including the sharing of benefits.[16] On December 24, 2017, the UN General Assembly adopted by consensus Resolution 72/249[17], to convene an intergovernmental conference and undertake formal negotiations for a new international legally binding instrument under the LOSC for the conservation and sustainable development of marine biological diversity in areas beyond national jurisdiction. The organizational meeting for the intergovernmental conference took place from 16–18 April 2018.

When considering the issue of MGR and the sharing of benefits in this BBNJ context, the international community has come a long way from Hugo Grotius's conception—but not that long. Grotius had a spatial approach to the freedom of the seas, arguing that access and navigation was the right of all for "the sea is common to all".[18] The international community has moved from sharing the ocean space freely to sharing its natural resources in an organised and regulated fashion, in particular commodities like fish and minerals.

Centuries later, the BBNJ process is now trying to govern and regulate the less tangible but nevertheless valuable biodiversity, with the aim of enhancing

14 UNGA Res. 69/292, UN Doc. A/Res/69.292, 6 July 2015, para. 1(a).

15 *Ibid.*, para. 2.

16 Report of the Preparatory Committee established by General Assembly Resolution 69/292: Development of an international legally binding instrument under the United Nations Convention on the Law of the Sea on the conservation and sustainable use of marine biological diversity of areas beyond national jurisdiction, UN Doc. A/AC.287/2017/PC.4/2, 21 July 2017, p.20. Available at www.un.org/ga/search/view_doc.asp?symbol=A/AC.287/2017/PC.4/2; accessed 30 October 2017.

17 Resolution 72/249 adopted by the General Assembly on 24 December 2017. International legally binding instrument under the United Nations Convention on the Law of the Sea on the conservation and sustainable use of marine biological diversity of areas beyond national jurisdiction. Available at https://undocs.org/en/A/RES/72/249; accessed June 2018.

18 Grotius (n 1), at p. 28.

access for scientific research on MGR in ABNJ and for the sharing of benefits arising from their utilisation.[19] This enhanced access to MGR cannot be regarded independently from the overarching objectives of sustainable use and conservation of marine biodiversity in ABNJ. In its modern and evolved version, the *Mare Liberum* of the 17th century thus finds its echo in the *Mare Geneticum* of the 21st century.

In recent years, many comprehensive scholarly studies have been written on the topic of MGR in ABNJ, analysing international cooperation issues, identifying legal gaps and illustrating possible interpretations. Hence, the present article will not introduce the history and diplomacy behind the BBNJ process,[20] neither will it analyse in depth the legal issues raised by a new treaty surrounding the discussion. Enshrined in the *Mare Geneticum* approach of shared access and utilisation, this article provides a pragmatic approach to the MGR in ABNJ component of the new ILBI, aiming to inform and inspire the BBNJ negotiations. The analysis will cover all three pillars of an access and benefit-sharing (ABS) regime: access; benefit-sharing; and compliance.

This article first gives an overview of the building blocks of the proposed governance regime. It then lays out the scientific and technical foundations forming the rationale of our proposal. This includes findings based on recent technical analyses on the market value of MGR in ABNJ and the gaps in research capabilities of states, and indications where relevant data are not available and further studies might be needed.

The core of this article further develops each building block of the proposed governance regime for MGR in ABNJ. This is followed by an illustration of how the scientific community implements in practice the concept of open access to data and samples as applicable to marine scientific research (MSR) in ABNJ, as we propose in this article. The final section illustrates a potential centralised compliance system, before summing up the whole proposed governance regime.

19 For a comprehensive description of access to MGR within national jurisdiction of coastal States, see LE Lallier, O McMeel, T Greiber, T Vanagt, AD Dobson and M Jaspars, 'Access to and use of marine genetic resources: understanding the legal framework' (2014) 31(5) *Natural Products Reports* 612–616; LE Lallier, A Broggiato, D Muyldermans and T Vanagt, 'Marine Genetic Resources and the Access and Benefit-Sharing Legal Framework' in LJ Stal and MS Cretoiu (eds.), *The Marine Microbiome—An Untapped Source of Biodiversity and Biotechnological Potential* (Springer International Publishing, Switzerland, 2016) 453–472.

20 A Broggiato, S Arnaud-Haond, C Chiarolla, and T Greiber, 'Fair and equitable sharing of benefits from the utilization of marine genetic resources in areas beyond national jurisdiction: Bridging the gaps between science and policy' (2014) 49 *Marine Policy* 176–185, at pp. 179–181.

2 Overview and Scope of the Proposed Building Blocks

The proposed governance regime can be divided into three steps that build on the CBD and its Nagoya Protocol: access, benefit-sharing and compliance. However, it is not the ambition or purpose of this article to provide detailed or final solutions, in particular with regard to enforcement or implementation measures. Rather, *Mare Geneticum* seeks to propose sound basic principles for the establishment of a realistic and functioning MGR regime in ABNJ. The principles are visualised in Fig. 1.

In this regime, *in situ* access to MGR in ABNJ is facilitated through a simple notification step: the Obligatory Prior Electronic Notification (OPEN). The online notifications submitted by (prospective) users should be managed by the international organisation that will likely be established or mandated by the ILBI. However, the user must accept certain conditions for the OPEN to be recorded: the obligation to share non-monetary and monetary (when applicable) benefits arising from the utilisation of the MGR. The OPEN is the starting point of a track-and-trace system that can benefit both the users and the regulator.

The main non-monetary benefit is based on the open access (OA) principle: releasing samples and raw data (metadata and, if applicable, genetic sequence data and biochemical data) to the public domain through openly accessible biorepositories and databases. Connecting various collections around the globe will strengthen existing and newly created networks of biorepositories, or "common pools" of MGR.[21] Their coordination, coupled with the OA approach, will therefore facilitate *ex situ* access as easily as *in situ* sampling through the same OPEN system.

To safeguard the interests of scientists and of commercial users, limitations to the OA principle can be awarded via an embargo period which will allow a user to keep material and data private for a certain period, e.g., to secure confidentiality while publishing the first results of research or while applying for a patent. When needed, the embargo could be extended, triggering the payment of an exclusivity fee as a counterpart. This will allow users to further

---

21 Broggiato *et al.* (n 20), at p. 181; T Greiber, 'Common pools for marine genetic resources: a possible instrument for a future multilateral agreement addressing marine biodiversity in areas beyond national jurisdiction', in EC Kamau and G Winter (eds.), *Common Pools of Genetic Resources—Equity and Innovation in International Biodiversity Law* (Routledge, London and New York, 2013), 399–414, at pp. 407–411; G Wright, J Rochette and T Greiber, 'Sustainable Development of the Oceans: Closing the Gaps in the International Legal Framework' in V Mauerhofer (ed.), *Legal Aspects of Sustainable Development* (Springer International Publishing, Switzerland, 2016) 549–564, at p. 556.

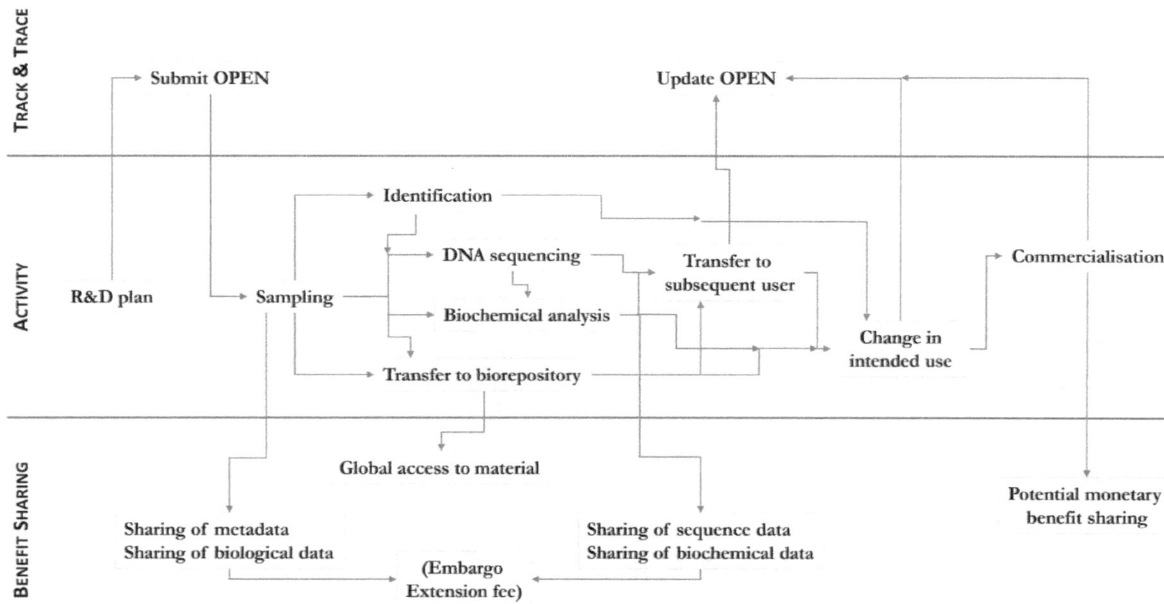

FIGURE 1 The flow diagram of Mare Geneticum—possible flows between various activities, benefit-sharing options and track and trace mechanisms. However, the diagram is not intended to give a complete picture in terms of access and benefit-sharing options associated with utilisation of MGR from ABNJ. For example, this figure does not capture all types of benefit-sharing options such as technology transfer or capacity building.

advance their research and to safeguard their investments. The exclusivity payments could be made into a biodiversity contribution fund. Such a fund should be dedicated to the functioning of an international organisation, if any is to be mandated by the ILBI, for the regular implementation and management of the relevant MGR provisions, as well as to contribute to the conservation efforts of the three other building blocks of the BBNJ package, namely environmental impact assessments, marine protected areas and technology transfer. The *Mare Geneticum* approach thus offers three possibilities to users:

- Open Access to MGR and data;
- Embargo period (relatively short);
- Exclusivity subject to payment.

If monetary benefits, additional to the exclusivity fee, would be agreed upon during the negotiation of the ILBI, we suggest these to be linked to the commercialisation of a product derived from MGR coming from ABNJ, and not to the act of research and development (R&D) itself. In this case to reduce the transaction cost and to maximize predictability, which are necessary to attract investments from the private sector, a fixed percentage would be preferable over case-by-case negotiations.

Compliance will be ensured through the centralised system of the OPEN registry whereby reports and additional conditions arising during the lifespan of MGR and data utilisation will be kept and tied to it, enabling easy tracking and tracing.

3 Rationale for *Mare Geneticum*

3.1 *Premises*

The premises of the present proposal are based on the need for a multilateral system to regulate MGR from ABNJ and the importance of sustaining scientific research undertaken by both public and private users. This article acknowledges that ensuring the sustainable use of MGR from ABNJ together with the fair and equitable sharing of the benefits arising from their utilisation is possible only by bridging the gap between those countries that hold knowledge, MGR and technologies, and those that do not,[22] in order to achieve a more "[…] equitable and efficient utilisation of their (seas and oceans) resources" as stated in the fourth paragraph of the Preamble to the LOSC.

Given the absence of national jurisdiction in the geographical area concerned, any regime regulating ABS of MGR needs to be multilateral in order to

22 Broggiato *et al.* (n 20), at p. 183.

be effective. Moreover, access should be granted upon pre-defined conditions, as a case-by-case negotiation of terms would increase the costs, lengthen the administrative procedure and, most importantly, impair legal certainty for the users. The ILBI must provide legal certainty and stability both for the scientific community and for the private sector. Indeed, being able to assess (financial) risks at the onset of R&D would provide companies with the stable environment in which they can make the necessary investments.

A multilateral approach also ensures consistency by not differentiating between the water column (High Seas) and the seabed (Area) in ABNJ as neither science nor the definition of MGR justifies such a differentiation.[23] Support for this overarching approach lies in the UN General Assembly Decision on the development of an ILBI, which, as well as requiring action under the framework of the LOSC, specifically decides that the question of MGR be addressed "together and as a whole"[24]

MSR is crucial to advance knowledge of the marine environment, which includes, e.g., marine biodiversity, ecology and ecosystem processes, and for its role in the provision of ecosystem services and the maintenance of ocean health for the benefit of not only humankind but also the planet. Advancing our knowledge of the marine environment brings many environmental, social and economic benefits,[25] by, e.g., contributing to food security, conserving and managing the marine environment and resources, helping to understand, predict and respond to natural events and to human impacts and processes, eradicating poverty and contributing to sustainable development.[26] In addition, scientific research on MGR may lead to applications in biotechnology. Therefore, the strategic purpose of an ILBI should be to promote MSR and further downstream research directed to advancing scientific knowledge and understanding of the oceans for the wider long-term benefit of the world.[27]

---

23 Conservation and Sustainable Use of Marine Biological Diversity of Areas beyond National Jurisdiction: Preparing for the PrepCom, Report of the BBNJ Workshop of the Centre for International Law, National University of Singapore, February 2016, available at http://cil.nus.edu.sg/wp/wp-content/uploads/2015/10/CIL-report-of-BBNJ-workshop-21-March-2016-final-2.pdf; accessed 18 January 2017.

24 UNGA Res. 69/292 (n 14), para. 2.

25 H Harden-Davies, 'The regulation of marine scientific research: addressing challenges, advancing knowledge' in RM Warner and SB Kaye (eds.), *Routledge Handbook of Maritime Regulation and Enforcement* (Routledge, Abingdon, 2016) 212–230, at p. 216.

26 UN Report of the Secretary-General UNGAOR, UN Doc. A/64/66/Add.2, 19 October 2009, para. 15.

27 Harden-Davies (n 25), at p. 228; P Oldham, S Hall, C Barnes, C Oldham, AM Cutter, N Burns, and L Kindness, '*Valuing the Deep: Marine Genetic Resources in Areas Beyond National Jurisdiction*' (Defra, London, 2014) 1–241, at p. 18.

Advances in science require the availability of research material, samples and data, together with advanced technologies and research capabilities. To facilitate access to MGR in ABNJ, the governance mechanism should be based on a principle of OA by coupling light-touch procedures with the obligation to share the raw data and to deposit samples in publicly accessible biorepositories (see *infra*). OA refers to research outputs that are free of all restrictions on access (e.g., access tolls). However, it does not necessarily mean free utilisation, as some restrictions or conditions of use may be attached to the accessed material or data. For example, some databases of images available online currently associate certain copyright and license restrictions on the use of such images (e.g., forbidden sales, limited modifications…), without restricting access as such.

To ensure that regulations arising out of ILBI are not overly burdensome or inapplicable in practice,[28] an excellent understanding of the MSR process is an absolute necessity. The involvement of the marine scientific community is therefore of paramount importance: we echo the need to bridge the gaps between science and policy.[29]

3.2 *Scientific and Technical Baseline*

3.2.1 Commercial Value of MGR in ABNJ

Prior to discussing potential benefit-sharing arrangements related to MGR in ABNJ, their actual commercial value should be assessed. Are the expectations of large financial gains from the utilisation of MGR in ABNJ realistic?

Uncertainty has been raised about the actual likelihood of commercialisation following R&D on MGR,[30] and too much emphasis has generally been placed on monetary benefit streams. Indeed, there is currently little evidence of

28 A Broggiato, 'Exchange of information on research programs regarding marine biodiversity in areas beyond national jurisdiction' in IUCN information papers for the intersessional workshop on marine genetic resources in ABNJ (IUCN Environmental Law Center, Bonn, 2013) 55–62, at p. 55; Harden-Davies (n 25), at p. 218. Available at http://www.un.org/depts/los/biodiversityworkinggroup/documents/IUCN%20Information%20Papers%20for%20BBNJ%20Intersessional%20Workshop%20on%20MGR.pdf; accessed 18 January 2017.

29 Broggiato *et al.* (n 20), at p. 176.

30 DK Leary and SK Juniper, 'Addressing the marine genetic resources issue: Is the debate heading in the wrong direction?' in C Schofield, S Lee and MS Kwon (eds) *The Limits of Maritime Jurisdiction* (Martinus Nijhoff Publishers, Leiden, 2014) 769–785, at p. 773; and D Leary, M Vierros, G Hamon, S Arico, and C Monagle, 'Marine Genetic Resources: A Review of Scientific and Commercial Interest' (2009) 33 *Marine Policy* 183–194, at p. 187.

systematic commercial-scale development of MGR from ABNJ.[31] Furthermore, it is important not to confuse the potential of MGR in ABNJ with the more prolific commercialisation of marine biodiversity products from shallower waters, primarily within coastal states' jurisdiction.[32] In theory, marine biodiversity has enormous potential. Biochemists are often effusively enthusiastic about the diversity of biomolecules produced by marine organisms compared to their terrestrial counterparts. However, to date, the realisation of this potential in relation to ABNJ has been slow compared to national jurisdictions.[33] Therefore, although the potential for development has been widely stated,[34] its appreciation still requires further study. Moreover, a comprehensive study reviewing the full spectrum of monetary and non-monetary benefits that could be derived from MGR in ABNJ would also be invaluable, as there appears to be none at this stage.[35]

At present, there are a number of patents and pending applications based on MGR in ABNJ, both from the Area and the high seas. This can be interpreted as evidence for commercial interest.[36] However, the existence of such patents does not necessarily indicate the eventual development of marketable products. Moreover, there is increasing evidence of academia seeking patents to protect their intellectual property (IP), even without true commercial intent.

Finally, distinguishing new MGR discoveries within national jurisdictions from those in ABNJ should be encouraged in a more systematic manner. To this end, the UNESCO Intergovernmental Oceanographic Commission added the option "areas beyond national jurisdiction" for geographical search in the new version of the Ocean Biogeographic Information System (OBIS) platform. OBIS is a global data-sharing platform and clearing house for marine biodiversity (biogeographic and biometric) data in all oceans, hosted by the International Oceanographic Data and Information Exchange (IODE). Marinlit, the Royal

31 Leary and Juniper (n 30), at p. 773; SK Juniper, 'Technological, Environmental, Social and Economic Aspects of Marine Genetic Resources' in IUCN information papers for the intersessional workshop on marine genetic resources in ABNJ (IUCN Environmental Law Center, Bonn, 2013) 15–21, at pp. 20–21.

32 Oldham *et al.* (n 27), at p. 197.

33 Juniper (n 31), at p. 19.

34 *Ibid.*; Oldham *et al.* (n 27), at p. 182.

35 L Glowka, 'Evolving Perspectives on the International Seabed Area's Genetic Resources: Fifteen Years after the Deepest of Ironies' in D Vidas (ed.), *Law, Technology and Science for Oceans in Globalisation* (Martinus Nijhoff Publishers, Leiden, 2010) 397–419, at p. 415.

36 M Vierros, C Salpin, C Chiarolla and SM Arico, 'Emerging and unresolved issues: The example of seabed and open ocean genetic resources in areas beyond national jurisdiction' in SM Arico (ed.), Ocean sustainability in the 21st century (Cambridge University Press, Cambridge, 2015) 198–232, at p. 212.

Society of Chemistry database, is also of interest as it gives the location, when available, of organisms from which compounds were derived, clearly showing that most are derived from the Exclusive Economic Zone (EEZ).[37]

3.2.2 Gaps in Research Capabilities of States

In order to propose the most widely acceptable options for the ILBI governance system, it is necessary to identify the areas where inequalities between states are most pronounced. The analysis should focus on the actual availability of MGR from ABNJ and the capacities needed to study and exploit them.[38] Genetic resources can be accessed in different ways: *in situ, ex situ,* and *in silico*. Access to *in-situ* resources means collecting samples of marine organisms (containing genetic material) within their natural surroundings. Access to *ex situ* MGR occurs when the resources are accessed away from their natural surroundings, such as from culture collections, museums and research institutions. *In silico* normally describes direct access to genetic data, such as whole genomes or isolated gene sequences, with or without functional annotations, or biochemical data on gene products, such as proteins, peptides and metabolites.

Recent technical analyses showed uneven levels of access to MGR between a small group of developed countries and the rest of the world, mostly for the following reasons:

1. The cost of technology to sample in international waters and the deep sea, and the cost of its maintenance;[39]
2. The scientific skills needed to undertake research on marine biodiversity;[40]
3. The cost of and scientific skills needed to undertake molecular screening and biodiversity assessment;[41]
4. The scientific skills needed to analyse the data thereby produced.[42]

---

37 MarinLit is a database dedicated to marine natural products research. http://pubs.rsc.org/marinlit/.

38 Glowka (n 35), at pp. 411–412.

39 Broggiato *et al.* (n 20), at p. 177; Juniper (n 31), at pp. 15–17; K Juniper, 'Use of Marine Genetic Resources' in M Banks, C Bissada, PE Araghi (eds), *The First Global Integrated Marine Assessment World Ocean Assessment I under the auspices of the United Nations General Assembly and its Regular Process for Global Reporting and Assessment of the State of the Marine Environment, including Socioeconomic Aspects* (UN, New York, 2016), Chapter 29, at p. 6.

40 Juniper (n 39), at p. 9; Juniper (n 31), at pp. 16–17.

41 Broggiato *et al.* (n 20), at p. 179.

42 Juniper (n 39), at p. 7; G Shimmield, 'Extent and Types of Research, Uses and Applications' in *IUCN information papers for the intersessional workshop on marine genetic resources in ABNJ* (IUCN Environmental Law Center, Bonn, 2013), 7–15, at p. 13.

In 1995, only six countries had the technological, financial and human resources to directly access MGR *in situ* in ABNJ (Finland, France, the United Kingdom, Japan, Russia and the United States of America).[43] In 2012, twenty-nine countries, both developed and developing, had access to MGR from hydrothermal vents, as members of InterRidge, (an organization for International Cooperation in Ridge-Crest Studies),[44] and of the Pacific Islands Applied Geoscience Commission.[45] However, notwithstanding the wider access to deep-sea sampling technologies, disparity remains.[46]

Another important capability to derive value from marine biodiversity is the specialist scientific skills required to identify species, both those species that are already known and those that are new to science.[47] These taxonomic specialists are mostly trained in developed countries with a long history of botanical and zoological scholarship in universities and museums. A recent review of the literature revealed that the majority of publications in the field of marine taxonomy come from relatively few developed countries.[48] These specialists are experts in the morphological identification of specimens (classical taxonomy) and, increasingly, the interpretation of DNA sequence information to identify marine plants, animals and microbes (molecular taxonomy). There is a global scarcity of taxonomists able to identify marine flora and fauna. This problem is particularly acute for a range of marine invertebrate phyla.[49]

Various scientific approaches to undertake molecular screening and analyse the acquired data, such as microbial metagenomics, also require sophisticated bioinformatics tools and training which are most accessible in developed countries.[50] Nevertheless, some capabilities in bioinformatics and genomics exist in developing countries, particularly in the health and agricultural science sectors, and these skills could be adapted and applied for use in the context of MGR.[51] Moreover, there are capacity-building initiatives aimed at lowering this disparity. The UK's Wellcome Trust, for example, provides training in genetic data analysis (mainly on human genome and human pathogens) to developing countries, as does Japan's National Institute of Technology and Evaluation.

43 Glowka (n 35), at p. 412.
44 Available at www.interridge.org; accessed 18 January 2017.
45 Glowka (n 33), at p. 412.
46 Broggiato *et al.* (n 20), at p. 179; Juniper (n 31) at p. 15–16; Juniper (n 39), at p. 6.
47 IE Hendriks and CM Duarte, 'Allocation of effort and imbalances in biodiversity research' (2008) 360(1) *Journal of Experimental Marine Biology and Ecology* 15–20, at p. 17; Juniper (n 39), at p. 7.
48 *Ibid.* Hendriks and Duarte, at p. 18.
49 Available at www.publications.parliament.uk/pa/ld200708/ldselect/ldsctech/162/162.pdf; accessed 18 January 2017.
50 Juniper (n 39), at p. 8; Shimmield (n 42), at p. 13.
51 Juniper (n 31), at p. 17; Juniper (n 39), at p. 8; Shimmield (n 42), at p. 17.

Technological advances are now radically changing life sciences:[52] the cost of sequencing has decreased significantly and new technologies have emerged, such as bioinformatics. OA bioinformatics databases are essential for the success of genetics as they enable the discovery of new genes unexplored by the depositor of the data and their comparison to large sets of genes and sequences deposited by others in the databases. The ability to mine public domain and OA databases containing genomic and proteomic data, and to subsequently use such data, could become as important as physical access to organisms or their genetic material.[53] This practice has led the genetics community to enthusiastically adopt the OA database model (see *infra*). As Glowka points out, "in theory, all that would be needed is internet access, appropriate software and skilled researchers",[54] allowing further engagement of developing countries' scientists.

To sum up, as underlined by the First Assessment of the Ocean made by the United Nations, the current uneven research capabilities across the globe are the primary source of inequity amongst states,[55] *more than disparities in accessing the resources in situ* (authors' emphasis). This requires efforts in capacity development related to MSR so that a greater number of countries can participate in the exploitation of MGR.[56] Therefore, after ensuring OA to samples and data as one of the main ways of benefit-sharing (see *infra*), the ILBI should promote and strengthen capacity building.

4 *Mare Geneticum*: Balancing Open Access and Commercial Interests

4.1 *Facilitated but Conditional Access*

The UNGA Resolution defines the subject of the ILBI negotiation in the 2011 package as "the conservation and sustainable use of marine biological diversity of ABNJ, in particular, together and as a whole, *marine genetic resources, including questions on the sharing of benefits…*"[57] without specifically mentioning the question of access to MGR. Notwithstanding the fact that access is a prerequisite to enforce subsequent benefit-sharing, *Mare Geneticum* proposes that the facilitated access procedure should be subject to notification rather than authorisation.

52 Glowka (n 35), at p. 408; Juniper (n 31), at p. 22; Leary and Juniper (n 30), at p. 777.
53 Glowka (n 35), at p. 415.
54 *Ibid.*
55 Juniper (n 39), at p. 8.
56 Juniper (n 31), at p. 21.
57 UN 69/65, UN Doc A/69/L.65, 11 May 2015, para. 3.

In situ access to MGR is generally done without commercial intent.[58] Indeed, most deep-sea and high-seas expeditions are publicly funded, rendering MGR sampling cruises in ABNJ non-commercial in character, or at least with intentions that are not solely or primarily commercial.[59] Moreover, most publicly funded institutions require the deposit of taxonomic and genetic discoveries in public collections and databases, usually within one year of the completion of a project. It should be noted, however, that extracts of marine samples collected for non-commercial purposes might be deposited in collections with a drug discovery objective, or be subsequently used for R&D purposes. Indeed, the majority of biodiscovery ventures with a commercial interest begin with *ex situ* or *in silico* access rather than *in situ*.

As strongly advocated by the scientific community,[60] in designing and implementing any ABS measures for MGR in ABNJ it is important to avoid excessive bureaucratic burdens that could hamper MSR. Within the present proposal, all the different ways to access MGR coming from ABNJ are facilitated.

4.1.1 Notification Procedure: Obligatory Prior Electronic Notification (OPEN)

The facilitated procedure to access MGR from ABNJ *in situ* consists of an Obligatory Prior Electronic Notification (OPEN) step, submitted electronically via a registration platform that will be publicly accessible in an online registry. The OPEN will require a minimum dataset of information to be recorded: it is important to underline that most of these data are already collected by scientists and there will be no extra burden on them. The dataset includes:

- Information about the collector and the corresponding contact point;
- Geographical area(s) of sampling;
- Period of sampling;
- Complete description of the research project and participating research entities. This may be based on the cruise plan that is often provided with funding applications;

58 Juniper (n 31), at p. 18.

59 Wright *et al.* (n 21), at p. 557.

60 Deep-sea marine scientific research and genetic resources in areas beyond national jurisdiction: DOSI submission to the Second Preparatory Committee—22 March 2016. Deep Ocean Stewardship Initiative (DOSI) is a union of experts from across disciplines and sectors formed to develop new ideas for sustainable use and management of deep-ocean resources. Available at www.un.org/depts/los/biodiversity/prepcom_files/DOSI.pdf; accessed 30 October 2017.

- Expected nature of what will be collected—this should be done by sample type, for instance: pelagic vertebrate, benthic invertebrate, sediment, core sample, plankton, water, etc.;
- Description of the targeted MGR when possible; The dataset to fill in will be accompanied by a click-wrap agreement to be signed, including the commitments:
- The commitment to release the collected samples or data in an openly accessible biorepository, with or without exceptional conditions depending on the intent of use (see *infra*);
- The commitment to update the OPEN information at certain milestones. This is critical to ensure compliance and monitoring.

Any OPEN will contain OA conditions and benefit-sharing obligations associated with the collected material, whether those are monetary or not. The lifetime of the samples and extracted data will be punctuated with milestones corresponding to the identification of samples, to the deposit of samples and/or duplicates in a collection, and to the transfer to users and change of intent for utilisation, as will be defined in the ILBI and for which any agreement on conditions of utilisation and benefit-sharing should be linked or annexed to the OPEN. It is advisable to link the OPEN platform to the CBD Clearing House database,[61] in order to ensure that all genetic resources accessed in ABNJ are recorded in the CBD Clearing House, therefore avoiding free riders.

A unique alphanumeric identifier will be associated with each OPEN and will keep track of the cruise information and the samples collected. Each code associated with these samples throughout their lifetime should reflect this identifier, allowing subsequent determination of the provenance and hence securing legal certainty and compliance (see *infra*). This is needed to harmonise MSR practice and will generate a valuable database on global marine biodiversity.

A chosen institution should manage the secure internet tool capable of collecting this information through a centralised mechanism, or coordinate a decentralised system. Whether a new organisation is established by the ILBI or whether an existing institution is mandated for this purpose will have to be determined by the international community's negotiations on the ILBI terms.

When MGR from ABNJ are accessed *ex situ* in a collection, a notification should be registered on the same online registry and linked to the existing OPEN, which may be amended with additional information or conditions of utilisation. In case of commercial intent, the user will be required to accept

61 Available at https://absch.cbd.int/; accessed 18 January 2017.

and be bound by possible monetary benefit-sharing obligations in addition to the already existing non-monetary benefits, entailing a subsequent payment to the biodiversity contribution fund upon commercialisation of any product as described further below, if agreed in the ILBI. These conditions can be easily encoded into the material transfer agreement signed with the collections in order to gain access to and use the requested MGR. This material transfer agreement should then be annexed to the OPEN to ensure traceability. As such, the OPEN travels with the material from one user to the next user, with the obligation for each user to keep the OPEN up to date.

In cases of *in silico* access a notification in the OPEN registry should be completed once the geographical origin of the MGR generating the data is known. Access to *in silico* data is quite challenging to track and trace, as is shown by the examples occurring within national jurisdictions under the CBD and Nagoya Protocol system. The Global Catalogue of Microorganisms (GCM),[62] a global OA bioinformatics database, is working on ensuring ABS compliance by means of linking the unique identifier of each strain of microorganism to the internationally recognized certificate of compliance (IRCC)[63] of the CBD Clearing House. The GCM provides authenticated access and material information and could accommodate all OPEN data or Nagoya Protocol IRCC. The GCM software uses the submitted strain identifiers to search for published patent records for the same identifiers and can provide reports on these. Therefore, the GCM software potentially allows anyone to trace any use of the material and identify any patents taken out or licenses granted under patent, contributing to the provision of legal certainty. The requirement to include the OPEN identifier in any record or publication could enable the system to run automatic searches and accrue records, as is being done by the GCM to some extent.

62 WFCC Global Catalogue of Microorganisms (GCM) is a system to help culture collections to manage, disseminate and share the information related to their holdings. http://gcm.wfcc.info/ Accessed 17 March 2017.

63 The internationally recognized certificate of compliance (IRCC) originates from the permit or its equivalent issued by State Parties to the Nagoya Protocol at the time of access as evidence that access to genetic resources was based on prior informed consent and that mutually agreed terms were established. When the permit is communicated to the ABS Clearing house of the Nagoya Protocol it becomes the IRCC.

In the field of *in silico* access, GenBank[64] operates under the INSDC policy,[65] which advocates full OA and prohibits restrictions or licensing requirements. Nevertheless, *Mare Geneticum*'s approach includes exceptions that will allow future commercial ventures and investments that would be discouraged. The ABS compliance with INSDC in linking gene sequences with eventual ABS strings attached might become an issue of discussion within the framework of the Nagoya Protocol. In this case, if compliance can be ensured with the collaboration of the INSDC, a similar project to the one run between the GCM and the ABS CH could be operated between GenBank and the CBD Clearing House in order to link the sequence data to the original material, its ABS conditions and to the OPEN registry. This would enable users to easily be aware of their obligation to share the benefits when utilizing sequence data of MGR from ABNJ.

4.1.2 Authorisation Procedure in the Case of Environmental Impact Assessment

Sampling at sea does not usually produce significant environmental disturbance, therefore no environmental impact assessment (EIA) should be required prior to the activity. However, there should be a screening stage that could trigger the need for EIA, for instance when sampling will occur in marine protected areas or in vulnerable marine ecosystems such as hydrothermal vents, or when destructive devices will be used. It must be stressed that the obligation to put the samples in openly accessible biorepositories should eventually minimise the need for subsequent sampling for the same MGR or in the same area, implementing the principle of avoidance of double sampling enshrined in the InterRidge Code of Conduct[66] and the ABS CIESM Charter.[67] One limitation, however, may be the fact that different types of research sometimes require different types of collection methods and storage. To this end, the effective coordination of the OPENs and of biorepositories will be required

---

64 GenBank ® is the NIH genetic sequence database, an annotated collection of all publicly available DNA sequences. GenBank is part of the International Nucleotide Sequence Database Collaboration (INSDC), which comprises the DNA DataBank of Japan (DDBJ), the European Nucleotide Archive (ENA), and GenBank at NCBI. These three organizations exchange data on a daily basis. Available at https://www.ncbi.nlm.nih.gov/genbank/; accessed 17 March 2017.

65 Available at https://www.insdc.org/policy; accessed 17 March 2017.

66 Available at https://www.interridge.org/node/16908; accessed 17 March 2017.

67 Available at http://www.ciesm.org/forums/index.php?post/2013/03/14/CIESM-Charter-on-ABS; accessed 17 March 2017.

to ensure the dissemination of information regarding samples and their availability amongst the scientific community.

Another trigger for EIA could be the harvest of species that can, following interesting discoveries on their genetic material, be deemed necessary for the development of a product. For instance, Chris Battershill and his New Zealand colleagues collected several tons of the *Lissodendoryx* sponge after a careful environmental survey in order to provide the US National Cancer Institute with sufficient supplies of the bioactive compound halichondrin B for clinical testing against cancer. This research eventually led to eribulin, a simplified synthetic analogue of halichondrin Bcompound, Eribulin™, which has been approved for clinical use as an anticancer agent. A case like this should trigger not only an authorisation process through the EIA requirement, but also the addition of an access fee to the OPEN process, considering the administration needed for an EIA.

4.1.3 Balancing Facilitated Research while Securing Future Commercial Ventures: Sharing Conditions and Exceptions

Bearing in mind the main disparity between countries as previously explained, it must be stressed that promoting or facilitating access to *ex situ* and *in silico* MGR for researchers worldwide provides a significant and public benefit. Free or 'at cost' access to *in situ* resources is to be conditional on the creation or strengthening of already existing "common pools"[68] of MGR coming from ABNJ and the associated raw data.[69] Facilitated *in situ* access, coupled with the sharing of *ex situ* MGR and *in silico* data, will ensure equal levels of opportunity in research to the scientific community worldwide, overcoming one of the main gaps in research capability between countries.

To this end, one must differentiate access from utilisation: access, the acquisition of samples or data, does not constitute utilisation. There is no direct and immediate commercial value at the access point, hence there should be no need for authorisation, and no discrimination, in this facilitated access procedure. No procedural distinction should be made between public and private entities, or between basic research and commercially driven research, as long as the users respect the set of conditions based on the OA principle and on benefit-sharing.

---

68 Broggiato *et al.* (n 20), at p. 181; Greiber (n 21), at p. 407–411; Wright *et al.* (n 21) at p. 556.

69 This would have to be delocalised as no single collection can do this. Using a virtual system can collate all the available data and perhaps even lead to reduction in the over-sampling of certain deep-sea areas, such as the Mariana Trench.

In practice, these conditions will need to be encoded into legal obligations: at the moment the OPEN notification is submitted the users sign clickwrap terms containing the obligations to share the raw data in public databases, such as GenBank, according to the principle of OA, and to deposit any existing duplicates of the samples in public biorepositories. The terms also should contain an obligation to make payments to the biodiversity contribution fund in cases of commercialisation of a product derived later from the accessed resources, in case monetary benefit sharing are agreed upon by the ILBI. A further obligation could include the payment of an exclusivity fee in return for an embargo on the release of the samples and data into the public domain, for a period to be determined, potentially renewable upon payment of a further fee, in order to secure R&D or potential commercial intent, regardless of whether such intent is known upstream or arises later in the process.

As a limitation to the obligation to share raw data and accessed materials, the grant of an initial embargo period should be left as an option for the users, to allow them to capitalise on their research material. The embargo period should be reasonable but fairly short, considering that only the raw data are to be released and not the detailed research results. It will nevertheless be possible to extend the embargo period by payment of an exclusivity fee. These possibilities should be clearly stated at the time of filling in the OPEN. The embargo period should secure biodiscovery investments and thereby future discoveries, start-ups, and innovative R&D, but should not in any case free the user from its benefit-sharing obligations: the ultimate release of samples and raw data to the public domain, and the payment of monetary contributions when a product is eventually commercialised, if the latter is agreed upon by the ILBI.

4.2 *Benefit-sharing Obligations*

The first benefit to be shared under *Mare Geneticum* is enabling and facilitating access to MGR and associated data, thus empowering humankind to make the best of the last frontier that is the ABNJ. Scientific research produces benefits *per se*, including the better understanding of the marine environment, marine ecology and the oceanic system, and the improvement of the sustainable use of the oceans and its resources. Hence MSR represents a benefit for all that goes beyond the availability of any products made from MGR,[70] even

70 T Greiber, 'Types of benefits and benefit sharing' in *IUCN information papers for the intersessional workshop on marine genetic resources in ABNJ* (IUCN Environmental Law Center, Bonn, 2013) 29–37, at p. 29.

though some of these may make important contributions to public health, bioremediation or food security, and also produce global benefits.[71]

There is, however, no guarantee of monetary benefits arising out of the utilisation of MGR.[72] In fact, only seven pharmaceutical products derived from marine organisms are currently on the market. Five of these are small molecule drugs discovered before 1990, all of which took more than fifteen years to develop into clinical products. By 1990, 5,800 small molecules of marine origin had been reported, meaning that just one compound for every 1,160 led to a commercial product. Given the long development timelines for pharmaceuticals, no compound discovered after the adoption of the CBD has reached the market yet. At the moment, twenty-eight marine natural products are in clinical trials and a further 250 are undergoing preclinical investigation.[73] In addition, it must be stressed that, of the seven marine-derived products in use, six come from organisms found in the EEZs of coastal states. The seventh product, a highly purified polyunsaturated fatty acid (Omacor®/Lovaza®) used by patients at risk of heart attack, is derived from a range of fish species appearing both within and beyond national jurisdiction. Whereas the other substances are developed by chemical or biochemical processes, Omacor/Lovaza requires the harvesting of fish in order to produce the product. One of the seven, Eribulin (trade name Halaven®, produced by Eisai) required 25 years of development before reaching significant sales, Y29,3 billion in 2014, or USD $282 million at the current conversion rate.[74]

Given the above, non-monetary benefits are considered the most practical and immediately valuable aspect of ABS, in particular because the chances of developing a commercial product are relatively slim. For this, OA databases are crucial. However, strengthening "common pools" not only requires the release of material, but also implies the need for global coordination, management, and institutional arrangements.

Even though the LOSC does not specifically provide for an ABS regime with regard to MGR in ABNJ, which will eventually be the role of the ILBI,

71 FO Glöckner, LJ Stal, RA Sandaa, JM Gasol, F O'Gara,F Hernandez, M Labrenz, E Stoica, MM Varela, A Bordalo, and P Pitta, 'Marine Microbial Diversity and its role in Ecosystem Functioning and Environmental Change' in JB Calewaert and N McDonough (eds), *Marine Microbial Diversity and Its Role in Ecosystem Functioning and Environmental Change,* Marine Board Position Paper 17 (Marine Board-ESF, Ostend, Belgium 2012) 17–41, at p. 25.

72 Greiber (n 70), at p. 32; Juniper (n 31), at pp. 19–20.

73 Available at http://marinepharmacology.midwestern.edu/; accessed 18 January 2017.

74 Eisai Annual Report 2014, available at http://www.eisai.com/pdf/eannual/epdf2014an.pdf; accessed 18 January 2017.

non-monetary benefit-sharing obligations applying to MSR in ABNJ are inherent in the Convention.[75] As a matter of fact, the scientific community already implements them as best practice (See *infra*). Accordingly, this aspect of our proposal is not inconsistent with LOSC.

4.2.1 Non-monetary Benefits: the OA Principle as the Core Benefit

Considering the above, non-monetary benefits will create direct, quasi-immediate benefits compared to monetary benefit-sharing. Moreover. they contribute to building capacity, creating opportunities, and promoting R&D in all countries.[76] Non-monetary benefits include, among others, training of scientists, transfer of research results and scientific information, transfer of technology, and access to *ex situ* collections and *in silico* data. As most of these advantages emanate from research practice, the scientific community is one of the main stakeholders to be listened to when drafting a benefit-sharing regime for MGR in ABNJ.[77]

Part XIII of the LOSC conceptually deals with MSR[78] occurring within national jurisdiction as well as in ABNJ, although without using this terminology.[79] Part XIII contains clear obligations on non-monetary benefit-sharing arising from scientific research.[80] In essence, it promotes international cooperation, and publication and dissemination of information and knowledge, especially in favour of developing countries.[81] Article 244(1) sets the obligation for "States and competent international organizations [to] make available by publication and dissemination through appropriate channels [...] knowledge resulting from marine scientific research". Articles 143(3) (applicable to the Area) and 244(2) aim at strengthening autonomous MSR capabilities of less technologically developed states rather than by the mere transfer of technologies.[82] The UN analysis of State practice indicates that data obtained through

75 Broggiato *et al.* (n 20), at p. 181. Greiber (n 69), at p. 44.

76 Glowka (n 35), at p. 9; Greiber (n 70), at p. 32.

77 Vierros *et al.* (n 36), at p. 212; Oldham (n 27), at p. 2.

78 Wright *et al.* (n 21), at p. 556.

79 Greiber (n 70), at p. 35.

80 Broggiato, (n 20), 176–185, at p. 182; Greiber (n 70), at p. 35.

81 Article 242–244 LOSC.

82 A Broggiato, T Dedeurwaerdere, F Batur ansd B Coolsaet, 'Introduction. Access and Benefit-Sharing and the Nagoya Protocol: the Confluence of Abiding Legal Doctrines' in B Coolsaet, F Batur, A Broggiato, J Pitseys, T Dedeurwaerdere (eds), *Implementing the Nagoya Protocol—Comparing Access and Benefit-sharing Regimes in Europe* (Brill/ Martinus Nijhoff Publishers, Leiden, 2015) 1–29, at p. 11.

MSR, particularly from ABNJ, are effectively shared via international data repositories such as OBIS, as well as via publication in international journals.[83]

These provisions constitute the legal basis for further development of a comprehensive and coherent non-monetary benefit-sharing scheme for MGR in ABNJ. To this extent, the OA principle at the basis of the *Mare Geneticum* governance is consistent with both these LOSC obligations and the current scientific practice and values.

Many scientific codes of conduct and guidelines[84] are already raising awareness and building up best practice in the MSR community in terms of sharing samples, data and research results, as well as strengthening capacity building and training in developing countries.[85] Various examples include the already existing gene banks, digital databanks, scientific journals and patent pools,[86] but also the common practice of joint research programmes. For instance, the Intergovernmental Oceanographic Commission of UNESCO (IOC-UNESCO)[87] widely promotes international cooperation in MSR, capacity building, technology transfer and data-sharing. The IOC collects, analyses and publishes information from states on practices in MSR and technology transfer.[88] It has published guidelines for states on the transfer of marine technology,[89] and has established a capacity-building development programme to strengthen MSR. It plays a role in international cooperation projects such as the International Oceanographic Data and Information Exchange (IODE), which facilitates

83 United Nations Division for Ocean Affairs and the Law of the Sea—Office of Legal Affairs, *Marine Scientific Research: A Revised Guide to the Implementation of the Relevant Provisions of the United Nations Convention on the Law of the Sea* (United Nations, New York, 2010) para 116.

84 See for example the InterRidge statement of commitment to responsible research practices at deep-sea hydrothermal vents; available at https://www.interridge.org/IRStatement, accessed 18 January 2017; and the ABS CIESM Charter, *supra* (n 67).

85 Broggiato (n 20), at pp. 176–185.

86 Patent pools are consortia of entities agreeing to cross-license patents relating to a particular technology in order to save time and money, to mitigate patent-related risks, and to create collective benefits.

87 IOC is a competent international organization under the UN Convention on the Law of the Sea for Marine Scientific Research under Part XIII and Capacity Development (CD) and Transfer of Marine Technology (TMT) under Part XIV. The IOC is the primary international organization responsible for marine science in the UN system, as also recognized by LOSC (Annex 8 Article 2).

88 EJ Tirpak, *Practices of States in the Fields of Marine Scientific Research and Transfer of Marine Technology: An Update of the 2005 Analysis of Member State Responses to Questionnaire No. 3*, UN Doc. IOC/ABE-LOS VIII/8 (19 March 2008).

89 Intergovernmental Oceanographic Commission, *IOC Criteria and Guidelines on the Transfer of Marine Technology*, IOC Information Document, 1203 (UNESCO, Paris, 2005).

international cooperation on data format standards to harmonise the use of data between states.

In 1996, leaders of the scientific community advocated the immediate release of DNA sequence data in public databases in the Bermuda Principles.[90] In 2007, the Organization for Economic Cooperation and Development (OECD) recommended wider and open sharing of data from public funding,[91] followed by the European Commission's policy instructions to Member States to "promote the broad dissemination of knowledge created with public funds, by taking steps to encourage open access to research results, while enabling, where appropriate, the related intellectual property to be protected".[92] From there national policies blossomed around the globe, in particular in the host countries of the main funding agencies that currently finance ABNJ research: the European Union (EU), the United States (US), China and Germany.[93]

What all these data policies have in common is the implementation of the OA approach, albeit to different extents. The National Science Foundation of the US adopted the Sample and Data Policy of the Division of Ocean Sciences in 2011.[94] This requires the Principal Investigator working under its funding "to submit at no more than incremental cost and within a reasonable time frame (but no later than two (2) years after the data are collected), the primary data, samples, physical collections and other supporting materials created or gathered in the course of work under NSF/OCE grants". It further requires submission of sequence data to a publicly accessible data repository. The EU published a Recommendation on access to and preservation of scientific information in 2012[95] encouraging all EU Member States to put publicly-funded research results in the public domain in order to strengthen science and the

---

90 For a summary of the principles agreed at the first international strategy meeting on human genome sequencing (commonly referred to as Bermuda Principles of 1996), see http://www.ornl.gov/sci/techresources/Human_Genome/research/bermuda.shtml, accessed 17 March 2017. For a historical analysis of the principles, see Eliot Marshall, 'Bermuda Rules: Community Spirit, with Teeth' (2001) 291 (5507) *Science* 1192.

91 OECD, OECD Principles and Guidelines for Access to Research Data from Public Funding, http://www.oecd.org/science/scienceandtechnologypolicy/38500813.pdf Accessed 17 March 2017.

92 EC recommendation C/2008/1329 of 10 April 2008, http://eurlex.europa.eu/LexUriServ/LexUriServ.do?uri=CELEX:32008H0416:EN:NOT; COMMISSION RECOMMENDATION of 17 July 2012 on access to and preservation of scientific information (2012/417/EU) Official Journal of the European Union L 194/39 21/07/2012.

93 See Oldham *et al.* (n 27), at p. 77.

94 Available at https://www.nsf.gov/pubs/2011/nsf11060/nsf11060.pdf Accessed 17 March 2017.

95 Commission Recommendation of 17.7.2012 on access to and preservation of scientific information. C(2012) 4890 final. Available at https://ec.europa.eu/research/science

knowledge-based economy. In 2014 the National Natural Science Foundation of China (NNSFC), one of the country's major basic-science funding agencies, and the Chinese Academy of Sciences (CAS) announced that researchers they support should deposit their papers into online repositories and make them publicly accessible within 12 months of publication. In 2015, the Deutsche Forschungsgemeinschaft (DFG) adopted Guidelines on the Handling of Research Data, calling for the long-term archiving of research data and OA to it.[96]

Although OA to sample material is less advanced, there is a global movement towards enabling the long-term maintenance of valuable biological, chemical and other materials resulting from research activities. In the field of deep-sea research, the scientific community advocates increased sharing of such samples and for research grants to include a budget for curation and long-term care. Samples arising from MSR carried out in ABNJ can often be accessed through international networks of collections. For example, the InterRidge statement of commitment to responsible research practice notes that the network is building open databases on available biological samples preserved in laboratories and museums around the globe, as an available resource and to minimise repeated sampling.[97]

In addition, many journals currently require unique material included in publications to be made available. The journal *Nature*'s policy states that:

> A condition of publication in a Nature journal is that authors are required to make unique materials promptly available to others without undue qualifications. It is acceptable to request reasonable payment to cover costs of distribution and reagents may be made available via commercial or non-commercial third party providers.[98]

Such a strong statement from a top international peer-reviewed journal sends a message that sharing of material is essential for a productive global research enterprise, although compliance with this requirement may still need

-society/document_library/pdf_06/recommendation-access-and-preservation-scientific-information_en.pdf; accessed 17 March 2017.

96 Available at http://www.dfg.de/download/pdf/foerderung/antragstellung/forschungsdaten/guidelines_research_data.pdf; accessed 17 March 2017.

97 See the InterRidge Code of Conduct (n 68).

98 Available at http://www.nature.com/authors/policies/availability.html; accessed 18 January 2017.

to improve.[99] This trend has resulted in best practice in open science, technological advances and the ever-growing practice of digitalisation of genetic data and other information, which has enabled more global accessibility than ever before.[100] Therefore, enabling and increasing access to relevant scientific data, publications and software to analyse these data is undoubtedly an important component of non-monetary benefit sharing.[101] However, the moderate optimism brought by new opportunities thereby created cannot obscure the reality faced by some researchers and users from developing countries, whose institutions do not always have the necessary licenses for access to journals, or the necessary internet access and bandwidth and other necessary resources. In this respect, the biodiversity contribution fund to be established by the ILBI could assist those in need of better access.

4.2.2 Monetary Benefit-sharing

The present section deals with the potential obligation to require monetary payments at different stages of the research pipeline. There could be two milestones at which monetary payments may be foreseen.

1. The OPEN entails payment of an exclusivity fee early in the biodiscovery process, when the user wants to extend the embargo period on releasing the MGR collected in ABNJ to the public domain. When the exclusivity option is exercised, payment of the exclusivity fee is compulsory and should be transferred to the biodiversity contribution fund to be established by the ILBI. The exclusivity fee's amount could be determined by a sliding scale, depending on various factors: the duration of the extension period, the MGR concerned by the embargo, the level of research funding employed to date, and the user's financial capacity.
2. If the ILBI would require monetary benefits linked to the utilisation of the genetic resource as such, we suggest this second payment step to be triggered by the commercialisation of a product developed on the basis of MGR from ABNJ. This form of royalty should be paid to the same international fund set up by the ILBI to manage exclusivity fees. The percentage of revenue to be shared should be predetermined and fixed, possibly by consultation with representative organisations and stakeholders of several biotechnology sectors, in order to provide for legal

99 D Cyranoski, 'Research materials: Share and share alike?' (2002) 420 *Nature* 602–604, at p. 604.

100 GM Garrity, LM Thompson, DW Ussery, N Paskin, D Baker, P Desmeth, DE Schindel and PS Ong, *Study on the Identification, Tracking and Monitoring of Genetic Resources*, UN doc. UNEP/CBD/WG-ABS/7/INF/2, of 2 March 2009, p. 19.

101 Greiber (n 70), at p. 35.

> certainty, predictability and equity amongst players. It should also be consistent with the market levels payable under ABS systems already in place within national jurisdictions (e.g., Brazil) and under development at regional levels, to avoid creating any perverse incentives.

Considering that it may take over 20 years to release a product onto the market, having the possibility to pay an exclusivity fee at an early stage of the research not only guarantees continuous investments in blue biodiscovery, but also secures early incoming monetary resources for the ILBI contribution fund.

With these governance principles, *Mare Geneticum* seeks to achieve the fair and equitable sharing of the benefits arising out of utilisation of MGR coming from ABNJ, and to enhance MSR and enable biodiscovery worldwide for the benefit of humankind. However, promoting fundamental research through OA whilst allowing users to take research results to the level of application and commercialisation of the biodiscovery pipeline will be a difficult balance to achieve.

4.3 *Enforcement and Compliance: Centralised Tracking System*

Ensuring compliance with and enforcement of benefit-sharing obligations is not an easy task, especially within a multilateral context. To this end, the OPEN registry would provide a centralised system where monitoring can be based on reporting and updating obligations. At the end of a non-commercial research project or at the moment of commercialisation of a product developed on the basis of MGR coming from ABNJ, a second OPEN notification could be envisaged and would need to be linked to the first one. An alternative could be additional information and potentially additional conditions (e.g., exclusivity) to be annexed to the pre-existing OPEN.

Effective compliance starts with the obligation to report activities to the institution that will be mandated or established by the ILBI for managing access to MGR and the OPEN registry, similarly to the International Seabed Authority's reporting requirements imposed on seabed mining contractors.[102] There would be an obligation to update, either on a regular basis (e.g., annually) or upon reaching certain milestones in the MGR lifetime, but should at the very least occur at every permanent subsequent transfer to collections or to different users, and when the type or the intent of the utilisation changes (e.g., when commercial intent arises). Using the OPEN as the central tracking system will ensure the smooth and effective monitoring of MGR utilisation. The obligation to update or report will first be imposed upon the responsible person of a

102 LOSC, Annex III, Article 17(1)(b).

research project accessing MGR *in situ,* but when signing the OPEN clickwrap agreement, it should also be binding for any subsequent user accessing MGR *ex situ,* or data *in silico* when possible. In other words, because it is quite often the case that multiple users conduct research on the same MGR and that third-party transfer is common practice in biodiscovery ventures,[103] the obligation should be tied to the MGR through the OPEN and its unique identifier, and not to the primary user only. Subsequent users can easily become subject to the OPEN conditions applicable when signing a material transfer agreement with peers or with a biorepository, containing as such a viral licence.

Low impact, cost-effective monitoring is advisable. Trust should be placed in researchers to report sample collection along with findings and transfers. Ocean scientists must be meticulous about recording when and where samples are collected *in situ* because it is an indispensable part of research methodology and protocols, hence it is unlikely to put any additional burden on researchers.[104] Moreover, as previously mentioned, most funding agencies and scientific journal editors require researchers to deposit genetic and proteomic data in publicly accessible archives where they are openly accessible. Reporting standards should be simple, consistent and interoperable.

Further along the research chain, potential R&D users of MGR coming from ABNJ should submit a new notification when a commercially oriented project begins, considering that such a change of intent might trigger the need for additional conditions of use other than just an embargo period on the public release of said MGR and associated data. In particular, there might be intellectual property rights to take into account, as well as payment requirements arising from the monetary benefit-sharing provisions of the ILBI. This new notification could either be in the form of an annex to the MGR's OPEN, or as a second OPEN that should be linked to the first one.

With today's powerful tools such as computer programmes and the Internet, setting up a centralised tracking system is not only possible but also relatively simple to establish and operate. This tracking format has been set up by the 2015 Brazilian legislation on access to and use of its genetic resources,[105] whereby users have to submit similar information to an ABS registry. However, its effectiveness cannot be evaluated, as it is not yet operational.

---

103 M Jaspars, D De Pascale, JH Andersen, F Reyes, AD Crawford and A Ianora, 'The Marine Biodiscovery Pipeline and Ocean Medicines of Tomorrow' (2016) 96(1) *Journal of the Marine Biological Association of the United Kingdom* 151–158.

104 Vierros *et al.* (n 36), at p. 212.

105 Brazilian Biodiversity Law, Federal Act No. 13.123/2015, 20 May 2015 ; Decree No. 8.772/2016, 11 May 2016.

The IOC-UNESCO could easily support the ILBI's implementation with regard to the OPEN mechanism, by providing:

(i) A global data-sharing platform and data clearing-house mechanism for marine taxonomic, genetic, biodiversity and associated data in all ocean basins, including ABNJ;

(ii) A mechanism for international cooperation in MSR, coordination in global ocean observation, and development of standards, manuals and guidelines and codes of conduct in MSR and data-sharing protocols;

(iii) A global network of regional centres to enhance capacity, by training the next generation of scientists and area managers in applying international standards and best practices.[106]

Although States are responsible for the implementation of international treaties, the centralised system for OPENs would alleviate the legislative and administrative means to be deployed in order to ensure compliance. Indeed, instead of managing ABNJ material and data through national registries to be coordinated at a global level, States would merely have to ensure that users comply with adequate and effective reporting. The failure to report or comply with the OPEN conditions, when observed by the mandated international organisation, or by funding agencies when possible, should be notified to the relevant State, and be subject to sufficiently and proportionally discouraging penalties in order to ensure the equal compliance of public and private research organisations. Compliance mechanisms will be the responsibility of State parties to the ILBI, and should serve as incentives to respect the *Mare Geneticum* governance established by it. Any international organisation put in place by the ILBI should coordinate and manage the OPEN mechanism with State parties, leaving enforcement to the States. To this end, there will be an important need to set globally accepted, and harmonised, minimum standards of compliance. It is thus within the hands of States, as both international law makers and subjects, to draft an ILBI reflecting the balanced regime necessary to efficiently share the benefits of MGR without impeding or slowing down research.

106 IOC-UNESCO 'IOC Potential Contribution To A New International Instrument Under UNCLOS On The Conservation And Sustainable Use Of Marine Biological Diversity Of Areas Beyond National Jurisdiction', Information Document IOC/INF-1338, Paris, 17 May 2016. Available at http://ioc-unesco.org/index.php?option=com_oe&task=viewDocumentRecord&docID=17286; accessed 18 January 2017.

5 Towards an Implementing Agreement

The governing principles and implementing mechanisms put forward in this article are intended to lay the basis for a new governance regime in the high and the deep seas that are, by nature and by law, international. Based on the idea that the utilisation of MGR should benefit the world as a whole, notwithstanding the intellectual property rights that may arise from associated discoveries, *Mare Geneticum*'s approach is about adequate regulation for better sharing, in a distant echo of Grotius:

> Now, as there are some things which every man enjoys in common with all other men, and there are other things which are distinctly his and belong to no one else, just so has nature willed that some of the things which she has created for the use of mankind remain common to all, and that others through the industry and labor of each man become his own.[107]

The international community has engaged in the process of developing an implementing agreement to the LOSC in ABNJ, the ILBI. It is going to be their task to draft a realistic and balanced system based on sound foundations. During the Preparatory Committee's sessions for an ILBI, several States have called for open access to research data, samples and knowledge, as well as the need for a data-sharing and clearing house facility. Although a number of databases and biorepositories already exist, what will be needed is a coordinated tracking system, such as the unique identifier of an OPEN record for MGR samples and data from ABNJ.

The new ILBI should adopt a simplified monetary benefit-sharing system in order to promote biodiscovery initiatives rather than to deter them, and to avoid implementation struggles, as may be seen with the LOSC Part XI regime on seabed mining.[108] Above all, the ILBI should emphasize and strengthen non-monetary benefit-sharing for the advancement of science and nature conservation through, *inter alia*:
- Open access to raw data and samples;
- Enhanced international research coordination and cooperation;
- Targeted training and sharing of expertise, methodology, guidelines and best practices;
- Standardised data management, taxonomy and species identification;

---

107 Grotius (n 1), at p. 2.

108 J-S Fritz, 'Deep Sea Anarchy: Mining at the Frontiers of International Law' (2015) 30 *The International Journal of Marine and Coastal Law* 445–476.

- Marine spatial planning in ABNJ, including protected areas;
- Ecosystem-based management;
- Development of marine conservation policies.

Indeed, because *Mare Geneticum* is not a stand-alone approach but part of a four-component package, sharing the benefits arising out of MGR in ABNJ should also mean attributing such benefits to the designation and management of marine protected areas, the systematisation of EIA processes, and the transfer of technology. Notwithstanding the fact that the world has a lot to gain from healthy and sustainably managed oceans, the LOSC Preamble is here to recall that the spirit and purpose of the Convention as a whole is to "promote the peaceful uses of the seas and oceans, the equitable and efficient utilisation of their resources, the conservation of their living resources, and the study, protection and preservation of the marine environment".

CHAPTER 11

Research for Regions: Strengthening Marine Technology Transfer for Pacific Island Countries and Biodiversity beyond National Jurisdiction

Harriet R. Harden-Davies
Australian National Centre for Ocean Resources and Security, University of Wollongong, Wollongong, NSW 2500, Australia

Abstract

Pacific Island Countries have limited capacity to engage in scientific research involving marine genetic resources in areas beyond national jurisdiction (ABNJ). Marine scientific research and capacity development are central to the regime for technology transfer established by the 1982 United Nations Convention on the Law of the Sea (LOSC), but gaps and ambiguities weaken this framework. In this article, options to strengthen scientific capacity in Pacific Island Countries, through the development of a new international legally binding instrument for the conservation and sustainable use of biodiversity in ABNJ under the LOSC, are examined. The international framework for technology transfer could be strengthened by fostering an integrated approach to the advancement, sharing and application of scientific knowledge. Coordination and collaboration at global and regional levels will be required to increase marine science cooperation, improve access to data and information, deliver training, and overcome barriers to develop institutional and individual scientific capacity.

Keywords

technology transfer – marine scientific research – capacity development – areas beyond national jurisdiction (ABNJ) – biodiversity conservation

 | DOI:10.1163/9789004391703_013

1 Introduction

Marine technology transfer and capacity building are critical cross-cutting elements in the development of a new international legally binding instrument (ILBI)[1] for the conservation and sustainable use of marine biological diversity in areas beyond national jurisdiction (ABNJ) under the 1982 United Nations Convention on the Law of the Sea (LOSC).[2] After a decade of discussions,[3] a preparatory committee (PrepCom) has been established to develop substantive recommendations on the elements of a draft text of an ILBI and report to the General Assembly by the end of 2017. The development of the ILBI is a historic turning point in the international law of the sea and seeks to address challenges facing biodiversity in the 64% of the ocean that lies in ABNJ, through: environmental impact assessments, area-based management measures, benefit sharing of marine genetic resources, and capacity building and technology transfer.

Scientific capacity development and technology transfer are crucial for the conservation and sustainable use of biodiversity in ABNJ; this has been recognised at the PrepCom.[4] The need to strengthen national and regional capabilities in marine science and technology to enable developing countries to share in marine scientific advances, and absorb and apply technology and scientific knowledge, has long been recognised. A resolution from the Final Act to the Third United Nations Conference on the Law of the Sea (UNCLOS III) stated that unless urgent measures were taken, the "scientific and technological

1 United Nations General Assembly Resolution 69/292 'Development of an international legally binding instrument under the United Nations Convention on the Law of the Sea on the conservation and sustainable use of marine biological diversity of areas beyond national jurisdiction'. 6 July 2015. Available at https://daccess-ods.un.org/TMP/1859741.2109375.html; accessed 10 September 2017.

2 United Nations Convention on the Law of the Sea, (Montego Bay, 10 December 1982, in force 16 November 1994) 1833 *UNTS* 396.

3 E Druel, J Rochette, R Billé and C Chiarolla, 'A long and winding road. International discussions on the governance of marine biodiversity in areas beyond national jurisdiction', IDDRI Study 07/13 (IDDRI, Paris, 2012); G Wright, J Rochette, E Druel and K Gjerde, 'The long and winding road continues: Towards a new agreement on high seas governance' IDDRI Study 01/16 (IDDRI, Paris, 2015).

4 R Long and M Rodriguez Chaves, 'Anatomy of a new international instrument for marine biodiversity beyond national jurisdiction. First impressions of the preparatory process' (2015) 6 *Environmental Liability—Law, Policy and Practice* 213–229; IISD Reporting Services. Earth Negotiations Bulletin. Summary of the Second Session of the Preparatory Committee on Marine Biodiversity Beyond Areas of National Jurisdiction: 26 August–9 September 2016. Vol 25. No. 118. Available at http://enb.iisd.org/oceans/bbnj/prepcom2/; accessed 11 September 2017.

gap between developed and developing States would widen further" and "endanger the very foundations of the LOSC regime".[5] Equitability is integral to the LOSC regime for technology transfer.[6] Capacity development and technology transfer, have been described as the 'equitable ingredients' of the ILBI, important for both intra-generational and inter-generational equity,[7] especially for Small Island Developing States (SIDS).[8] The importance of technology transfer and scientific capacity development to implement the LOSC and benefit from sustainable development has been recognised by the United Nations General Assembly (UNGA).[9] Sustainable Development Goal 14a calls on States to increase scientific knowledge, develop research capacity and transfer marine technology to improve ocean health and to enhance the contribution of marine biodiversity to the development of developing countries, particularly for SIDS.[10]

---

5 'Resolution on the development of national marine science, technology and ocean service infrastructures'. Adopted by the Conference at the 182nd meeting on 30 April 1982. Third United Nations Conference on the Law of the Sea 1973–1982, Concluded at Montego Bay, Jamaica on 10 December 1982. A/CONF.62/120. Available at http://legal.un.org/diplomaticconferences/1973_los/docs/english/vol_16/a_conf62_120.pdf; accessed 10 September 2017.

6 LOSC Preamble; LOSC Art. 266(3) calls for the creation of favorable economic and legal conditions for the transfer of marine technology on an equitable basis.

7 For example, equitable sharing of benefits of marine genetic resources from ABNJ could be considered as intra-generational equity, and the conservation and sustainable use of biological diversity for future generations could be considered as inter-generational equity.

8 See, for example, "Supplementary view of the Government of the Federated States of Micronesia on the elements of a draft text of an international legally binding instrument under the United Nations Convention on the Law of the Sea on the conservation and sustainable; use of marine biological diversity of areas beyond national jurisdiction following the conclusion of PrepCom 2". Available at http://www.un.org/depts/los/biodiversity/prepcom_files/rolling_comp/Federated_States_of_Micronesia.pdf; accessed 14 February 2017, at pp. 1–2.

9 United Nations General Assembly Resolution 71/257 'Oceans and Law of the Sea'. 23 December 2016. at Preamble and para 13, available at https://documents-dds-ny.un.org/doc/UNDOC/GEN/N16/466/62/PDF/N1646662.pdf?OpenElement accessed 10 September 2017; United Nations General Assembly Resolution 70/235 'Oceans and Law of the Sea' 23 December 2015. at Preamble, available at https://documents-dds-ny.un.org/doc/UNDOC/GEN/N15/456/94/PDF/N1545694.pdf?OpenElement; accessed 10 September 2017.

10 Sustainable Development Goal 14 "Conserve and sustainably use the oceans, seas and marine resources for sustainable development". In: United Nations General Assembly Resolution 70/1 'Transforming our world: the 2030 Agenda for Sustainable Development', 25 September 2015, at p. 14; available at http://www.un.org/en/ga/search/view_doc.asp?symbol=A/RES/70/1; accessed 10 September 2017.

SIDS face capacity constraints which hinder their ability to participate in and benefit from scientific research in ABNJ,[11] as highlighted by the Alliance of Small Island Developing States (AOSIS) and Pacific Small Island Developing States (PSIDS) at the PrepCom.[12] The Federated States of Micronesia has suggested that the ILBI should include measures for the acquisition of scientific knowledge relating to biodiversity in ABNJ and training in marine science and technology.[13] The Group of 77 (G77) plus China have stated that the ILBI should promote increased scientific knowledge, research capacity development and marine technology transfer.[14] One of the key challenges facing States in the development of the ILBI is to enhance the implementation of LOSC Part XIV (Development and Transfer of Marine Technology) to enable equitable participation in the conservation and sustainable use of biodiversity in ABNJ, without undermining existing regional frameworks.[15]

In this article, options are examined to strengthen marine technology transfer and scientific capacity development for Pacific Island Countries to benefit from marine genetic resources in ABNJ under an ILBI. First, the LOSC regime for technology transfer is examined, illustrating the linkages between scientific research, capacity development and knowledge exchange. Second, the opportunities and challenges facing Pacific Island Countries to access and use marine genetic resources in ABNJ are discussed, highlighting technology

11 C Salpin, V Onwuasoanya, M Bourrel and A Swaddling, 'Marine Scientific Research in Pacific Small Island Developing States' (2016) *Marine Policy*, online, https://doi.org/10.1016/j.marpol.2016.07.019HY.

12 "Alliance of Small Island States (AOSIS) Submission on Capacity Building and Transfer of technology at the Second Session of the Preparatory Committee on the Development of an International Legally Binding Instrument under the United Nations Convention on the Law of the Sea on the Conservation and Sustainable Use of Marine Biological Diversity". 5 December 2016. Available at http://www.un.org/depts/los/biodiversity/prepcom_files/rolling_comp/AOSIS-capacity_building_and_transfer_of_technology.pdf; accessed 14 February 2017; "PSIDS Submission on Institutional Arrangement. BBNJ Preparatory Committee". 5 December 2016. Available at http://www.un.org/depts/los/biodiversity/prepcom_files/rolling_comp/PSIDS-institutional_arrangements.pdf; accessed 14 February 2017.

13 FSM (n 8).

14 G77, "Development of an internationally legally binding instrument under the United Nations Convention on the Law of the Sea on the conservation and sustainable use of marine biological diversity of areas beyond national jurisdiction (A/RES/69/292) Group of 77 and China's Written Submission. 5 December 2016" available at: http://www.un.org/depts/los/biodiversity/prepcom_files/rolling_comp/Group_of_77_and_China.pdf; accessed 14 February 2017.

15 UNGA Resolution 69/292 states that the development of the ILBI "should not undermine existing relevant legal instrument and frameworks and relevant global, regional and sectoral bodies", UNGA (n 1) at para 3.

transfer and capacity development needs. Third, options to strengthen the implementation of the LOSC framework provisions for technology transfer and scientific capacity development under an ILBI, through the generation, sharing and application of scientific knowledge, are identified. The article concludes that development of an ILBI is an opportunity to strengthen the international framework for technology transfer and scientific capacity development, but resource and coordination challenges need to be overcome.

2 International Legal Framework for Marine Technology Transfer

The purposes of technology transfer identified in the LOSC range from social and economic development[16] to the protection and preservation of the marine environment.[17] The framework established by the LOSC for the development and transfer of marine technology[18] is strongly interlinked with scientific capacity development. For example, increasing scientific capacity is identified in Article 266(2) as an aim of technology transfer, and the development of technological infrastructure and human resources (through training and education) are among the basic objectives of technology transfer articulated in LOSC Article 268.[19] Technical, human and institutional scientific capacity development provisions in the LOSC include: the acquisition of technological infrastructure,[20] development of human resources through training and education,[21] and the establishment of national and regional marine science and technology centres.[22]

The acquisition, evaluation and dissemination of marine scientific and technological knowledge, information and data are emphasised in the LOSC as a basic objective[23] and modality of technology transfer.[24] It is also an obligation

16 LOSC Art. 266.

17 LOSC Art. 202.

18 LOSC Parts XIV (development and transfer of marine technology), XIII (marine scientific research), and XI (the Area).

19 LOSC Arts. 268(c) and (d).

20 LOSC Art. 268(c).

21 LOSC Arts. 275(2), 277(a), 268(d).

22 LOSC Arts. 274–277.

23 LOSC Art. 268(a).

24 LOSC Art. 277(f) identifies "prompt dissemination of results of marine scientific and technological research in readily available publications" as a function of regional [marine science and technology] centres.

for marine scientific research;[25] Article 244 of the LOSC provides that States shall publish and disseminate knowledge resulting from marine scientific research and promote the flow of scientific data and information, especially to developing States. Article 244 further provides that States shall strengthen the autonomous marine scientific research capabilities of developing States, including through technical and scientific training programmes. Sharing the outcomes of marine scientific research, and building capacity to assist developing States to make use of those outcomes, are therefore obligations for the conduct of research in ABNJ, whether exercising the freedom of marine scientific research in the high seas[26] and/or fulfilling the duty to conduct marine scientific research in the Area for the benefit of mankind.[27]

However, there are gaps, weaknesses and ambiguities in LOSC Part XIV that constrain effective implementation. Despite the various objectives and measures of technology transfer described in Part XIV, the LOSC does not include a definition of "technology" or "technology transfer". Absent or unclear institutional and funding mechanisms render many provisions of Part XIV little more than weak inducements for States. This also creates challenges to monitor or evaluate technology transfer. The provisions of Part XIV are somewhat ambiguous given the requirement that technology transfer should be conducted on reasonable, fair and equitable[28] terms to States that "need and request" it.[29] International cooperation in marine scientific research (facilitated through scientist exchanges and conferences),[30] especially at the regional and subregional level,[31] is the primary method to achieve technology transfer identified by the LOSC.[32] As a result, the implementation of the LOSC regime for the development and transfer of marine technology, including scientific capacity development, is a main focus in the development of the ILBI. The example of marine genetic resources[33] in Pacific Island Countries illustrates the practical

25 All States have the right to conduct marine scientific research (LOSC Arts. 87, 143, 238), subject to responsibilities. For example, LOSC Art. 240 elaborates principles for the conduct of marine scientific research.

26 LOSC Art. 87(1)(f).

27 LOSC Art. 143(1).

28 LOSC Arts. 266(1), 269(b).

29 LOSC Arts. 266 and 275.

30 LOSC Art. 269, 277(d).

31 LOSC Art. 268(e).

32 LOSC Arts. 266(1), 268(e), 269(a), 270, 272, 273, 278.

33 "Marine genetic resources" are not defined in the LOSC, but could be considered to include material from marine animals, plants, microbes or other organisms, and parts thereof containing functional units of heredity of actual or potential value. For discussions on the definition of marine genetic resources. See for example: M Vierros, C Suttle,

challenges and opportunities for strengthening the implementation of technology transfer under the ILBI.

3 Marine Genetic Resources beyond National Jurisdiction: Opportunities and Challenges for Technology Transfer in Pacific Island Countries

The high marine biodiversity of the South-West Pacific region encompasses rich genetic and biochemical diversity,[34] making the region a significant source of marine genetic resources and target for marine bio-discovery activities. The South-West Pacific was a major source of natural products from invertebrates in the 1990s.[35] Although this has mainly been in shallow coastal waters, the growing number of deep-sea natural products[36] described from the region indicates some level of research activity in deep-sea marine genetic resources. Examples of deep-sea natural products derived from the Pacific include: compounds with anti-cancer properties derived from sponges collected in Guam and Palau and from fungal strains collected off Fiji; and sterols with anti-fungal properties from a starfish collected off New Caledonia.[37] Marine genetic resources patents associated with the North Fiji Basin, Manus Basin, Tonga Trench and Kermadec Trench.[38] Nevertheless, the South-West Pacific deep sea remains one of the most under-sampled areas of the global ocean, leaving significant gaps in knowledge of its deep-sea biodiversity.[39] Increased

---

H Harden-Davies and G Burton, 'Who Owns the Ocean? Policy Issues Surrounding Marine Genetic Resources' (2016) 25(2) *Limnology and Oceanography Bulletin* 29–35; H Harden-Davies, 'Deep-Sea Genetic Resources: New Frontiers for Science and Stewardship in Areas Beyond National Jurisdiction' (2017) 137 *Deep Sea Research Part II: Topical Studies in Oceanography* 504–513.

34 TF Molinski, DS Dalisay, SL Lievens and JP Saludes, 'Drug Development from Marine Natural Products' (2009) 8(1) *Nature Reviews. Drug Discovery* 69–85.

35 MC Leal, J Puga, J Serodio, NCM Gomes and R Calado, 'Trends in the Discovery of New Marine Natural Products from Invertebrates over the Last Two Decades—Where and What Are We Bioprospecting?' (2012) 7(1) *PLoS ONE* e30580.

36 D Skropeta, 'Deep-Sea Natural Products' (2008) 25(6) *Natural Product Reports* 1131–1166; D Skropeta and L Wei, 'Recent Advances in Deep-Sea Natural Products' (2014) 31(8) *Natural Product Reports* 999–1025.

37 Skropeta and Wei (n 36).

38 P Oldham, S Hall, C Barnes, C Oldham, M Cutter, N Burns and L Kindess, 'Valuing the Deep: Marine Genetic Resources in Areas Beyond National Jurisdiction' (One World Analytics, London, 2014) 1–241, at pp. 81, 82, 143, 158.

39 C R German, E Ramirez-Llodra, MC Baker, PA Tyler and the ChEss Scientific Steering Committee, 'Deep-Water Chemosynthetic Ecosystem Research During the Census of

scientific research would be necessary to access, use and derive benefits from marine genetic resources in South-West Pacific ABNJ.[40]

The financial and technological requirements of undertaking research in ABNJ are, however, beyond the capacity of Pacific Island Countries alone. Low population, large geographic area, remoteness, and limited human, financial, technical and scientific resources pose significant obstacles to the research capacity of Pacific Island Countries.[41] Limited scientific and technological capacity, such as a lack of offshore ocean research vessels and sampling equipment[42] and of onshore laboratory equipment and information technology infrastructure, constrains the capacity of Pacific Island Countries to access, use or benefit from marine genetic resources in ABNJ.[43] Pacific Island countries are therefore reliant upon foreign research institutions, resources and expertise to access and use marine genetic resources from ABNJ. Technology transfer and scientific capacity development would therefore be needed for Pacific Island Countries to engage in, and benefit equitably from, marine genetic resources in ABNJ.

Marine Life Decade and Beyond: A Proposed Deep-Ocean Road Map' (2011) 6(8) *PLoS ONE* 1–16.

40 Data, technology transfer, knowledge and capacity development are examples of 'non-monetary' benefits from marine genetic resources, Harden-Davies (n 32).; The UNGA has recognised the importance of research on marine genetic resources for the "purpose of enhancing scientific understanding, potential use and application and enhanced management of marine ecosystems", UNGA Resolution 71/257. 'Oceans and Law of the Sea'. 23 December 2016 at para 246; available at https://documents-dds-ny.un.org/doc/UNDOC/GEN/N16/466/62/PDF/N1646662.pdf?OpenElement; accessed 10 September 2017.

41 Salpin (n 11) observed that the challenges facing Pacific SIDS to participate in, and fully benefit from, marine scientific research include: lack of research infrastructure; limited education opportunities and expertise; and limited funding. See also: RJ Morrison, J Zhang, ER Urban Jr, J Hall, V Ittekkot, B Avril, L Hu, GH Hong, S Kidwai, CB Lange, V Lobanov, J Machiwa, ML San Diego-McGlone, T Oguz, FG Plumley, T Yeemin, W Zhu and F Zuo, 'Developing Human Capital for Successful Implementation of International Marine Scientific Research Projects' (2013) 77(1–2) *Marine Pollution Bulletin* 11–22.

42 Salpin (n 11).

43 P Bernal and A Simcock, 'Marine Scientific Research' in L Inniss and A Simcock (eds), *The First Global Integrated Marine Assessment: World Ocean Assessment I* (United Nations, New York, 2016) at p. 18; SK Juniper, 'Technological, Environmental, Social and Economic Aspects. Information Paper 3' in *IUCN Information Papers for the Intersessional Workshop on Marine Genetic Resources 2–3 May 2013, United Nations General Assembly Ad Hoc Open-Ended Informal Working Group to Study Issues Relating to the Conservation and Sustainable Use of Marine Biological Diversity Beyond Areas of National Jurisdiction.* (IUCN Environmental Law Centre, Bonn, 2013) at p. 15.

3.1 *Technology Transfer*

According to the Intergovernmental Oceanographic Commission (IOC) Criteria and Guidelines on the Transfer of Marine Technology (CGTMT)[44] marine technology includes:

- Information and data (marine sciences, operations and services);
- Expertise, knowledge, skills, methods (technical/scientific/legal);
- Equipment (*in situ* sampling and observation, laboratory analysis and experimentation);
- Computer software, models and modelling techniques;
- Manuals, guidelines, criteria, standards, reference materials.

The IOC CGTMT have been acknowledged by many States as a useful tool in the development of the ILBI,[45] although the G77 plus China suggest[46] that further elaboration of the guidelines would be useful. A wide range of technology could be included in the scope of marine genetic resources in ABNJ. This could include scientific research hardware such as at-sea observation and sampling equipment, on-shore laboratory equipment, and data management and analysis software (e.g., for biodiversity and climate change modelling, oceanography and sea-bed mapping). Information sharing could also include manuals and guidelines for the collection, storage and curation of biological samples.

Technologies that can be applied for multiple purposes could be particularly important for capacity development. The merits of multi-use technologies are illustrated by the Centre of Drug Discovery and Conservation of the University of the South Pacific, which has a dual focus on marine biodiscovery and ecological surveys. For example, 'shot-gun DNA sequencing' could be used for marine biodiscovery research as well as other purposes, such as water quality monitoring. Low technology, low-key and long-term approaches to technology transfer and capacity development are often more effective in Pacific Island Countries than short-term, high-technology approaches.[47] For

---

44 Intergovernmental Oceanographic Commission (IOC), 'IOC Criteria and Guidelines on the Transfer of Marine Technology'. IOC Information Document 1203 (IOC-UNESCO, Paris, 2005), para A.2 at p. 9.

45 See for example: "Development of an International Legally-Binding Instrument under UNCLOS on the Conservation and Sustainable Use of Marine Biological Diversity of Areas Beyond National Jurisdiction (BBNJ Process). Written Submission of the EU and its Member States. Capacity Building and Transfer of Marine Technology. 31 January 2017" at para 17. Available at http://www.un.org/depts/los/biodiversity/prepcom_files/rolling_comp/EU_Capacity-Building_and_Transfer_of_Marine_Technology.pdf; accessed 16 February 2017; AOSIS (n5).

46 G77 (n 14), at p. 5, para 8.

47 See, for example, C Kaluwin and A Smith, 'Coastal vulnerability and integrated coastal zone management in the Pacific Island region' (1997) 24 *Journal of Coastal Research* 95–106.

technology transfer to be useful in the long term requires considerations of issues such as the cost of maintenance and operation.

Data and knowledge are forms of technology, access to data and knowledge is a form of technology transfer.[48] Access to data is also a regional priority identified in the Pacific Islands Regional Ocean Policy.[49] Data and information on marine biodiversity, natural products and genetics, as well as biological samples collected from ABNJ, could enable Pacific Island Countries to benefit from marine genetic resources. However, the usefulness of access to data, knowledge and samples is largely dependent on scientific and technological capacity, including skilled personnel, scientific equipment, and technical infrastructure, such as computers and reliable internet access.[50] Information communication technology limitations have been highlighted by Pacific Island Countries at the PrepCom.[51]

Information technology could therefore be particularly important to enable Pacific Island Countries to access data and information relating to ABNJ. Various existing data-sharing mechanisms are in operation at regional[52] and global[53] levels that could be relevant. However, resource constraints, limited funding and overlapping functions can impede the efficiency of data management systems in the region. For example, the Pacific Island Marine Portal[54] was established as a collaborative project between the Pacific Islands Marine Resources Information System (PIMRIS) and the IOC International

48 IOC (n 43); Harriet Harden-Davies, 'Marine Science and Technology Transfer: Can the Intergovernmental Oceanographic Commission Advance Governance of Biodiversity Beyond National Jurisdiction?' (2016) 74 *Marine Policy* 260–267; see also LOSC Art. 277(e).

49 Pacific Island Forum Secretariat (2002) 'Forum Communiqué: Annex 2 Pacific Island Regional Ocean Policy', Fiji: 33rd Pacific Islands Forum (15–17 August 2002). Theme 2. Available at http://www.forumsec.org/resources/uploads/attachments/documents/PIROP.pdf; accessed 10 September 2017.

50 Salpin (n 11) observed that the "value and use of research results and data is [sic] largely correlated to the suitability of data management systems, as well as expertise of local scientists—lack of adequate handling and storage, processing technology and expertise has been an obstacle to fully benefiting from marine scientific research results, data and samples".

51 PSIDS (n 12).

52 For example: Enhancing Pacific Ocean Governance project (EPOG), http://msp.csiro.au/; accessed 15 February 2017; PacGeo, available at www.pacgeo.org; accessed 15 February 2017.

53 For example: IOC International Oceanographic Data and Information Exchange (IODE), Ocean Biogeographic Information System (OBIS), available at www.iobis.org; accessed 20/02/017.

54 Available at http://www.pimrisportal.org/about; accessed 20 October 2016. See also J Veitayaki, GR South, 'Capacity building in the marine sector in the Pacific Islands: The role of the University of the South Pacific's Marine Studies Programme' (2001) 25 *Marine Policy* 437–444.

Oceanographic Data and Information Exchange (IODE) to improve access to Pacific marine information for the Pacific Islands community. However, although some regional organisations appear to be using the portal to share information, resource constraints inhibit its effectiveness. This illustrates the importance of coordination and sustained resourcing for data management systems at regional and global levels.

3.2 *Scientific Capacity Development*

3.2.1 International

International organisations, such as the International Seabed Authority, Food and Agriculture Organization, and the IOC are involved in facilitating capacity development in the region. The IOC is recognised in the LOSC as a competent international organisation for marine scientific research.[55] The IOC offers a forum for Pacific Island Countries to seek support for marine science capacity development and technology transfer, and the IOC SIDS Action Plan[56] provides a renewed impetus for IOC's 148 Member States to support marine science capacity development and technology transfer. It also has a role in implementing the SIDS Accelerated Modalities of Action (SAMOA) Pathway.[57] Eleven Pacific Island Countries are Member States of IOC.[58] Increasing the participation of Pacific Island Countries in IOC could help promote regional capacity development priorities at the international level. However, resource constraints limit IOC's activities in Pacific Island Countries. The IOC Capacity Development fund (which sources contributions for projects ranging from monitoring ocean acidification impacts to tsunami preparedness) is dependent on voluntary Member State contributions.

---

55 LOSC Annex VIII, Article 2(2).

56 IOC, 2016. *IOC SIDS Action Plan: A follow-up to the Small Island Developing States SAMOA Pathway Outcome Document.* Item 4.1.2., 49th Session of Executive Council, UNESCO, Paris, 7–10 June 2016. IOC/EC-XLIX/2 Annex 5. Available at http://unesdoc.unesco.org/images/0024/002449/244941e.pdf; accessed 09 September 2017.

57 The SAMOA Pathway outlines priorities and pathways to reach sustainable development for SIDS, including enhancing oceanographic research capacity. Small Island Developing States Accelerated Modalities of Action (SAMOA Pathway). Report of the third International Conference on Small Island Developing States, Apia, Samoa, 1–4 September 2014. A/CONF.233/10. At Annex paras 58a and 68f. Available at http://www.un.org/ga/search/view_doc.asp?symbol=A/RES/69/15&Lang=E; accessed 10 September 2017.; IOC Decision EC-XLIX, Dec. 4.1(II) 'IOC Contribution towards Agenda 2030: IOC SIDS Action Plan' at p. 16; available at http://unesdoc.unesco.org/images/0024/002449/244991e.pdf; accessed 10 September 2017.

58 Nauru, Cook Islands, Fiji, Vanuatu, Tuvalu, Tonga, Solomon Islands, Samoa, Papua New Guinea, Palau, Niue.

The IOC regional Sub-Commission for the Western Pacific (IOC-WESTPAC), established in 1989 and hosted by the Government of Thailand since 1994, has a mandate to promote and coordinate international cooperation in marine scientific research and capacity development in the region. IOC-WESTPAC capacity development[59] activities include: training courses and summer schools; and international scientific symposia held every three years with associated young scientist awards, travel grants and internship programs. The IOC Regional Network of Training and Research Centres on Marine Science (RTRCs) was established in 2008 to improve regional capacity on marine science,[60] recognising the "disparity in capacity and capability among the Member States of the region, and high capability of several Member States in marine science, ocean observations and services".[61] However, only three Pacific Island Countries[62] are IOC-WESTPAC Member States.[63] Most of the activities of IOC-WESTPAC take place in South-East Asia. Resource constraints limit the implementation of IOC-WESTPAC activities. IOC-WESTPAC has expressed "deep concern over the long-time overloaded and unstable staffing situation at the WESTPAC Office".[64] IOC-WESTPAC has requested assistance from IOC Member States to implement regional capacity-building activities, including the RTRC,

59 IOC-WESTPAC 'WESTPAC Approach to Capacity Development in Marine Science'. (IOC-WESTPAC, Bangkok, 2014) 1–10. Available at http://iocwestpac.org/online%20doc/Capacity%20Development.pdf; accessed 11 September 2017.

60 The RTRC initiative was adopted by the Sub-Commission at its Seventh Intergovernmental Session (WESTPAC-VII, 26–29 May 2008, Sabah, Malaysia, http://unesdoc.unesco.org/images/0021/002185/218502e.pdf; accessed 10 September 2017) and endorsed by the IOC at its forty-first session of the Executive Council (24 June–1 July 2008, Paris, France, http://unesdoc.unesco.org/images/0017/001798/179861e.pdf; accessed 10 September 2017). The first RTRC was established at the First Institute of Oceanography, State Oceanic Administration of China (FIO, SOA) with a focus on ocean dynamics, climate change and modelling. Discussions with other RTRCs are ongoing with Indonesia, Thailand, Malaysia and Vietnam. Available at http://iocwestpac.org/capacity-development/49.html; accessed 26 September 2016.

61 IOC-WESTPAC. *UNESCO-IOC Regional Network of Training and Research Centres in the Western Pacific*. 7th Intergovernmental Session of the IOC Sub-Commission for the Western Pacific, Sabah, Malaysia, 26–29 May 2008. UN doc IOC/SC-WESTPAC-VII/3s. Annex II, at p. 3; http://iocwestpac.org/file/1641/ref/Adopted%20Guideline%20and%20Procedure.pdf; accessed 26 September 2016.

62 Samoa, Solomon Islands, Tonga.

63 There are 22 IOC-WESTPAC Member States, including USA, UK, France, Australia, New Zealand.

64 IOC. Tenth Intergovernmental Session of the IOC Sub-Commission for the Western Pacific (WESTPAC-X). Bangkok, 25 May 2015. IOC/SC-WESTPAC-X/3s, at paras 4 and 5; available at http://unesdoc.unesco.org/images/0023/002341/234134E.pdf; accessed 10 September 2017.

by encouraging Member States, donors, organizations, and institutions to engage in the regional network.[65] To date, IOC-WESTPAC has not been active in capacity-development activities in Pacific Islands. Increasing the participation of Pacific Island Countries in IOC-WESTPAC could elevate Pacific Island engagement in regional IOC capacity-development and technology-transfer activities. However, this would be largely reliant on enhanced resources and coordination.

In practice, capacity development in the region is supported through multilateral and bilateral arrangements with donor countries, or through *ad-hoc* international research collaborations. For example, the University of the South Pacific (USP) Centre of Drug Discovery and Conservation has been the recipient of three consecutive International Cooperative Biodiversity Grants from the US National Institutes of Health (2005–2018) in a consortium with the Georgia Institute of Technology and Scripps Institute of Oceanography, aiming to support sustained international research engagement in the South-West Pacific. Another example, the memorandum of understanding between the Republic of Korea Institute of Ocean Science and Technology (KIOST) and the Secretariat of the Pacific Community (SPC), illustrates how bilateral links aim to support sustainable Pacific development through science and technical innovation, including through technical meetings, joint lectures, exchange initiatives, sharing samples and instrumentation.[66] Strengthening and enhancing these types of collaborations and capacity-development initiatives would be crucial to ensure long-term meaningful technology transfer to Pacific Island Countries and equitable participation in the implementation of an ILBI.

3.2.2 Institutional

Few Pacific Island Countries have established marine scientific research institutions.[67] Scientific research capacity in the South-West Pacific region is largely concentrated in regional organisations and institutions. For example, the USP, established in 1968, is a regional university jointly owned by the

65 IOC-WESTPAC (n 62).

66 Convention for the Protection of the Natural Resources and Environment of the South Pacific Region (Nouméa Convention) (Nouméa, 24 November 1986, in force 22 August 1990) PITSE 15; see also United Nations General Assembly Resolution 70/235 'Oceans and Law of the Sea' 23 December 2015. at Preamble, available at https://documents-dds-ny.un.org/doc/UNDOC/GEN/N15/456/94/PDF/N1545694.pdf?OpenElement; accessed 10 September 2017, at para 248.

67 Salpin (n 11).

governments of twelve member countries.[68] The main campus is in Fiji, the School of Agriculture and Food Technology is in Samoa, the School of Law is in Vanuatu and there are campuses in all member countries.[69] USP is a regional hub for international marine research collaborations, provides education and training, and represents all Pacific Island Countries in the International Council for Science (a role usually reserved for Learned Academies).[70] The USP marine studies program, established in 1978, has relied on foreign donor programs, as well as on funding from USP member countries,[71] highlighting the challenges facing the region to secure human, financial and infrastructure resources. The USP's 'Centre of Drug Discovery and Conservation' of the Institute for Applied Science has some research infrastructure for genetic resources research; however, research capacity remains limited and USP is not currently capable of undertaking research in ABNJ.

Other regional organisations could play a role in technology transfer and capacity development. For example, the SPC is the regional scientific and technical organisation, it has a role to facilitate international cooperation in scientific research and deliver scientific and technical services (including conservation, deep sea minerals, maritime boundary delimitation and genetic resources).[72] The South Pacific Regional Environment Program (SPREP) in Samoa also has involvement in marine scientific research, including as the regional point of contact for the Pacific regional alliance for the Global Ocean Observing System (PI-GOOS).[73]

The establishment of national and regional marine science and technology centres is promoted in the LOSC to advance the conduct of marine scientific research, enhance capabilities to utilise and preserve marine resources and

68 Cook Islands, Fiji, Kiribati, Marshall Islands, Nauru, Niue, Solomon Islands, Tokelau, Tonga, Tuvalu, Vanuatu and Samoa.

69 USP's mission includes tertiary education and the application of research to deliver benefits and solutions to communities and countries in the Pacific region. Available at https://www.usp.ac.fj/index.php?id=usp_introduction; accessed 6 July 2016.

70 Of the 121 Members of the International Council for Science, USP is the only Member that is a university that represents multiple countries. Available at http://www.icsu.org/asia-pacific/about-icsu-roap/asia-pacific-members; accessed 4 July 2016.

71 Veitayaki and South (n 54).

72 Pacific Community, 2016, 'Pacific Community Strategic Plan 2016–2020'. Pacific Community, Nouméa, pp. 5–7. Available at http://www.spc.int/images/publications/en/Corporate/Strategic-Plan-2016–2020.pdf. Accessed 30 October 2016.

73 PI-GOOS is a long-term sustained scientific cooperation program between SPREP, USA and Australia to monitor the Pacific Ocean, as part of the Global Ocean Observing System; http://www.goosocean.org/index.php?option=com_content&view=article&id=40&Itemid=140. Accessed 30 June 2017.

transfer marine technology.[74] The UNGA has recognised the importance of coordinating activities with regional and national marine science and technology centres to achieve development objectives,[75] and the SAMOA Pathway has highlighted the "establishment of dedicated regional oceanographic centres" and the provision of technical assistance.[76]

Existing marine science and technology institutions in the region, such as USP, fit the criteria of 'regional marine science and technology centres' referred to in LOSC Article 277, such as for education and data exchange. These regional marine science and technology centres function as a decentralised but interconnected network, illustrating that a network model could be more appropriate for SIDS than individual centres.

Coordination is critically important for effective ocean governance in the region.[77] Therefore, in addition to strengthening the capacity of individual institutions, increasing links between organisations (inside and outside the region) is important to avoid duplication of activities and enhance the existing network of marine science and technology centres. The coordination and delivery of technology transfer and capacity development initiatives, however, will depend on the availability of resources, as highlighted by Pacific SIDS.[78]

3.2.3 Individual

For Pacific Island Countries to make use of marine genetic resources in ABNJ, training and skill development could be required in disciplines such as taxonomy, ecology, genetics, molecular biology, microbiology, chemistry, oceanography and bio-informatics.[79] Participation in research cruises in the region could provide an opportunity for research training and access to *in situ* marine genetic resources. Research collaborations and post-cruise mentoring

74 LOSC Arts. 269, 274, 277.

75 UNGA Res 70/235 (n 9) at [249].

76 SAMOA Pathway (n 55) at [58.f].

77 See for example: E Druel, P Ricard, J Rochette and C Martinez, *Governance of Marine Biodiversity in Areas Beyond National Jurisdiction at the Regional Level: Filling the Gaps and Strengthening the Framework for Action.Case Studies from the North-East Atlantic, Southern Ocean, Western Indian Ocean, South West Pacific and the Sargasso Sea*, Study 4/12 (IDDRI, Paris, 2012); A Wright, N Stacey and P Holland, 'The Cooperative Framework for Ocean and Coastal Management in the Pacific Islands: Effectiveness, Constraints and Future Direction' (2006) 49(9–10) *Ocean & Coastal Management* 739–763.

78 PSIDS (n 12).

79 Note: LOSC Art. 277(a) refers to training and educational programmes across a number of disciplines relating to marine scientific and technological research, including marine biology, conservation and management of living resources, oceanography, hydrography, engineering, geological exploration of the seabed, mining and desalination technologies.

could enhance research training opportunities for Pacific Island Countries. Training in 'on-shore' research skills could be more useful than 'at-sea' skills, given the technological limitations in the region.

A flexible and adaptable approach is necessary to provide training opportunities that are fit for the needs of the region.[80] USP, for example, offers short-term training opportunities, such as workshops, as well as long-term academic education programs (pre-degree, undergraduate and post-graduate) in various marine scientific research disciplines. Distance learning enables participation across different Pacific Island countries; for example, more than half the students at USP use distance learning.[81] Information technology infrastructure is required to enable distance-learning opportunities and support knowledge diffusion across the region. International research collaboration links and access to academic experts could help address gaps in expertise and develop human capacity in the region.[82]

3.3 *Coordination for Implementation: a Regional Science and Technology Strategy?*

For capacity development and technology transfer to meet national and regional needs, those needs must first be identified. LOSC Articles 266(2) provides that States shall promote the development of the marine scientific and technological capacity of States which may need and request technical assistance. Furthermore, LOSC Article 275(2) provides that States shall support the establishment and strengthening of national marine scientific and technological research centres so as to provide for advanced training facilities and necessary equipment, skills and know-how as well as technical experts to such States which may need and request assistance. This underscores the importance of enabling technology transfer needs to be identified and ensuring there are avenues through which assistance can be requested.

Although few Pacific Island Countries have articulated national marine scientific research policies, the Pacific Islands Regional Ocean Policy sets a vision to improve understanding of the ocean in three ways: identifying and meeting information needs; access to information; and science education and training.[83] Strengthening the international framework for science and

---

80 J Veitayaki and PE Manoa, 'Building Capacity in the Marine Sector in the Pacific Islands and the role of The University of the South Pacific'in MR Dakuidreketi and GI Lingram (eds), *Higher Education and Community Engagement in the Pacific: Development and Policy Issues* (University of the South Pacific Press, Suva 2014) 70–91. at p. 76.

81 Veitayaki and Manoa (n 78) at p 72.

82 Veitayaki and South (n 54).

83 Pacific Islands Regional Ocean Policy (n 47).

technology transfer and capacity development through the development of the ILBI would therefore align with these existing regional priorities.

However, fragmentation in regulatory and institutional frameworks for marine scientific research hinders the prioritisation of research needs in Pacific Island Countries.[84] The development of a regional marine science and technology needs assessment could be useful to identify technology transfer and scientific capacity development priorities, including to benefit from marine genetic resources in ABNJ. Such a strategy could consider how to identify and meet the scientific capacity development needs of the region at international, institutional and individual levels. Existing regional arrangements such as the Council of Regional Organisations in the Pacific,[85] which facilitates coordination between regional organisations engaged in science and technology, and the Office of the Pacific Ocean Commissioner[86] could be appropriate avenues to progress such a strategy.[87]

4 Towards an Enabling Environment for Technology Transfer?

4.1 *An Integrated Approach to Acquire, Share and Apply Knowledge*

The development of the ILBI is an opportunity for States to strengthen the implementation of the LOSC framework provisions for technology transfer. Due to the different needs within and between regions, there will be no 'one size fits all' solution for technology transfer and capacity development. The development of the ILBI could, however, create an enabling international

84 Salpin (n 11).

85 Council of Regional Organisations in the Pacific comprises the heads of regional organisations in the Pacific, including USP, SPC and SPREP. http://www.forumsec.org/pages.cfm/about-us/our-partners/crop/?printerfriendly=true; accessed 10 September 2017.

86 Office of the Pacific Ocean Commissioner; http://www.forumsec.org/pages.cfm/strategic-partnerships-coordination/pacific-oceanscape/pacific-ocean-commissioner.html; accessed 10 September 2017. See also *Framework for a Pacific Oceanscape* in C Pratt and H Govan, 'Our Sea of Islands, Our livelihoods, Our Oceania: Framework for a Pacific Oceanscape: a catalyst for implementation of ocean policy' (Report prepared for the Council of Regional Organisations of the Pacific Marine Sector Working Group, Suva, 2010), at p. 59; available at http://www.forumsec.org/resources/uploads/embeds/file/Oceanscape.pdf; accessed 10 September 2017.

87 For a discussion of the role of the Council of Regional Organisations in the Pacific and the Office of the Pacific Ocean Commissioner in regional coordination and cooperation see G Quirk and H Harden-Davies, 'Cooperation, Competence and Coherence: The Role of Regional Ocean Governance in the South West Pacific for the Conservation and Sustainable Use of Biodiversity beyond National Jurisdiction' (2017) 32(4) *International Journal of Marine and Coastal Law*, this special issue.

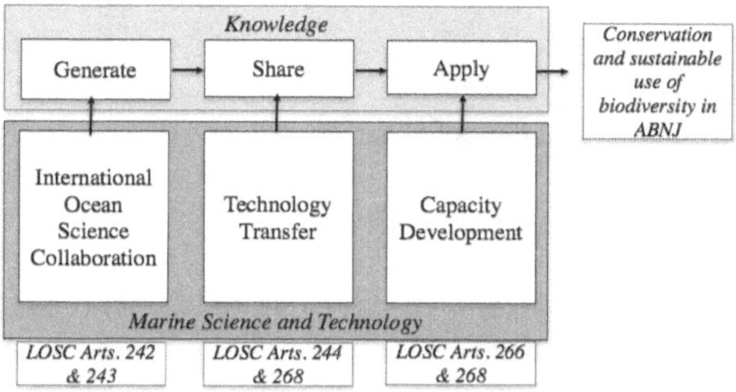

FIGURE 1 Three pillars to create an enabling international environment for scientific capacity development

environment for scientific capacity development where different needs could be better identified and met. The acquisition, dissemination and application of scientific knowledge could be progressed through strengthened international marine science cooperation, technology transfer and capacity development (see Fig. 1).

The acquisition, dissemination and application of scientific knowledge are important in the context of ABNJ. The 1970 Declaration of Principles Governing the Sea-Bed and the Ocean Floor, and the Subsoil Thereof, Beyond the Limits of National Jurisdiction,[88] for example, called on States to promote international cooperation in scientific research through: (a) participation in international programs including by encouraging participation of personnel from different countries; (b) publication of research programs and dissemination of results; (c) strengthening research capabilities.[89] In 2015 and 2016, the UNGA recognised that realising benefits of the LOSC could be enhanced by international cooperation, technical assistance and capacity-building.[90]

An integrated approach to the acquisition, sharing and application of scientific knowledge could be particularly important to share benefits from marine genetic resources. The importance of technology transfer and international cooperation to build research and innovation capacity for 'adding value to genetic resources' for developing countries is recognised by the 2010 Nagoya Protocol on Access to Genetic Resources and the Fair and Equitable Sharing

88 UNGA Resolution 25/2749, 'Declaration of Principles Governing the Sea-Bed and the Ocean Floor, and the Subsoil Thereof, Beyond the Limits of National Jurisdiction', 17 December 1970; available at https://documents-dds-ny.un.org/doc/RESOLUTION/GEN/NR0/350/14/IMG/NR035014.pdf?OpenElement; accessed 11 September 2017.

89 *Ibid.*, at para 10.

90 UNGA (n 9).

of Benefits Arising from Their Utilization to the Convention on Biological Diversity.[91] The 2001 International Treaty on Plant Genetic Resources for Food and Agriculture[92] (ITPGRFA) identifies information exchange, access to technology and capacity-building as forms of benefit sharing of genetic resources.[93]

This notion that sharing benefits from marine genetic resources can be progressed through scientific investigation, technology transfer and capacity development is pertinent to the development of the ILBI, as illustrated in the discussion of Pacific Island Countries. The ITPGRFA calls on Parties to cooperate to "promote an integrated approach to exploration, conservation and sustainable use [of genetic resources]"[94] including through surveys, collection of samples and associated information and metadata. The merit of an integrated approach is also reflected in UNGA Resolution 69/292, which states that the elements of the ILBI should be considered "together and as a whole". An integrated approach to the investigation, conservation and sustainable use of marine genetic resources in ABNJ could foster potential 'spill-over' benefits whereby technology could be applied for sustainable development purposes that go beyond biodiversity in ABNJ.

4.2 *Acquiring Scientific Knowledge: International Collaboration for Regional Participation*

International cooperation is crucial to enhance scientific knowledge of marine biodiversity in ABNJ, especially in regions with low marine research capacity. The ILBI could seek to strengthen the implementation of LOSC Articles 242 and 243 through international cooperation in marine scientific research in order to advance knowledge of biodiversity in ABNJ and increase participation of scientists from developing countries.

Increasing scientific knowledge of biodiversity in ABNJ would require sustained support for existing initiatives, as well as resources for new investigations. The development of new observation technologies and understanding of the roles and functions of biodiversity in ABNJ, and the transfer

91 Nagoya Protocol on Access to Genetic Resources and the Fair and Equitable Sharing of Benefits Arising from Their Utilization to the Convention on Biological Diversity (Nagoya, 29 October 2010, in force 12 October 2014) at Preamble; available at https://treaties.un.org/pages/ViewDetails.aspx?src=TREATY&mtdsg_no=XXVII-8-b&chapter=27&lang=en; accessed 10 September 2017; Convention on Biological Diversity (Rio de Janeiro, 5 June 1992, in force 29 December 1993) 1760 *UNTS* 79. Arts. 16, 19.

92 International Treaty on Plant Genetic Resources for Food and Agriculture (Rome, 3 November 2001, in force 29 June 2004) 2400 *UNTS* 303.

93 ITPGRFA Art. 13.1.

94 ITPGRFA Art. 5.1.

of marine technology to share knowledge and enhance capacity of SIDS are among the aims of the 'International Decade of Ocean Science' proposed by the IOC.[95] This illustrates international recognition of the need to enhance international marine science cooperation for SIDS. The International Indian Ocean Expedition,[96] organised under the auspices of IOC, is an example of internationally collaborative, regionally coordinated research. Similarly, to fill gaps in scientific knowledge of biodiversity in Pacific ABNJ, an 'International South Pacific Ocean Investigation' could be considered. This could aim to galvanise political will to increase scientific knowledge of biodiversity beyond national jurisdiction, develop research capacity and transfer technology. IOC, perhaps through IOC-WESTPAC, could facilitate cooperation between Pacific Island Countries and nations with stronger research capacity active in the region, such as Japan, Korea, Australia, New Zealand, USA, France and UK. However, this would be entirely dependent on resources to support research activities.

4.3 *Disseminating Scientific Knowledge: Data and Knowledge Exchange*

Access to data and knowledge will be crucial to enable technology transfer and implement the ILBI. Global science increasingly supports open data; for example, an international accord published in 2015 by Science International stated that "open data should be the default position for publicly funded science" and updating historical values for "a new era of technology" is essential to achieve full benefit to society.[97] The obligation to publish and share data and knowledge enshrined in LOSC Article 244 could be further implemented under the ILBI.

The United Nations Agreement for the Implementation of the Provisions of the United Nations Convention on the Law of the Sea of 10 December 1982 Relating to the Conservation and Management of Straddling Fish Stocks and Highly Migratory Fish Stocks[98] (UNFSA) offers an example of how this can be achieved by elaborating provisions and standards for the collection and

---

95 UNESCO-IOC. 2017. One Planet One Ocean. Proposal for an International Decade of Ocean Science for Sustainable Development (2021–2030) at p. 1. Available at http://www.unesco.org/new/fileadmin/MULTIMEDIA/HQ/SC/pdf/IOC_Decade-Ocean-Science_Handout_Final.pdf; accessed 28 February 2017.

96 Second International Indian Ocean Expedition 2015–2020, http://www.iioe-2.incois.gov.in/; accessed 10 September 2017.

97 Science International, "Open Data in a Big Data World" (2015) at p. 3. Available at http://www.science-international.org/; accessed 22 September 2016.

98 United Nations Agreement for the Implementation of the Provisions of the United Nations Convention on the Law of the Sea of 10 December 1982 Relating to the Conservation and Management of Straddling Fish Stocks and Highly Migratory Fish Stocks (New York, 4 December 1995, in force 11 December 2001) 2167 *UNTS* 3.

sharing of data. For example, UNFSA Article 14 provides for the collection and exchange of scientific data,[99] international cooperation in research, scientific capacity development in line with a set of standard requirements for the collection and sharing of data as elaborated in UNFSA Annex I. Similarly, an elaboration of data-sharing principles, standards and requirements could be included in the ILBI to implement the LOSC obligation to publish and disseminate data. International standards and best-practice guidelines for data management and informatics provide a basis which the development of the ILBI could draw from.

4.4 *Applying Scientific Knowledge: Capacity Development*

4.4.1 Institutions: a Global Network of Regional Marine Science, Technology and Innovation Clusters

Regional marine science and technology centres could increase absorptive capacity, provide a hub for technology and research infrastructure and a focal point for regional research and engagement. The ILBI could reinforce the need to develop a global network of regional and national marine science, technology and innovation clusters. Linking regional centres via a virtual global network could support the participation of developing countries in international research collaborations. Existing models highlight the importance of training courses, workshops, lecturer exchanges, visiting professorships and post-graduate teaching programs.[100]

This also illustrates the advantages of intergovernmental coordination to aid international and regional cohesion. Stronger coordination with competent international organisations, such as the IOC, as stipulated in Article 276 of the LOSC, could support the development of an internationally connected regional network of marine science and technology centres. The ITPGRFA recognises a role for International Agricultural Research Centres of the Consultative Group on International Agricultural Research (CGIAR) in making samples available as part of the multilateral system of access and benefit sharing.[101] This offers an example of how international research arrangements could be integrated into the ILBI.

4.4.2 Individuals: Training and Skill Development

Scientific research skills and training are an important priority for developing human capacity to participate in the conservation and sustainable use of

99 UNFSA Art. 14(1)(a).
100 IOC-WESTPAC (n 69).
101 ITPGRFA Arts. 11.5, 15.1.

biodiversity in ABNJ. The LOSC obligation under Article 266 to promote the development of marine scientific and technological capacity could be further implemented under the ILBI by providing opportunities for scientific training and education and enabling the implementation of Article 269 (e.g., researcher exchanges[102] and joint international scientific research programs).[103]

Long-term collaborations could be supported by a mentoring scheme linking early career researchers in developing countries with senior scientists in developed countries facilitated through existing international scientific networks. Workshops and training courses targeted to ABNJ research could be delivered through a variety of means: in person; facilitated by regional networks such as IOC and its regional commissions and training centres; or online, such as IOC Ocean Teacher Global Academy. Researcher training opportunities, from undergraduate to Ph.D. level and beyond, could be facilitated through regional centres and international scientific networks. However, to attract to and retain researchers at regional science and technology centres, it will be necessary to increase absorptive capacity through, for example, teacher exchanges, continuous professional development opportunities and incentives, such as sustained international collaborations and resources.

4.5 *Challenges Ahead*

A number of challenges relating to technology transfer and capacity development remain for the development of the ILBI. In particular, the scope of technology transfer will need to be understood and agreed, and implementation options established.

4.5.1 Clearinghouse

A clearinghouse mechanism has been proposed as a means to provide a centralised portal to access and exchange information on activities related to biodiversity in ABNJ[104] and promote international collaboration. This could facilitate technology transfer by improving linkages between technology recipients and donors, and enabling knowledge exchange. Questions remain, however, on the types of information that would be included and how it could be managed. A clearinghouse would require sustained resources and stakeholder engagement (especially from scientific communities) to ensure that quality information was made available to users. Building on the strengths

102 LOSC Art. 269(d).

103 LOSC Art. 269(e).

104 See for example PSIDS (n 12); AOSIS (n 12); and EU (n 44) at paras 13 and 14.

of existing mechanisms, such as the Ocean Biogeographic Information System of the IOC, would be important.

However, the capacity constraints of SIDS, illustrated in Pacific Island Countries, mean that web-based clearinghouses could be quite limited in effect without corresponding capacity development and technical infrastructure.

4.5.2 Scope

The development of the ILBI will consider "capacity building and technology transfer" as it relates to the conservation and sustainable use of biodiversity in ABNJ. However, technology and capacity building for ABNJ cannot be considered in isolation, as it could be equally applicable in areas within national jurisdiction. Furthermore, technology can have multiple applications; for example, technology required for marine genetic resources research could also be useful for area-based management or even broader purposes.

Fostering a broad scope of technology transfer, including technologies that can be used for multiple purposes, could support meaningful capacity development. A broad scope of technology under the ILBI could be the best option to ensure efficiency and effectiveness of research efforts. However, a balance between specificity and flexibility to support effective implementation will be needed. Promoting technology *development*, as well as transfer, into the scope of the ILBI will be important, to facilitate investigation of biodiversity in ABNJ and advance scientific knowledge to support conservation and sustainable use. However, although LOSC Part XIV concerns the "*development* and transfer of marine technology"[105] (emphasis added), UNGA Resolution 69/292 refers only to "transfer of technology".[106]

A holistic scope of technology-transfer development could reduce duplication of activities and resources, and have wider advantages for sustainable development. The importance of technology transfer and capacity development in marine scientific research for sustainable development is recognised in UNGA Resolutions[107] and in Sustainable Development Goal 14. Marine scientific research is an important ingredient for sustainable development for SIDS, in a range of areas including marine genetic resources, fisheries and minerals.[108] The potential for the ILBI to strengthen capacity development in pursuit of sustainable development has been recognised

105 LOSC Art. 268(b) calls on States to promote the development of marine technology.

106 UNGA (n 1) at p. 1, para 2.

107 UNGA Res A/71.L.26 at [247] (n 9).

108 Salpin (n 11).

by New Zealand,[109] Australia[110] and the European Union (EU).[111] Although the ILBI cannot function as an overarching implementing instrument for Part XIV as a whole, it does provide a substantial opportunity to strengthen the international framework for scientific capacity development.

4.5.3 Funding

Sustained funding will be crucial for technology transfer and capacity development, including to generate, share and apply knowledge from ABNJ. International collaboration will be crucial to advance knowledge of biodiversity in ABNJ given the high cost of conducting marine scientific research in deep and remote open ocean ABNJ, especially in the Southern Hemisphere. AOSIS and PSIDS have suggested including a fund with a specific allocation for capacity development, technology transfer and scholarship in SIDS.[112]

However, it is unclear whether a financial mechanism will be established under the ILBI. The Global Environment Fund (GEF), UNESCO-IOC Capacity Development Fund and the Addis Ababa Action Agenda technology and facilitation fund could provide examples for funding capacity development and technology transfer. Furthermore, the agencies identified in the 'Resolution on the development of national marine science, technology and ocean service infrastructures' could also provide examples: "World Bank, the regional banks, the United Nations Development Programme, the United Nations Financing System for Science and Technology and other multilateral funding agencies".[113] New mechanisms, such as an "Ocean Sustainability Bank" and innovative blue finance partnerships have also been proposed.[114] Coordination and ease of

109 New Zealand, 2016, "Preparatory Committee on Conservation and Sustainable Use of Marine Biological Diversity of Areas Beyond National Jurisdiction, New Zealand Submission, December 2016". Available at: http://www.un.org/depts/los/biodiversity/prepcom_files/rolling_comp/New_Zealand.pdf; accessed 14 February 2017, at p. 8.

110 Australia, 2016, 'Preparatory Committee on Conservation and Sustainable Use of Marine Biological Diversity of Areas Beyond National jurisdiction (BBNJ). Submission by Australia. December 2016'. Australian Mission to the United Nations, New York, 6 December 2016. '*Australia: "capacity building can assist developing country partners to engage, consistent with SDG Goal 14, in the conservation and sustainable use of the oceans, seas and maritime resources*'. Available at http://www.un.org/depts/los/biodiversity/prepcom_files/rolling_comp/Australia.pdf; accessed 14 February 2017, at p. 8.

111 EU (n 44).

112 PSIDS (n 12).

113 'Resolution on the development of national marine science, technology and ocean service infrastructures' (n 5).

114 T Thiele and H Harden-Davies (2016), "Technology Transfer". Nereus Policy Briefs. Available at http://www.nereusprogram.org/policy-brief-bbnj-technology-transfer/; accessed 14 January 2017.

application will be a crucial priority to ensure that SIDS can access funding opportunities. Many developing States, including SIDS, call for a non-voluntary or binding mechanism,[115] others call for a mixture of voluntary and mandatory measures.[116] On the other hand, the EU[117] and various developed nations favour voluntary measures. The question of whether technology transfer should be voluntary or mandatory under the ILBI remains unanswered.

5 Conclusion

Marine technology transfer and scientific capacity development are crucial for the conservation and sustainable use of biodiversity in ABNJ. The LOSC framework for technology transfer is strongly interlinked with scientific capacity development and emphasises the acquisition, evaluation and dissemination of marine scientific and technological knowledge, information and data. However, gaps and ambiguities weaken this framework. The development of the ILBI is an opportunity to strengthen the implementation of Part XIV of the LOSC and foster a new paradigm of technology transfer and innovation based on knowledge exchange, open data and scientific capacity development.

Improving the international framework for technology transfer and capacity development could also advance regional objectives for Pacific Island Countries and have broader sustainable development benefits. The institutional, technological, financial and human capacity constraints that limit the ability of Pacific Island Countries to engage in scientific research involving marine genetic resources in ABNJ illustrate the need to increase technology transfer and develop scientific capacity in the region, at institutional and individual levels. These are already identified as broad priorities for the region; however, the development of a Pacific Islands regional marine science and technology strategy could enable clearer identification of technology transfer and scientific capacity development needs. Enhancing the capacity of existing regional organisations in strengthening international links could help achieve a well-resourced and cooperative network of marine science and technology centres, providing hubs for research infrastructure and focal points for science and skills.

An integrated approach to the investigation, conservation and sustainable use of biodiversity in order to promote the acquisition, dissemination and

---

115 See for example FSM (n 8).

116 Fiji, 2016, "Fiji's submission for BBNJ PrepCom" at p. 4, http://www.un.org/depts/los/biodiversity/prepcom_files/rolling_comp/Fiji.pdf; accessed 14 February 2017.

117 EU (n 44).

application of scientific knowledge could provide a useful focus for the development of technology transfer under an ILBI. Based on lessons from Pacific Island Countries, this could enhance the international framework for technology transfer through: sustained support for sharing of global marine scientific data and information; strengthened links between research institutions to form a global network of regional marine science and technology clusters; and increased skill development opportunities, including distance learning and workshops. A broad scope of technology, including multi-purpose technologies, could enable meaningful capacity development. However, a number of questions remain in relation to the scope and implementation of technology transfer. International cooperation, at the global and regional level, will continue to play a crucial role to secure the required resources for implementation, avoid duplication and ensure that technology transfer meets identified needs.

Index

www.ingramcontent.com/pod-product-compliance
Lightning Source LLC
Chambersburg PA
CBHW031320230926
51848CB00001B/29
* 9 7 8 9 0 0 4 3 9 1 6 9 7 *